Giants of the Sky

Giants of the Sky

The biggest aeroplanes of all time

by
Bill Gunston

Patrick Stephens Limited

First published in 1991

British Library Cataloguing in Publication
Data

Gunston, Bill, 1927-
  Giants of the sky.
  1. Aircraft
  I. Title
  629.133

  ISBN 1-85260-258-9

Printed in Great Britain
Typesetting by MJL Limited, Hitchin,
Hertfordshire

10 9 8 7 6 5 4 3 2 1

Patrick Stephens Limited, a member of the
Haynes Publishing Group, has published
authoritative, quality books for enthusiasts for
more than twenty years. During that time the
company has established a reputation as one of
the world's leading publishers of books on
aviation, maritime, military, model-making, motor
cycling, motoring, motor racing, railway and
railway modelling subjects. Readers or authors
with suggestions for books they would like to see
published are invited to write to: The Editorial
Director, Patrick Stephens Limited, Sparkford, Nr
Yeovil, Somerset BA22 7JJ.

Contents

Acknowledgements

I would like to thank the following friends for supplying photographs, drawings, information, criticism and much more besides: John Batchelor, Jack Bruce, Nigel Eastaway, George Haddow, Mike Hooks, Phil Jarrett, Malcolm Passingham, Richard Riding, Robert J. Ruffle, John Stroud and Harry Woodman. I couldn't have done the book without them.

Introduction

Roger Bacon, the mythical sage of *Flight International*, has frequently observed that it's tough designing aeroplanes. You have to defeat gravity, the omnipotent downwards pull of our planet. As he has pointed out, 'It's easier making mauve shirts'.

This basic fact certainly has something to do with our fascination for very large aeroplanes. I must emphasize that this book is concerned only with fixed-wing aerodynes, aerodynes being the pedantic term for heavier-than-air aircraft. They are the ones that have to fight to defeat gravity. Aerostats — balloons and airships — have often been enormous, some airships rivalling ocean liners for size, but they cheat by being naturally buoyant at a certain level in the atmosphere. I am old enough to have known what it was like to walk close underneath a giant airship moored at ground level. We didn't have the expression then, but it was enough to blow your mind. Yet, while your mind almost refused to believe the size of it, you inwardly felt that building a gigantic collection of gasbags was somehow not as impressive as building an enormous heavier-than-air machine that had to lift itself with its wings.

Aviation buffs must often have wondered at some of the Giants of the Sky. Today we live in a hard-bitten world where people are interested mainly in 'the bottom line'. Things tend to happen only if they are obviously necessary for defence of for airline profit, and even then they often have to fight for years for proper funding. Yet in days gone by many giant aircraft were designed, built and flown for no very obvious purpose. I have divided this book into sections, each dealing with the aircraft which made their first flight in a particular 10-year period. Looking at the aircraft in the first two sections one feels that often the objective of the designer was simply to create a giant aircraft. Apart from Igor Sikorsky's IM series, the NC-4 which managed to fly in stages across the Atlantic, and a handful of Staakens, none of them ever accomplished anything to justify their costly creation.

Even into the 1930s, 40s and 50s the practice continued of creating leviathans of the sky which, at the end of the day, accomplished nothing. But by this time there were more valid explanations. Usually the reason was simply the onward march — or rather gallop — of technology. Time after time a design team would set out with high morale and high hopes, only to find that, during the five, six or seven years it took to translate paper into hardware, the entire scene had changed. Famous examples include the Hughes H-4 Hercules, Bristol Brabazon, Saro Princess and North American XB-70.

Some chronicles have criticized these aircraft, or the people who ordered that they should be built. Some of these criticisms have appeared in a book entitled *The World's Worst Aircraft*. Such comment is thoughtless and unjust. Hindsight is all very well, but it must never be used to scorn the best efforts of those who lacked undiscovered knowledge. I go into this in more detail in the stories of the particular aircraft, but in fact the Brabazon, Princess and XB-70 (for example) were outstanding achievements. Their structures, aerodynamics, systems and the way they flew were all first-class. But it is very easy to promote the idea that a big aeroplane that does not go into production must be a useless 'white elephant', and a scandalous waste of money.

Aerodynamically I do not believe very large aeroplanes gain much over smaller ones. Many features add to their efficiency. The drag-producing cockpit windows, radio masts and blades, drain pipes and similar items are proportionately smaller, piston engines could be tucked away internally in the wing or fuselage, and the whole aircraft can approach more closely to an ideal shape. On the other hand, structural flexure is likely to be greater, and the boundary layer — the turbulent layer of air which scrubs across the skin of the aircraft — always gets ever-thicker and more draggy with increasing distance from the leading edge or nose. With huge airships the boundary layer became so thick that, in 1918, gunners on top of Zeppelins could squat entirely within it, feeling the true slipstream quite viciously ruffling their hair at perhaps 70 mph while they were otherwise surrounded by almost flat calm.

Another omnipotent factor is the square/cube law. Common sense indicates that lengths vary directly, areas (and therefore structural strengths) vary as the square of the dimensions, and weights vary as the cube. For example, suppose we start with an aeroplane with a span of 100 ft, a wing area of 1,500 sq ft and a weight of 60,000 lb (figures typical of a Lancaster). Then, if we do nothing to alter the shape, the same aircraft enlarged to a span of 200 ft will have a wing area of 6,000 sq ft ($2 \times 2 = 4$ times) and a weight of 480,000 lb ($2 \times 2 \times 2 = 8$ times). The square/cube law applies universally, and is used to explain why an elephant does not have legs like those of a mosquito.

Indeed, so powerful is the square/cube law that one might be forgiven for marvelling that giant aeroplanes could ever be built. But, whereas I have doubted that giants of the sky can gain much aerodynamically, they do gain a little structurally. If your brain cells are not very active, it is the simplest thing in the world to imagine a series of geometrically similar structures ranging from very small to very large. In this case, the fact that the load the structure can withstand varies at the square of the linear dimensions, while the structure weight varies as the cube, soon does get you into trouble. Indeed, a very erudite paper written in 1912 proved mathematically that, mainly because of the square/cube law, no

aeroplane could ever leave the ground if it weighed more than 8,000 lb.

On the contrary, the percentage structure weight (weight of the structure expressed as a percentage of the MTO [maximum take off] weight of the whole aircraft) has tended to get lower and lower as time has gone by and aircraft have got bigger and much heavier. This is partly because of better detail design, partly because of the introduction of new materials, and partly because we have learned how to use these materials to the limit. Of course, structural design is just one of many facets of aircraft engineering, but it is one that is particularly important in the creation of the very largest aircraft.

It would be easy to write a book about Giants of the Sky which simply described the aircraft and said, in effect, "Cor, ain't 'arf big!" Maybe that would be enough for some readers, especially those who merely want to look at pictures, but to me there is little point in writing such a book unless it also addresses itself to the original requirement, the background politics, the reasons for the design choices, and why it did or did not get anywhere. When this is done we often get a different perspective; for example, as I have said, instead of being some kind of abject failure, the Brabazon emerges as a quite remarkable achievement, which just happened to take too long in a time of rapid technical change.

Today we have gone quite a bit beyond 8,000 lb. The biggest of today's 'big twins', the Airbus A330, has an MTO weight more than 57 times greater. This weight is similar to that of the biggest airships ever built (of course, I mean the total weight of the airship and its load, ignoring the lift of the gas). The Soviet An-225 is about three times heavier still. There is not the slightest doubt that we could build a thousand-ton aeroplane if we so wished, but it would be restricted to only a few of the biggest airfields. For example, the captain would certainly have difficulty following existing taxiways. In the more distant past airfields were tiny by modern standards, and it is for this reason that such a high proportion of the giants were flying boats. But I don't think we shall see any more of that species. The reasons are discussed in several of the following stories, notably in that of the SR.45 Princess.

I have arranged the giants as nearly as possible in chronological order of first flight, but this posed problems as soon as I began to include aircraft that never flew, and even projects that never got off the drawing board. There are a lot of the latter, and I feel their interest certainly warrants their inclusion, though in a few cases (for example, the General Development monoplane and the Shin Meiwa flying boat) I may have allowed in things no self-respecting designer would take seriously. In any case, where do you put an unbuilt project in a chronological book? I have tended to insert them a little while after their cancellation, which in the case of modern aircraft might have been many years before the aircraft could actually have flown.

I must make one further point. Obviously there is a grey area populated by aircraft which might, or might not, be considered a giant. You can never hope to please every-one, and I apologise in advance if I have omitted any particular favourites of my readers. For example, in the pre-1920 section, though I included the Sikorsky IM series, and most certainly the German R-series, I have left out the British Handley Pages. On the other hand I have included many other British monsters such as the Kennedy, Felixstowe Fury, Fairey N.4 and Tarrant Tabor. The author cannot hope to write precisely the same number of words on each entry, nor should he attempt to. Each entry comes out the way it comes out. For example, if the IM family were built today they would come, in terms of gross weight, somewhere between a Cessna Caravan and a Cessna Citation, or in other words half the weight of a Shorts 360. But over 75 years ago things were a bit different, and I have given them one of the longest stories in the book (and I am grateful to Harry Woodman for correcting errors in what I wrote). I think a lot of these stories are quite interesting, and I hope many others will agree.

Bill Gunston
Haslemere, Surrey
1990

Pre-
1920

The 30 years from 1891 to 1920 saw the birth of the practical heavier-than-air flying machine, and its development (perhaps predictably) not as a transport vehicle but into a weapon of war. In World War 1 many tens of thousands of aeroplanes operated from rough front-line fields and from the surface of the sea, in almost every kind of weather. Most were quite small, but a few were enormous.

In Germany, especially, the R (*Riesenflugzeug* or giant aircraft) series were produced by many manufacturers in a sustained effort to create a strategic bombing force that could alter the course of the war. With the realization after 1916 that airships were too vulnerable for such missions, the R-programme received extra impetus. A basic requirement of all these aircraft was that mechanics should be able to repair any engine faults in flight, so, while some R-aircraft had large nacelles accommodating mechanics who also manned machine-guns, others had their engines grouped inside the fuselage, driving via gearboxes and shafts. The problems may be imagined, as can the working conditions in the engine room.

At the end of the war the R-aircraft had taught the Germans to think big, some of their projects being among the largest aeroplanes ever designed (for example, 20 engines inside a wing of 479 ft span!), but as they lost the war these colossal machines never got built. To some degree history was to repeat itself in 1945. What the Germans *were* able to use was their pioneer work on metal aircraft. Junkers stuck to somewhat crude structures using plain tubing and corrugated skin, but Rohrbach concentrated on the use of advanced sections, made by rolling, pressing and even machining, with smooth Duralumin skin able to play a major role in bearing the loads.

This 'stressed-skin' construction was fully used in the Staaken E.4/20 airliner of 1920, but 10 years later it had still made only a limited impact in the USA and virtually none in other countries. Yet it was to turn the large aeroplane from a vast acreage of flimsy fabric into a tough bird with a metal skin, with a single wing needing no external struts or wires. This quickly doubled the speed of aircraft, and by 1940 had in some cases multiplied it by four, as explained in later chapters.

Previous page *Scraperboard drawing by Harry Woodman of Sikorsky IM-B* Kievskii II.

1 Maxim biplane

This aeroplane certainly merits a place in this book on the grounds of its size, even though it never made a proper flight and had little impact on the development of successful aeroplanes. Of course, the author never knew Maxim and so must rely on the opinions of others. And some of the opinions could hardly be more different.

Hiram S. Maxim was born in Maine, in the United States, in 1840. Self-taught, he was an engineer and inventor of great ability, and he also had sound business sense. In 1881 he visited Europe and, among many other things, found everyone wanted newer and better weapons. Accordingly he rented a small office and workshop at 57D Hatton Garden, London, and designed the machine-gun that became world-famous. In 1884 he went into partnership with Vickers, who couldn't produce them fast enough, and Maxim soon became almost a millionaire. He took British nationality and was knighted in 1901.

One of his abiding interests, in the face of universal public scorn (because everyone knew that man cannot fly), was the possibility of making a successful flying machine. Unlike almost all the other nineteenth-century would-be aviators, Maxim had all the money he needed. Many have scorned his work, almost as if they were jealous of his resources, but I have found little to criticize when one bears in mind the totally ignorant environment in which he worked. Like the Wrights a decade later, he was methodical and meticulous. He carefully considered everything before even beginning to draw, and at the start of this work he built an impressive wind tunnel with flow straighteners and a force-measuring balance on which to mount test specimens.

Typical of the man was the enormous size (for the period) of the biplane he designed. It has been said he did not intend to fly it in the fullest sense, but merely to make it

Maxim's huge biplane resting on its railed track. The high-pressure boiler is in the bows, with a mechanic standing behind it. (Via Philip Jarrett)

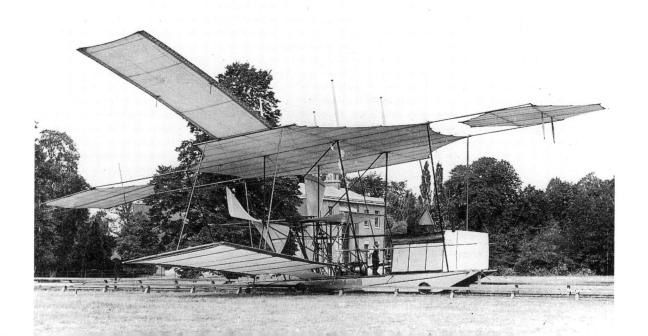

lift from the ground. I doubt this; the reader can judge from what follows. Certainly the criticism that Maxim was just one of the 'chauffeur' type aviators, ignorant of the need for proper flight control, is completely unwarranted. He conducted years of thoughtful research, and showed in his writings how hard he tried to 'get it right'.

He began in 1889 by testing model wings and propellers on a whirling arm, and later in his wind tunnel. Then he conducted detailed research into structures, finally deciding to use a basic framework of steel. As for propulsion, he made the startling choice of steam engines! This sounds ridiculous, especially as it needed two extra men in the crew, but he carried it through in masterful fashion. He designed and built two extraordinarily advanced compound engines, drawing steam at no less than 320 lb/sq in from a water-tube boiler and each delivering a measured 180 hp to one of the two propellers. He even added a large condenser above the upper wing, calculating that on a long flight it would save more than its own weight in water. The audacity of this propulsion system is almost beyond belief, and the fact that it actually worked and never blew up speaks for itself.

The giant airframe was really a sesquiplane, a biplane with the upper wing much larger than the lower. At top centre was a gigantic wing with a large root chord which rapidly tapered towards its outward extremities. To this were attached rectangular outer wings with considerable dihedral (upward slope) to give the aircraft stability. The lower wings were very similar to the rectangular outer upper wings, but were attached directly on each side of the long four-wheeled car which housed the boiler, engines and crew of four. The enormous 17 ft 10 in pusher propellers were mounted between the upper and lower wings at the rear. Span was 104 ft, length about 95 ft, wing area (including the front and rear elevators, described later) about 4,000 sq ft, and weight about 8,000 lb including a tank of naphtha fuel and 600 lb of water.

Maxim did everything with care, and wrote down the reasons for his actions. He was, in my view, the first person ever to organise a flight-test programme in the modern manner. He specified the checks that should be made of water-pump operation, water temperature and the efficiency of the condenser. He also measured propeller slip and thrust at varying rpm, and the rapidity with which propeller speed could be varied, because he intended to steer by differential thrust. He continued:

A flying machine must be steered in two directions — right or left, and up or down. We should first experiment with the more difficult one — namely the up or down or vertical motion. We should attach two long arms to our aeroplane in such a manner that they would project a considerable distance in the rear. To these arms we should pivot a very large and light, silk-covered horizontal rudder, and connect it with ropes so that it could be turned up or down by a small windlass from the machine. We should then take a run on the track and see if changing the angle of this rudder would increase or diminish the load on the forward or hind wheels...

As built, his machine also had another 'horizontal rudder' (elevator) at the front. He leased Baldwyn's Park, south of Bexley, Kent, and by 1894 was ready to test his huge machine on its track. This track is often described as circular, but in fact it had long straight sides, as surviving photos show. The machine ran on steel rails, but for the initial series of tests was restrained against rising more than about a foot by wooden upper restraining rails. After further careful tests of control and stability about all three axes, he recorded:

Having all things in readiness ... we should take our first flight, running the engines and doing the right and left steering ourselves. A day should be selected when there was a fresh breeze of about 10 mph. We should first travel slowly around the circular track until we came near that part in which we should face the wind. Speed should then be increased until it attained a velocity of 38 to 40 mph. This would lift the machine off the track and would probably slightly change the centre of effort, but it would be quickly corrected by the man at the wheel. While the machine was still in

the air, careful experiments should be ascertained to what degree the controls had to be tilted in order to produce the desired effect on the machine. The machine should also be run at a speed less than 35 mph in order to allow it to approach the earth gradually; then the speed should be increased again to more than 35 mph in order to rise, at the same time trying the effect of running one propeller faster than the other, to ascertain to what extent this would have to be done in order to cause the machine to turn to the right or left...

Many writers have suggested he only actually ran his monster round the track once. He clearly did so many times, because he gave numerous people rides at five shillings (25p) each, on many of which 'lift off' was obtained. Four people who rode on his monster were Griffith Brewer, F.H. Wenham, F.W. Breary (Secretary of the Aeronautical Society) and, as a boy, C.C. Walker, later a lifelong aide of Geoffrey de Havilland. It must have been an awesome sight to see the vast machine proceeding under full steam pressure and striving to escape from its restraining track. Unfortunately, on one of its runs it did just that. Maxim calculated that its lift reached 10,000 lb, and the 2,000 lb excess over the machine's weight was enough to break one section of restraining rail. Wisely, Maxim did not feel ready to proceed up into the sky, and he immediately shut off steam and tilted the machine nose-down, though it slewed off its track.

There the matter rested. He could easily have repaired the damage, but decided to think a bit harder before exploring the skies in a way that could easily have proved fatal. I have always been surprised that no less an authority than Charles Gibbs-Smith should have thought the 1894 biplane 'the greatest amount of wasted money and effort in the history of flying. Maxim was the victim of his mental inflexibility, overweening conceit and lack of humility which, where aeronautics was concerned, perpetually baulked his undoubted talent.'

2 Sikorsky IM series

Today the name of Igor Ivanovich Sikorsky means the greatest pioneer of helicopters. We have to think for a bit to recall that over 50 years ago he made some of the biggest technical strides in the design of large flying boats (see later). And over 75 years ago he designed aeroplanes that were not only the biggest in the world but were also built in quantity. Not much new technology was involved; he just took what was available and used it to the limit.

We can easily go wrong on the history. A standard work, *Igor Sikorsky*, by Frank Delear (at the time, 1969, PR Manager of Sikorsky Aircraft), states that the Sikorsky S-6B three-seater won the 1912 Russian military aeroplane competition and that, before the result was announced, Sikorsky was invited to dine with M.V. Shidlovsky, Chairman of the

RBVZ (Russo-Baltic Wagon Works, a big industrial combine). Sikorsky had long dreamed of building a giant four-engined aircraft, and to his delight Shidlovsky said 'Start at once'. The result was the *Grand*, with four engines, four rudders and many other advanced features. First flight 13 May 1913.

Every one of these statements is erroneous. What actually happened was that, under Shidlovsky, the RBVZ was given a thorough shaking up, and in order to be near the money and the government contracts the existing aviation department was moved from Riga to St Petersburg. Young Sikorsky was taken on as Chief Designer in April 1912. The S-6B was not accepted for series production, but in late 1912 Sikorsky was given permission to build an aeroplane

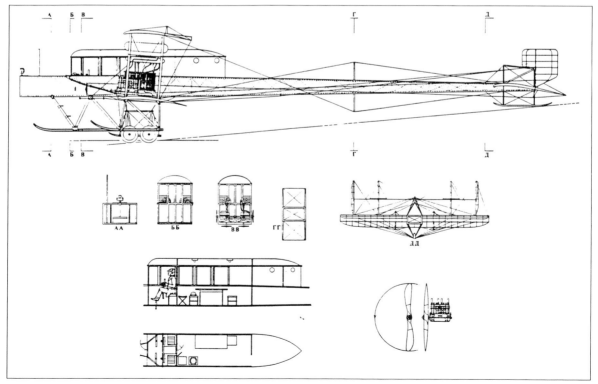

Below left *Side elevation and cross-sections of Sikorsky's S-21*, Grand. (Harry Woodman)

Right *Sikorsky talking with Czar Nicholas II in the nose of* Russki Vityaz, *with four engines. The occasion was the Czar's army manoeuvres at Krasnoye Selo in July 1913.* (H. Woodman)

of unprecedented size, but it had two engines and two rudders, and was first flown by its designer on 2 March 1913 (15 March in the old Julian calendar used in Czarist Russia).

We must bear in mind that in 1913 very few aeroplanes existed with a span greater than 50 ft, power greater than 150 hp or gross weight heavier than 2,000 lb. This underscores the magnitude of the advance made by Sikorsky with the *Grand*, which as originally built had a span of 88 ft 7 in, length of 65 ft 7 in, two 100 hp engines, and empty and loaded weights of 6,614 and 8,818 lb respectively (these seemingly precise weights are actually conversions of '3 tonnes' and '4 tonnes', so we should not take too much notice of their precision). The structure was of wire-braced wood, the spar booms being pine, the fuselage longerons ash, and the spar webs, ribs and fuselage skins being ply. The main wing spars were of box type with two webs of 5 mm ply and upper and lower booms 18 × 20 mm. By sheer chance Sikorsky made his wings with a very high aspect ratio — having noticed the good effect of extra span on a preceding design — and this enabled the big aircraft to fly on only 200 hp. One of its outstanding features was the dangerous-

looking slenderness of the rear fuselage. Sikorsky braced it with wires above and below, but despite this the plywood skin can be seen in photographs to be warped by the stress. One most unusual decision was to put the wings ahead of the CG and use a large lifting tailplane. In theory this ought to result in the aircraft being longitudinally unstable; conventional aeroplanes have tailplanes which push downwards, the CG being just ahead of the centre of lift.

Though not the world's first enclosed cabin aeroplane (that was the Avro Type F of 1912) the huge Sikorsky was on a totally different scale. In its cabin you could walk about, the internal dimensions being 18 ft 10 in long and 73 in wide. At the front of the cabin were large glass windows around the seats for the two pilots, in front of whom double doors led to an open nose balcony. Behind the pilots was a plywood bulkhead with double glass doors to the passenger cabin, with camp stools, a small sofa, a small table, water closet (of the type used in RBVZ passenger coaches), wardrobe, curtains at the all-round panoramic windows, carpet and electric light! The engines were Argus II four-cylinder upright inline watercooled, driving two-blade tractor propellers. The undercarriage comprised a large tailskid and a rather clumsy arrangement of struts at the front carrying two large inner skids, two smaller outer skids and two groups each of four wheels, sprung by rubber cords, carrying small skids between them. Cylindrical brass tanks above the engines, attached to the upper wings, held 330 lb of fuel, and upright water radiators were attached to the interplane struts just outboard of the engines.

Thus, Sikorsky did not necessarily set out with the objective of building a four-engined aeroplane, but it was immediately apparent that more power was needed. His big aeroplane, which was also known as the *Bolshoi Baltiskii* (Great Baltic), could not climb higher than 330 ft. On the other hand, it had quite an effect on the army of experts who had confidently said the whole enterprise was madness, and that it was obvious that so big a flying machine could never leave the ground.

After the first flight Sikorsky had the aircraft brought back into the hangar at the Komendantskii aerodrome for various modifications. He added two more engines, identical to the first, and, because he was justifiably apprehensive about the asymmetric problem following failure of an engine, he added the two extra engines as pushers directly behind the original ones. To make doubly sure that control could never be lost, he also replaced the original rudders with larger surfaces with a cambered (sideways-lifting) profile, concave on the outward faces, to provide a balancing effect in the slipstream. The new rudders had large horn balances; as before, there were no fins. The second flight, with four engines, took place on 10 May 1913. Sikorsky found no problems with engines throttled back on one side; indeed, he found he could make turns against the good engines. This was the first flight by a four-engined aeroplane.

Sikorsky was well aware that tandem engines are inefficient. Working in the slipstream of the front engines, the rear propellers are extremely difficult to design and usually give much less thrust for a given

power input than they would if they worked on undisturbed air. (It is perhaps remarkable that tandem propellers were chosen for so many aircraft in this book, right up to a Saro monster sketched in 1952.) Accordingly, he took courage in both hands and modified the aircraft yet again, with the extra engines installed as tractors like the first, further outboard, just inboard of the next set of interplane struts. Fuel tanks and radiators were arranged as before, the two radiators on each side being in tandem. Just to make certain there would be no difficulty in asymmetric flight Sikorsky added an extra pair of rudders halfway between the original rudders and the centreline.

As finally modified, the big Sikorsky was renamed *Russki Vityaz* (Russian Knight). It can fairly be regarded as the prototype of all subsequent large aeroplanes, and it was a complete success; Sikorsky was awarded the official title of Engineer. In its final configuration the aircraft's weight went up to 7,716 lb empty and 9,259 lb loaded. Maximum speed rose from the original 50 mph to slightly over 56. Even so, performance was modest, ceiling being about 2,000 ft. Sikorsky was confident that, with the experience gained, he could build a better aircraft, with more power. In any case, the pioneer big aeroplane had a short life, though it flew 53 times. On 11 September 1913 (30 August in our calendar), during the third military aeroplane competition, the engine fell out of one of the competing aircraft and crashed on to the parked *Vityaz*. Rain soaked the structure, previously protected by the varnished fabric, and Sikorsky decided the aircraft was not worth repairing. Nobody thought it might have been worth repairing merely as an historic exhibit.

This pioneer large aeroplane was an enormous achievement in every way, particularly in view of young Igor's very limited training and experience. A critic might say that it extended existing technology to the limits, and avoided structural failure only because of its unimpressive performance, but it was obviously not an end but a beginning. In a more sensible world it might have been the beginning of a series of commercial transports, but it was actually the beginning of a series of valuable reconnaissance aircraft which also served as bombers. The first contract, for 10 aircraft, was placed in July 1913, but all 10 were different. Ultimately 80 of these great machines were constructed, most of them seeing many months of extremely arduous missions until — and even after — the Russian capitulation. I do not propose to describe them in detail, one of the reasons being that it has been suggested that no two were alike!

All, however, were known as *Il'ya Mouro-metz*, or IM aircraft. There are as many ways of spelling the name as of spelling Shakespeare; he was a 10th Century legendary hero, the last Bogatyr, who defended Kiev. The first IM was RBVZ factory No 107. Compared with *Vityaz* it had a completely new fuselage, still slender but robust enough to need no external wire bracing except for the wing/fuselage drag wires. This was the first fuselage ever built in the modern manner. Whereas the original aircraft had had a fuselage looking almost like a telegraph pole, with a large box-like cabin at the front, No 107 had what we would today call a normal cross-section, a man being able to walk upright along the full length of the cabin.

The nose scarcely projected ahead of the wings. There were large windows all round to a point well behind the wings, aft of which there were portholes on each side. Few changes were made to the wings and engines, apart from considerably increasing the span (upper wing 105 ft, lower 72 ft 2 in) to give a wing area of 1,959 sq ft; and the upper wing was mounted higher. The engines were installed between pairs of interplane struts, one pair of struts being close on each side, and the radiators were mounted edge-on behind the engines.

The first IM was completed in October 1913, and had an amazing appearance because it was a huge quadruplane, but with tandem pairs of wings. Sikorsky, and especially his assistant K.K. Ergant, may have been influenced by Gustave Eiffel, who some years earlier had advocated tandem wings for large aircraft as a means of avoiding unwieldy wing spans. The weight of a second biplane cellule (admittedly not as big as the original wings) made the first attempts to fly, in late October or early November 1913, unsuccessful. Accordingly,

Maj-Gen Shidlovsky (with beard), commander of the EVK and director of the RBVZ, inspecting an IM-B (English, type V) at Jablonna in February 1915. This ship, Kievskii II, *was the first B with a sharp nose; the extra tanks and cowled Argus engines were not standard.* (H. Woodman)

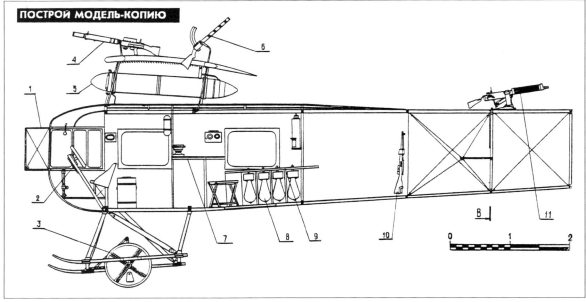

ПОСТРОЙ МОДЕЛЬ-КОПИЮ

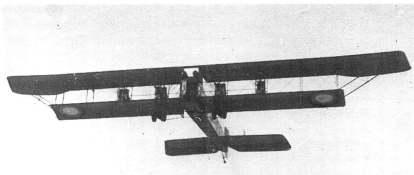

Above *A recent Soviet drawing showing armament of an IM-B. The bombs are 16.4 kg (36 lb); the guns are (4) Lewis, (6) Madsen, (11) Maxim.* (Copyright *Modellist-Konstruktor*)

Left *IM-B* Kievskii II *flying over Jablonna in February 1915. The port inner engine was leaving a smoky exhaust.* (H. Woodman)

the tandem biplane cellule was replaced by a monoplane wing, again half-way to the tail, braced to a large kingpost structure above the fuselage and to a prominent sledge-like structure underneath. The tail had a large central rudder with a smaller one on each side. The next attempt to fly, probably in late November, was a qualified success, the machine just managing to remain airborne but barely under control. So the tandem wing was removed entirely, though the upper kingpost structure was retained. A ladder was installed inside the rear fuselage leading to a hatch in the top decking, which was paved with ply to form an open-air 'promenade deck', with handrail! At last the aircraft made a fully successful first flight on 12 December 1913.

In early 1914 the engines were raised on steel trestles to a level almost halfway between the wings, the wings were given raked tips, with the ailerons having increased chord and washout, and there were other minor changes. The modified No 107 then made a record-breaking flight on 12 February 1914 with 12 men and a dog on board. One of the best-known of all IM photographs shows No 107 making a low pass across Komendantskii airfield with two passengers standing on the promenade deck. At that time, with snow on the ground, it had skis. Later these were replaced by seaplane floats, and the engines were replaced by 200 hp Salmson water-cooled radials inboard and 115 hp Argus outboard. No 107 was moored at Libau when World War I began on 1 August 1914 (Britain and France joined in on the 4th), and it is believed to have been destroyed by its crew to prevent its capture.

The next IM, No 128, was slightly longer, had smaller wings and more instruments and equipment, the engines being 140 hp Argus inboard and 125 hp Argus outboard. At the rear it had a promenade deck but no portholes. It was a very successful aircraft, reaching 10,000 ft and also being a little faster than its predecessors at up to 62 mph. It set records for load/height and distance/duration, and on 4 June 1914 (which may have been its third flight) it flew 1 hr 27 min with Sikorsky piloting and 10 passengers. Its greatest achievement was a truly remarkable flight from St Petersburg to Kiev and back on 16-17 June 1914. The aircraft had to fly overweight, with a crew of four, 2,073 lb of fuel, and heavy loads of spares, tools, baggage and oil. Refuelling stops were made at Orsha southbound and Novosokolniki on the return, total flight time being 30 hr 30 min. Much of the flight was blind, in cloud, rain and often turbulence, and more than once Sikorsky or other crew members had

to walk out on the ply catwalk along the wings to minister to the engines, extinguish a fire, repair a broken fuel pipe and screw the cover back on a carburettor. Just once Sikorsky climbed to the rear observation platform and was entranced by the beauty of the cloudscape. Any pilot will appreciate how wonderful it must have been to stand up on top of the big IM at slow cruising rpm, feeling the bumps as the aircraft passed over each upthrusting 'mushroom' of cumulus. No 128 was subsequently known as *Kievskii*, a name allegedly bestowed by the Czar.

In the Cyrillic alphabet the first six characters are A, Б(B), B(V), Г(G), Д(D), and E(Ye). These letters were assigned to the different IM versions, Nos 107 and 128 being the Type A or IM-A. Some authorities include these two as Type Б, the first production model, which (leaving out 107 and 128) numbered five aircraft. No 135 had four 140 hp Argus V engines, and Nos 136-139 had 14-cylinder 200 hp Salmsons inboard and nine-cylinder 130 hp Salmsons outboard. Despite the extra power the drag of the Salmsons and their radiators was so great that performance was actually reduced, so the IM-Б was used for

The first IM-E (English, type Ye) at the EVK base at Pskov in spring 1916. This first version, the E.1, had a single rudder. Engines were aircooled Renault vee-12s. (H. Woodman)

training. They were among the first aircraft assigned to the special unit formed to operate the IMs, the EVK (Eskadra Vozduchnykh Korablei, squadron of flying ships). It was a strategic reconnaissance/bomber unit formed and commanded by Shidlovsky from December 1914.

Received in February 1915, the first combat-ready aircraft of the EVK comprised two Type Б (V in English), of which about 30 were produced in eight versions which in service were repeatedly subjected to individual modifications. Except for No 179, which was bigger, the IM-Bs were smaller than their predecessors, the wings having even narrower chord (but huge ailerons) giving a total area of 1,292 or 1,346 sq ft. All had a completely glazed nose, the first five or six having a sharp vertical knife-edge nose and all the rest a flat blunt nose, as well as a wider fuselage and other improvements. Most had four 150 hp Sunbeam watercooled vee-8 engines, but the early sharp-nosed aircraft had Argus III or V, and some unarmed machines used as trainers had just two Salmson 14s or two pusher 225 hp Sunbeam vee-12s.

Next, from December 1915, came the IM-Г. The Г (G in English) was essentially a super-B, with the upper wing extended to 101 ft 3½ in and increased in chord to that of the outer panels and ailerons, most having an area of 1,718 sq ft. Loaded weight was typically 12,125 lb and maximum speed around 72 mph, though there were many variations with different arrangements of Argus, Sunbeam, RBVZ, Renault, Beardmore or Hall-Scott engines, the inboard engines often being of a different type from the outers. All were six-inline watercooled except for the Sunbeam and aircooled Renault engines which were vees. The four main groups were: Г.1, the most common version, with a single large rudder and two small ones; Г.2, twin rudders to allow a tail gun position to be installed (in 1916, more than two years before Handley Page and Mackenzie Kennedy applied to patent the

idea in idea in Britain); Г.3, with an improved tail gun position and strengthened wings; and Г.4, very similar to the Г.3, first produced in summer 1917.

The Type Д (D) was not a success, and the wonder is that as many as 10 were built, from January 1916. Though it had some advanced features, and reduced span and length, the four 150 hp Sunbeams in tandem pairs only just got it off the ground, the ceiling being put at 656 ft (200 m). One feature of the IM-Д was that the fuel tanks above the fuselage were faired in, giving a humpbacked appearance. This was retained in the ultimate version, the biggest and best of all, the IM-E (Ye). The eight of this type all had four 220 hp Renault aircooled vee-12 engines. Most had a span of 113 ft 2 in, wing area of 2,368 sq ft, gross weight of 16,446 lb and maximum speed of 85 mph. The first two Es had large single rudders and yet another new defensive idea: a retractable 'dustbin' for a gunner. The rest had twin rudders and the tail gunner. Production was not completed until 1918, after the Bolshevik revolution.

The EVK began what might be called operational training sorties prior to the first actual combat mission on 15 February 1915. Operating from Jablonna, Poland, this was the first of over 400 raids by IMs, the thrilling stories of which are omitted from most Western histories of air warfare. At first many (if not most) of the Czar's officers disbelieved in aeroplanes, just like their counterparts elsewhere, but within days the superb and valuable pictures the IMs obtained forced a reversal of opinion. Whenever a target of opportunity presented itself they bombed it, though this was at first a secondary role. Soon the IMs were having such an effect on German morale that the German high command issued an official notice mentioning the rumours of giant Russian aircraft and proclaiming 'such aircraft do not exist!'

IM missions were flown with crews numbering from three to six. Most bombs were of the 16 or 32 kg size, carried in rows of six suspended nose-down in cassettes which were slid along steel rails on the right side of the cabin to bring each bomb over the opened bomb bay. Smaller bombs were thrown by hand through the bay or out of the door, while heavier bombs, such as the 15 Pud (240 kg, 529 lb), were strapped externally under the CG. Defensive armament comprised up to six guns, including the massive Maxim, the Lewis, the Danish Madsen (whose drawback of not working when inverted did not arise, but which gave trouble because the Russians tried to make it fire rimmed 0.303 in ammunition) and a few Colt-Brownings and hand-held carbines. Tail gunners tended to get airsick from flexure and swaying of the fuselage, so they normally manned guns elsewhere. If attacks came from astern the gunner lay on his back on a trolley and, using the transverse bracing wires, pulled himself along rails in the constricted rear fuselage (with only fabric below) until he reached the tail cupola where he could set up his gun, preferably a Lewis, to fire astern.

Altogether, despite their tendency towards lack of power and a basically fragile and flexible airframe, the IMs proved to be adequately tough and very useful. They sustained a remarkable pace and magnitude of development which saw gross weight doubled and engine power more than quadrupled in less than four years. Only two were ever shot down. On 6 July 1915 one of the ships given the honour title *Kievskii* was shot about so badly that it virtually fell apart after force-landing just inside the Russian lines. The other was lost on 12 September 1916 after it had accounted for three German fighters. On 21 February 1918 about 30 Sikorskys were deliberately destroyed as their base, Vinnitsa, was being overrun by German troops. Even so, a number of IMs survived to wear the Bolshevik red star, some having quite long careers at the Serpukhov gunnery school and others becoming the Soviet Union's first civil transports.

3 Staaken R series

Many people today do not know that towns in eastern England, and especially London, were repeatedly bombed in World War 1. Two names were on the lips of recipients: Zeppelin and Gotha. But not all the airships were Zeppelins and not all the aeroplanes were Gothas; indeed, it so happened that the biggest and most capable of all the raiding bombers were Zeppelins!

The VGO.I was the ancestor of all the Staaken giant bombers. The newly built aircraft is seen parked next to a Halberstadt B.II. (H. Woodman)

A photograph taken by the right upper-wing gunner of the R.IV (R.12/15). He was standing on his ladder above the right engine nacelle. Note the two pilots and two left-engine mechanics. (H. Woodman)

At the start of the war, on 1 August 1914, there were no large aeroplanes in Germany. Hellmuth Hirth, already famous as a pilot (and much later famous for his engines), wanted to build and fly a huge seaplane to the 1915 World's Fair in San Francisco, but the war made this impossible. He had, however, obtained backing from Gustav Klein of the giant Bosch electrical firm, as well as the promise of large six-cylinder engines of no less than 240 hp from May-bach. This activity attracted the attention of the old but dynamic Count (Graf) Zeppelin. He had become obsessed with the damage that could be caused by large bombs, and he was thinking not of battlefronts but of enemy ports and cities. He urged his Zeppelin airship works to build a bomber capable of carrying a 1,000 kg (2,205 lb) bomb for 600 km (373 miles). There is some confusion about the requirement; I am sure the Graf meant a *range* of 1,200 km. At the same time he asked Claudius Dornier, at another of his factories, to start building giant flying boats, as described later.

Of course, there were hurdles to be over-come. Many in high places, including the war office in Berlin, disapproved of the idea of a giant bomber. Colsman, director of the airship works, even thought such diversion of effort 'unpatriotic', while Robert Bosch wanted to gather all the talent and organise the project himself. Zeppelin was a remark-able man, and before August was out he had organised the whole enterprise as the VGO (Versuchsbau Gotha-Ost GmbH, or East Gotha experimental works), with a strong team which included Klein and Hirth (and nearly included Dornier and Heinkel), with Prof Alexander Baumann in overall charge of design. Work on the VGO. I proceeded rapidly, the last drawing being issued in December and the almost completed aircraft being left in January to await its engines. At last Hirth made a successful first flight on 11 April 1915. It was then the largest aero-plane in the world.

A straightforward biplane, the VGO. I established an overall design of airframe which, with very minor changes in either size or design, was to endure throughout the whole subsequent series of bombers. Both wings were similar in plan, but while the upper wing was horizontal the lower had dihedral outboard of the centre section, bringing the tips nearer together. Construc-tion was of wood, the spars basically being ash in the upper wing and spruce in the lower, the finished spar being wrapped in glue-soaked cotton fabric. The completed cellule, with a span of 138 ft 5½ in and area of 3,572 sq ft, was a four-bay structure with struts made from high-tensile steel tubing, those carrying the engine nacelles being round and the rest streamlined. The fuselage had spruce upper and ash lower longerons, welded-tube frames and cover-ing of ply over the nose and top, and fabric elsewhere. The biplane tail, with four fins and rudders, was mainly of aluminium except for the wooden structure of the fixed tailplanes, all covering being fabric. Ailerons, on the upper wings only, were steel-tube structures with fabric covering. A

Right *On the ground the R.VI invariably had its nose in the air. This was R.27/16, built by Schütte-Lanz. (Via H. Woodman)*

Below *An Aviatik-built R.VI, probably R.33/16, after delivery to Döberitz in October 1917 and inspection by the Idflieg acceptance commission. (H. Woodman)*

simple 'tricycle' landing gear was fitted, each of the three units having two pairs of wheels on one axle. At rest the VGO. I looked acutely nose-down, but because of the large positive wing incidence the aircraft could leave the ground without having to rotate.

Three 240 hp Maybach HS engines were fitted, one in the nose and the others in pusher nacelles. Much of the structure of the nacelles and nose was aluminium or steel, and there was a seat for a mechanic adjacent to all three engines. Two pilots sat side-by-side in the open cockpit, and immediately behind them in the fuselage was the commander/navigator. Communication with the mechanics involved 'engine-room telegraph' bells and hand signals while the mechanics replied with engine data chalked on blackboards! Each engine drove a 14 ft two-blade propeller and had a water radiator mounted edge-on on each side. Gross weight was 20,992 lb, maximum speed 68.4 mph and endurance about 8 hr.

While the basic airframe proved excellent, the massive engines, which were based on Maybach's airship engines, proved unreli-

able. Despite this, VGO. I survived several crashes and rebuildings to enjoy a long career, latterly as RML.I (German navy landplane 1). After the first crash it emerged in February 1916 with larger fins and rudders, gunner cockpits in the front of each engine nacelle and a single transverse radiator above the centre engine. After carrying out various bombing missions RML.I was again rebuilt with five new high-compression engines giving far greater power. Each nacelle housed two 245 hp Maybach Mb IVa engines, geared to a single (larger, four-blade) propeller. In the nose was a fifth Mb IVa engine (one report, certainly mistaken, states the nose propeller was driven by two 160 hp Mercedes D III). Large parts were covered with transparent Cellon to make the bomber less visible, a 'stealth' practice experimented with on dozens of aircraft since 1913. Sadly, on its first flight after the final rebuild the rudders jammed hard over, causing a fatal crash.

VGO.II, first flown in September 1915, became R.9/15 in the 1916 category of *Riesenflugzeug* (giant aeroplane), meaning R No 9, funded in 1915. It differed only in details — such as a twin-finned tail — from its pre-

An R.VII in flight, one of very few genuine World War 1 air-to-air photographs. (H. Woodman)

decessor, though it carried out firing trials with a 130 mm gun firing downwards near the CG. I believe this to have been the largest-calibre gun fired from an aircraft. VGO.III, or R.10/15, first flew on or just before 1 June 1916. Again it was very like its predecessors, but — fed up with the Maybachs — the engines were six of the reliable 160 hp Mercedes D III. The nose propeller was driven by two engines side-by-side, while each nacelle had one engine low at the front with a long drive-shaft passing under the high rear engine, both shafts driving a common gearbox. All radiators were of the standard block type, mounted broadside-on above the engines. VGO.III made about seven bombing missions, fitted with a pioneer two-way radio served by a generator driven by its own petrol engine (for some reason trying to drive it by a windmill or from the main engines did not work). By this time gross weight, with fuel more than doubled to 770 gal, had climbed to 25,578 lb, and speed to 75 mph.

In the summer of 1916 VGO was transferred to Staaken, a suburb of Berlin, and after being renamed Flugzeugwerft GmbH became, in January 1918, the Zeppelin-Werke Staaken. Hence, the next bomber was designated the Staaken R.IV, or R.12/15. First flown on 16 August 1916, it differed mainly in that the nacelle engines were 220 hp Benz, giving a total horsepower of 1,200. This aircraft enjoyed a distinguished career with Rfa 500 on the Eastern Front and Rfa 501 on the Western Front, among other things surviving flying into the cables of a balloon barrage over London's docks. It had powerful defensive armament, with two dorsal gunners, one ventral, one in the front of each two-man nacelle and two in the upper wing above the engines.

The R.V (R.13/15), the last built at Gotha, experimented with an all-tractor layout. Five 245 hp Maybach Mb IVa engines were fitted, those in the nacelles being staggered laterally as well as vertically. The rear fuselage was shortened and the armament

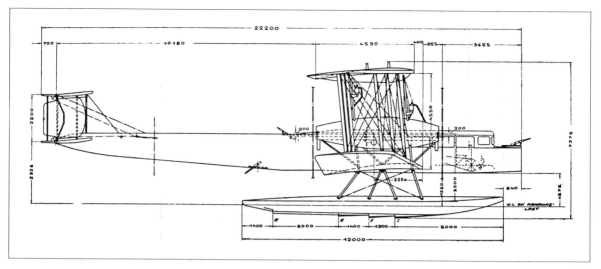

included gunners in the rear of the nacelles and in a *Schwalbenest* (swallow's nest) in the centre of the upper leading edge. R.13/15 flew 16 combat missions, on one occasion carrying a load of 10,519 lb at 10,800 ft in a 7 hr mission, but its engine transmissions were troublesome. In contrast, the R.VI eliminated all transmission problems and not only went into production but established a remarkable record of combat missions.

The first R.VI was R.25/16, first flown in late 1916. The availability of the 260 hp Mercedes D IVa gave reliable power adequate for four engines to be used, and these were arranged in simple push/pull tandem nacelles. Normal two-blade (usually Garuda) propellers were fitted, but R.26 had four-bladers and R.30 was flown with pioneer variable-pitch propellers. R.30 also had a 120 hp Mercedes D.II in the fuselage driving a large blower to supercharge the main engines, making a considerable difference to altitude performance. R.30 was one of several R.VIs with gun positions in the upper wing. Another innovation in the R.VI was that, to avoid trouble on soft airfields, there were 16 main wheels, with two quadruple groups on each axle.

Staaken built six R.VI bombers, while three were built by Schütte-Lanz, six by

Side elevation of the Staaken Type L seaplane, a works drawing dated 22 June 1918. Dimensions are in millimetres.

Aviatik and three by OAW (Ostdeutsche Albatroswerke). The final three, R.52-54, all built by Aviatik, ended up with 245 hp Maybach engines (R.52 having started with the big but unreliable 300 hp Basse und Selve) and R.52 also differed in having a revised forward fuselage, with an open cockpit at the rear and the glazed enclosed compartment taken right to the nose without a gunner cockpit. Most had successful operational careers, R.39 dropping 57,320 lb of bombs in 20 missions, including three bombs of 2,205 lb each dropped on London. Some had as few as three guns (the Lewis was preferred), while a few had seven. Equipment was outstanding. Full night lighting and landing lights were standard, as were two-way radio, extremely comprehensive instrumentation, and intercom by means of light bulbs and messages sent along pneumatic tubes. Some R.VIs had oxygen and, in late 1918, the radio-navaid which enabled repeated bearings to provide a fix, as in the naval airships. An R.VI could fly up to 10 hr, and though 11 were lost only two of these were actually shot down.

The R.VII (R.14/15) was basically an R.IV with the rear fuselage, tail and wheels of an R.VI. The R.XIV (R.43, 44 and 45/17) was basically a more powerful version of the R.VI No R.30, initially with four (push/pull) 350 hp Austro-Daimler engines, in which form R.43 flew in February 1918. These were soon replaced by the Basse und Selve, but all three R.XIV giants finally settled for five 245 hp Maybach Mb IVa, R.45 having the open pilot cockpit just behind the wings. R.43 was one of the Staakens to be shot down, by Capt A. B. Yuille, flying a Camel of No. 151 squadron, the RAF's first night-fighter unit. Staaken followed with the R.XIVa (R.69-72/18), basically a five-engined XIV with balanced controls, engines with reduction gears and smaller nacelles. The R.XV (R.46-48/17) were again very similar to the XIV. Last of the landplane Staakens, R.49-51 were built by Aviatik as the R.XVI. The airframe was that of R.52 (R.VI), but strengthened for greater weights and engine power. Streamlined nacelles housed the 300 hp Basse und Selve BuS IVa in the front and the massive 530 hp Benz Bz VI vee-12 at the rear, but before the first flight of R.49 (probably in

August 1918) the front engines had been replaced by the 220 hp Benz Bz IV. The third R.XVI was never finished, but R.49 and 50 performed admirably.

The final five Staakens were seaplanes. First came the Model L, virtually an R.VI with a large central fin added to counter the effect of having twin floats. The L was built to meet numerous needs of the Imperial German Navy for reconnaissance, bombing and torpedo carrying. It flew with land wheels in September 1917 and was delivered as a seaplane in November. It was followed by four production machines, Navy numbers 8301-8304, with the fuselage raised almost to be midway between the wings. The pilots sat in the enclosed nose, and the upper and lower rear gun positions each had a 20 mm Becker cannon, three machine-guns being in the nose (between and ahead of the pilots) and in the upper wing above the nacelles. The floats were duralumin, and maximum speed was about 81 mph. None of these seaplanes saw active service, but in terms of span and wing area they remain the biggest float seaplanes ever built.

4 Dornier Rs series

Claudius Dornier worked on airships for Count Zeppelin, but was transferred on the outbreak of war in August 1914 to design large flying boats of all-metal construction. From the outset this challenging assignment was carried through with boldness and skill, leading to a succession of flying boats which included the Do X and Do214 featured on later pages.

Dornier headed the Zeppelin-Werke Lindau, at Seemoos on the Bodensee (Lake Constance), near the parent firm at Friedrichshafen. Work on designing the Fs.I (*Flugboot Seemoos*), later called the Rs.I, began at once, and the monster boat — in

span the largest aircraft in the world — was completed in October 1915. Superficially it seemed a normal biplane, with an upper-wing span of 142 ft 9 in. In fact it abounded in unusual features, the most important being its structure of steel strip rolled and joined into special sections, with lightweight Duralumin used for various secondary parts. The three 240 hp Maybach Mb IV engines drove pusher propellers; one engine was mounted above the hull but the others were in an internal engine room and drove via shafts and gearboxes. Only the fore part of the hull had a planing bottom, the rear part curving sharply up to the unusually

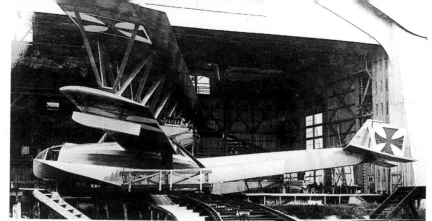

Right *In overall dimensions the Rs I was the largest of all the wartime Dornier boats. She is seen here on the railed Track at Seemoos after being rebuilt with external engines.* (Dornier DWF 3034/28)

Right *The unusual nose of the Rs I showing how the pilots looked ahead through transparent Cellon plastic. On top, a wind anemometer and the front gunner cockpit.* (Dornier DWF 3034/32)

Below *The Rs II as originally built, with internal engines with shaft drives. This form was later designated IIa.* (Dornier DWF 3034/42)

lateral stability when afloat, and an untapered rectangular monoplane wing of enormous chord. One might have thought the extremely broad tips very inefficient, but Dornier persisted with such wings up to World War 2. As before, wing incidence could be varied by screwing up or down the lower attachments of the two large forward struts joining the wing to the hull. There was also a completely separate very small lower wing. Inside the short hull were three 245 hp Maybach Mb IV engines driving a row of pusher propellers. The odd tail, with three horizontal and two vertical surfaces, was carried on an uncovered boom made of wire-braced steel tubes.

Though the Rs.II never went into naval service it had a quite long and very useful life, in the course of which it was subjected to numerous modifications. The first flight, on 30 June 1916, was very brief, but subsequent tests led to repeated redesign of the tail, the boom structure, both wings and, especially, the powerplant. In its final form the Rs.II had four of the improved 250 hp Maybach Mb IVa engines in tandem pairs mounted above the wide hull. The hull and tail were also redesigned, which doesn't leave much unchanged! In its final form the span was 108 ft 11 in and maximum speed 79.5 mph. Designation was Rs.IIb.

The Rs.III was yet again a totally different design. Though some of its features had been tried previously — for example in a Gotha-Ursinus design — it was an extremely bold machine of striking appearance. Major elements were arranged in vertical layers. At the bottom was the short but very broad hull, with a complicated planing bottom fitted with various strakes or skegs. The side-by-side open cockpit was just behind the bow gunner. Next came the four Mb IVa engines in tandem push/pull nacelles each mounted on four pairs of braced struts. Above the nacelles were further pairs of braced struts to which was attached the extremely broad monoplane wing, braced to the hull by cables. The tips were slightly

modern tail, with a single tailplane/elevator and single fin/rudder which seemed to be leaning backwards. Most of the hull was, like the wings, fabric covered, but the planing bottom and sides (everywhere susceptible to wave impact) was skinned with Dural. The two pilots were enclosed in a strange Cellon (celluloid) cockpit in the bows. Another unusual feature was that the entire wing cellule could be rocked about a central pivot, braced by a large forward strut, to vary incidence, the interplane struts being of diagonal Warren type of V-shape in side view. Design gross weight was 20,943 lb.

The Rs.I suffered a propeller breakage during ground running, and in any case Dornier's dissatisfaction with the outboard drives led to a rebuild. In December 1915 it reappeared with the three engines in a single row carried on broad diagonal pylons between the wings. Unfortunately, before its first flight, the huge machine was driven on to rocks in a gale and wrecked.

With remarkable speed Dornier then built the Rs.II, which began taxi tests on 17 May 1916. It differed greatly from its predecessor, though the advanced steel/Dural construction was hardly altered. In particular the Rs.II pioneered Dornier's use of an extremely broad hull, needing no external

Left *The completely rebuilt boat, now designated Rs IIb, with two tandem pairs of Mb IVa engines. Almost every part was different.* (Dornier DWF 3034/42)

Right *The Rs III, with experimental extended tail fins. The Dornier boats were often photographed on the turntable at Seemoos.* (Dornier DWF 5333)

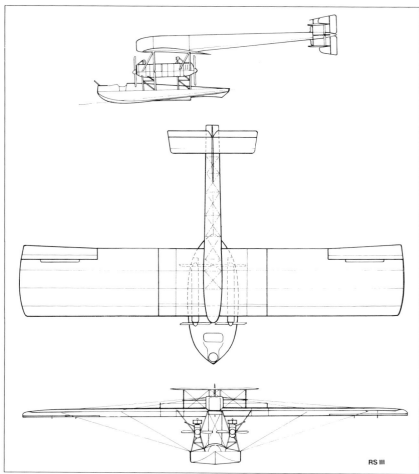

RS III

Right *Three-view of the Rs III in its final form, with normal fins and unraked but slightly curved wingtips.* (Dornier DWM 98/131083)

raked (almost square), and the ailerons were assisted by 'park bench' aerofoils. Finally, above the wing was attached the fuselage, or tail boom, of square cross section and light-alloy monocoque construction, with a wireless cabin in the nose and a twin-gun dorsal cockpit further back. On the aft end of the fuselage, well over 20 ft above the water, was the biplane tail with symmetric upper and lower rudders.

The Rs.III first flew on 4 November 1917. By this time the Maybach engines had matured, the Dornier engineers were capable and experienced, and the Rs.III was a very successful machine from the start. Apart from minor tinkering, for example by adding very long tail fins, little needed to be done, and on 19 February 1918 the Rs.III made a 7-hr delivery flight from Lindau to the navy seaplane station at Norderney, with only one occasion when a mechanic had to climb up to look after an engine. It made several flights from Norderney of up to 12 hr duration, and spent 1919-20 on mine-sweeping duties. With 691 gal of fuel it weighed 23,523 lb, giving an edurance at about 75 mph of 10 hr.

In 1918, with some rapidity, the Lindau works built the Rs.IV. This had the same engines, same span of 121 ft 5 in, and almost the same fuel capacity, weights and performance as the Rs.III. It differed significantly, however. The hull was longer but had a narrower beam, and a completely different

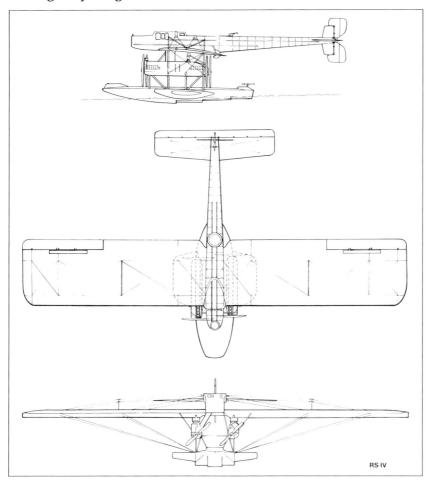

RS IV

Left *Three-view of the Rs IV in its original military form.* (Dornier DWM 98/131088)

Above right *The Rs IV finished its career as a civil aircraft before being scrapped by order of the Allies.* (Dornier DWF 13016/31)

planing bottom. The wingtips were not raked, and were rounded at the front. The narrower hull meant that the engine nacelles had to be closer together, so to provide propeller clearance the left nacelle was about a foot further back than that on the right. For stability afloat, tapered sponsons were added on each side of the hull. The latter had bow and stern gunner's cockpits, but the pilots were relocated in an enclosed cabin in the high fuselage, just ahead of the leading edge, along with the commander and radio operator. Mechanics' cockpits were provided in the middle of the nacelles. Finally, the tail was cleaned up, with a single large tailplane/elevator.

The Rs.IV first flew on 12 October 1918. Like the Rs.III it was a good sea boat — so far as one could judge in fine weather — and handled well in the air, though rate of roll was unimpressive. The only adverse feature appeared to be the flat planing bottom, which gave high drag in the air and very high drag when accelerating on the sea to get up on to the step. On an early flight the Rs.IV alighted heavily enough (or it may have been a wave hitting the flat underside) to buckle the lofty rear fuselage; this may have been deliberate, to spite the Allies. The war over, it was rebuilt as a civil aircraft, though it was never furnished. Before the

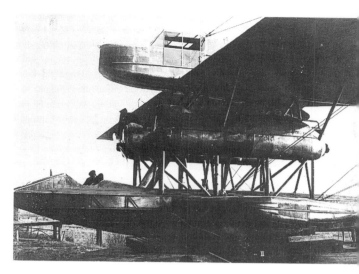

Allies had the Rs.IV scrapped in 1920 they examined it carefully, and were impressed at the structure. A French report noted that not a single piece of plain tubing was used; all members were special sections.

At the Armistice there was a project for a bigger Rs.V, with a span of 144 ft 4.3 in. One version would have had eight Mb IVa engines in the hull driving four push/pull propellers on shafts passing through the leading and trailing edges. A second would have had wing nacelles housing tandem pairs of 600 hp Mb VI vee-12 engines. Construction of the Rs.V was never begun.

5 Other German R-types

Most students of World War 1 are quite familiar with the British Handley Page bombers, and some with the pioneer Russian Sikorsky and Italian Caproni bombers. Where German bombers are concerned little is known beyond the Gotha and perhaps AEG types, which made up the bulk of the forces raiding England. Until Messrs Haddow and Grosz published a classic book on the subject hardly anyone knew the enormous effort expended in Germany on what

were called R-aircraft, from *Riesenflugzeug* (giant aeroplane). They were intended to change the course of the war, but (I'm afraid like a lot of the aircraft in this book) all they did was consume a lot of skilled man-hours and aviation-grade raw material. But what an interesting lot of aircraft they were!

Two families of R-aircraft were important enough to have their own entries in this book. These are the early Dornier flying boats and the Zeppelin Staakens. That still

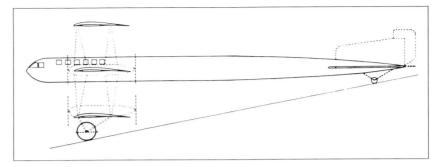

The ten-engined Poll triplane was one of the largest aircraft being built during World War 1. (G.W. Haddow)

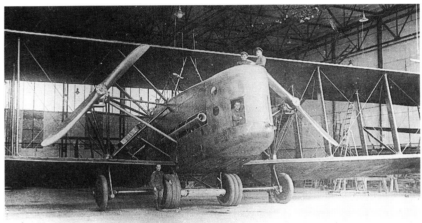

The AEG R.I (R.21/16) in its final form, with open cockpit and the radiators mounted on the diagonal wing bracing struts. The bell-mouth inlet helped cool the exhaust pipes. (H. Woodman)

leaves a fascinating group of aircraft, many of which were built and flown, and some of which even saw active service. Of course, as it was wartime, almost all the R-aircraft were heavy bombers. A few, among them one of the biggest, were planned as transports.

One has to remember that this was an era of structures which consisted of a relatively flimsy wood or steel skeleton whose strength and rigidity depended crucially upon being braced by struts and, especially, by strong wires. These struts and wires served as compression struts and tension ties, both inside and outside the covering skin of fabric. When very heavy loads had to be carried the answer was to use enormous wings. With a wing loading of 8 lb/sq ft a 40,000 lb aircraft thus had to have 5,000 sq ft of wing area (four times that of a Lancaster), and it was the job of the struts and wires to harness the large forces generated

by the gently lifting 5,000 sq ft and transmit them to the fuselage, along with the rolling moments generated by the huge ailerons which often needed all the strength of two pilots to achieve anything approaching full deflection. The technology was vaguely akin to that of sailing ships.

It was also an era of massive but, by modern standards, terribly unreliable engines. Such things as shaft keyways, valve springs, cotter pins, exhaust-pipe flange bolts (and flanges!), and oil or fuel-pump drive shafts not infrequently had lives in the order of five to 20 hr. As R-aircraft could fly missions lasting from 6-12 hr, or ever more, then, statistically, something was likely to break that would result in partial or total engine failure on every flight. It was part of the underlying reason behind the R-aircraft that, unlike smaller aeroplanes, skilled crew members could attend to and repair the engines in the course of each mission. This

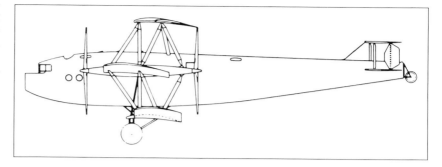

The enormous AEG-Aviatik would have been powered by four of the massive 12-cylinder Benz engines mounted transversely. Wing area was to be 6,671 sq ft. (G.W. Haddow)

DFW adopted the unusual arrangement of top-wing tractor propellers and bottom-wing pushers. This was the first R.II (R.15/16). (H. Woodman)

was the only time in history when such a possibility was laid down as a basic requirement for each fresh design.

There were two ways in which this particular requirement could be met, and I have divided this entry into two groups in consequence. In one group the engines were installed well away from the fuselage in nacelles large enough for mechanics accommodated inside them to have access in flight to almost all parts of the engines. In some designs the nacelle mechanics also manned machine-guns. In the alternative scheme, which was in general the favoured answer, all the engines were grouped in an intolerably hot and deafening 'engine room' occupying a large part of the central fuselage. From here their power was transmitted by various arrangements of clutches, gearboxes and shafts to propellers mounted outboard along the wings. Almost all of the R-aircraft had both tractor and pusher

propellers. Most were biplanes, some were monoplanes (especially those projected at the war's end) and a few were triplanes. Most were slow, even by the standards of the day, and unwieldy to fly. Like so many aircraft in this book, their technical achievements were enormous but their actual achievements very little.

Nacelle engines

The following brief outline is alphabetical, not chronological. Thus, the first of this group is the Aviatik R.III. The famous aircraft firm unofficially called its two batches of licence-built Staaken bombers Aviatik R.I and R.II aircraft, but the R.III was its own design. Dating from the beginning of 1919, it was an attempt to enter the civil transport market, but the R.III was never completed, and possibly not even started. A straightforward design with biplane wings and tail and four 250 hp Benz Bz IVa engines in push/pull tandem nacelles, it was to have had nine single seats down each side of the central aisle, and (having ducked under the floor of the open cockpit) a forward observation cabin with a door to an open nose deck resembling that of Sikorsky's *Grand*.

The next of this family was also never built, but the design was patented in November 1917. The overall shape almost exactly resembled the Handley Page O/100, but the R-aircraft proposed by Lt Dipl-Ing Ernst Neuber was far bigger, the span being nearly 179 ft. Close inboard were the two push/pull nacelles, each propeller being driven by a tandem pair of 245 hp Maybach engines (thus each nacelle contained four engines in a row). Armament comprised a 105 mm gun firing obliquely down at ground targets from the centre fuselage. Defensive firepower comprised eight machine-guns in four pairs.

One of the biggest and strangest of all the R-aircraft was the Poll Grosseflugzeug, a huge triplane which was actually well advanced in construction at the Armistice. Financed by Brüning und Sohn, the Deutschebank and (initially) by the Imperial German Navy, it was intended to drop leaflets (some reports said bombs) on New York. The slender fuselage, 111 in square in section and 150 ft long, was centred on the middle wing, which had a span of 165 ft. The upper and lower wings were of 102 ft span. Power was provided by 10 tandem engines in four push/pull nacelles centred on the middle wing and a fifth nacelle above the lower wing on the centreline. Surprisingly, there were only two pairs of mainwheels. One wheel is stored by London's Imperial War Museum; it is made of wood with a steel hub and steel rim, the diameter being 93.5 in. Perhaps the least credible figure relating to the Poll is its planned flight endurance of 80 hr.

The only other nacelle-engined R-aircraft were project drawings emanating from Adlershof, discovered many years later at Wright Field, Ohio. Little is known about them, and they certainly did not come from any of the well-known manufacturers. As described later, all were bombers and all were gigantic, the nacelle-engined types being the smallest, and the only biplanes.

Internal engines

Writers who study such British aircraft as the Bristol Tramp and Parnall Possum are liable to think putting all the engines in an internal engine room a strange idea. In fact the vast majority of the wartime German R-aircraft types adopted such a layout. Most had engines grouped in the fuselage, but others arranged them longitudinally or transversely inside a thick monoplane wing. The fact that they were wholly inside the aircraft made no measurable difference to flight performance, because most of these aircraft seldom exceeded 65 mph, and the biggest contribution to powerplant drag came from the large radiators broadside-on to the oncoming air. In all the many German internal-engine schemes the inevitable unreliability of the engines and associated devices was accentuated by the need for long and heavy shafting, clutches and high-power gearboxes. To cut down weight the torque in the transmission was reduced by running the shafts at high speed, sometimes even higher than the engine crankshaft speed, but this in turn often brought problems with the bearings and with whip and vibration. Despite great and sustained efforts I consider the problems of such a propulsion system were nothing like completely solved at the Armistice. Suffice to say, such installations were not proceeded with after the war, even by such companies as Aviatik, Dornier, Junkers or Rohrbach.

Alphabetically, the first of this family was R.21/16 (the 21st R-aircraft, which was funded in 1916), the only AEG R.I to be flown. The giant electricity firm had cut its teeth with successful smaller bombers, and with ample design and engineering talent their R.I might have been expected to be a success also. Painstaking development delayed the first flight until 14 June 1918. The structure was mainly metal, almost all of it high-tensile steel, with equal-span biplane wings and a small tail. The latter comprised a single very broad but short-span tailplane, pivoted and trimmable by an electric screw-jack just as is often done today, an extremely small central fin, and a 'slab' elevator pivoted to the top of the fin and to the two rudders pivoted between the elevator and the tail-plane. The ailerons were equally unconventional, being pivoted to the interplane struts midway between the wings, with pronounced inverse taper. The main landing gear comprised two wide wheels each with three tyres (many R-aircraft had multiple tyres on each wheel if the tyres were not steel rims) connected via universal joints with extra single wheels further outboard which normally took little load. The pilots sat side-by-side in an open cockpit at the back, in line with the trailing edges.

Gunner's posts were in the nose, above a big observation cabin, and above and below the rear fuselage. But the whole of the main fuselage was occupied by the engines, with a narrow gangway between them. Four massive 260 hp Mercedes D IVa engines — six-cylinder water cooled inlines, like almost every German engine used in R-aircraft — were arranged in a front and rear pair on each side. Each pair of engines was arranged nose-to-nose so that both drove a common bevel gearbox between them. From this a shaft sloped up away from the fuselage to drive that side's single tractor propeller. Endless trouble was experienced with vibration, shaft misalignment and other purely mechanical problems. The gears themselves gave relatively few problems, but the leather cone and dog clutches were always a source of weakness, and the same went for every other engine-room R-aircraft. All exhaust on each side was grouped into a large pipe surrounded by a cooling manifold with a ram inlet at the front. At first each engine had its own radiator close beside it on the side of the fuselage, and the pairs of engines drove four-blade propellers. Soon two-blade propellers were fitted, and a little later the cockpit was modified by removing various top deckings and fairings to leave a plain open cockpit, while the radiators were replaced by paired groups mounted on the diagonal inboard struts bracing the lower wing. (See the photograph on page 36.)

On 3 September 1918 the R.I was destroyed in flight by structural failure of a modified propeller. Three incomplete R.Is were scrapped after the Armistice.

AEG had several orders from the Idflieg (army) and navy for huge R-aircraft, but none was anything like complete in late 1918. One (R.II) was to have been a thick-winged monoplane of 151 ft span powered by eight Mercedes D IVa engines. Another incomplete aircraft was the AEG-Aviatik R-aircraft, a triplane with a span of 180 ft 5 in powered by four 530 hp Benz Bz VI vee-12 engines supercharged for high-altitude missions by a centrifugal compressor in the fuselage driven by a 120 hp Mercedes D II. This again was an arrangement used in several German bombers of both world wars.

One of the greatest exponents of the central engine-room aircraft was DFW, a well-known producer of aircraft of normal dimensions. Its first giant, the R.I No 11/15, was designed in 1915 by Hermann Dorner (later the Hannover designer), assisted by an experienced team. The R.I made its first flight on 5 September 1916. It was a biplane of equal span, with a biplane tail with twin rudders, a central fin being added later. The capacious well-streamlined fuselage, skinned with plywood, housed the four 220 hp Mercedes D IV engines in almost superimposed groups, which at the expense of large frontal area kept the engine room virtually within the chord of the wings. Unlike all other R-giants each engine drove its own propeller, the high-mounted front engines driving tractor propellers on shafts just beneath the upper wing and the low rear engines driving pusher propellers rotating just behind cutaway portions of the lower wing. Seen from the front the tractor and pusher propeller discs hardly overlapped. (See the photograph on page 37.)

The DFW R.I suffered its share of problems, and eventually appeared with extended upper wings, different radiators, a large gravity fuel tank above the fuselage and, most importantly, a more rigid engine mounting structure and additional provisions for reducing or absorbing vibration. In June 1917 it made an operational mission, dropping 1,500 lb of bombs, but in September it was wrecked in a forced landing.

Generally favourable experience with the R.I led to an order for six R.II aircraft, construction of which began at the end of 1916. Similar to the R.I but bigger, they were powered by four 260 hp Mercedes D IVa engines. The first, 15/16, flew on 17 September 1917 but crashed a few months later. The second, 16/17, flew in February 1918, and was later fitted with a large Brown Boveri compressor ahead of the engine room, driven by a 120 hp Mercedes D II, supercharging the main engines via external air pipes. The other R.IIs were not completed.

In September 1918 the Idflieg (inspectorate of aviation troops) ordered two DFW R.III aircraft. These were perhaps Germany's late-war equivalent of Handley Page's 'bloody paralyser', but about two years too late because even the paper design was incomplete at the Armistice. They followed the established DFW philosophy, but doubled-up. In the engine room were four engines on each side, the four front engines having forward drives and the aft engines rear drives. Various propeller arrangements were studied, but that on which most work was done featured front and rear eight-blade contraprops, each driven by one pair of engines. As in 16/17 a separate supercharging installation was provided, the blowers being driven by two D II engines just ahead of the main group. Span was 175 ft 6 in. An unusual feature was that, while the two-

pilot cockpit was aft of the engines, the navigator had a separate open cockpit near the nose with pedals for making heading corrections for navigation, bomb-aiming or during landing. He would have been the aircraft commander.

As explained later in the story of the G.38, Junkers was a pioneer of all-metal construction, of the thick monoplane wing devoid of external bracing, and (on paper) of the flying-wing aircraft. In March 1917 Prof Junkers completed the basic design of the R.I bomber, with four 260 hp Mercedes D IVa engines mounted in transverse pairs inside a thick monoplane wing of 114 ft 10 in span, driving 16 ft 5 in propellers via twin bevel boxes on a common shaft. For its day it was an extremely advanced and impressive aircraft, but the first was incomplete at the Armistice. A second R-aircraft, with paired engines mounted in normal nacelles projecting ahead of the 126 ft 3 in wing, remained on paper.

Next, alphabetically, comes Linke-Hofmann. In early 1916 this railway firm began building established aircraft types under licence, and on its own account received a contract for an R-aircraft. Under Paul Stumpf, previously designer of AEG bombers, the work proceeded rapidly, and the Linke-Hofmann R.I made its first flight in January 1917. Its outstanding feature was

Below left *Even by 1915 standards the Linke-Hofmann R.I had a bluff unstreamlined fuselage, yet the first example managed a creditable 87 mph. This, the second (R.40/16), was heavier and somewhat slower. (Peter M. Bowers via H. Woodman)*

Left *The engine group of the Linke-Hofmann R.II on test in the factory: A, four Mercedes engines; B, exhaust from one engine; C, decompression lever (for starting); D, Bosch magnetos; E, central gearwheel; F, propeller shaft; G, direction of propeller. (MTU archives)*

Below *The nose of the Linke-Hofmann R.II contained four big engines mounted nose-to-nose all driving on one gearwheel. A similar arrangement was proposed for a Junkers project, the Vickers Vigilant and possibly the English Electric Phoenix Pulex. (G.W. Haddow)*

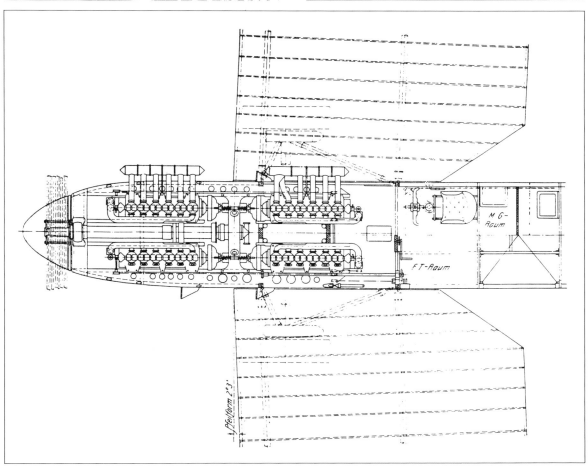

ALL·15

Left *Without anything to give it scale it is hard to believe that the Linke-Hofmann R.II was one of the largest aircraft of the entire war era!* (Via Philip Jarrett)

Right *For sheer concentration of power the central nacelle of the Schütte-Lanz R.I took some beating. The engines were the enormous BuS IVa, almost like marine engines.* (G.W. Haddow)

the grotesque depth of the stumpy fuselage, which filled the space between the biplane wings. At the top was the lofty cockpit, with a roof but open on each side. At the next (main) level were the four 260 hp Mercedes D IVa engines, arranged axially so that the left and right pairs drove a common transverse cross-shaft geared to the two tractor propellers. At the lowest level was the bomb-aiming station and four fuel tanks. The tail comprised a tailplane with elevators, central fin, two outboard rudders and a slab elevator pivoted on top of the three vertical surfaces. The neat landing gear had two large wheels with steel tyres.

Many aircraft of the Central Powers had been skinned with transparent Celluloid type materials, such as Emaillit and Cellon, in low-visibility experiments. Some results appear to have been encouraging, the aircraft proving difficult to see despite the noise betraying its location. The biggest Cellon experiment was the first Linke-Hofmann, which had Cellon covering the upper part of the nose, ahead of the pilots, and the entire rear fuselage and tail. In this case it was found that the shiny covering often made the aircraft more visible rather than less, and the pilots sometimes had to look through almost opaque condensation (and there were other problems). Accordingly, the

second R.I, No 40/16, was covered with normal hexagon-print camouflaged fabric. No 40 differed in many other respects, one being its unfashionable use of coil springs instead of rubber cords in the main landing gear.

One of the most unusual of all R-aircraft, the R.II looked at first glance like an ordinary single-engined scout or day bomber. In fact it was the biggest of all the Linke-Hofmanns, with a span of 138 ft 4 in and loaded weight of 33,070 lb. Yet, seen in a photograph, the single open cockpit, simple two-wheel landing gear and single two-blade propeller utterly belie the enormous size of the R.II. In the nose were four 260 hp Mercedes D IVa engines arranged nose-to-nose on each side. Each pair drove a central spur gear meshing with a central gear, of 30 in diameter, which via a huge tubular shaft drove the Garuda laminated wooden propeller. At almost 23 ft diameter this was (I believe) the biggest propeller ever actually used on an aeroplane, though it would have been surpassed by the Vigilant (see later). It turned at 545 rpm, slow enough for the test pilot to describe being pulled through the air by it as 'an extraordinary sensation'.

Next, alphabetically, comes Schütte-Lanz, famous as a builder of airships. The firm's first R-aircraft, never built, would have had

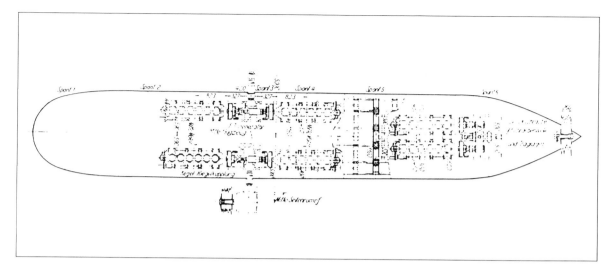

four 300 hp Robur (Salmson type) water-cooled radials in outward-facing pairs in the fuselage driving tandem push/pull propellers on slim nacelles midway between the wings. It was replaced in the final two years of the war by the R.I, a huge biplane with both wings having a span of 144 ft 4 in. The tail was carried on two large booms, which housed the fuel and four (dorsal and ventral) gunners. In the central nacelle were six Basse und Selve BuS IVa engines, whose six cylinders were big enough to produce 300 hp. The forward pair on each side were mounted nose-to-nose to drive a shaft running out to a tractor propeller on the front of the adjacent boom. The aft pair were geared to a pusher propeller on the tail of the nacelle. A fifth gunner was installed amidships in the upper wing. This machine was to have weighed 36,603 lb, and was nearly complete in November 1918.

Some of the oddest R-aircraft were made by SSW (Siemens-Schuckert Werke). The early ones were hardly giants, but after Franz and Bruno Steffen joined, as both designers and test pilots, a series of remarkable machines emerged. The first, still not really a giant, was the indestructible R.I, first flown as early as May 1915 and still flying (after repairs and rebuilds) at the Armistice. An unequal-span biplane, it had an extra-ordinary rear fuselage in the form of upper and lower tapering triangular booms. From a distance the aircraft in flight somewhat resembled two monoplanes, one inverted on top of the other. This odd rear-fuselage structure (which in a patent was to be adjustable by means of screw threads to adjust the incidence of the tail) was used in the SSW R.I to R.VII inclusive.

The nose of the R.I housed three 150 hp Benz Bz III engines, one in front and two side-by-side behind, all driving into a large common gearbox from which tubular shafts drove the two tractor propellers. Three prominent radiators filled the front and sides of the nose. Immediately to the rear the fuselage (or, rather, nacelle) suddenly grew upwards to fill the entire space between the wings. Altogether it sounds a most odd design, and performance was predictably unimpressive (maximum speed 68 mph), but the R.I proved a sound basis on which to build bigger and more powerful machines.

The SSW R.II to R.VII followed the same odd configuration but were significantly bigger, and generally better-looking. The R.II, III and IV were all built with three 240 hp Maybach engines and an upper-wing span of 92 ft 7 in. They were rebuilt with 220 hp Bz IV or 260 hp Mercedes D IVa engines and

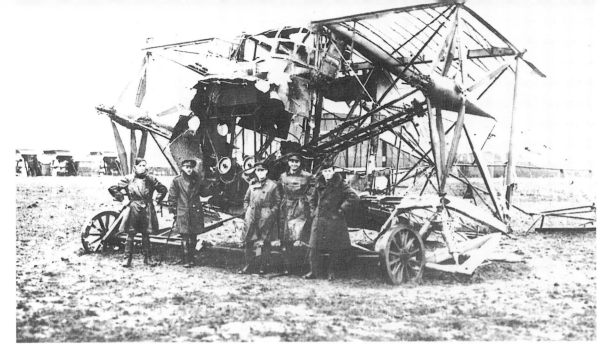

British officers intrigued by the remains of the SSW R.III (R.3/15) on the airfield at Bickendorf near Cologne in December 1918. The engines and transmission are exposed. (Australian War Memorial via H. Woodman)

a span increased to between 112 ft 7 in and 124 ft 8 in (all different). The R.V. VI and VII were generally similar to the II, III and IV as rebuilt. Much time and money was wasted trying to solve problems with the unsatisfactory Maybach engines, and another problem was the desperately cramped engine room (so that, to renew the exhaust gaskets on a right-hand engine, the opposite left-hand cylinder head had to be removed!).

SSW's final R-aircraft was the biggest aeroplane of its day actually to be completed, though its power was the same as that of the Schütte-Lanz, and its loaded weight (35,053 lb) slightly less. The R.VIII, ordered in mid-1917, in some ways represented the culmination of the R-aircraft technology, though this technology still remained highly imperfect and prone to structural and mechanical failure. Outwardly it was a conventional biplane, looking much like an enlarged Handley Page V/1500. The equal-span wings had slight sweepback, the short fuselage had a deep rectangular section, the tail comprised a high tailplane with balanced elevators, low elevators for trimming and three rudders, the four ailerons had Flettner servo tabs, and the neat main gears had steel coil springs. In the engine

room were six 300 hp Basse und Selve IVa engines, the front pair driving two-blade tractor propellers and the nose-to-nose remainder driving four-blade pushers. Water and oil for the three engines on each side were cooled by compact circular radiators in profiled diffuser ducts which look as if they had been designed to give net thrust. Altogether the R.VIII was an impressive machine, with a span of 157 ft 5.76 in and wing area of 4,736 sq ft, but it was not completed until after the Armistice, and never flew.

An enlarged and refined version, the R.IX, was started as a bomber and changed to a 36-seat transport, but never built. Another project, the SSW Kann, was to have been a monoplane of 197 ft span with four tractor propellers driven by 750 hp steam turbines! Common sense suggests that the Kann was wholly impractical.

The Zeppelin-Werke, Staaken, was rapidly building very advanced monoplane bom-

bers at the war's end, using Duralumin structure designed by Dr Rohrbach. The only type of which details are known is the R.VIII, with a span of 180 ft 5.4 in and powered by eight engines (almost certainly Mercedes D IVa) in a series of compartments inside the leading edge. The Allies were shortsighted in refusing permission for this potentially very important aircraft to be completed.

As noted earlier, most of the gigantic Adlershof projects, discovered after the war

Above *Emergency landing by the SSW R.VI (6/15) in a ploughed field near Vilna, Poland, in December 1916. (H. Woodman)*

Below *Internal arrangement of the enormous SSW R.VIII, with the six massive engines carried on a deep braced truss girder of steel tubes. (G.W. Haddow)*

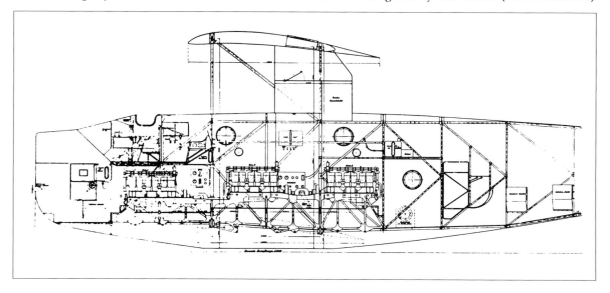

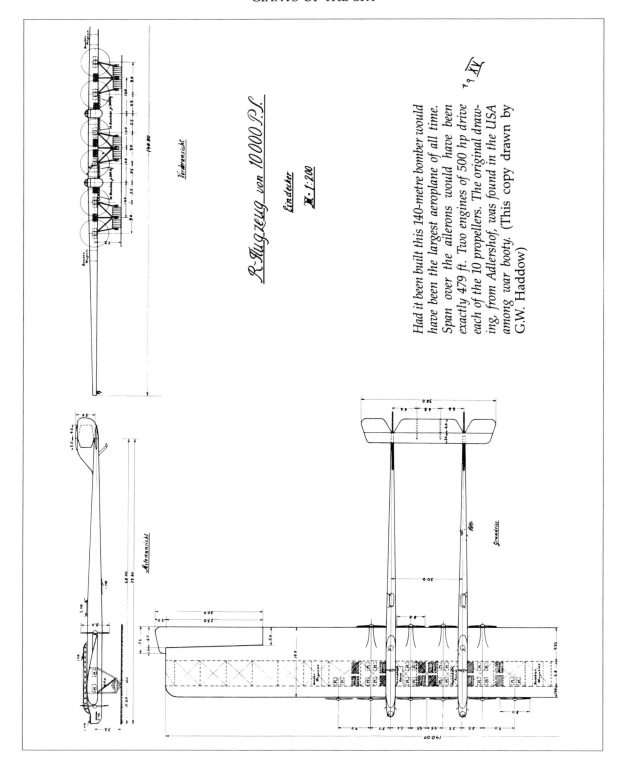

R-Flugzeug von 10000 P.S.

Eindecker

M. 1:200

Had it been built this 140-metre bomber would have been the largest aeroplane of all time. Span over the ailerons would have been exactly 479 ft. Two engines of 500 hp drive each of the 10 propellers. The original drawing, from Adlershof, was found in the USA among war booty. (This copy drawn by G.W. Haddow)

among Zeppelin material at Wright Field, had engines mounted inside a monoplane wing. The smallest, of 2,000 and 3,000 hp, had conventional layout. The rest, from 4,000 to 10,000 hp, had two slim fuselages carrying a monoplane or biplane tail with up to four rudders. All the biggest projects had three main landing gears. The 500 hp Benz watercooled vee-12 engines were in each case mounted axially in engine rooms between the main spars of the wing, one pair of engines being geared to each pusher or tractor propeller.

The smaller projects were accompanied by full specifications, in every case the wing loading being 35 kg/sq m and the power loading 10 kg/hp. The biggest and most powerful, and for this reason the one featured in this book, was fully dimensioned but without any breakdown of weight. Assuming the same wing and power loading, gross weight would have been 221,000 lb. It would have had a rectangular wing with a span of 459 ft 4 in over the fixed surface and of exactly 479 ft including the projecting balanced ailerons. The main wing box tapered in depth but not in plan view, and it contained the fuel and 20 engines, the latter driving six tractor and four pusher propellers. Eight engines (two pusher propellers and two tractor) were between the slim fuselages, which were 66 ft apart and gave the monster an overall length of

The SSW R.VIII was completed on 1 March 1919, but never flew, suffering severe damage when a pusher propeller disintegrated during ground testing. (Via Philip Jarrett)

290 ft 8 in. There was to be a long 'greenhouse' canopy above each forward fuselage, and 14 defensive machine guns. Up to 40 bombs of 661 lb would be carried under the wing, and others in cells inside the outer wings. The three main gears each had two sets of five tyres on one axle, giving 30 in all with a track of 161 ft. Adlershof is a suburb of Berlin, and was Germany's chief official flight-testing centre.

Could such a gigantic bomber have been built in the 1918-21 time frame? My own view is that, by spreading the load across a huge wing and two fuselages the design might have been capable of fulfilment. Obviously there would have been many problems, and even with both greenhouses full of pilots the rate of roll, and possibly of other manoeuvres, would have been extremely slow. Perhaps the most damning criticism is that an aircraft with a span of 479 ft and wheel track of 161 ft would be beyond anything that could be handled conveniently at today's major airfields. When one considers the small patches of grass used 70 years ago, such colossal aircraft appear unrealistic. A pity, because I consider the basic layout of these monsters excellent.

6 Kennedy Giant

Though it hardly took the world by storm this intended heavy bomber was planned and advertised as 'the world's largest aeroplane'. It also seems to be the only type in this book actually to have been *called* a giant (apart from the German-language Me321/323), though in those days designations were often vague. It was also called the Kennedy No 3, the Kennedy Giant Biplane, the Sikorsky-type bomber and the Super Sikorsky.

Chessborough J. H. Mackenzie Kennedy sailed from his native Scotland in 1905 with £3 in his pocket, and started a remarkably successful career in Czarist Russia. He was obviously well-connected, and busied himself with warships, guns, railways and many other enterprises, including aircraft. In 1912 he built a primitive (Voisin-type) biplane. After the war started he returned to Britain, where predictably he got involved with munitions magnates, one of whom may have been the shadowy figure named Hamilton Edwards. He let it be known that he had assisted Sikorsky in the design and manufacture of the IM aeroplanes. This has often been reported as fact, but when in 1960 I asked Sikorsky about this he replied, 'Mr Kennedy never worked for me, but I believe he visited us at the RBVZ factory'. My own opinion is simply that Mr K was a talented engineer (and smooth talker) who thought the big Sikorsky a good thing to copy. He soon had what were called 'palatial offices' in Cromwell Road, London, and got down to designing a giant bomber which at first was almost pure IM, 1914 pattern. The War Office contract was actually with Hamilton Edwards. Dated 7 July 1915, it described the aircraft as 'one Sikorsky, four 200 hp Salmson'. On 6 July 1916 the contract was transferred to Mr K. Serial number of the aircraft was 2337.

Having no factory, Mr K (or perhaps Edwards) let subcontracts for the actual detail design, stressing and manufacture of the aircraft to two companies at Hayes, Middlesex: Fairey Aviation, and The Gramophone Co (later EMI). Parts were trucked to the new aerodrome at Northolt, where they began arriving in November 1916. As no hangar was big enough, the Giant had to be assembled in the open. Many photographs show it surrounded by ladders and trestles, and on one occasion, when teams of men and two lorries were trying to manoeuvre it on the boggy ground, it broke its back. Construction was completed in about March or April 1917.

The Kennedy Giant, as it is most often called, was an unequal-span biplane. It was unquestionably based on the 1914 Sikorsky IM. Structure was wood, with steel joints and struts, with a mix of ply and fabric covering. The upper wing was rectangular, and carried the wide ailerons. Span was 142 ft, just exceeded by the Dornier Rs.I. The lower wing had the same chord of 10 ft but much shorter span, and no ailerons. The fuselage was like a box, almost a rectangle in side elevation; in plan the extremely short nose was rounded and the rear fuselage tapered to the stern post, to which was hung a ludicrously small rudder. Just in front, half-way down the fuselage, were the normal-size tailplane and elevators. A detail I find puzzling is that, as built, the Giant had prominent drag struts linking the very short forward fuselage to the lower wing, as well as two horizontal members which appeared to link the interplane struts immediately outboard of the engines, passing straight through the fuselage. The drag struts later vanished, to be replaced by yet another transverse member just above the lower wing. These transverse 'rods' appear to have been pipes, but they are more prominent than fuel or water pipes need

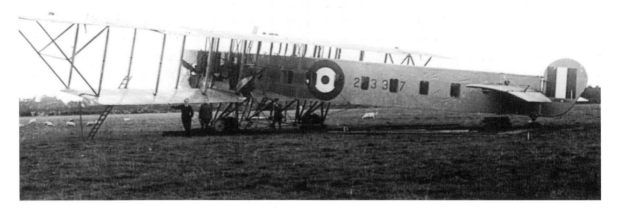

have been. I cannot see them serving a structural purpose (see photo, page 50).

Jack Bruce has recorded, 'Unfortunately for Kennedy, the only engines which the authorities would release for his machine were British-built Salmson watercooled radials of 200 hp each'. They were among the first to be produced under licence by Dudbridge Iron Works. It may be that the Giant was underpowered, but on the other hand it had more power than the same-size Staaken VGO bombers and four times the power of the original Sikorsky giant, so doubtless Kennedy was not bothered on this score. The engines were arranged in push/pull tandem pairs, and with such a tiny rudder one can say 'Thank Heavens for that!', though it was a layout Sikorsky had already rejected. It is doubtful that Kennedy was aiming to achieve more than about 70 mph, but even so the rather clumsy design of his Giant would have had high drag. On each side of each pair of engines was a totally unstreamlined radiator, and the Salmson was notorious for high drag, as Sikorsky had discovered. Almost certainly Kennedy intended to enclose the installations in a streamlined cowl, because later in 1917 the front propellers appeared with huge dome-like spinners while the rear propellers had conical spinners. All propellers had two blades. Another source of drag was the main landing gear, with 20

The Kennedy after the nose had been lengthened, but with the original rudder. (Via J.M. Bruce)

struts for the two pairs of wheels and four skids.

The entire nose was glazed, like a bay window. There is some evidence the pilot sat on the left, with the navigator on his right. There would have been at least two other crew members in a production bomber. In his several patents Kennedy described how he would have carried the bombs, hung nose-down with cups steadying their noses. The bomb-aimer would have had a control panel with electrical switches and indicators enabling him to drop any chosen selection of bombs and see which remained. He also tried to patent a scheme of defensive armament with guns in nose, dorsal and tail positions, but obviously neither nose nor tail guns could have been fitted to the Giant. Another odd design choice was to drive the ailerons and tail controls via external push/pull pods. Aerodynamicists would say that such rods running (as they did) along the top of the leading edge of the wing was the surest possible way to destroy airflow across the wing and promote an early stall!

Some time in the summer of 1917 the first test flight was attempted. The pilot was Lt Frank Courtney, RFC, an instructor at No 35

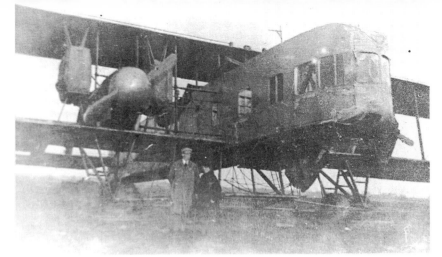

Training Squadron at Northolt. Subsequently he was to become one of the best-known British test pilots, but on this occasion he found 800 hp was not enough to overcome the pull of Mother Earth. Into wind, at full power, he found that eventually the rumble of the wheels ceased, but there was argument afterwards over whether or not the tailskid also left the ground. Certainly, No 2337 was tail-heavy, and in any case Courtney felt that, had the machine really climbed away, he would not have had sufficient strength to control it.

In my view the failure to fly must have been at least partly due to the aileron rods destroying the attached flow over the upper wing. Another factor was probably that the CG (centre of gravity) was dangerously far aft. We do not know how professionally the Kennedy was designed, and one could speculate on the structure being overweight; but it does not need much specialist knowledge to get the CG in the right place, and to check its location. Despite this, Kennedy had about 8 ft added to the length of the previously extremely short nose. This made the Giant look a bit more like 1917 instead of 1912, but by this time Courtney may have declined to try again. He, or someone else, may have suggested that the rudder was nothing like big enough — especially with the now huge side-area ahead of the wing — and so the Giant was then fitted with a new rudder of about 60 per cent greater area and a horn balance. By this time Kennedy may have run out of willing test pilots.

At least the fact that the Giant did get its wheels off the ground sufficed to extract the promised payment for the aircraft from the War Office, but there was no question of any further development. By this time, in 1918, Kennedy had probably recognised that the basic design was obsolete. He was busy with a smaller but better bomber, which after the Armistice he recast as a 'tonnage carrying' civil aircraft, to be made in partnership with John Dawson & Co of Newcastle-upon-Tyne. But soon Dawson decided to build nothing but furniture, and after a few further ventures and patent arguments Kennedy was declared bankrupt in early 1921. At this time No 2337 was still lying derelict in Northolt's north-west corner.

7 Felixstowe Fury

Almost all the big flying boats used by the RNAS and RAF, and many of those of the US Navy, in World War 1 owed a great deal to John Porte. As a lieutenant in the Royal Navy he learned to glide and then to fly, but in 1911 he was invalided out with tuberculosis. His flying went from strength to strength, and he held senior positions in British companies before, in 1914, joining Curtiss in the USA, initially to design a flying boat to fly the Atlantic, as explained in the next story. The war intervened, but Porte designed the Curtiss H-4, H-12 and many other boats, as well as the excellent Felixstowe series in Britain, of which the F.2A and F.3 were the most widely used.

Towards the end of the war there was so much of what we today would call 'defence funding' that it was easy to add the odd extra very large aircraft. The RNAS Seaplane Experimental Station at Felixstowe, by this time under the command of Sqn Cdr Porte, had done so much brilliant work, nearly all on aircraft derived from his pre-war basic design, that it was eager to show what could be done with the proverbial clean sheet of paper. Though there does not seem to have been a direct operational requirement for such a machine — and the same goes for the

big Fairey boats described later — it is hardly surprising that Porte's team set about building a very large boat that was much better than anything seen previously. The result became known as the Porte Super Baby, though its official title was the Felixstowe Fury.

In many respects it was a completely conventional design. One of the exceptions was that, to keep the span down to 123 ft, it was a triplane, with the bottom wing similar in chord to the others but of considerably shorter span. Only the middle and top wings had ailerons, with large horn balances. Wing area was 3,108 sq ft. The tail was also most unusual: there was a large central fin which was sharply swept back on both leading and trailing edges, and to it were attached biplane tailplanes. The upper

Ground running the five engines of the Fury, with a Sopwith Camel in the foreground. (Via J.M. Bruce)

tailplane was considerably larger than the lower and carried the main elevator. The lower elevator was smaller and was used for trimming, in a way described later. Twin rudders were mounted between the tailplanes, and a third smaller rudder was carried above the upper tailplane at the rear tip of the swept fin.

The Fury was designed to be powered by three 600 hp Rolls-Royce Condor engines, but these were not ready in time. Accordingly five 334 hp Rolls-Royce Eagle VII engines were fitted; these, like the Condor, were massive watercooled vee-12s. All were mounted on the middle wing, there being two tandem push/pull nacelles plus one pusher engine on the centreline. The tractor engines drove two-blade propellers and the three pushers four-blade units. The bluff upright water radiators were mounted between and above the tandem engines and ahead of the central engine. To accommodate the three pusher propellers in the correct position, a long section of trailing edge of the middle wing was removed.

Of course the structure was all-wood, apart from steel joints and a few steel struts. The hull was a typical Porte design, in the form of a flat-sided fuselage riding on a very much wider planing-bottom hull. As usual the top line was straight and the bottom a curve, with a single step well aft, but a new feature was that the actual planing bottom, on each side of the keel, was slightly concave instead of forming a flat 150° vee. Internal structure was mainly in the form of lattice girders and strong transverse frames, and the skin was multiple diagonal veneers of cedar, or, in the case of the bottom skins, cedar and mahogany. Historian Jack Bruce recorded that 'Great pains were taken to avoid the splitting which occurred at the joints of earlier hulls; the diagonal planking was steamed and bent round the chines and fin tops.' All fuel was in metal tanks in the hull, with the pumps driven by two windmills which fed the fuel up to a gravity tank (which looks very small) under the

centre of the top wing. Stabilizing floats were attached directly under the bottom wings which, as in previous Porte boats, had two bracing struts each side running diagonally to the chine of the hull.

Certainly the most interesting and advanced feature of the Fury was the fact that 'servo motors' were fitted in the flight-control system, to apply augmented power to all the movable surfaces. The arrangement was possibly the first powered flight-control system in history, and was developed with an installation on N90, an otherwise normal Felixstowe F.5. For example, the aileron control wires passed over pulleys until they emerged from the top of the hull in line with the front of the central wing strut, one cable well to the left of the centreline and the other to the right. The two cables were brought together at a central yoke where small pulleys turned them vertical to run up the strut to the top wing. When the pilot applied aileron the tension in the pulled cable rocked the pivoted yoke to that side. The greater the tension, the greater the lateral movement of the yoke. At a certain level the pivoting of the yoke engaged a worm gear which was continuously driven throughout flight by a large two-blade propeller. Normally this ran free, causing very little drag, but when the gear was engaged it drove a sprocket and long chain connected to the aileron cables. Rocking the yoke to the left pulled down the left aileron. Rocking it to the right reversed the drive and pulled down the right aileron.

There was more advanced technology (for the day) in the tail. The following is taken from the Royal Aeronautical Society paper read on 18 January 1923 by Maj J.D. Rennie, Chief Technical Officer at Felixstowe:

An adjustable tailplane may, however, present some difficulty, as in the case of a biplane tailplane, of which the fins and rudders form an integral part; the effort required to operate it under its own weight, apart from air load, may be beyond the capability of the pilot, unless

The Fury with its modified tail unit. (G.S. Leslie/ J.M. Bruce collection)

some auxiliary motive power is used, such as an oil pump and ram. Anticipating this trouble on the Fury, the elevator on the lower plane was operated separately by a long lever on a quadrant centred on the elevator control shaft. This was used to obtain trim and the upper elevator for extra control in the usual way. The result was quite satisfactory, but owing to hull interference the efficiency of the lower plane was relatively low.

With regard to fin and rudders, owing to the long forebody, these are of relatively large area. The rudder area on the F boats was barely sufficient for control with one engine cut out completely. The Fury, however, was very satisfactory in this respect; the arrangement there used, namely, three propellers abreast, and three fins and rudders in their respective slipstreams would seem to solve the problem of one engine cutting out. Little data appears to be available on the subject; calculations are liable to be greatly in error as the yaw taken up by the machine after one engine has cut out is difficult of determination with any degree of accuracy. A figure of some interest in this connection and not generally available is the air drag of a stationary propeller. Tests of a fair variety of different propellers gave from 12 to 13 lb/sq ft of projected area at 100 ft/sec.

Altogether the Fury was an excellent aircraft. It incorporated all the countless lessons learned with previous Porte designs. Back in 1916 Porte had built a biplane flying boat of almost precisely similar size, humorously named the Baby (it was followed by 10 production Babies). Compared with these machines the Fury had more wing area, being a triplane, more power (five Eagles, each of a more powerful version, instead of three) and considerably greater capability, with a gross weight increased from 18,600 lb to a maximum of 33,000 lb. Moreover, the Fury's hull was probably the best of any wartime flying boat.

The single Fury, serial N123, was completed in September 1918. From the start its handling qualities, both on the water and in the air, were outstanding. In fact, though there is no evidence that the system did not give satisfaction, the flight-control servo motors were soon removed because they were complicated and simply not needed. The design gross weight was 24,000 lb, but at 28,000 lb the launching, seaworthiness and take off characteristics were found to be better than those of previous boats, and Col Porte made at least one take off at 33,000 lb. Maximum speed was just short of 100 mph, and service ceiling 12,000 to 14,000 ft.

Various modifications were made, the most obvious of which was to fit a different tail unit. This retained the same horizontal surfaces but joined them by three identical fins and rudders, as noted in Rennie's paper. Following model tests in the NPL Froude towing tank, the hull was given various — mostly minor — modifications. The most visible change was to add first a second step and then a third, the hull finally reverting to the two-step layout. The middle engine was given a four-blade propeller like the outer pushers, and for some reason the hull and interplane struts were painted white. Maj T.D. Hallam made a test flight with 24 passengers, 5,000 lb of sand ballast and fuel for seven hours.

The Fury never saw active service, and probably never carried its armament of four to six machine-guns and 'a substantial load'

of bombs. With its fuel capacity of 1,500 gal the Fury could probably have flown across the North Atlantic in either direction (Jack Bruce has no doubt of it). This was in fact planned shortly after the Armistice, but there was never enough money to allow it to happen. In any case the Fury was soon written off. In 1919 Col Porte and Maj Rennie were demobilised. Maj Ronald Moon took the Fury off, apparently with the CG in the wrong place, and (so the evidence suggests) at too low a speed. The big boat stalled, and the planing bottom caved in on impact with the water.

8 Curtiss NC series

Despite all the problems of giant aeroplanes, notably the basic one that lift (wing area) varies as the square of the dimensions while weight (such as fuel load) varies as the cube of the dimensions, it can be shown for various reasons that, for any given kind of tech-

nology, big aeroplanes can be made to fly further than small ones. Thus, from 1913, designers who sought to win a prize offered by the *Daily Mail* of £10,000 for the first non-stop flight across the North Atlantic all thought in terms of a very large machine.

The most prominent of these designers was the American pioneer Glenn Curtiss. Funded by the wealthy department-store owner Rodman Wanamaker, who was determined to win the prize, Curtiss hired two Britons to help with the design of a giant flying boat: Lt John Porte (see Felixstowe Fury) led the hull team, and personally designed the planing bottom, while B. Douglas Thomas, late of Sopwith Aviation, designed the wings. This 1914 boat was sized to accomplish a non-stop leg of 1,100 miles, which was the longest single overwater stretch. Today it seems amazing that it should have been designed with just two 90 hp engines (both pushers). In fact the *America*, as it was named, proved in June 1914 to be underpowered, and a third engine was added. Then in August war broke out and the flight was abandoned, but this boat was the starting point for Porte's outstanding series of wartime designs.

Porte returned to England and, as we have seen, masterminded the subsequent development of British seaplanes at Felixstowe. Wanamaker, however, saw no reason to give up and, having the perfectly reasonable idea that it should be possible to build a really capable transatlantic machine, con-

tracted with Curtiss for a second time to do just that. This time there was to be no pussy-footing about with two 90 hp engines; the design power was four Curtiss vee-12 engines of 250 hp each, all arranged as tractors driving four-blade propellers. The result was the Curtiss Model 3, or Wanamaker Triplane. Wanamaker, however, faded from the picture, and instead of being a civil transatlantic machine it turned into a military patrol boat called the Type T. When completed in 1916 it was one of the world's largest aircraft, the span of the top plane being 134 ft. The middle and bottom wings were progressively smaller.

There is every reason to believe that the Type T was a good boat, despite its exceptional size. The Royal Naval Air Service ordered 20, allotting serial numbers 3073-3092, but received only the first to be completed. Whilst at Felixstowe No 3073 was re-engined with 240 hp aircooled Renaults,

Though intended to be the first of 20 this Curtiss Type T Triplane, RNAS No 3073, was the only one to reach Felixstowe. This head-on view, taken after 3073 had been re-engined, shows the odd cross-section of the Porte hull. (Via Philip Jarrett)

and it certainly saw some operational service. The main mission of the giant triplanes was to be anti-Zeppelin patrol, the boats having the power and endurance to stand off hundreds of miles from the British coast and engage the airships with various weapons manned by the crew of six.

Had the whole batch been completed, it was planned that the huge boats would have been flown across the Atlantic. Just as in World War 2 with the Kaiser-Hughes concept for a 'flying Liberty Ship', the idea of a giant transatlantic flying boat had a natural appeal for Americans in World War 1. Certainly Curtiss continued to think about the problems in 1916-17.

After the entry of the United States into the war in April 1917 the US Navy swiftly grew in power, capability and ambitions. The biggest single factor in drawing the USA into the conflict had been Germany's unrestricted U-boat warfare, and the US Navy's No 1 task was to defeat the U-Boat. From late 1917 various aircraft were shipped across the Atlantic, including 60 Curtiss H-16 patrol flying boats and another 50 constructed at the Naval Aircraft Factory (NAF) at Philadelphia (all 50 were shipped by 7 July 1918). This was no mean achievement, because the contract to build the NAF on virgin ground

at the Philadelphia Navy Yard was only let in August 1917, and everything — choosing tools, hiring and training personnel (many of whom had never seen an aeroplane) and deciding on raw materials — had to be done from scratch. The CO was Cdr. F.G. Coburn, and the two senior design engineers were Cdrs Jerome C. Hunsaker and Holden C. Richardson.

On 25 August 1917 the Chief Naval Constructor, Adm David W. Taylor, issued a statement advocating aerial attack on U-boats. He said 'The ideal solution would be big flying boats or the equivalent, that would be able to fly across the Atlantic to avoid the problems of delivery &c'. The result was that Curtiss was invited to Washington to discuss the design of such a flying boat with the Bureau of Construction and Repair. The NC (Navy Curtiss) was thus a true collaborative effort, the preliminary design being handled jointly at the NAF by Hunsaker and Richardson and by Curtiss staff at Garden City, New York. An exception was the hull, the complete design of which was carried out in September 1917 by Richardson and his assistants at the NAF. Curtiss received a contract to build four NCs, and it was intended that the NAF should build six more. All were to be combat-ready boats,

Left *Navy Curtiss 1 immediately after being launched. Note three engines, the 'fighting top' for a gunner and primitive stabilizing floats. (Via H. Woodman)*

Right *The NC-2 was always the odd man out, with paired tandem engines and the pilots in a nacelle high up above the hull.*

delivered by air across the Atlantic in accord with Adm Taylor's suggestion.

In many ways the NC design was conventional, roughly the size and (as designed) power of the Type T triplane boat, but a biplane. The most unconventional feature was the fact that the hull was short (45 ft), the tail being carried on a framework of braced struts. The idea was that long hulls tended to break, especially in heavy seas, and that what did not exist could not be weak. There is no evidence to suggest that this arrangement was any better or worse than the conventional layout.

The wings were of unequal span, the top measuring 126 ft and the lower (which had dihedral) 114 ft. Chord was 12 ft. Structure was of spruce, with all fittings of chrome-vanadium steel and covering of doped fabric. The hull had an NAF shape; instead of having a Porte-style narrow upper part and very wide planing bottom, the cross section was almost a circular arc (turtle deck) meeting the planing bottom at the full-beam chine. This was structurally efficient and increased internal space. The planing bottoms were slightly concave, and there was a single transverse step. Keel structure was oak or rock elm, the rest being cedar, with cedar or spruce planking and the skin over

the upper turtle deck being cottonwood/birch plywood. The tail was carried on three braced tubular steel struts, and comprised upper and lower tailplanes of unequal span, each carrying a balanced elevator, and two fins and three rudders. The large balanced ailerons, on the upper wings only, extended well beyond the tips with projecting horn balances. As was often the case with boats of this period, the upper wings carried prominent stabilizing fins above the outer interplane struts to serve as kingposts for the anti-lift bracing wires.

Power comprised three 400 hp Liberty watercooled vee-12 engines, all mounted as tractors just above the mid-level between the wings. Each drove a four-blade propeller, immediately behind which was the flat rectangular water radiator projecting vertically upwards ahead of the engine. Except for the cylinder blocks each engine was cowled in a box-like streamlined nacelle, mounted between pairs of interplane struts. A total of 1,573 gal (all gallons in this book are Imperial) of fuel was housed in nine drums in the hull, pumped by windmills up to a gravity tank in the upper wing. A hand-cranked emergency pump was provided. The usual slipstream-driven windmills also rotated above the hull to drive electric generators to charge the lead/acid batteries supplying interior lighting, radio, navigation and landing lights, all very rare in 1918.

Ahead of the wings were separate side-by-side cockpits for two pilots. In the nose was a navigation desk for plotting charts, with sextant, drift sight and even a radio direction-finding receiver. Gunners occupied cockpits in the bow, aft of the wings and above the middle of the upper wing. The bottom wing made structural provision for a bomb load, such as 230 lb A/S bombs; for the anti-Zeppelin role no racks were installed.

Hulls were to be made by Lawley & Sons of Boston, other parts mostly being produced by Curtiss at the factory at Garden City, which was enlarged for the purpose. Completed sections were trucked to the Rockaway Beach Naval Air Station (NAS), at Far Rockaway, Long Island (very near Garden City). Here NC-1 was completed in late September 1918 and first flown by Cdr Richardson and Lt David H. McCulloch on 4 October. On 27 November NC-1 flew with 51 men on board, at the time a world record. Nevertheless, it was clear that the big boat was underpowered.

The Armistice on 11 November resulted in immediate cancellation of many Navy contracts, and at the NAF only those machines that had reached assembly Stage 6

were to be completed. NC-5 to NC-10 had not reached this stage, so they were delayed until 1920-21. Work continued on NC-2, 3 and 4. No two were ever alike, though after numerous modifications NC-1, 3 and 4 did end up closely similar. NC-2 was always very much an odd one out. She was completed with the centre engine arranged as a pusher, and with the two pilots in a single side-by-side cockpit in the extended front portion of this engine nacelle, high above the hull. NC-2 first flew in February 1919, but by this time it was clear that the NC boats as a class would be improved by having extra power. NC-2 was therefore rebuilt with four Liberty 12 engines arranged in push/pull tandem pairs, with simple cowlings covering just the crankcases and driving two-blade propellers in front and four-bladers behind. The four radiators were directly in front of and above each engine. A major change was that the previous engine-bearing interplane struts were removed, the two tandem nacelles being mounted on groups of steel struts attached to the lower wing, braced to four interplane struts at the centreline, which still carried

---

The launch of NC-4, with three tractor engines and one pusher, improved floats and the pilots in the hull. (Via J.M. Bruce)

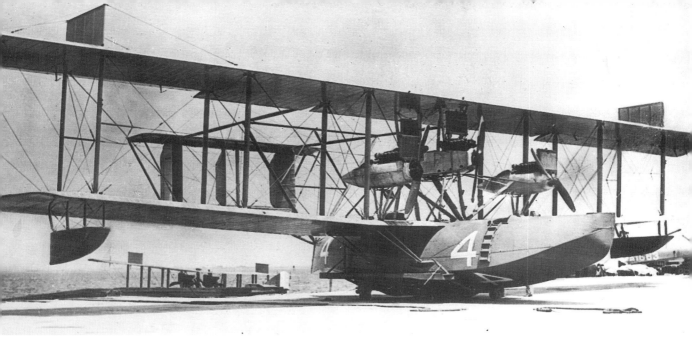

the pilots' cockpit but in a shortened nacelle. NC-2 flew in this strange configuration on 12 April 1919. Finally, the central nacelle was removed and the pilots were given a normal cockpit in the hull. As rebuilt NC-2 was redesignated NC-T, for Tandem, but she was never fully satisfactory.

Meanwhile, NC-1 had likewise been modified, with a totally new arrangement of engines and interplane struts, all previous struts and nacelles being removed. On the centreline was constructed a mounting of six struts on which was carried a tandem nacelle (not identical to those of NC-2) with two Liberty engines, with six further struts linking the nacelle to the upper wing. Except for the upper part of the cylinder blocks the engines were cowled, and the rear radiator was mounted half-way between the rear of the aft engine and the top wing. The other two engines were carried on the lower wing on braced arrangements of struts, much lower than previously and inboard of the innermost interplane struts. Again, the tractor screws were two-blade and the pushers four-blade.

Another modification was to fit new stabilizing floats under the outer wings. Originally these had been of the crude form common on early float seaplanes, with a

NC-4 immediately before its transatlantic flight, on beaching chassis and with specially built ladder to cockpit. (Via H. Woodman)

trapezoidal side elevation (high front and low stern) and rectangular, almost square, cross-section. The new floats had a proper vee-type planing bottom and a rather unusual side elevation, with a high bow and full-depth vertical knife-edge at the back. They appeared to be remarkably narrow, though clearly they possessed adequate buoyancy.'

NC-3 was completed to the revised NC-1 configuration, flying on 23 April 1919. NC-4 was again very similar, but her hull was built by Herrescholl Co of Rhode Island. She first flew on 30 April 1919. The last three boats made no provision for armament, and were completed in order to attempt a transatlantic flight to gain prestige for the Navy. They were formed into Seaplane Division One, at NAS Rockaway Beach, under Cdr John H. Towers, the boats being redesignated as type NC-TA (trans-Atlantic). They were fitted with extra fuel tanks and navigation equipment, new and more powerful radio able to transmit about 300 miles in the air and 150 on the sea, and new propellers

designed by the Bureau of Steam Engineering in place of the original Olmsteads. NC-1 was severely damaged in a storm, so NC-2 was dismantled and her wings were fitted to NC-1. Thus, three boats remained to take off from Rockaway Beach on 8 May 1919.

The rest of the story is the best-known part. On 16 May the three big NC boats left Trepassey Bay, Newfoundland, heading on the great-circle course for Horta, in the Azores. NC-4 alighted there on the 17th to find no sign of the others. Eventually NC-3 arrived, commanded by team-leader Towers, having been forced down 45 miles southeast of Fayal and having to taxi the next 200 miles, arriving 52 hr out from Newfoundland. NC-3 could not continue. NC-1 fared even worse, having to alight 100 miles west of Flores and sinking after suffering damage from the heavy seas, the crew being rescued. On 20 May NC-4 went on alone, travelling via Ponta Delgada, Lisbon and Ferrol de Caudillo, to a triumphant arrival in Plymouth on 31 May, escorted by three RAF F.2A boats. Lt-Cdr A.C. Read and his

NC-9, one of the six boats built post-war. Two were lost, and the other four converted from three to four engines. (Via Malcolm Passingham)

crew were fêted, and today NC-4 still exists at the Naval Aviation Museum at NAS Pensacola, Florida.

To avoid arguments, NC-4 made the first crossing of the North Atlantic by stages. Less than a month later Capt John Alcock and Lt Arthur Whitten Brown, both of the RAF, made the first non-stop crossing in a Vickers Vimy, on 14/15 June, at the excellent average speed of 118 mph. In July RAF airship R.34, with a large crew, made a completely successful round trip (which obviously included the first westbound crossing). Altogether 91 aviators flew the Atlantic before Charles Lindbergh made the first solo crossing, in May 1927, which was also the first between major cities (New York and Paris). And Lindbergh did it in a small aircraft.

9 Tarrant Tabor

In July 1917 the British Air Board, following general agreement that the war was likely to last into 1919, authorized the con-

struction of aircraft able to carry significant bombloads over unprecedented distances; in particular, able to bomb Berlin from bases in England. One of these aircraft was the Handley Page V/1500, a perfectly straightforward design which, despite the non-appearance of the intended engines, went into production and saw successful service. Though an impressive machine, the V/1500 does not quite rate inclusion here. But another 'Berlin bomber' most certainly does. This was the first, and last, aircraft produced by W.G. Tarrant Ltd, of Byfleet, Surrey.

Tarrant specialized in wooden buildings. On the outbreak of World War 1 a lot of the firm's capacity was turned over to mass-production of aircraft tails, wings and sometimes fuselages. In 1917 Mr Tarrant decided to 'have a go' himself, and he thought a good thing on which to learn the business might be the biggest aeroplane in the world!

Put like this it sounds nonsensical, but in fact the project was managed perfectly reasonably. Design was entrusted to the Small Drawing Office at the Royal Aircraft Factory at Farnborough, the head of which was Walter H. Barling. Thus all the basic design was professionally handled, while the structural stressing was in the capable hands of Letitia Chitty, who at the age of 19, whilst reading mathematics at Newnham College, Cambridge, was pitchforked into the intricacies of aircraft structures in the Admiralty Air Department — along with

One of the bombloads specified for the Tabor was 16 bombs of 250 lb, but this photograph shows no hint of any attachments under the bottom wing. It has just been pulled out from the Farnborough Balloon Hangar on railed trucks. (Via Philip Jarrett)

such others as Capt. A.P. Thurston, A.J. Sutton Pippard, H.B. Howard, Capt T.M. Wilson and Capt J. Laurence Pritchard, later a noted Secretary of the RAeS (who, incidentally, was disgusted when in 1951 I 'threw away a career' to become 'a mere aviation writer'). In other words, the people who designed the giant knew what they were about.

While the work was proceeding, in 1918, the Air Board placed contracts for two of the Tarrant bombers, allocating serial numbers F1765 and 1766. The aircraft was blessed with the name Tabor, which I only know as 'a small drum like a tambourine'. Maybe in this case it had some other meaning (derived from people's names?).

Predictably, the Tabor was made entirely of wood, except for steel joints and steel tubes for the engine and landing-gear struts and similar highly stressed parts. Miss Chitty recalled that it was the last aircraft she worked on. 'Mr Tarrant was an inspired timber merchant who dreamed of a super-Camel. It hadn't a chance. It was too big, too heavy — that wasn't its fault, but Grade A spruce had by now run out and it had to be built of American white wood (tulip). In my language 3,500 instead of 5,500 lb/sq in.' In other words, the Tabor was never going to be a sparkling performer.

Perhaps the most impressive thing about it was the superb semi-monocoque fuselage, of almost perfect streamline shape, with ring frames looking like those of an airship, the inner and outer rings being joined by numerous short diagonal links serving variously as ties or struts. This beautiful fuselage was mounted midway between the lower and middle triplane wings, which were of unusual design. The middle wing was larger than the others. and was the only one to have ailerons. The arrangement of struts can clearly be seen, and if we treat the slightly inclined pairs of 40 ft struts on each side of the engines as all adding up to one column then the Tabor comes out as a two-bay machine, which is pretty impressive for

a span of over 131 ft. The smaller V/1500, for example, had four bays, and some biplanes had even more.

Originally the Tabor was designed for four of the big Siddeley Tiger engines, all arranged as tractors. Two were to be about half-way between the bottom and middle wings on each side and the other two directly above, mid-way between the middle and top wing. The Tiger, which had only a faint family link with the much later Armstrong Siddeley Tiger, was a watercooled vee-12 based on the cylinder blocks of the Puma, and it was hoped to produce 600 hp. Unfortunately neither it, nor any of the other high-power engines, such as the Rolls-Royce Condor or Beardmore Atlantic, could be made ready in time, and the Tabor had to be redesigned to be powered by six Napier Lions. These superb 450 hp engines, each with three watercooled 4-cylinder blocks arranged in W or 'broad arrow' formation, were no problem to instal, though it meant that the bottom engines would be in tandem push/pull pairs. The four tractor engines drove 12 ft 6 in two-blade propellers and the pushers 10 ft 7.25 in four-bladers. All fuel was carried in the fuselage, all engines had long exhaust pipes and the six water radiators were fixed broadside-on directly beneath each engine, there being (so far as photographs show) no attempt at any cowling.

With so lofty a giant, starting the engines posed problems. I have never understood why one of the available methods of gas starting was not used, in which a compressor supplied a compressed over-rich mixture to each cylinder in the correct sequence. One such system was actually tested on a Lion. Instead, the standard Hucks was used. This was a car chassis whose engine could be coupled to a shaft carried overhead whose front end terminated in a two-pin dog clutch. The height and inclination of the shaft were adjustable. The clutch mated with a female connection on the front of the propeller looking like a giant lamp bayonet

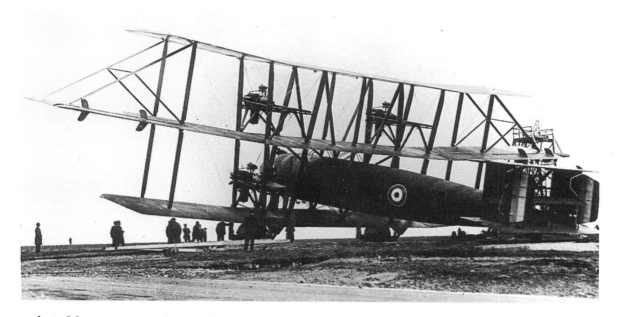

The Tabor was painted with a khaki POV (pigmented oil varnish) which looked dark brown. Small white serial numbers were on the fins. Here the engines are running. (Via Philip Jarrett)

socket. I have seen a photo of the Tabor in which the Hucks is starting a lower engine while the engine directly above is turned by a mighty belt, but Jack Bruce has pictures showing the whole Hucks apparatus hoisted by lift on a giant tower to crank the upper engines. They must have hustled to get all six engines started on the same day! And I salute the mechanics who serviced the upper engines, some 33 ft from the ground.

Predictably, the undercarriage was also interesting. At the back was a suitably massive tailskid. The main units, of which there were two, each comprised three wheels on one axle, the latter being attached to a surrounding frame in the form of three sides of a square, pin-jointed to large triangular brackets at the rear and to the almost vertical lower ends of the main interplane struts at the front. The latter incorporated telescopic shock-absorbing struts. The overall effect was quite neat, in comparison with the clumsy arrangements on some other large aircraft. The tail was also neat by the standards of the day, but it was not quite what it seemed. It was supported by the fixed lower tailplane, mounted quite low on the fuselage. This carried twin fins, each

with a rudder whose horn balance was inset into the fin, on top of which was the upper tailplane. The catch came in the fact that, whilst there were indeed two elevators, the lower one was hinged to the lower tailplane and the other was pivoted half-way up the fins. The 'elevator' hinged to the upper tailplane was for trimming only.

There are many things I do not know about the Tabor. The only entrance appears to have been a small circular hatch in the lower left side of the rear fuselage. There was clearly a side-by-side open cockpit for the two pilots, and one or two other windows or open hatches can be seen, but I know nothing of the crew positions, nor of the armament, other than that provision was made for 4,650 lb of 'bombs and associated gear' and 380 lb of 'guns and ammunition'. One obvious problem is that any internally stowed bombs would have had to pass through the bottom wing, so the bomb racks must have been under the bottom wing.

Though W.G. Tarrant made all the major airframe parts these were trucked to Farnborough, where the aircraft was erected in one of the two giant Balloon Sheds (actually, in 1918, airship sheds). In May 1919 F1765 was completed, and to get it outside it had to be mounted on small four-wheel trucks running on rails, the aircraft emerging sideways. After some ground running, the first flight was set for 26 May. The pilots, Capt F.G. Dunn AFC, assisted by Capt P.T. Rawlings DSC, carried out successful taxi tests, with Miss Chitty's colleague Capt Wilson in the tail gun position. Dunn increased speed on the lower engines, lifted the tail and then opened up the upper engines. It

proved fatal; the Tabor majestically tipped on to its nose, despite full up-elevator, and came to rest just past the vertical, resting on its shattered leading edges. Both pilots were thrown out and killed, but Wilson scrambled down the fuselage almost unhurt, there being no fire.

At the inquest Mr Tarrant described how his consulting engineers had argued with RAE experts about nose- or tail-heaviness, and how, to avoid the latter, about 1,000 lb of lead-shot bags had been loaded into the nose. But it seems more likely that the reason for the uncontrollable nose-down pitch was the thrust of the upper engines so far from the ground, possibly combined with some abnormal drag from the wheels. The second Tabor was never completed.

The
1920s

Aircraft constructors, and especially their designers, might have been expected to be fast-moving people, ever alert to the emergence of new technology and, in a world of intense commercial and military competition, eager to be the first to put each new technology to use. Not a bit of it! In fact there seems to be a kind of 10-year gap which the decision-takers need in order to collect their thoughts. After all, we don't want to rush into anything new, do we?

Thus, whereas in 1920 the world might have been expected to be on the brink of a swift and total move towards all-metal stressed-skin construction, as so impressively demonstrated by the Staaken E.4/20 four-engined cantilever monoplane airliner (not quite a giant) of 1920, in practice nothing much happened. Even the giant aeroplanes continued to be designed in traditional ways, and when a big stressed-skin aeroplane *was* built (the Inflexible) everyone contrived to (in my opinion, that is) make the proverbial pig's ear of it.

To some extent it was a chicken-and-egg situation. Because nobody — except for a handful of Germans — had any experience of stressed-skin construction, nobody appeared to appreciate the advantages. Because nobody appreciated the advantages, there was no pressure from any of the customers. Thus, when in the mid-1920s the Royal Air Force (RAF) did begin to recognise the advantages of structures made of metal, rather than wood, they were thinking only in terms of resistance to tropical humidity and white ants, and of general robustness. The British industry merely went on producing wire-braced biplanes with fabric covering, but with the underlying skeleton translated into metal. Some designers specially allowed for wooden parts to be inserted during repairs in remote areas where there were no facilities for working in metal. One might as well design a car so that a horse could be attached at the front.

Only at the very end of this decade of the 1920s do we begin to encounter giant aircraft that are all-metal. Both were German — the Dornier Do X and Junkers G38 — but they were by no means stressed-skin aircraft. This is surprising, because Rohrbach, the greatest pioneer of stressed-skin structures, had been on Dornier's payroll during World War 1. Instead, the vast acreage of wing skin of both these monsters was corrugated, to give it greater robustness. This meant that, while mechanics could walk on it, it could not bear high tensile loads as could flat sheet. The latter would not only be lighter but would also have less drag, as explained much later in the Ju90 story.

Even more surprising, Rohrbach spent the 1920s directing his own company's production of commercial transports, both landplanes and flying boats, which had modern smooth-skinned cantilever wings, and ought in consequence to have been the most efficient in the world. Perversely, and perhaps predictably, these sold only in small numbers, and Rohrbach was merged into Weser Flugzeugbau. It was left to Jack Northrop in far-off California to show the world how to make aeroplanes — but in the next decade.

Leaving aside the question of structural methods, the 1920s began with a lot of the Northern Hemisphere littered with ex-wartime aircraft, which you could buy for almost nothing. This made it hard for the once-fat planemakers, yet many of them nevertheless contrived to build colossal aircraft, such as the Ca60, which never had a hope of finding a customer. Those built under contract, such as the Tabor, N.4, XNBL-1 and Inflexible, accomplished nothing to justify their cost. Sadly, some of the most advanced projects were German, and the Allies wouldn't allow these to be built.

Previous page *Since long before the Wright Brothers visionaries have drawn giant flying machines. This delightful 'strategic airlifter' appeared in the Australian magazine* Aircraft *for 1 September 1931 to accompany a piece by Louis Breguet in which he wrote of aeroplanes that could carry a whole battalion. (The artist* was *joking.)*

10 Grahame-White 24-seater

Claude Grahame-White was one of the greatest pioneers of aviation in Britain. Before World War 1 his flying school at Hendon was the busiest in the country, so it is only right that today's RAF Museum should be located on Grahame-White Way. In 1910 he built his first aeroplane, and these grew in numbers, size and complexity, as did his Hendon factory. His first really big machine was the E.IV Ganymede bomber, with a span of 89 ft and powered — in the absence of 400 hp Libertys — by three 270 hp Sunbeam Maoris. I cannot resist quoting from H.B. Howard's contribution to the special 1966 Centenary edition of the *Journal* of the Royal Aeronautical Society:

In the winter 1917-18 I spent several weeks at Grahame-White's works at Hendon. Grahame-White was then building a new type of bomber which had two fuselages and three engines, one in the nose of each fuselage and one mounted in a nacelle on the lower plane in between the two fuselages. The first flight of this ungainly contraption was quite an occasion. Grahame-White was at the time married to Ethel Levy, a revue star of the period whom those of my generation may well

remember. Before take-off Ethel Levy christened the aircraft with the traditional bottle of champagne, the 'top brass' and press photographers etc all standing round. The aeroplane lumbered heavily over the ground for some fifty yards and sat down heavily, one undercarriage having collapsed. In self-defence I should add that in those days we did no check-stressing on undercarriages.

The Armistice put paid to the Ganymede's career as a bomber, so G-W turned it into G-EAMW, a rather clumsy airliner with two 450 hp Napier Lions and the central nacelle extended into a full-length fuselage for about 12 passengers.

He thereupon got down to the design of an even bigger machine, to accommodate passengers in style similar to 'the first-class carriage or Pullman car', with cabins 'neatly panelled' and seats 'tastefully upholstered'.

Side elevation of the Grahame-White 24-seater. Small circles in the centre wing show the position of the drive shafts to the left tractor propeller (front shaft) and right propeller (rear). The ladder was 'ground support equipment'. (Via J.M. Bruce)

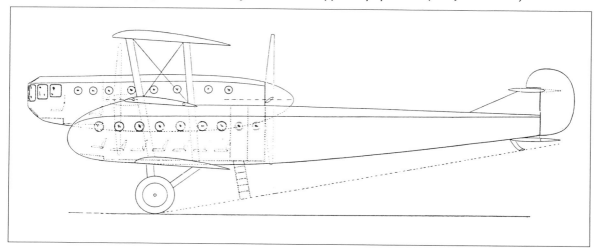

To achieve his objective he decided to keep the engines and similar unspeakable lower-class things, such as the flight crew, completely remote from the passengers. In effect, he adopted the configuration of the Ganymede, but in reverse. In the central nacelle were the engines and flight crew, while the passengers were in the twin fuselages which carried the tail.

I think he was optimistic in estimating the gross weight, with 24 passengers and six crew, at 'from 8 to 8.5 tons', which is scarcely more than that of the Ganymede, though whereas the bomber had fuel for 9 hr the big passenger machine had fuel for only 3 hr. The civil machine was a triplane, with a span of 100 ft, and wing area of about 2,800 sq ft, compared with 1,660 for the bomber, which I would have thought matched a weight nearer to 28,000 lb. All three wings differed in chord. In the central nacelle were three engines. Two, of 500 hp (Lions?), drove shafting to tractor propellers on the centre wing. The third, of 800 hp (Napier Cub?), was in the rear of the nacelle driving an enormous four-blade pusher propeller. The 'navigator or captain' was to sit in 'the very front of the nacelle', the pilot (obviously having the status of a bus driver) being behind him. Each fuselage was to seat 12 passengers, with a 13th 'lookout' seat in the nose. Each passenger had a porthole, and an attendant in each car was to 'point out landmarks', though in the drawing the portholes are too high for anyone to see out! The tail was of the biplane type, with three fins and two rudders. Cruising speed was estimated at 100 mph, and list price as £20,000. This was more than double the price of a Handley Page O/400 heavy bomber; but several hundred O/400s were made, while the G-W triplane stayed on paper.

11 English Electric Phoenix Pulex

During World War I one of the numerous companies brought in to help produce aircraft was the works at Bradford, Yorkshire, of the Phoenix Dynamo Co. This had become one of the chief aircraft contractors to the Admiralty, and it even built up its own design team, led by W.O. Manning. After the war it became part of the giant English Electric Company, and as it had done quite well building aeroplanes it was decided to stay in the business and form a permanent Phoenix Aircraft Branch. It is ironic that, whereas the aircraft that actually got built to Manning's design, the Wren, was reputedly the lowest-powered British aeroplane ever to fly, the ones left on the drawing board included the most powerful of their era. For example, there was the Eclectic (try saying English Electric Eclectic a few times quickly!). This biplane flying boat would have had six Rolls-Royce Condors and a span of 201 ft 6 in. But even this would have been dwarfed by the English Electric Phoenix Pulex. I include the original brochure drawings, and readers can work out

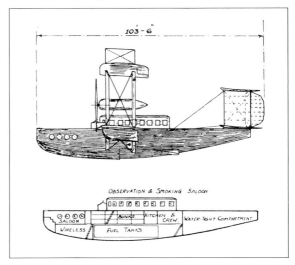

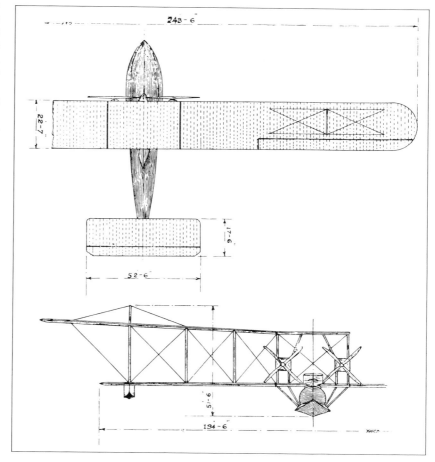

Below and right *This dimensioned drawing enables readers easily to calculate the wing area. What is much more difficult is how four Condor engines drove each propeller! (English Electric via J.M. Bruce)*

for themselves how the two propellers would have been driven by eight 600 hp Condors! The Pulex was to weigh 100,000 lb, and with 50 passengers and baggage fly for 20 hr at 80 mph. What the firm overlooked was that in the immediate post-war era the infant airlines were going broke even with small secondhand machines.

12   Gosport G.9

The Gosport Aircraft Company, located on the west side of Portsmouth harbour, was a wartime licence-builder of FBA and Felixstowe F.5 flying boats. At the Armistice its principals, Sir Charles Allom and Charles Nicholson (of Camper and Nicholson), both yacht builders, decided to produce a large civil transport flying boat. They hired John Porte, who not unnaturally chose the Felixstowe Fury as the basis for the planned G.9. The structure was almost unchanged, though the planned engines were three 600 hp Condors, the middle one a pusher. The hull was slightly extended to give an overall length of 64 ft 6 in, and it was to be furnished for 10 passengers and 4,000 lb of mail and cargo. Fuel capacity was reduced to 6,500 lb, to give a loaded weight of 28,800 lb. The design performance was to fly 900 nautical miles (1,036 miles) at 95 kt (109 mph). In late 1919 the hull was nearing completion at Gosport, under the direction of Nicholson who took over technical control

(Porte having succumbed to his long illness in October 1919). The intention was that the hull should be conveyed to Phoenix Dynamo at Bradford for completion, but — probably in 1921 — the project was abandoned.

13 Supermarine 3,000 hp

In 1921-22 the Supermarine Aviation Works made several announcements to the effect that they were building a giant flying boat. The power of 3,000 hp suggests five Rolls-Royce Condor engines, possibly three tractor and two pusher. This is speculation, as is the belief that the aircraft would have been a biplane. Supermarine said 'It will be in many respects of a progressive nature', but it was never completed.

14 Vickers Vigilant

It is ironic that the Vickers Vigilant that was actually built (indeed, by the thousand, in the 1950s) should have been the smallest man-portable anti-tank guided missile of all time, with a span of 11 in. The 1919-22 Vigilant would have had a span nearly 300 times greater, and it would have been one of the largest aeroplanes ever to fly. We know very little about it, beyond the fact that it would have been a traditional biplane flying boat, with the wings and tail covered mainly with fabric. Span would have exceeded 250 ft, and estimated gross weight was 110,000 lb. Power was to be provided by eight 650 hp Rolls-Royce Condors 'in modified airship nacelles'. Quite a few drawings survive, one showing tandem engines geared to four-blade propellers of no less

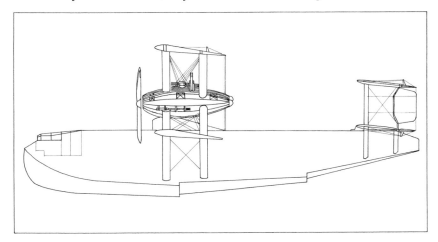

Left *Side elevation of the Vickers Vigilant, redrawn from works drawing No. 5089 (undated). Most drawings showed tandem engines in each of four nacelles.* (Vickers)

Above right *Three-view of one form of the Vigilant, with two engines geared to each tractor propeller. Span was to be 209 ft.* (Via Eric B. Morgan.

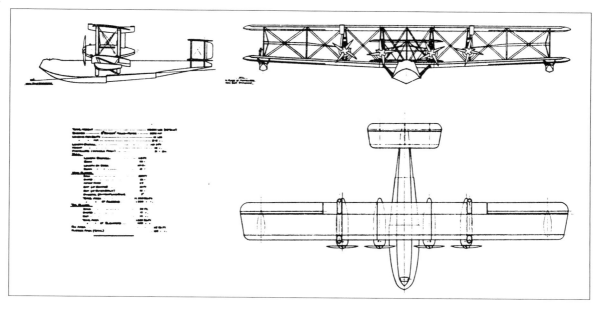

than 25 ft 6 in diameter. Major differences between the drawings show that even the basic configuration was not settled when work was abandoned, probably in 1922.

15 Junkers projects

Few aircraft designers 'thought bigger' than Prof Hugo Junkers. On Armistice Day, 11 November 1918, he called his staff together and told them that, at least for the immediate future, they would work only on civil aircraft. Their F13 small civil transport, first flown in June 1919, was a smash hit, 322 being sold all over the world (309 more than the most successful British rival). But the JG1 airliner, construction of which also began in late 1919, was deemed by the Inter-Allied Control Commission to have military potential, and so it was ordered to be destroyed. The occupying power certainly had a plausible argument, because the JG1 was a civil version of the second Junkers R-type bomber. It would have been an impressive machine, with four 230 hp Junkers L2a engines buried in the front of the wing, of just under 125 ft span, driving tractor propellers. Later Junkers decided to fit 400 hp

Liberty engines, but this was a tiddler compared with the unbuilt projects.

First of the monsters was the R-Flugboot (giant flying boat), of which a drawing exists dated 26 June 1918. It was intended to be powered by four of the massive Junkers vee-12 spark-ignition oil engines, each with two of the cylinder blocks of the 500 hp FO2 engine, which was actually running. These 1,000 hp engines were each to be buried inside the 262 ft 6 in wing, driving a 22 ft tractor propeller. The hull was rather shallow but amazingly broad, the maximum beam of 33 ft being more than 50 per cent greater than that of a Boeing 747. Warren bracing joined this wing to the hull and to a much smaller lower wing just above the wavetops. Wing area would have been a record 10,760 sq ft, and loaded weight 48 tonnes (105,820 lb).

After the war this project was replaced by

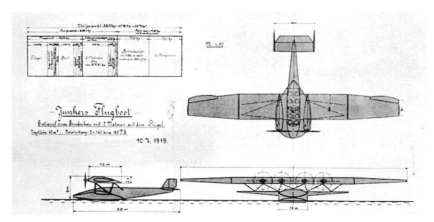

Simple three-view of the Junkers R-Flugboot. (Junkers)

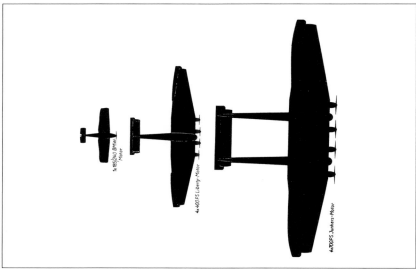

Comparative silhouettes of the F13 (left), JG1 and the huge Junkerissime. (Junkers)

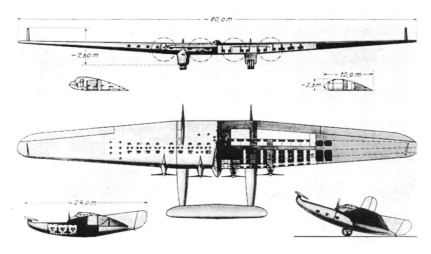

Junkers drawings of the extraordinary J1000. (Junkers)

the *Junkerissime* of 1921-22. This followed Junkers' belief in the all-wing aeroplane, in that the four 700 hp two-stroke diesel engines (which Junkers had not yet produced) were to be housed in the 206 ft wing along with the 60 passengers, cargo, fuel and crew. The tail was carried on twin booms, which at the front housed the tandem wheels, and aft of the wing contained the doors, from which corridors led to staircases to the main deck in the wing, with roof windows. There was also to be a flying-boat version, but in this case the need for large planing bottoms meant that the twin booms became proper hulls, housing part of the accommodation.

Junkers had factories in Sweden and the Soviet Union where, beyond the jurisdiction of the Inter-Allied commission, many kinds of military aircraft were produced. At Dessau there were growing production lines of civil aircraft, all with all-metal construction and corrugated skins. Yet Junkers chafed and fretted, forever wishing to build colossal aeroplanes of all-wing layout. By 1925 he had completed the project design of the J1000. This was clearly to be the realization of his dream, yet to me it appears quite unnecessarily unconventional, and indeed grotesque in appearance. The J1000 had a tail-first twin-hull all-wing configuration! Almost everything, including the fuel and nearly all the 100 passengers, were to be housed in the surprisingly graceful wing (previous Ju wings had had square tips and overhung horn-balanced ailerons). Span was 262 ft 6 in, and the centre section was to have a chord of 32 ft 10 in and maximum depth of 7 ft 7 in. On the centreline was a relatively tiny crew nacelle. On the leading edge were four tractor propellers, but there is no information available on the engines. Between the two propellers on each side was an odd stumpy fuselage, housing three landing wheels abreast on the underside, curved up at the rear to form a fin and rudder and curved up at the front to carry the one-piece pivoted foreplane. There were additional fins and rudders above the wingtips, toed inwards (presumably as an inbuilt counter to the asymmetry caused by engine failure). The whole design abounded in odd features; for example it sat on the ground in a grotesquely nose-high attitude while everyone boarded up stairs from the trailing edge.

Altogether the J1000 seemed hardly the work of a practical design team, yet even bigger all-wing schemes were quite seriously committed to paper. One wing profile for a 'cantilever wing for 100 to 1,000 persons' showed a double-deck layout inside a wing whose chord must have been 19 or 20 m (62-66 ft). This implied a span of some 425-450 ft, bigger than anything except the Adlershof and Tupolev projects. Suffice to say that none of these enormous all-wing Junkers designs ever got off the drawing board, but that still left the G38. A minnow by comparison, the G38 was still quite impressive as it visited Europe's capitals in the service of Deutsche Luft Hansa at the start of the 1930s, as described later.

16 Caproni Ca60

At the start of World War 1 the only place where you could see aircraft not very far short of Sikorsky's giants was Italy. The commander of the Battaglione Aviatori, Col Giulio Douhet, was a rare thing among high-ranking officers in 1913: he was a visionary who could see the whole concept of strategic air power. He wrote a classic book on the subject which influenced every air commander. The struggling aircraft fac-

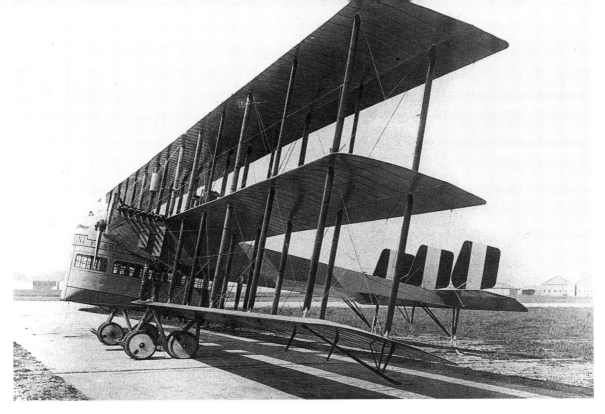

tory of Gianni Caproni quickly produced a large aeroplane intended as the prototype of a bomber. Like many contemporary designs it had a pusher propeller in the rear of a central nacelle, and a tail carried on two slender booms. It was most unusual in that the nacelle contained no fewer than three 80 hp Gnome rotary engines in a row, the rearmost driving the pusher screw and the other two driving bevel gearboxes and shafts to wing-mounted tractor propellers. This aircraft was followed by a better design with one pusher and two conventionally installed tractor engines. Subsequently more than 1,000 large trimotor bombers were built, mostly at Caproni's factory at Milan-Taliedo but including a few made under licence in France and the USA.

The big Capronis started bombing against Austro-Hungarian targets on 20 August 1915, over 15 months before the first raid by a British Handley Page. Readers may imagine what it was like to be a top gunner standing in a completely open cage just inches in front of the huge pusher propeller of a bomber of the Ca3 or Ca5 series, on missions

which took perhaps five hours doing a double crossing of the Alps in winter. The biggest version, quite different from the others in being a triplane, was the Ca4 series. This family looked odd, because the nacelle and slim tail booms were attached to the middle wing, resulting in an acute ground angle notwithstanding the use of a tailskid nearly 9 ft high. Up to 3,197 lb of bombs were carried in a box on the bottom wing, between the 16 mainwheels. In 1918-20 several civil versions were built, one being illustrated.

Caproni was therefore well used to large biplane or triplane wings and various arrangements of tractor and pusher engines. What he clearly lacked was knowledge of either aerodynamics or the stability and control of aeroplanes, because immediately after the war he, with assistants, designed what I think can fairly be called the most unlikely flying machine since 1910 — except, perhaps, for a rotary-winged entry in a 1962 man-powered aircraft competition. I remember seeing a picture of this machine when I was a boy: it was cryptically labelled 'The

Caproni Trans-Aereo triplane', without comment. It looked rather like a vast houseboat mating with a squadron of Caproni's giant triplane bombers. I think it was Frank Robertson of Shorts who, told that the Skyvan was unstreamlined, said (the expurgated version) 'You can make a brick outhouse fly if you give it enough horsepower and wing area', and this was clearly believed by Caproni.

The Ca60, to give it its proper designation, was a flying boat. The hull had an almost constant cross section for most of its 77-ft length, and looked vaguely like a passenger train. Caproni had built smaller flying boats so it had a proper planing bottom, with two steps in tandem to aid in unsticking. As in a 747 the pilots sat high above the nose, enabling the huge multi-pane passenger windows to go right around the nose and back along both sides. Seating was intended to be provided 'for 100 passengers in comfort'. Alternatively 17,635 lb of mail was to be carried, or, in a military version, eight 1,600 lb torpedoes *and* eight 650 lb bombs.

This strange hull was to be lifted by three sets of triplane wings, all having similar span (98 ft 5 in) and chord, giving gross wing area of 8,073 sq ft (7,962 net). All three sets were rigidly attached to the hull, the front and rear sets being mounted on top of the hull and the middle group being lower, so that the spars passed through the hull forming an obstruction between the front and rear cabins. All nine wings were fitted with ailerons, and those on the front and rear groups of wings could operate in unison so that they also served as elevators. Thus, to command a climb by hauling back on the control wheel had the effect of lowering the six front ailerons and raising the six at the rear. For lateral stability on the water two floats were mounted well inboard under the bottom midships wings. Against the bulk of the whole edifice these floats seemed rather inadequate.

For propulsion Caproni chose eight 400 hp Liberty watercooled vee-12 engines. These were excellent engines, and I am sure no aircraft of any kind had ever previously had 3,200 hp installed. Like almost everything else about the Ca60 the engine arrangement

Above left *The Caproni Ca48 was a 1918 transport based on the Ca4 series triplane bombers. This example once flew Milan-London with 23 passengers.* (Caproni)

Right *One advantage of the Ca60 was that it afforded excellent shelter from the rain. This photograph was probably taken shortly before the monster was launched.* (Via R.T. Riding)

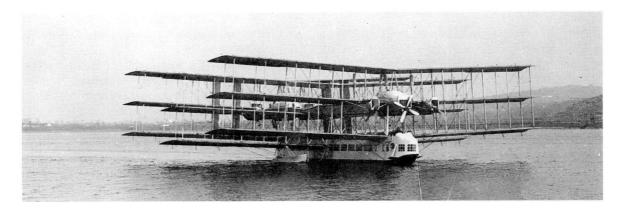

was unique, with four engines at the front and four at the back. Two of the engines, driving four-blade propellers, were arranged in a tandem pair, one tractor and the other a pusher, mounted at the centre of the front middle wing. Two more were installed in an identical push/pull arrangement at the centre of the rearmost middle wing. Two more, driving two-blade tractor propellers, were installed on each side of the front middle wing at the front of a long slim box structure which at the rear tapered off where it joined the middle wing of the midships group. The final pair of engines were a kind of mirror image; driving two-blade pusher propellers, they were mounted on the rear ends of identical long box structures which tapered at the front to join the middle centre wings, thus greatly increasing the overall rigidity and strength of the structure. The long bracing boxes could be walked along for ground servicing; in flight a mechanic could crawl along inside them to get at the backs of the engines (though changing a faulty plug might have required the arms of an orangutan). The water-cooling radiators were in each case above and in front of the relevant engine. Fuel was carried in upright cylindrical tanks attached to the interplane struts. For directional stability and control four of the groups of interplane struts at the rear, just outboard of the engines, were made in the form of large fins and rudders, equal in area above and below the middle wing. Empty and loaded weights were

The Noviplano, *or* Capronissimo, *riding at anchor on Lake Maggiore. Can you believe it?* (Via Philip Jarrett)

30,865 lb and 55,116 lb, and cruising speed was to be 68 mph.

The amazing contraption — one could hardly call it an aeroplane — was launched, in the presence of the US Ambassador, on 21 January 1921. The Ca60 slid down the slipway at Sesto Calende and floated on the previously beautiful Lake Maggiore, and that was about all it ever accomplished. I do not know what Trans-Aereo was supposed to mean, but its popular name *Capronissimo* was obvious. Another appellation, *Noviplano,* did not mean 'new plane' but 'nine wings'. What everyone thought of the monster, especially test pilot Semprini, I have no idea. By 1921 the public were growing out of the 'It'll never fly' era, and beginning to regard flying machines as a source of enthusiastic excitement and, certainly in the case of Italy, of national pride. Where the Ca60 was concerned, I think one could indeed feel enthusiasm and pride, provided one knew nothing about aircraft design!

The Caproni team, working to a specification and patent (9 February 1921) by Caproni himself, had certainly studied and solved many of the problems involved in designing a large aeroplane. Unfortunately, as any aircraft designer will tell you, you have to solve them all. The *Capronissimo* was not just clumsy but lethal. To quote *Jane's*:

The general arrangement of the machine indicates that the load . . . is distributed over the whole length of the machine, and that the engines are concentrated at the extreme ends. Consequently the longitudinal moment of inertia is colossal — which in any case would call for extremely powerful longitudinal stabilizing and control surfaces. But the distribution of the load is such that all three sets of wings must be nearly equally loaded, a condition entirely opposed to the generally accepted principles of stability . . .

Semprini had a distinguished wartime career flying Caproni bombers, so perhaps he was able to replace whatever doubts he must have had by blind faith in the maestro. But on the very first tentative hop across the lake's surface, on 4 March 1921, it was clear that the contrivance was both unstable and uncontrollable. At least nothing broke. Sand equivalent to the weight of 60 passengers was loaded, and Semprini then took the huge machine into the air. It left the water cleanly enough, climbed to about 60 ft and then simply nosed down majestically straight into the lake, with Semprini valiantly holding the wheel in the full-aft position. Fortunately he survived, but the Ca60 was broken into pieces. Amazingly, the wreckage was to have been repaired, but (for good or ill) it was soon destroyed by fire. Doubtless it was well insured.

Could such a machine have been a success? Even if it had had the entire area of the three aft wings pivoted to serve as elevators I do not believe it would have been controllable. Certainly the pilot would have had to 'fly' such a longitudinally unstable arrangement continuously from take-off to alighting. Caproni even had dreams of a yet bigger *Noviplano* to carry 150 passengers across the Atlantic. I prefer the comment of Giorgio Apostolo, that 'The whole structure would not have looked out of place in 1588 sailing up the English Channel with the Spanish Armada'.

17 Fairey N.4

On 31 October 1917 the British Admiralty issued specification N.4, also known after April 1918 by its RAF No. XXII, calling for a large flying boat for open-sea reconnaissance and co-operation with surface fleets. By this time Britain's aircraft industry, virtually non-existent in 1914, had grown to have technical capabilities surpassing those of any other country. Apart from a reluctance to build monoplanes, which in the longer term was to prove serious and to make virtually all large or powerful British aircraft of 1934 obsolete, the British companies were better served in 1918 by designers and technicians, and by supporting manufacturers of engines and equipment, than anywhere else in the world. In particular, the giant flying boat envisaged by the N.4 requirement could have been produced by the Seaplane Experimental Station at Felixstowe, or by English Electric, Vickers, Fairey, Supermarine, Phoenix Dynamo, Short, S.E. Saunders, Dick Kerr, Blackburn or May, Harden & May.

In fact the contract for the N.4 was awarded to Fairey Aviation, of Hayes, Middlesex, and Hamble, on Southampton Water. It was obvious from the start that a very large machine was required, and as there were plenty of long stretches of sheltered water available this was thought to present no problem, whereas landplanes of similar size would have required bigger aerodromes. Indeed, in comparison with some contemporary projects, the N.4 boat was a tiddler.

Nevertheless it was one of the largest aircraft of its day, and it is just unfortunate that, because of the end of the war, no N.4 flew until almost six years had elapsed. Of course, it had been intended to put the N.4 into series production, perhaps to a total of 20 or more, but in the event only three serial numbers were allotted, N118, 119 and 129, and N118 was never flown. All three boats were the result of collaboration between several companies, working to Fairey drawings. The first to be completed, N119 *Atalanta*, had a hull subcontracted to May, Harden & May, at Hythe on Southampton Water, and wings and tail assigned to Dick Kerr at Lytham St Annes, Lancashire. The only other one to be completed, N129 *Titania*, had a hull built at Fyffe's yard on the Clyde, and wings and tail built by Fairey at Hayes, with assembly at Hamble. The third, N118, was to have had a hull designed by Camper & Nicholson, but made at Gosport, and wings and tail made by Phoenix Dynamo at Bradford, who were also the assemblers. Someone commented that these boats probably travelled further by road than in the air!

Though completely conventional, the Fairey N.4s were excellent boats, whose powerful engines gave them all-round performance considerably higher than their wartime predecessors. Aerodynamically I doubt if they were very much better; wing aerofoil profiles had not developed, engines were uncowled and I doubt if overall drag figures showed any improvement. One of the significant advances was the use of a Linton Hope hull. Lt Linton Hope was a pre-war yacht designer. In 1915 he joined the Admiralty Air Department and proposed an improved form of hull, which was promptly used in the AD boat, with a hull built by May, Harden & May and assembled by Pemberton-Billing (Supermarine). The results were excellent, one AD in 1916 being deliberately stalled at 10 to 12 ft and allowed to drop on to the water with a crash, this being done 36 times without damage!

Linton Hope's hull was a semi-monocoque, with light wood formers to give the desired cross section with a rounded (turtle deck) top and wide planing bottom with a projecting chine. These formers were joined by numerous light stringers, around which were then strapped strips of wood to serve as attachments for the multiple diagonal-grain sheets of veneer. The result was light, strong and remarkably flexible. The patentee emphasized the advantage of having no places where the distributed loads imparted by the water could be concentrated by the structure of the hull. The whole hull was therefore exceptionally elastic, able to absorb shocks on take off and landing.

Linton Hope principles were first used in a large boat in the Phoenix P.5 Cork, designed by W.O. Manning. They were one of the firms assigned N.4 manufacture. Fairey bought the rights to this form of hull, and (it is reported) considered six variations of hull design for the N.4 boats. Apart from the fact that the large sloping and projecting chines must have created high drag, the N.4 hulls appear to have been excellent in all respects. The wide planing bottom under the fore-part of the hull tapered inwards at the single step amidships, which was not a vertical step but an inclined one. The planing bottom tapered at the rear to a shallow knife-edge which was two or three feet under water when the normally trimmed boat was at rest.

Both wings had the same chord of just over 11 ft, but they differed greatly in span, the upper wing's figure of 139 ft being one of the largest in the world at that time. The lower wings had considerable dihedral. Good-looking stabilizing floats were attached under the outermost interplane struts, while above them were the huge kingpost structures supporting the upper-wing bracing wires, skinned with fabric to form prominent stabilizing fins. Large balanced ailerons were attached to the upper wings only. The tail was in no way exceptional, comprising upper and lower

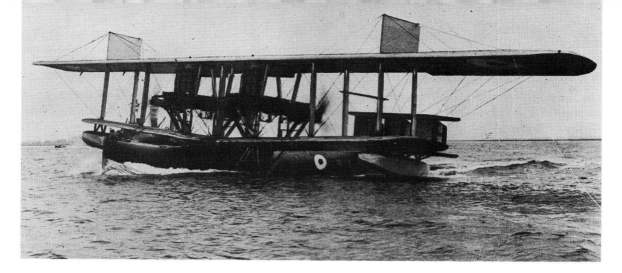

The first N.4, Atalanta, *probably returning from a flight at the Isle of Grain.* (Via R.T. Riding)

fixed tailplanes, each carrying an elevator, joined by three fins each carrying a rudder. The only surprising feature is how so large a boat could have been flown manually with no visible aerodynamic balance or servo assistance on the control surfaces. Wind-driven aileron power was not installed.

The power units were four Rolls-Royce Condor IA engines, each rated at 650 hp. These were massive watercooled vee-12s, very like enlarged Eagles, with epicyclic reduction gears to remarkably small (12 ft 6 in) four-blade propellers. An innovation on the Condor was an electric starting motor, which today seems obvious but which was extremely rare 70 years ago. The huge radiators for each pair of engines formed a single square matrix completely filling the space between the front engine and the fuel tank under the upper wing. As already noted, the N.4s were fast for their day, maximum speed at sea level being 115 mph (compared with about 85 mph for many wartime boats) yet the engines were completely uncowled.

The crew numbered six. In the nose was the side-by-side open cockpit for the pilots, and a bow position for a gunner in which could be put such weapons as twin Lewis guns, a Davis recoilless gun or a 37 mm Coventry Ordnance Works quick-firing cannon. Above the upper wing was provision for two fighting tops, box-like 'howdah' attachments containing cockpits for gunners. H.F. 'Rex' King believes these may

actually have been installed on the second N.4. Immediately aft of the wing were large oval cutouts in each side of the hull for beam gunners. Presumably their guns would have been mounted on outboard arms enabling them to fire downwards or astern. As H.A. 'Tony' Taylor has recorded that there were 'six Lewis-gun positions' (*Fairey Aircraft*, Putnam) presumably there was also a gunner's cockpit in the tail, or under the rear of the hull, but I know of no evidence for this. The bombload was 1,000 lb, carried under the lower wings. Gross weight (*Titania*) was 31,612 lb, and endurance was up to nine hours.

After the Armistice there was no sense of urgency, and parsimonious funding, and this combined with the multitude of contractors to delay the first flight of *Atalanta* by some six years. This must have seemed a poor reward for the eight woodworkers and two apprentices at Hythe who had built the hull in a mere 13 weeks. In 1919 this huge hull was transported — via a special route which wound its way through Wales — to be fitted with the wings and tail at Lytham. After assembly N119 remained incomplete for two years until, in 1921, it was dismantled and conveyed to the Isle of Grain experimental station on the Thames estuary. Here at last it was completed, and flown on

4 July 1923. A year later the station became the Marine Aircraft Experimental Establishment (MAEE) at Felixstowe. This N.4 certainly flew there, but was probably scrapped in the mid-1920s.

The second N.4, N129 *Titania*, managed to take advantage of the delays by being completed to a later standard. The most important change was to fit Fairey's patented camber-changing gear. This was what we today would call a plain flap. The rear part of the wing, typically the rearmost one-third of the chord, was arranged to pivot downwards, under an irreversible mechanical drive, to adjust the wing's camber: fully depressed for slow flight and landing and fully up in cruising flight. The second N.4 was the largest aircraft thus fitted. The upper wing had variable camber over the entire span between the ailerons, the hinged portion having the same chord as the ailerons. The lower wings had hinged trailing edges from root to tip.

Another change was to fit Condor III engines. These had the same power of 650 hp as the Mk IA but were totally redesigned (by A.J.Rowledge, who had come from designing the Lion at Napier), with greatly improved mechanical details. Among other things the weight of each engine was reduced from about 1,600 lb to only 1,320. There were numerous changes to the engine installations, the fuel tanks under the upper wing were of square section instead of half-round, and the water radiators above the forward engines were of unusual circular shape, almost certainly having lower drag. Another obvious change was to remove the fabric from the kingposts above the upper wing, eliminating the prominent 'stabilizing fins'.

N129 was assembled at Fairey's Hamble works, the hull having arrived from near Glasgow and the wings and tail from Hayes. The hull needed further work — Tony Taylor says 'modifications' — and, though this could surely have been done at Hamble, the hull then went to Hayes! Eventually the second N.4 was completed, in 1923, but for some reason it was not then flown. Instead

The second N.4, Titania, *on the slipway at Felixstowe.* (Via Philip Jarrett)

it was dismantled and taken to the Isle of Grain. Taylor suggests it was reassembled there, but as the establishment was then about to move to Felixstowe this seems unlikely. What is certain is that the second boat never flew until 1925, at the newly opened MAEE at Felixstowe. It flew occasionally until 1928 or possibly 1929, when it too was scrapped.

The third N.4, N118, was apparently assembled at the Phoenix works at Bradford, though of course it could not be flown there. At some later date it was dismantled and the hull was used for flotation tests at the Isle of Grain. It never flew.

18 Engineering Division XNBL-1

Many aviation enthusiasts, on reading the above title, will think 'Eh? Never heard of it!' But quite a few more would have heard of this beast's popular name, which was 'The Barling Bomber'. It was another of the numerous giant aircraft whose chief positive contribution was a negative one: it showed what *not* to do. Unfortunately, it did this in an environment of American hostility towards weapons, extreme parsimony in military funding and intense interest in unearthing any suggestion that politicians or generals were wasting the money contributed by taxpayers.

This aircraft was not a left-over from World War 1. That war had involved US Army and Navy air units in tactical missions on the Western Front and in offshore sorties against U-boats. After the Armistice the US Army Air Service took stock and decided that it ought to have a strategic bombing capability. Right up to World War 2 isolationists used to proclaim 'Don't waste money on such a capability; who are we going to fight?' After all, nobody expected a war with Canada or Mexico, and everyone else was out of reach. The Army usually answered by saying 'We need strategic bombers to destroy a hostile invasion fleet', though that did not make much sense either, because a seaborne invasion of the USA would be quite some operation! Despite this the Army did create a strategic bomber force, and I think by 1945 everyone was very glad they did.

All this was in a murky crystal ball in 1919 when the Army began considering the need for powerful bombers. At this time the Army's shrinking Air Service was eyeing Britain's RAF, and trying to flex its muscles by lobbying for an independent US Air Force, equal in stature to the Army and Navy. It even got the Secretary of War's Cromwell Commission to recommend this, but the Navy's opposition was predictably violent. The Navy insisted that it alone could fight off enemy fleets, and that aeroplanes could 'never sink a battleship'. This claim was sustained even after Army Martin and Handley Page bombers *had* sunk a battleship, during tests in 1921. So passionate were the feelings that one began to think the Army really wanted its anti-battleship capability in order to sink the US Navy.

By 1920 the Martin MB-2 was in full production as the standard Army heavy night bomber, most having the designation NBS-1, from Night Bomber Short-range. In the same year design began of the much bigger XNBL-1 (Experimental NB Long-range). The Army placed a contract for two, with serial numbers 64215 and 64216, in June 1920. It was expected the total cost would be just under $100,000. The whole programme was naturally assigned to the US Army Engineering Division at McCook Field, Dayton, Ohio. Chief designer was Walter H. Barling, who had previously gained experience of large structures with the Tarrant Tabor. In many ways he planned the XNBL-1 along similar lines, though as he had rather less power at his disposal he made the aircraft a little smaller, and to avoid the Tabor's lethal problem he kept all the thrust lines fairly low.

Aerodynamically the XNBL was conventional. As in the Tabor, the fuselage was an all-wood semi-monocoque of such beautiful aerodynamic form that one might have been forgiven for thinking the aircraft was intended to reach high speeds. This fuselage was lifted by triplane wings, the middle wing being slightly smaller in span than the others, and much smaller in chord — the exact opposite of the Tabor — and its inner bays sloped downwards (ie, they had sharp dihedral) to make a good joint with the fuselage. Pivoted bodily to the tail end of the fuselage, so that its incidence could be adjusted, was the biplane tail unit. The horizontal surfaces each carried one-piece elevators with large horn balances, and were joined by four rectangular fins each carrying a rudder with a similar horn balance.

The six Liberty watercooled vee-12 engines, each uprated to a short-term maximum of 420 hp, were all mounted on steel-tube pylons, plus the interplane struts, at such a level that they were quite close under the middle wing. The inner engines were tandem push/pull installations, the outers being singles. The engines drove wooden two-blade propellers, had water cooling radiators installed along the side of each nacelle and oil coolers arranged above the middle wing, and drew fuel from four tanks in the fuselage. Drag and thrust loads on the middle wing were reacted by large diagonal struts joining the leading edge to the fuselage just behind the cockpits.

A particularly unusual feature was the landing gear. Each of the two main units comprised a four-wheel truck rather reminiscent of those used on today's Lockheed C-5 Galaxy, with two wheels close together in front and a second pair further apart at the rear. What made this arrangement doubly unusual was that, prior to

landing, the front pair of wheels could be extended forwards by lengthening the struts. After landing on the eight wheels the aircraft, if the CG was in the right place, would tip back on its tailskid, the front wheels taking little load and if necessary raised off the ground. As originally built, the aircraft also had two wheels under the nose to protect the structure in the event of a Tabor-type nose-over. When it looked as if this would never happen these wheels were removed.

The cockpit was arranged for two pilots side-by-side. Immediately in front was a tall drum-like cupola for the standing nose gunner. Thus, either pilot had a view to one side only, and the view was further limited by enclosing the flightdeck and giving each pilot a cutout at the side preceded by a tapering windscreen. In some ways the arrangement was similar to the so-called bug-eye cockpits fashionable at the end of World War 2 (see Douglas Globemaster p.182). Steps led down to the navigator, radio operator and engineer, aft of which (between the lower and centre wings) was the bomb bay, with the fuel tanks above. Behind this were dorsal and ventral gun positions. Up to seven 0.300-in guns could be fitted, the normal type being the Lewis. Maximum bomb load, all carried in internal racks, was 5,000 lb. With this load on board the full fuel capacity of 1,665 gal was to be possible, but the bomber proved so slow that the range was only 170 miles.

Predictably the project took longer than expected, and cost much more. Accordingly the contract for the second aircraft was cancelled, though despite this the basic construction of the single XNBL was later published as $350,000 — and that was before they built the huge hangar for it. Manufacture of the aircraft was assigned to the Witteman-Lewis Co, of Teterboro, New Jersey. Major sections began to appear in October 1922, to be sent on flat trucks to Dayton for assembly. It had been hoped to erect the bomber in a special hangar, but

An unusual air-to-air view of 'the Barling Bomber', or XNBL-1. (Via Philip Jarrett)

funds for this were not then available and, as the machine grew larger, it eventually had to be kept out on the field. Eventually it was completed, painted olive drab and, on 16 August 1923, Lt H.R. Harris began engine runs and ground trials (in May 1984 Gen Harris gave a Wings Club lecture in which he gave this as the date of the first flight). Lt Harris actually made the first flight on 22 August and on the whole there were few problems. With four ailerons (two more than the Tabor), two elevators and four rudders the monster responded adequately to control inputs.

The only real problem was that it was obvious that the aircraft was underpowered. Even lightly loaded it had a very poor rate of climb, though after 36.3 min at full power it once reached 7,275 ft, which was regarded as the ceiling. In level flight it reached 95.5 mph, but the cruising speed was found to be 61 mph. Any pilot will tell you it is not entirely satisfactory flying an aeroplane whose cruising speed is 61 mph and landing speed 55 mph. Small wonder that the

Air Service report said the XNBL-1 had 'disappointing speed, load and endurance'.

On 2 October 1923 Maj-Gen Mason M. Patrick with crew flew the giant to St Louis to show it off at the National Air Races. Late in the same month it set several US and World records, for example by climbing to 6,722 ft with a payload of 4,409 lb (2 tonnes) and then climbing to 5,344 ft with a load of 6,614 lb (3 tonnes). These and several other tests were flown by Lt Harris. He recalls one test climb to absolute ceiling with full load. 'Descending from the climb top, a stream of liquid was observed coming out of the trailing edge of the top wing. All fuel was in the fuselage, so that wasn't it. Investigation on the ground showed that the wing had been full of rain water, and the test was valueless since the actual weight at take off was unknown. All testing had to be stopped until a hangar large enough to house the plane could be built.'

My immediate thought is that if the top wing had really been 'full of rain water' the Barling would never have departed from Mother Earth! As it was, the huge hangar was built, costing (Gen 'Hap' Arnold said) more than the bomber itself. Then the NBL-1, having lost its X for experimental, hardly flew again. I think what finally scuppered it was that on a planned flight to Washington it proved unable to climb across the Appalachian Mountains! It last flew from McCook Field on 7 May 1925. Subsequently it was stored at Fairfield Air Depot until in June 1928 it was scrapped.

19 Beardmore Inflexible

Back in 1912 it seemed to people in senior positions at the War Office that monoplanes, as a class, were dangerous because of a proneness to structural failure. Accordingly, military monoplanes were banned, and as late as the mid-1930s almost all British aircraft — especially the military aircraft — were biplanes. This was both the cause and effect of a chicken-and-egg situation. Because the customers wanted biplanes, which were braced with wires and covered in fabric, there was no incentive to learn any new structural methods. Because nobody had any experience of stressed-skin construction, the only way to make a monoplane was to make the wing very large and either extremely thick or else braced with struts and wires, so the resulting monoplanes were if anything inferior to the biplanes.

We could easily have had nothing but fabric-covered biplanes at the start of World War 2, but we were jolted out of our complacency by the MacRobertson race from Mildenhall to Melbourne in 1934. Among the types on the starting line were two American airliners, a Boeing 247D and a Douglas DC-2. Both were all-metal stressed-skin machines with thin cantilever wings, and no struts or wires. We had nothing remotely like them. (Specially to compete in the race, de Havilland had built a racer called the Comet, but this had to be made of wood.) The first result of this shock was the Bristol 142 high-speed executive transport, later called Britain First, built for newspaper tycoon Lord Northcliffe. Bristol was exceedingly reluctant to build this machine, because it was desperately afraid it would gain publicity despite being an all-metal stressed-skin monoplane, and totally contrary to the policies of its best customer, the Air Ministry!

Yet, of course, the experts at the Air Ministry had watched the progress made in other countries since the end of World War 1. Fokker had achieved enormous worldwide success with cantilever monoplanes, but using very thick wings made of wood. So too had Junkers, but using very thick wings with numerous spars taking the load and high-drag corrugated covering (see Junkers G38 p.99). But there was another constructor who, though he was less successful commercially, was actually the world leader in aircraft structures. He was Dipl-Ing Adolf Rohrbach, a senior designer at the Zeppelin-Lindau works during World War 1. He had led the team which, among many other things, designed the Dornier Do D1 fighter of 1918. Though a biplane, this was the first aircraft in the world to have all-metal stressed-skin cantilever wings. (The British Short Silver Streak of 1920 was an all-metal aircraft, but merely a translation into metal of the traditional braced biplane, its wings each having an unstressed skin.)

As noted earlier, the Zeppelin-Werke at Staaken, immediately after the Armistice, designed an extremely advanced four-engined airliner with a completely cantilever stressed-skin wing. It would have done Britain a lot more good if, instead of ordering the E.4/20's destruction, we had instead brought Rohrbach, by this time Technical Director, to Britain and asked him to carry on designing. What he actually did, in 1922, was to form the Rohrbach Metallflugzeugbau GmbH. At the start it had virtually no customers, though in early 1923 the British Air Ministry did open negotiations. There was at first no question of buying a German aircraft, but the Air Ministry was interested in getting experience of stressed-skin aircraft, which (surely obviously?) seemed to be superior and which were unknown in Britain. To our enduring misfortune we misplayed the whole thing, so that at great cost we got practically nowhere. What we did was to appoint a British licensee; then we placed orders through the licensee.

To return to Rohrbach, he continued to refine his structures, and once the German airlines had been merged into Lufthansa in 1926 orders began to come in, for landplanes and flying boats, such as the Ro VIII Roland and Ro X Romar. The Romar, powered by three 650 hp BMW engines, was an impressive flying boat with the extremely useful weight of 42,000 lb (heavier than all the wartime R-aircraft). The 121-ft wing was a pure cantilever, hardly any thicker than biplane wings would have been. Its structure looks modern even today. It was built up on a broad full-depth box spar with machined angle and T-section booms and sheet or braced truss webs. Front and rear rib portions were attached to the box, with stringers added before riveting on the stress-bearing light-alloy skin. The whole wing looked perfectly smooth externally. To avoid the Inter-Allied Control Commission all these aircraft were made by Rohrbach Metallflugzeug A/S of Copenhagen.

The British licensee appointed to use Rohrbach's patents was William Beardmore & Co of Dalmuir, Scotland. I cannot imagine why they were chosen. They had a long and proud heritage of marine work and had made many distinguished aero engines, and in the 1920s were devoting much effort to the massive diesel engines of the R.101 airship. Beardmore had also made aircraft during World War 1, including one of their own design derived from the Sopwith Pup, but all were small fabric-covered biplanes. Despite this, in 1925 the company contracted with the Air Ministry to deliver three advanced stressed-skin aircraft, two of them flying boats and the third an exceedingly large landplane.

The flying boats were in turn subcontracted to Rohrbach in Copenhagen. They were duly delivered to Britain, by air, in 1926 and 1927, where they were called by the name Beardmore Inverness. Each powered by two 450 hp Napier Lions, they were somewhat similar to the Rohrbach Ro V Rocco. Thus they added nothing to the technology, and did nothing for Beardmore either, which rather missed the point of the exercise.

The giant landplane was a different matter entirely. This was to be an all-Beardmore aircraft, and it was given the inappropriate name Inflexible (because properly designed stressed-skin aircraft flex at least as much as traditional wire-braced biplanes). Obviously this aeroplane was going to take some time to produce and cost a lot of money, and it would have seemed reasonable to design it to serve some useful purpose, such as a bomber or a transport — or, as was in vogue in those days, a bomber-transport. Instead it was designed merely as a very large aeroplane, and about the crudest large aeroplane imaginable. I hate saying this, because leader of the design team was W.S. 'Bill' Shackleton, who in later life built up a global business selling aeroplanes from an office in Piccadilly. He was a super chap, but the Inflexible hardly looked like the work of professionals. Shackleton said 'We were not particularly proud of it, but it met the requirements, and at minimum cost. Nobody was looking for performance, it was basi-

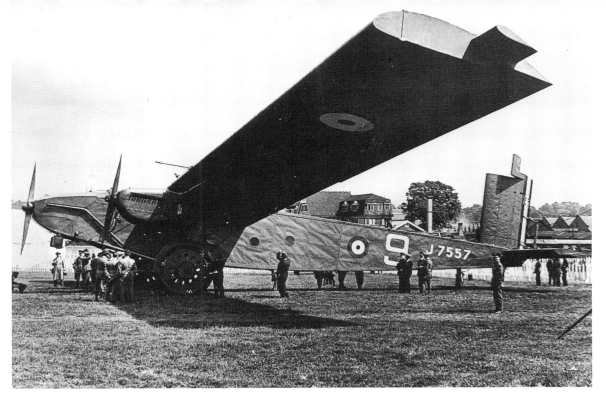

cally a structural exercise. Unfortunately, the basic design was not very good and the whole thing came out miles overweight.'

Of course, Rohrbach himself was supposed to assist, but quite early in the project, perhaps as early as 1925, he and Beardmore disagreed — possibly on the policy, the financing and the management, but certainly on the design itself. By 1926 Rohrbach and his experienced team had ceased to play much part in the design of the Inflexible, which to some degree explains the resulting simplicity and poor weight control. Moreover, there were severe aerodynamic problems which resulted in considerable redesign. These affected the wings, tail, engine installations and flight controls. Thus the aircraft was not completed until 1928, almost two years later than planned. Beardmore made nearly all the airframe. The parts were trucked to the Aeroplane & Armament Experimental Establishment (A&AEE) at Martlesham Heath, Suffolk, where Sqn Ldr Jack Noakes made the first flight on 5 March 1928.

There is not much to say about this brutishly simple machine. The rectangular wings, of the remarkably high aspect ratio of 12.6, were built up on a box spar extending from about 12 to 60 per cent chord, and had Warren truss ribs and smooth Duralumin skin. Left and right wings were attached, with considerable dihedral, by multiple bolted connections around the root rib to a massive bridge girder in the fuselage. The latter was just a rectangular box with metal skin. The tail surfaces were also pure rectangles, and the most prominent feature of the whole aircraft was the fact that each control surface carried a giant rectangular horn balance. The rudder also had a servo surface carried well downstream, this being the only part moved directly by the pilot's pedals. Wing span was 157 ft 6 in.

There was nothing much wrong with the power, except that there should have been at least four 650 hp Rolls-Royce Condor engines instead of three. One was in the nose and the others in very short tractor nacelles under the leading edge of the wings. All drove two-blade propellers and had plain unducted radiators, those for the wing engines being hung inboard under the wing. One odd feature is that, while the nose engine had a long exhaust pipe on each side, the wing engines had no fewer than 24 aft-facing exhaust stubs, two per cylinder. Fuel was contained in the wing box spar behind the engine nacelles.

One of the memorable features of the Inflexible was its wheels. I believe these had a diameter greater than any other aircraft wheel/tyre combination used previously. The overall diameter was fractionally under 8 ft. Each wheel had a rubber tyre on a steel rim riveted to 'a light-alloy disc of advanced design', though the wheels had different appearance at different times. Most photographs show outer discs with 12 dished depressions, painted Nivo dull green like the rest of the aircraft. Some show flat discs, painted white (or some other colour which looks white in photographs). Several show daylight visible through wire-spoked wheels. Be that as it may, another unusual feature was that the Inflexible not only had brakes but automatic brakes, designed by Dipl-Ing Kurt Tank, subsequently wartime Technical Director and test pilot of Focke-Wulf! Armed by the pilot on touchdown, the brakes were applied equally to both main wheels by a piston in the tailwheel bracket. At this time most aircraft, even large ones, had tailskids and no brakes.

There was no provision for armament, and the interior was virtually empty. Steps led up to the side-by-side open cockpit. The serial number was J7557, and the big number 9 was applied for display in the New Types Park at the 1928 RAF Pageant at Hendon.

The flying at Martlesham was shared by Noakes and Sqn Ldr Rollo de Haga Haig. They were agreed that the monster was absolutely stable, viceless and really not much of anything. With a bit of effort it answered to all control inputs, but its structural weight was so far beyond prediction that the three Condors could not confer the anticipated performance, and the useful load was unimpressive. The alleged empty and loaded weights of 24,301 and 31,400 lb do not sound particularly worrying, and I have often wondered if perhaps the true empty weight was nearer to 30,000 lb. Certainly the overall impression given by the Inflexible was that aluminium and steel stressed-skin construction was not a very good idea, which was one of the reasons why Rohrbach went off in a huff.

The Inflexible never did anything of interest. On 19 May 1929 Sqn Ldr E.S. Goodwin flew it to Mousehold aerodrome, Norwich, where it joined Sir Alan Cobham's flying circus. It was not exactly an ideal passenger machine, and its operating costs outweighed its undeniable crowd appeal, so after a rather undistinguished career the Inflexible was dismantled at Martlesham in 1930. Some of its parts were used to test anti-corrosion surface treatments, but both wheels were preserved, one in the Science Museum in London and the other in Dunlop's aviation museum in Coventry.

So why was the Inflexible such a so-so aeroplane? At the risk of too much speculation and wrong conclusions, suppose someone — for whatever reason — had wanted it to turn out that way, how could they arrange for this to happen? One obvious way would be to ensure that the structure came out very much overweight, and this could almost be guaranteed by specifying an aspect ratio of 12.6. Today the designers of the very latest commercial transports are striving to get near such a figure. We may note that the McDonnell Douglas MD-11 (handicapped by having almost a DC-10 wing) hits 7.5, the Boeing 767 reaches 7.9, the Airbus A310 8.8, the A320 9.4 and the A330/340 9.5. This is the very best that can be done today, using materials and design techniques far better than anything available more than 60 years ago. Most of Rohrbach's wings had an aspect ratio of about 6, and were tapered. The Roland airliner had an untapered wing, but the aspect ratio was 7.6. To design the Inflexible with an untapered wing of 12.6 aspect ratio was to guarantee that the inboard sections would be almost solid metal, and awesomely heavy. I cannot believe anyone in the mid-1920s would design such a wing unless instructed to do so. Perhaps the Air Ministry technical staff were merely trying to give Beardmore — a firm with no experience whatever of such construction — a really

severe challenge, to prove that stressed-skin construction really worked. The result in practice was to make the Inflexible so heavy that it had poor performance and could not carry anything. *Flight* called it the 'Weird-more Inexplicable'.

One of the stressmen working at Beardmore on the Inflexible was a young Swiss, H.J. Stieger. He was convinced he could make a lighter wing, and invented and patented a simple arrangement of pyramidal Warren-truss assemblies which became famous as the Monospar system of construction. But that put everyone back in the fabric era.

20 Caproni Ca90

For obvious reasons, only a limited number of design organisations have had both the capability and the funding to produce giant aircraft. Moreover, many who have enjoyed both assets have never had the motivation; or perhaps they have recognised that pushing the state of the art in terms of sheer size is likely to result in ponderous and unattractive aircraft.

One company which, despite the problems, periodically did produce monsters was that of Gianni Caproni. Founded in 1910, and thus the first aircraft company in Italy, Caproni has already appeared in this book, with a series of bombers which were 100 per cent successful and with a transport aircraft which was (predictably) an utter failure. The bombers were to some extent victims of their own success. After the Armistice, when money for such products was scarce, the wartime designs were simply continued in limited production, with minor improvements. For example, the Ca3M, called Ca36 by the company, was made to the tune of 153 examples between 1923 and 1926 even though by any sensible yardstick the basic design was obsolete.

This was a time when manufacturers tended to produce new designs, and even new prototypes, at the drop of the proverbial hat. Caproni's staff completed 25 completely (or largely) new designs between the Armistice and 1926, many of which were actually built. Several were of the inverted sesquiplane layout. The term sesquiplane means a biplane in which the lower wing is significantly smaller than the upper. One can argue for ever, because the idea is loosely defined, but in 1915 Gustav Delage, famed designed of fighters for the Nieuport company, explained why making the bottom wing half as big as the top wing resulted in superior aircraft. I came to the conclusion that his entire argument was fallacious, about the only real advantage of such a layout being a better pilot view downwards. Suffice to say the NiD29, designed by Delage in 1917-18 and a standard French fighter of the 1920s, had wings of equal size.

Just to confuse the issue, Caproni's designer of large aircraft, Ingeniere Rodolfo Verduzio, firmly latched on to the idea that the best formula was the inverted sesquiplane, in which it is the upper wing that is small. Both he and Caproni himself delivered papers explaining the idea. The reasons were partly aerodynamic and partly structural, and I am afraid that again I failed to be convinced. Suffice to say the inverted sesquiplane always remained a very rare species, and Caproni was the only company to persevere with it.

By far the most important of these distinctive Capronis were the bombers and transports which stemmed from the Ca73 passenger aircraft of 1924. There were numerous variants, all powered by a single push/pull tandem pair of engines mounted on struts above the fuselage, and not connected to the upper wing. The Ca73ter (company designation Ca82) remained in active service until 1935, seeing action against the helpless inhabitants of Libya and Abyssinia and possibly even Albania.

In 1926 Verduzio prepared the design of a Ca73 scaled up to be a real monster. There is not the slightest doubt it was Count Caproni's wish that he should do so, though doubtless they did get a contract from the Italian Air Ministry first. We have already seen how Caproni yearned to produce enormous flying machines, and in the second half of the 1920s the company was able to

go ahead because very powerful engines were being developed for seaplane racers to compete for the Schneider Trophy. Verduzio picked the biggest member of the Isotta-Fraschini Asso (Ace) series, the Asso 1000. This had three banks each of six cylinders arranged in W (broad arrow) formation, with a total capacity of no less than 57.26 litres (for comparison, the Merlin's capacity was 27 litres). For Schneider racers this monster engine gave 1,400 hp, but for the huge bomber, the Ca90, it was rated at 1,000 hp.

Verduzio decided to size the Ca90 to use six of these engines, in three push/pull tandem pairs. One pair were mounted close together in a nacelle above the fuselage; the others were mounted directly on top of the lower wing in nacelles so long that the propellers cleared the enormous wing. The rest of the machine was almost a direct scale of the Ca73, apart from changes to the detail structure, fitting a more modern monoplane tail and a different form of landing gear.

The huge Ca90 was by far the biggest of a family of bombers and transports noted for their 'inverse sesquiplane' layout. (Caproni via John Batchelor)

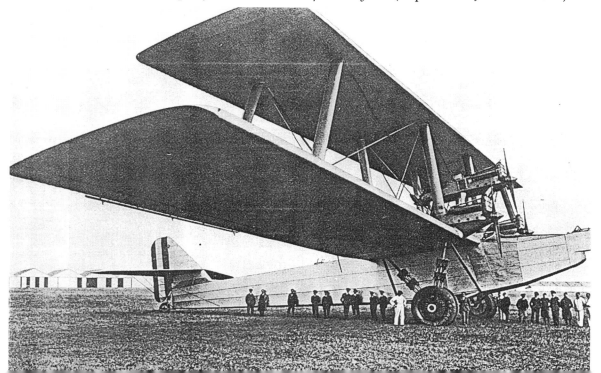

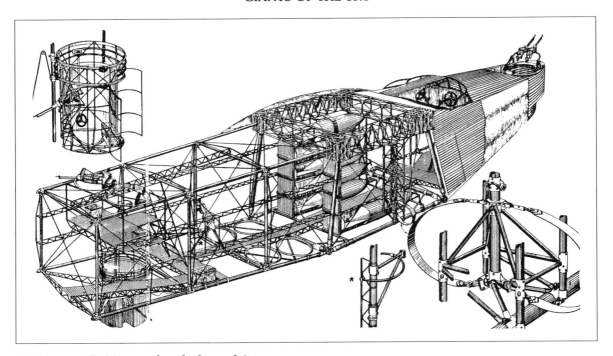

Only one Ca90 was funded, and it was a heavy bomber. The planned passenger version was never built, one reason being that no airline wanted to pay for it or thought it could fill it.

Whereas much of the structure of the wartime bombers had been of wood, the Ca90 airframe was entirely metal. Most of the greatest stresses were borne by steel tubes, four of which were used from tip to tip in each of the widely spaced wing spars. Most of the remaining structure comprised lattice girders reminiscent of airship construction, with suitably strong wire bracing: the main lift wires in the wing cellule were quadruple, each of 20 tons breaking strain. Despite the enormous size of the Ca90 — span of the lower wing was 152 ft 10 in — it was only a two-bay aircraft, the inboard interplane struts being vertical and the outboard struts inwards-sloping. Each was a four-tube lattice girder encased in a streamlined skin of fine-pitch corrugated Dural. Covering was fabric, except along the leading edges of the wings and the fuselage ahead of the wings, which were all corrugated Dural.

Contemporary Caproni drawing showing Ca90 fuselage structure, with insets showing 'dustbin' turret, beam gun mount (asterisk) and bomb retaining straps. (Caproni via John Batchelor)

The large tailwheel and four mainwheels were all mounted on pivoted arms with shock-absorbing by tensioned rubber loops. Each main wheel was loaded by two struts, one to each wing spar, each with upper and lower sets of 12 rubber cords, 48 in all above each axle. Flight control surfaces were of excellent design, the ailerons (lower wing only), elevators and rudder all having inset hinges and almost full-span servo tabs along the trailing edge.

In contrast to its predecessors, and indeed to many other aircraft of the day, the engines of the Ca90 were fully cowled. In conformity with common practice, the tractor engines drove two-blade propellers and the pushers four-blade, all with pointed spinners. Engines were handed, so that all propellers revolved anti-clockwise as seen from the front. I believe it is bad aerodynamics to make a propeller work in a spirally rotating slipstream whose direction of rotation is in the same sense. So far as I can determine, in every other tandem installation (in this book at least) the rear propellers worked in opposition to the incident propwash. The tractor engines had flat frontal radiators above the reduction gearbox, just ahead of the cylinder blocks. The central pusher engine radiator was left out in the slipstream beneath the middle of the nacelle, while the outer pusher engine radiators were of a different pattern mounted vertically up the rear interplane strut above the nacelle. Some 15,500 lb of fuel could be carried in eight cylindrical tanks filling the wing between the spars inboard of the outer engines.

Up to 17,637 lb (8 tonnes) of bombs could be carried, probably — like many other aspects of the Ca90 — a world record at the time. Bomb sizes could be 100, 250, 500 or 800 kg. A drawing shows how bombs were carried horizontally inside and alongside the centre fuselage, each restrained by a loop of springy steel pin-jointed at its upper end and held at its lower end by a cable-operated release. This drawing also shows the side-by-side cockpit, open on each side but with a central roof joined to the multi-pane windscreen. Defensive armament was all that one might have expected on so huge a bomber. In the nose was a cockpit with twin Lewis guns on a Scarff ring. Aft of the wings were two dorsal cockpits, side by side, each with a single gun. Immediately in front of these were two beam guns on pivoted mounts enabling the gunner to aim directly down or to the rear. Underneath was a rotatable 'dustbin' with a single gun (twin guns could be fitted). Finally, in the centre of the upper wing was a further cockpit with a Scarff ring for one or two guns, making a maximum of 12 guns in all.

The Ca90, devoid of markings apart from the Italian tricolour on the rudder, was completed in 1929, making a very successful first flight in the spring of that year. At the time, and until the appearance of the ANT-20 five years later, it was the largest landplane in the world; indeed, it was the largest aeroplane of any kind until the Do X took off later in 1929, and to this day not many aircraft have surpassed the Ca90's wing area of 5,346 sq ft. It is also a reflection on methods of construction to note that, despite its size, the equipped empty weight of the Caproni bomber was only 33,070 lb, less than half as much as that of the Do X and precisely half the maximum loaded weight. Note also that the Ca90's installed power was close to that of the Do X. Altogether, with a bomb load of eight tonnes, combined with an endurance with this bomb load of seven hours, the

Count Gianni Caproni gives scale to the Ca90's wheels. These are resting on trollies enabling the bomber to be pulled sideways out of its hangar. (Via Philip Jarrett)

Ca90 was no mean performer, though predictably it was rather slow, maximum speed being 127 mph. On 22 February 1930 it set several records for height and duration with load, in a 1 hr 31 min flight during which it lifted a useful load of 10 tonnes (22,046 lb) to a height of 3,231 m (10,600 ft).

After 1930 it was increasingly evident that the basic formula of the Ca90 was outdated. Caproni switched to monoplanes, and never again built anything approaching the Ca90 in size. I was told he drew a gigantic monoplane in 1940, weighing 50 tonnes, but never built it.

21 Dornier Do X

One of my earliest memories is of visiting this monster flying boat. It must have been November 1930, so I would have been three, and to put it mildly I was awed — one could almost say frightened. Easily the biggest heavier-than-air machine of its day, it would look quite impressive even today. On the other hand it was not a very good performer (two built for Italy were slightly better) and, in the words of John Stroud, 'The boat received large-scale publicity in the world's press, out of all proportion to its achievements'.

As we have seen, Claudius Dornier had

been a pioneer of large aircraft, and he continued his studies after the Armistice. Like Junkers, Rohrbach and other constructors, he evaded the Inter-Allied Control Commission by setting up shop in a neutral country. In his case he merely moved a few miles round the shore of the Bodensee to Altenrhein, in Switzerland. He kept his project team at Manzell, however, where from 1919 to 1926 a succession of enormous commercial flying boats were drawn. All had the Dornier hallmark of a thick untapered monoplane wing, and most had sponsons (fat wing-like projections on each side of the

hull just above the water) instead of wing-tip floats to give lateral stability when afloat. By 1925 most of these studies had a span of 48 m (157 ft 5.75 in) and 12 Siemens-built Bristol Jupiter nine-cylinder aircooled radial engines, each of 525 hp. Dornier left abundant records, among other things explaining that he preferred proven engines, even at the penalty of having to use 12 of them. Incidentally I do not believe any other aircraft of any kind has flown with more than 12 propulsion engines, though, if we regard the DB613 double engine as being in reality a pair of DB603s joined together, then the Do214 (described later) would have been a 16-engined machine.

Out of Dornier's various studies came one called 51335P. On 22 December 1926 this went ahead as the Do X. The letter was out of sequence, and was adopted (Dornier said) to signify 'the unknown'. The company type letters were puzzling, later types including the P, Y and F bombers, respectively with four, three and two engines. The monster Flugschiff (flying ship) was of course a huge programme, involving extensive wind-tunnel and towing-tank testing and prolonged structural and systems research.

Actual construction at Altenrhein began in December 1927, and Flugschiff D-1929 (an appropriate registration) was first flown by Richard Wagner on 12 July 1929. Construction required 240,000 man-days. Nobody seems to know who paid for it, but I believe that half the funding came from the German navy. Almost certainly the rest was provided by the Reichsverkehrsministerium (transport ministry), though Luft Hansa made no commitment to purchase or use the monster. No route could have supported it, though it might have earned a living making short pleasure trips, rather like Delag Zeppelin airships before 1914.

With so large a boat it was possible to mount the wing directly on the hull, through in fact it was attached to a raised portion which incorporated the cockpit and other flight crew compartments before sloping down at the rear, following the aerofoil profile of the wing, to meet the horizontal top line of the tapering rear part of the hull. The wing structure, wholly of Duralumin light alloy, comprised three full-span spars with sheet webs, lattice truss ribs and spanwise stringers. Corrugated metal skin covered the leading edge, the tips and the

Left *The Do X as originally built, with an auxiliary wing linking streamlined pylons carrying the 12 Siemens Jupiter engines.* (Dornier DWF 3081/67)

Right *The massive control wheels would have obscured the pilot's view of the instruments, had there been any! The desk on the extreme left belonged to the navigator.* (Dornier DWF 18592/11)

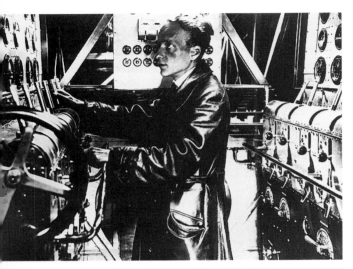

Top *One of the (usually two) flight engineers adjusting power on Engine 9. Note that he is not wearing intercom.* (Dornier DWF 26014/2)

Above *One of the compartments of D-1929 set for a meal. Nobody had even heard of plastic wineglasses!* (Dornier DWF 16408)

the aspect ratio *looked* far too low, just as that of the Inflexible looked far too high.

The hull was typical Dornier, and nothing like the old wartime boats. Constructed totally of Duralumin, it had a beautiful ship-like bow, sloping sides and a rounded top. There was no outward projection at the chine, the maximum beam being about 16 ft. The planing bottom surfaces were concave, there being a flat projecting section along the keel. The planing bottom tapered off not far behind the wings to terminate in a large water rudder. The rear fuselage tapered in plan and elevation to carry the tail high above the water. On each side was a sponson (*Bootsstummel*), about 86 in deep and with a span of 34 ft 9.4 in. Overall length was 131 ft 4.8 in.

The tail was rather strange, in that it incorporated small auxiliary surfaces which might well have been left out. The main surfaces comprised a central fin and rudder, carrying a fixed tailplane and divided elevators half way up. The tailplane was braced by two struts on each side. In addition there was a small fixed tailplane lower down, mounted directly on top of the hull, carrying at its tips small auxiliary rudders whose tops were pivoted to the main tailplane. The elevators had enormous 'park bench' balancing surfaces. So too did the huge (38-ft span) ailerons. The elevators and main rudder were fabric covered; all the rest of the tail was skinned in corrugated Dural. Altogether the tail, almost wholly in the wake of the propellers, appeared small in relation to the size of the aircraft.

The vertical distance from the water surface to the underside of the wing was 10 ft 10 in, yet Dornier still elected to put the engines high above the wing. Some of his earlier schemes had engines in the trailing edge or even entirely below the wing. Putting them all above the wing made the thrust lines very high. The six push/pull tandem nacelles were carried on streamlined pylons which were all joined along their tops (ie, just beneath the nacelles) by a

walkway along the top as far as the outer engines, the rest being fabric. The aerofoil profile was enormous, about 5 ft deep and with a chord of nearly 31 ft. Indeed, the low aspect ratio of 5 was a cause of poor flight performance, and especially of sluggish climb and low ceiling. As in the Rs boats,

narrow-chord wing which projected beyond the outer nacelles to have a span of just over 72 ft. As originally built, all the engines drove four-blade wooden propellers. The tips would have touched had not the nacelles all been staggered; thus, engines 1/2, 5/6 and 9/10 were mounted further ahead than 3/4, 7/8 and 11/12. This made the Do X asymmetric, though as in the Rs IV it was not very obvious. The vertical pylons contained steps giving access to the interior of each nacelle from which the engines (apart from the aircooled cylinders) could be reached in flight. Hatches in the top of the nacelles gave access to the two tubular oil radiators mounted on top of each nacelle on struts. To reach the pylons there was a walkway along the inside of the wing. Alternatively, when the boat was moored, engineers could walk along the top of the wing and enter through doors in both sides of each pylon.

As befits a 747 of its day, the Do X hull had three decks. Another similarity is that the main (passenger) deck was full length, though there was no view ahead. For much of its life D-1929 was not fully furnished, but when it was it had various seating arrangements, usually for 50 to 60 and with comfortable saloons and a restaurant. Without such amenities the normal seating plan provided twin seats each side of the aisle for 66 passengers or, with three rows of triple seats amidships, for 72. One could comment that on similar floor area today one might find 120 seats or more. On the lowest level were the four drums each holding 660 gal of fuel, as well as a startling 285 gal of oil and bays for baggage and cargo. A further 66-gal fuel tank was in each wing leading edge. All fuel and oil was pumped up electrically. At the upper level was the cockpit, seating two pilots side-by-side. Each had a huge 'steering wheel' and a battery of handwheels for elevator trim, rudder trim and for controlling the water rudder. In front were hardly any instruments, apart from a compass and climb/descent indicator (driven by

a prominent 'thermos flask'), with a box between the pilots housing tiny repeater tachometers and warning lamps for the 12 engines. Later the Do X was given proper instrument panels on each side. Eight square vertical windows surrounded the pilots, the two on either side of the centre pair being hinged to open outwards. Immediately to the rear, with four more windows, was the navigator's room with a plotting table, chart storage, repeater instruments

D-1929 late in life, with Curtiss watercooled engines on unfaired strut groups and a D/F loop above the bows. (Dornier DWF 6022)

(including clock and altimeter), drift sight and many other items. Next, in the thickest part of the wing, came the *Maschinenzentrale*, the flight engineer's domain. This contained an impressive bank of instruments and controls on each side, one lot for the six forward engines and the other for the aft engines. On the rear wall, actually one of the massive spar webs, was the main electrical panel. Below this a triangular doorway (it had to be this shape because of the Warren bracing struts of the spar) admitted to the radio compartment, with bulky communications sets. Later, in 1930, D-1929 was fitted with a D/F (direction finding) receiver, served by a giant loop antenna above the nose. At the extreme rear of the upper deck, where the ceiling (ie aft upper wing skin) sloped downwards, was the auxiliary generating plant, driven by a 12 hp two-stroke engine whose exhaust pipe projected high above the wing.

This was perhaps the only possible arrangement, but it was not really satisfactory. The *Funker* (radio operator) had to pass messages in the form of handwritten chits handed forward via the engineer. Likewise, his cabin separated the engineer from the auxiliary generating plant. As the engineer had to be where he was in order to have immediate access to the catwalks which led along the wings to the engines, it would have been much better if the radio operator could have been further forward on the right-hand side of the navigator's compartment.

Three prominent longitudinal beads (V-stiffeners) ran along the outer skin almost the full length of the hull. Of course, the three wing spars were attached to three specially strong hull bulkheads. To these, at the top of the hull on each side, were attached three diagonal bracing struts which disappeared into the sponson to join up with three more strong struts running horizontally out from the same three bulkheads inside the sponsons. The joints formed a solid attachment for three bracing

struts for the wings, running diagonally out to pin joints on the three spars. The inner struts helped people climb up the sloping aft face of the sponson to reach the main doors, one on each side. At the rear, 52 ft further aft, was another door, used (for example) for servicing the galley and toilet.

The flight on 12 July 1929 was really only a hop, made before the Do X had been painted. It was then painted and, after a second short flight, made a much longer flight on 29 July. There followed a prolonged period of testing, during which it was established that, while some aspects of performance — such as seaworthiness and, to some degree, the maximum and cruising speeds of 131 and 109 mph — were adequate, the take off was rather protracted, climb very slow, ceiling unacceptably low and general handling sluggish. On 21 October 1929, a flight was made with a crew of 10, 150 invited passengers and (it is always said) nine stowaways; the total of 169 stood as a record for almost 20 years. On one of the guest flights Claudius Dornier suddenly called all the passengers together amidships to drink champagne. One guest realised that this was done to help the pilot make a turn. When asked what he thought of 'my great *Luftschiff*' he replied 'Exactly the same as you do, my dear Herr Doktor!'

More serious was the severe overheating of the rear engines, which in consequence could not maintain their proper power settings. The designer of the Jupiter, Roy (later Sir Roy) Fedden, was never happy about the Do X installation, and in fact refused to give his blessing to it, though in many other types of aircraft uncowled Jupiter and Pegasus engines worked perfectly well as pushers, a later example being the Walrus. Dornier published the ceiling as 900 m (2,953 ft), whereas almost everyone else said it was more like 1,000 ft. Wherever possible the giant boat operated almost in ground effect, separated from the sea by about one wing span. For whatever reason, on 14 February 1930 the Do X made its last flight

One of the very few occasions when, even after being re-engined, the Do X climbed to about 1,000 m. (Dornier DWM 10/36196)

with Jupiter engines. It went back into the works to be fitted with American Curtiss Conqueror engines.

These were large watercooled vee-12s, completely cowled in box-like nacelles each mounted on four struts. These struts picked up at the same points in the wing as the previous installations, but instead of being enclosed in a streamlined casing the access ladder was now out in the open. The auxiliary wing was likewise removed, and replaced by simple pairs of horizontal struts linking the six nacelles. Altogether this was considered to lose hardly any lift and to save quite a lot of drag. At first the front engines drove four-blade propellers and the rear engines two-bladers — the reverse of the most usual arrangement — but before long all 12 engines had four-bladers, which could not have been those used with the Jupiter engines. The front engines had plain frontal radiators, while the radiators for the rear engines retracted vertically inside the nacelle and could be cranked out into the slipstream by the flight engineer just enough to keep the temperatures satisfactory. The oil coolers were in tandem on the right side of each nacelle.

The change of engines added 1,380 hp, the maximum power of each engine going up from 525 to 640 hp, but it also added nearly 10,000 lb in empty weight (increased from 62,280 to 72,035 lb). The first flight with the new engines was on 4 August 1930, the boat henceforth being known as the X 1b, the original configuration becoming the X 1a. The modification was on the whole an improvement, though Fedden always maintained that one reason for the change was that Dornier hoped to sell one or two of the giant boats in the USA, and could do so more easily with American engines. Certainly there was no very marked increase in performance. Cruising speed, according to Dornier, was unchanged, and most observers said there was little improvement in ceiling, though Dornier claimed 'about 1,250 m' (4,100 ft).

In October 1930 D-1929 was made somewhat heavier by being more extensively painted, the sides of the hull being white and the sponsons and planing bottom red. This was in readiness for the aircraft's one great publicity flight. It left Altenrhein on 5 November 1930 and, after a fire at Lisbon and take-off damage at Las Palmas, the Do X reached Bubaque, an island off Portuguese Guinea. Here, despite unloading crew and stores, the weight of fuel for a transatlantic crossing made the boat refuse to leave the water, so the crossing was finally made between the Cape Verde islands and Fernando de Noronha, 2,374 km (1,475 miles) in a little over 13 hrs. Subsequently the boat flew south to Rio, and then north again in many stages to New York. D-1929 wintered at Glenn H. Curtiss airport (today La Guardia), finally leaving in May 1932. The overload take-off at 53.3 tonnes (117,500 lb)

from Conception Bay, Newfoundland, took a nailbiting 106 secs, and for several hours the cruising height was the same '10 ft' as on the westbound leg across the South Atlantic. The Do X completed its journey by alighting on the Müggelsee in Berlin on 24 May 1932.

D-1929 made a few further flights, and in May 1933 the name LUFT HANSA appeared on the bows instead of the name of the maker. Harald Seabrook-Smith and John Stroud both report that the giant never went into revenue service, but it stayed with Luft Hansa until September. In 1934 it received the new national red/black swastika tail markings before being taken to the Berlin Luftfahrtmuseum. Here it was the largest exhibit until it was destroyed by bombs in 1945.

In 1930 Dornier received a contract from the Italian Government for two Do X boats of a slightly improved design. The changes were mostly confined to the systems and, especially, to the engines. The latter were Fiat A22R watercooled vee-12s, each rated

The Carabinieri is trying to decide how to climb on to the sponson of one of the Italian boats, moored at Venice Lido. The Fiat engine installations were attractive. (Dornier DWM 98/140800)

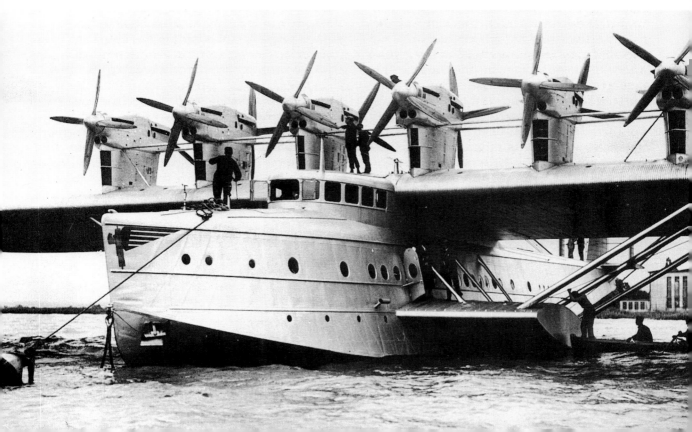

at 580 hp. They were installed in more streamlined nacelles, driving four-blade propellers with large spinners faired into the engine cowlings. Though the six nacelles were still linked only by pairs of struts, the vertical pylons reverted to having stream-lined casings to ease inflight access to the engines. The skin over these pylons was not corrugated, and the leading edge incorpo-rated the main cooling radiators, with slid-ing adjustable apertures at the front and flush exits along the sides. The oil coolers were side-by-side under the front engines, inside the cowling.

Despite the reduced power, and a con-siderable further increase in empty weight, to 76,764 lb (but not in maximum loaded weight), the Fiat-engined boats were slightly faster than their predecessors, had a simi-lar range and such a dramatically improved altitude performance (Dornier claimed 3,200 m, 10,500 ft) that they were able to cross the Alps on delivery. They were equipped as transports, though they bore civil registra-tion and were intended to be used by the airline SANA on a route from Trieste to Cadiz. They were designated as Do Type X2 (some historians, I believe erroneously, call them X2 and X3). The first, I-REDI, *Umberto Maddalena*, was first flown, with no mark-ings except a Fascist emblem on the bows,

on 16 May 1931. She was delivered, fully painted in white/red and with Italy's green/white/red tail stripes, to La Spezia on 28 August 1931. Her identical sister, I-ABBN, *Alessandro Guidoni*, was delivered on 13 May 1932. There are several photographs of the two Italian boats flying in formation, but they seem to have been little used, and probably did no flying at all after 1935.

Dornier never built the 1936 project known as the Do20. By this time the main works was at Friedrichshafen, a few miles from Altenrhein. The Do20 resembled a modernised Do X, with a simple tail unit and more streamlined hull. The main differ-ence from the Do X was that it would have had four tractor propellers on the leading edge, each driven by two Junkers Jumo 207 (or similar) diesel engines, each of about 900 hp. The paired engines were separately geared to coaxial propellers, so that all eight engines could be started individually. The Do20 was planned to carry 60 passengers across the Atlantic non-stop at 180 mph. It led to the much more powerful Do214.

Data for D-1929 as built include: span 157 ft 5¾ in, length 131 ft 4¾ in, wing area 4,844 sq ft, empty weight 62,280 lb (Italian boats, 76,764 lb), maximum weight 99,868 lb (with Curtiss engines, 105,820 lb), cruising speed 109 mph.

22 Junkers G38

As described earlier, Hugo Junkers had since 1909 been the greatest advocate of the all-wing (or almost all-wing) aeroplane. Yet, though he was perpetually scheming colos-sal all-wing aircraft, he was destined never to build one. After his death Junkers did build a huge all-wing glider (which we shall see later) which could hardly have been a greater flop. The nearest Junkers ever came to realising his dream was in the G38, work on which began in 1928. A critic might say

it combined most of the disadvantages of both the fuselage and the all-wing configu-ration, because it could be regarded as a nor-mal fuselage transport whose wing was so large it got in the way of almost everything in the fuselage.

Span was 144 ft 4.3 in and area (as origi-nally built) 3,122 sq ft. Root chord was 35 ft and thickness about 6 ft 7 in. Of course, the entire structure was metal, almost all being corrugated Dural, including the skin.

There were three main spars, with six tubular booms of high-tensile steel, and six auxiliary spars. The 18 tubular joints served to attach the left and right wings to the huge root fitting which formed most of the side wall of the fuselage. A small nose projected ahead of the leading edge and a modest rear fuselage carried the biplane tail, with one fin and three rudders. Engines comprised two of the massive Junkers L88 vee-12s of 800 hp, in the inner positions and driving four-blade propellers, and two 400 hp Junkers L8 engines in the outer positions, driving two-blade propellers. All engines were inside the wing, fully accessible in flight, driving via extension shafts. The water and oil cooling radiators were mounted on vertical guides on which they could be retracted inside the wing or extended by any desired amount. Fuel for no less than 20 hr was housed in 28 upright cylindrical tanks.

The quite small cockpit was only just wide enough to accommodate the side-by-side control wheels. The front spar of the wing had to stop at the root rib because of the presence of the pilots' seats. Below the cockpit was the radio operator, and in the extreme nose was the navigator. Behind the cockpit was the central station for the (usually two) flight engineers, who could walk out to any of the engines. Seating was provided for 30 passengers, most of whom had no external view, including those in the front and rear 11-seat cabins, though the front cabin had four transparent portholes in the roof. At the rear was a four-seat cabin,

next to the double entrance door, where smoking was permitted; they could see above the trailing edge of the monster wing. The lucky ones were the four who could occupy unique two-seat cabins in each inboard wing leading edge, looking ahead through curved glass panels.

The main landing gears were particularly neat. Each comprised a vertical shock strut, sprung by 36 rubber loops, carrying at its lower end two girders cast in Elektron magnesium alloy to which were attached the axles for single front and rear wheels. The whole assembly was braced laterally to the fuselage. When the first G38 was initially completed each main gear was faired by a giant spat, which extended up to encase the leg. As in the even bigger ANT-20 the spats were removed before the first flight, the rubber looms and upper leg then being protected by streamlined fairings. All four wheels had pneumatic brakes, the compressed air for this system, and for starting the main engines, being provided by a 30 hp diesel compressor in the port wing. There was also an electrical system for the full navigation lighting, radio (including D/F), and electric cooker in the galley. The crew of seven included three stewards.

The G38 made its first flight, quite successfully, on 6 November 1929. Registered D-2000, it began trials with Luft Hansa in June 1930, but it was not registered to the airline until May 1931. John Stroud watched its first visit to Croydon, on 1 July 1931, and was intrigued by its powered approach (the first he had seen). Performance was not bril-

Seldom illustrated, the first G38 carried out taxi tests with huge spats. These were removed before first flight. (Junkers)

Above *Radiators are fully extended as the much-improved second aircraft makes a typically short take-off. By this time (1936) it was called the 38ce, with four L88a engines. (Via Mike Hooks)*

Right *Compared with the Do X, the G38b had something almost resembling a modern airline cockpit. Note the wing leading-edge structure at left. (Lufthansa via Mike Hooks)*

liant, for at less than maximum weight of 46,296 lb the maximum speed was 118 mph, cruising speed 106 mph and time to 3,280 ft (1,000 m) no less than 9.5 min. Service ceiling was put by Junkers at about 8,200 ft.

Despite this modest performance, the G38 was destined to make a sustained impact, and not only in Europe. By late 1930 the decision had been taken to build a second G38, to an improved specification, and also to design a heavy bomber version for con-

struction under licence in Japan. The second aircraft, registered D-2500, made its maiden flight at the beginning of 1932 (Junkers appear not to know the actual date). It was known as the G38b, and differed from its predecessor in many respects. The most fundamental difference was that the fuselage was slightly longer (overall length 76 ft 1.5 in compared with 69 ft 8.2 in) and very much deeper, it now having passenger accommodation on two decks for up to 34.

Left *Aboard D-APIS in the late 1930s, with coffee and biscuits or an aperitif dispensed from a litre bottle. Note the pull-down blinds, cigar-extinguishing ashtrays and portrait actually signed 'von Hindenburg 29.9.33'.* (Lufthansa via John Stroud)

Below right *The artist has drawn Lindbergh's Ryan NYP perilously close to the General Development monster!* (General Development via R.T. Riding)

The trailing edge was fitted with the company's patented 'double wing' flaps and drooping ailerons which, despite a major increase in weight, reduced landing speed from 95 to 78 km/h (a scarcely believable 48.5 mph). The tail was redesigned with three fins and rudders, and there were many other changes, including hydraulic brakes. Virtually all passengers now had external view, and the four extra passengers all had nice seats, two in what had been the nose navigation cabin and the others in the leading-edge compartments which now seated three on each side.

D-2500 entered Luft Hansa service not later than July 1932. Over the next three years both aircraft underwent progressive modification. The G38 was brought back to Dessau and completely rebuilt to the standard of the second aircraft, plus four 800 hp L88a engines all driving four-blade propellers. It thus became the G38a, and it was then re-registered D-AZUR and named *Deutschland*, finally being fitted with four

750 hp Jumo 204 two-stroke opposed-piston diesel engines (much more conveniently installed through the underside of the wing instead of from above) before crashing at Dessau in 1936. As a boy I watched it take off from Croydon, leaving smoky exhaust trails. The G38b was likewise upgraded as the G38ce, at first with four L88a engines and finally four Jumo 204s, maximum weight being increased to 52,910 lb. This aircraft was named *Generalfeldmarschall von Hindenberg* and re-registered D-APIS, seeing intensive service with Luft Hansa until, on the outbreak of war, it was impressed into the Luftwaffe. It served with KGrzbV 172 (call sign GF+GG) until on 17 May 1941 it was destroyed at Athens by the RAF.

As for the heavy bomber version, this was the K51, but Junkers produced plans only. These were sent to Japan, where Mitsubishi used them in 1932-34 to build six Ki-20 (Army Type 92 Super Heavy Bombers). These had four L88 engines driving four-blade propellers, and three fins, but were otherwise broadly similar to the original G38. No less than 11,023 lb of bombs could be carried on external racks under the fuselage and wings. Most descriptions give the defensive armament as one 20 mm cannon and three machine-guns, but there are plenty of photographs showing twin guns in the upper nose turret, two more in the dorsal position, two in each of the gunner nacelles above the trailing edge of the wing and at least one in each of the glazed 'dustbin' turrets beneath the wings at the same location, in other words a total of not less than 10 guns. At least one Ki-20 was still flying in Japan in 1943.

23 General Development monoplane

I don't know much about the General Development Company, of Connecticut, but in 1929 it was allegedly building the biggest aeroplane in the world. More than that, it was a landplane, at a time when giants tended to operate from water. More even than that, it was building four of the monsters! Not to worry, it was bound to be all right, because the designer was E.Eliot Green, who had been 'aeronautical engineer to the Department of Commerce'. Anyway, the bills were all being met by Reid, King & Co, bankers and brokers of Hartford, Connecticut. The moving spirit behind the enterprise was Dr. W. Whitney Christmas, General Development's vice-president.

Like most of the truly gargantuan landplane projects, the Christmas-Green creation had twin fuselages on a colossal wing. Span was to be 262 ft, and wing area

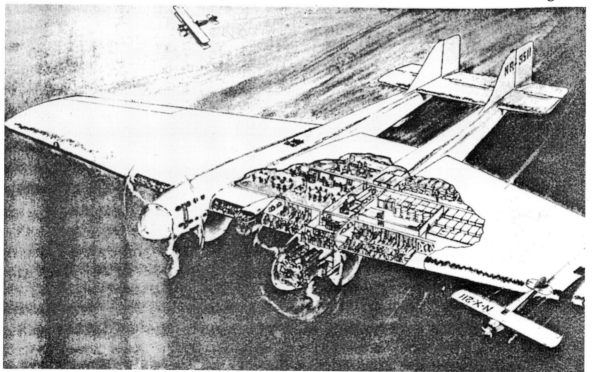

10,370 sq ft. Structure was mainly steel tubes. In the front of each fuselage was a small matter of a 34-ft propeller driven by four engines each of 1,100 hp. Plenty of detail is available on the installation, engine starting, the fuel system and many other considerations, but nobody said anything about what engine would be used. I could go on for hours about the furnishings, for the crew of 17, 160 passengers and their baggage, and consumable stores. Gross weight was to be 145,000 lb, and the 2,665 gal of fuel were to take the monster 800 miles in 7 hr. Each fuselage had two 6-ft wheels inside a trouser. The brochure told us: 'Inside the wheel fairing is a waste heat boiler which supplies heating to the interior of the machine, and here also terminate the exhaust pipes from the engines.' Isn't that how people commit suicide?

The
1930s

Whereas the 1920s saw practically no adoption of all-metal stressed-skin construction, by the early 1930s such aircraft as the Northrop Alpha and Martin Bomber had caused such a stir that the new form of structure simply could not be shrugged off any longer. A few constructors tried to produce modern-looking aircraft (such as the de Havilland Comet and Heinkel He70) but had to use wings made of wood. Such an answer was impossible for very large aircraft. The 1930s really sorted the men from the boys, and the companies that led the way in stressed-skin wings tended to have the global market at their feet. An obvious example is the Douglas DC-2/DC-3.

Of course, a key factor in building giant aircraft at this time was the engine. There was really only one type of engine to choose from: the four-stroke (Otto cycle) piston engine. Such engines impose fairly immutable limitations on the aircraft in which they are fitted. The basic aerodynamics of the traditional propeller tend to limit the speed that can be achieved to about 500 mph, and throughout the 1930s the cruising speeds for bombers and transports were usually less than one-third of this. Another basic limitation was sheer power. If you make the cylinders too big you run into trouble with the time taken for the flame to spread from the sparking plug throughout the charge; a rule of thumb that endures to this day is that the practical upper limit of cylinder radius is 3 in (76 mm). Increasing the stroke either means excessive piston speeds and insoluble problems with the balancing of the rotating and oscillating masses, or else severe limitation on rpm. Either way, it means a limit to the attainable power. So what about simply using more and more cylinders? The 1930s saw the launch of virtually all the ultimate high-power piston engines, and few had more than 24 cylinders. The successful R-4360 Wasp Major had 28, and the unsuccessful Lycoming XR-7755 had 36 (and they were big). What it added up to was that giant aircraft tended to need many engines.

By the end of the 1930s virtually every large aeroplane was an all-metal stressed-skin design, using engines of at least 1,500 hp each. This is from two to three times the power available from the biggest engines in the 1920s, yet the 1930s was a time of consolidation. Manufacturers concentrated on what might be termed 'sensible' bombers and transports, none of them anything like as large as the biggest projects of earlier times (with the sole exception of the A.N. Tupolev 26 and 28, which were never completed). Perhaps surprisingly, the biggest projects were civil transport flying boats intended to meet a specification issued by PanAm (which many observers consider to have been a purely political move never intended seriously by the airline). Not very far behind were three civil transport flying boats produced in France, which were actually flown.

But it was not really a vintage decade for giants. Most people were far too busy mass-producing normal-size warplanes for the coming terrible war that seemed increasingly inevitable.

Previous page *This artwork appeared in the London magazine* The Sphere *in June 1933. It was triggered off by a Rumpler project, and was to have a span of 600 ft, length of 335 ft (twin hulls), 1,500 passengers in a total payload of 450 tons, take-off weight of 1,600 tons and '100,000 hp from 12 engines each driving a 50 ft propeller'.*

24 Sikorsky flying boats

Obviously, in any book of this nature, there are grey areas between the aircraft which are obviously 'giants' and those which are not. For example, the most famous British airliner of the early 1930s was the HP42/45, with a span of 130 ft and wing area of 2,989 sq ft; but it had a gross weight of only 29,500 lb and little over 2,000 hp. The next generation was the AW27 Ensign, which had a span of 123 ft and wing area of 2,450 sq ft; but it began life weighing 48,500 lb and with 3,520 hp and grew to weigh 55,500 lb with 4,800 hp. The Ensign was Britain's first large stressed-skin landplane, and it showed how difficult it is for a dog to learn new tricks. To compare its huge and ungainly bulk with that of the DC-4 (described later) shows why large British airliners found no export market.

The Ensign's stable-mate was the Short S.23 Empire flying boat, and this ultimately led to the story of the Shetland. In fact, in almost all respects the Short boat, for all its beautiful appearance, was inferior from the operator's viewpoint to the previous US generation, the Sikorsky S-42. We left Igor Sikorsky in Russia, designing IM bombers. At the time of the Bolshevik revolution he got out and, with little more than his clothes, arrived in New York. Here he very gradually managed to build a viable aircraft company, and in 1926 one of its prototypes was the S-34, a neat six-seat amphibian with a short nacelle-type hull and high monoplane wing. From this was developed the slightly larger S-36, and this in turn led to the S-38, first flown on 25 June 1928. Powered by two 425 hp Pratt & Whitney Wasp engines (almost the first P&W engines sold for a civil aircraft) the S-38 could carry a crew of two and eight passengers, cruising at 103 mph for 500 miles. It proved a smash hit around the world, 114 being built.

It provided a basis for greater things, and the key to the future lay with PanAm. Delighted with the S-36 and 38, the growing airline wanted much bigger, longer-ranged equipment. When PanAm consultant Charles Lindbergh saw the drawings of the S-40 he was disappointed. 'I used to call the S-40 "the flying forest" because of all its struts. But Igor sold me on the S-40. André

Sikorsky's S-40 followed the layout of the very successful S-38 and its predecessors — and, in fact, of the much earlier Curtiss NC boats. (Pan American via Mike Hooks)

Priester was even quicker to see that Igor was correct, that this approach would give us a plane of proven design in a short time, and that a cleaner, faster plane would have to come later as a second step.' So PanAm ordered three S-40s in December 1929, and put the first into service in November 1931.

At the time the S-40 was the largest aeroplane built in the USA, as well as the world's biggest amphibian. The underlying structure was all-metal, but much of the 114 ft wing was fabric covered, and the design merely extrapolated S-38 technology to a bigger size. Gross weight was 34,000 lb, and the four 575 hp Hornets gave a cruising speed of about 115 mph, carrying 40 passengers for 500 miles or 24 for 950 miles. Sikorsky himself had a vivid dream at the age of 11 in which he was walking down the walnut-panelled aisle of a giant flying machine, seeing bluish lights above and feeling distant vibrations (this in the year 1900). One day aboard the S-40 he suddenly realised his dream had come true, in every detail. The three S-40s, named *American/Caribbean/Southern Clipper*, established outstanding service records, ending their days as US Navy trainers for the pilots of large flying boats in World War 2.

Of course, PanAm never lost sight of its need for the more advanced next generation, devoid of such a forest of struts, and it issued a requirement on 15 August 1931. The main demand was to carry 12 passengers 2,500 miles at 145 mph. The result was orders for Sikorsky's S-42, and also for Martin's M-130 described later. Sikorsky

aimed slightly lower and already had the experience of the S-40, so the S-42 flew first. There is no question but that, when it first flew on 29 March 1934, it was the best flying boat in the world; indeed, nothing rivalled it for a long time. Compared with the S-40 it had more powerful 700 hp Hornet engines, driving Hamilton Standard two-position controllable pitch propellers and installed in efficient cowlings, a 118 ft 2 in wing with a stressed-skin main (inter-spar) box, a conventional full-length hull carrying a neat twin-finned tail, and a very much cleaner exterior. What was less obvious was that Sikorsky had quite deliberately aimed at a wing loading which, for a normal production aircraft, was unprecedented: almost 30 lb/sq ft. For example, the equivalent British aircraft, the Short 'Kent' class, used 2,640 sq ft of wing to support a weight of 32,000 lb, whereas the S-42 had only 1,340 sq ft to support a gross weight which began at 38,000 lb, grew to 40,000 lb in the S-42A and finished at 42,000 lb in the S-42B. A key factor was the use of split flaps, extending from aileron to aileron, which at 40° reduced the stalling speed to 65 mph.

Sikorsky designed the hull for minimum drag and weight, accepting that pylons would be needed to carry the wing and tail at the correct height. In normal configuration there were four cabins each seating eight. The first S-42 increased the USA's holding of FAI-approved world records from nine to 17, with a shoal of speed/range/altitude records. Cruising speed was typically 157 mph, the height reached with a 5-tonne (11,023 lb) payload was 20,407 ft, and the range was about 1,200 miles with a payload of 7,000 lb or 3,000 miles with 1,500 lb. The S-42A and B had extended range, enabling them to survey the PanAm routes across the Pacific and North Atlantic (though commercial services on these routes were flown mainly by the M-130 and Boeing 314, as explained later). Ten S-42s were built, four surviving World War 2. The S-42 was the obvious inspiration for the Japanese Kawanishi H5K, very important in World War 2.

In the mid-1930s the US Navy was not well-equipped with large seaplanes, and Rear-Adm Joe Reeves asked United Aircraft, parent of Sikorsky, whether a big flying boat could be built capable of patrolling far into the Pacific. The result was the Sikorsky XPBS-1, hailed as *The Flying Dreadnought*. Ordered on 29 June 1935 and first flown on 13 August 1937, it was really very much in the class of the previously existing Martin 130, with four 1,050 hp Twin Wasp engines, a span of 124 ft, wing area of 1,670 sq ft and gross weight of 48,540 lb. The single XPBS,

BuNo 9995, was a good-looking machine with a hull deep enough to carry the wing at the correct height without a pylon. Though it had a single fin it had a tail turret, the first on any American aircraft. This turret, like that in the nose, mounted a 0.5 in gun; two 7.62 mm guns could fire from waist positions.

The Navy eventually adopted Consolidated's Model 29 (PB2Y Coronado) instead, but Sikorsky — by this time Vought-Sikorsky — developed the XPBS into the VS-44A civil airliner. The VS-44A was restressed to operate at a maximum weight of 57,500 lb, carrying sufficient fuel for the remarkable range of 4,545 miles with 16 passengers. Maximum cruising speed was 210 mph, though 160 was typical on long sectors. In May 1939 a new US flag carrier, American Export Airlines (AEA), applied for CAB permission to operate services to Britain and France, and ordered three VS-44As. The war intervened, but on 12 January 1942 the Navy gave AEA a contract to operate transatlantic services, offering a totally different level of comfort

---

Unconvincing artwork showing Sikorsky's submission to meet the 1938 PanAm specification. The caption is datelined 'for release Wednesday afternoon, June 22'. (Sikorsky Aircraft via John Stroud)

from that available in B-24s and other alternatives. One VS-44A, used post-war by Antilles Air Boats, survives in the museum at Windsor Locks, Connecticut, next to its birthplace.

Sikorsky was one of the four companies which responded to a challenging requirement issued in 1937 by PanAm. Popularly called the Lindbergh Specification, because of the famous pilot's work for PanAm as Chairman of the airline's Technical Committee in 1929-35, it was in fact issued two years after Lindbergh had resigned this appointment. Living in England, where he commuted around Europe in his specially designed Miles Mohawk, he knew nothing of the specification until he read about it, and his name was used by the airline merely to lend credibility to what posterity regards as a purely political ploy to stave off threat of competition from another US flag carrier. By issuing an essentially impossible demand to the US industry, the airline succeeded in impressing the politicians in Washington and staving off all threats. When the airline announced that none of the industry's proposals was acceptable it was the manufacturers that were seen to have failed.

The specification called for an aircraft with a payload of 25,000 lb, with staterooms for 100 passengers carried over a range of 5,000 miles. Of course, today this is peanuts. The Airbus A330, with only two engines, can carry four times the specified payload over the stipulated distance, though of course today we do not think in terms of 'staterooms'. But in 1937 the PanAm demand was totally unrealistic. One factor alone, the availability of engines, ruled it out as impractical. Wright's R-3350 Duplex Cyclone was running on the test bench at powers approaching 2,000 hp, but it was at least five years away from airline service. Even after five years, in 1942, by which time one of the PanAm aircraft might possibly have been ready for flight, the difficulty of getting enough horsepower could have been immense. The four responders to the PanAm requirement were Boeing, Consolidated, Douglas and Sikorsky. Predictably, all proposed giant flying boats. All featured engines buried in the wing, which was mounted high on the hull, and retractable stabilizing floats. Presumably, all assumed that accommodation would be pressurized. The Sikorsky submission had a hull of almost circular section, with two decks, overall length being 155 ft 6 in. The wing, mounted surprisingly far aft, would have had a span of 236 ft and the almost unbelievably small area of 4,670 sq ft.

25 Short S.14 Sarafand

Like every other British aircraft manufacturer in the 1930s, Short Brothers had no experience of modern stressed-skin construction, though back in 1920 the firm had produced a beautiful little all-metal biplane, the Silver Streak, which in any sensible environment might have been expected to be a beginning rather than an end. Instead, Short simply followed the requirements of the RAF and Imperial Airways and made fabric-covered biplanes, mainly with a metal skeleton underneath. Yet, when he saw the Do X, Oswald Short apparently thought his company could produce a much better flying boat despite the use of this outmoded fabric-covered biplane technology. Oswald Short often told me how calculations had shown his firm could 'build a Do X for two-thirds of the weight', carrying a useful commercial payload over stages of up to 1,000 miles (then considered very long).

I do not doubt that this was true, but what

You can almost hear the shouts as they push S1589 on its beaching chassis up the slipway at the maker's Rochester works. Test pilot John Lankester Parker always wore his trilby hat. (Short Brothers via Mike Hooks)

Short did — having convinced the Chief of the Air Staff that the project should be paid for — was to build yet another fabric-covered biplane flying boat which just happened to be bigger than all the others. There are plenty of anecdotes concerning the Sarafand, whose name was that of a tiny village in Palestine between Tyre and Sidon, today in strife-torn Lebanon. One such tale is related in another of my books for PSL, *Plane Speaking*. Another is that it was impossible to put the top wing on inside the erecting shop at the Rochester (Kent) factory, so the huge boat was launched with a clumsy arrangement of jury struts extending from the top of one lower wing, across the tops of the engine nacelles and back to the other wing. After launching, the Sarafand was hauled back on dry land in what was called the barge yard where, enclosed by two huge gantries, and with the lower wings supported by trestles under the floats, the jury strutting was removed and the 120-ft upper wing put on. J. Lankester Parker made the first flight on 30 June 1932.

With Air Ministry serial S1589, the Sarafand was built to reconnaissance specification R.6/28. This all seems odd to me, because while on the one hand Oswald Short wanted to produce a giant flying boat as a civil transport, on the other the Chief of the Air Staff insisted the RAF had no requirement for a huge military boat. Just to make the whole procurement process even more lunatic, to quote Chris Barnes, in the Putnam *Shorts Aircraft Since 1900* '...the contract was signed after a suitable specification, R.6/28, had been drafted to define the project; this necessarily had to be issued to other manufacturers with an invitation to tender, and resulted in a comparable design for a 40-passenger civil monoplane being ordered from Supermarine.' From that point, things went from merely lunatic to completely nonsensical, as explained in the next story (on the Supermarine boat).

Gross weight of the Sarafand was 70,000 lb, wing area 3,460 sq ft and fuel capacity no less than 3,382 gal. Power was provided by six Rolls-Royce Buzzard IIIMS water-cooled vee-12 engines, in push/pull tandem nacelles midway between the wings. Each engine was rated at 825 hp, driving a 16 ft two-blade wooden propeller and with the radiators and oil coolers for each nacelle faired into the interplane struts underneath. All control surfaces had inset hinges, and control forces were commendably light. The rudder was driven by a large servo rudder downstream, and on each side of the central fin was a delta-shaped auxiliary fin, half above the single tailplane and half below, driven irreversibly by the pilot to trim out any engine-out asymmetry. Scarff ring mountings for Lewis guns were in the tail and on the left and right sides (slightly staggered) above the rear hull. In the nose was

a fourth mount which could carry a 37 mm COW gun, as in other big RAF boats of the day.

Altogether the Sarafand was a good example of British biplane flying boat technology. Its range was recorded as 1,450 miles, and maximum speed 153 mph. Appearing three years after the Do X, it hardly seemed an improvement — except possibly in ceiling — and unlike the German boat, which did at least tour the Americas, the Sarafand (so far as I know) never went further than 100 miles from Southend-on-Sea. It was scrapped in 1936.

26 Supermarine 179

In the story of the Short Sarafand it is recorded that, in its wisdom, the Air Ministry decided to invite other manufacturers than Short Brothers to tender to the same specification and that, as a result, a large flying boat was ordered from Supermarine Aviation, a Vickers company with works at Southampton. One thing that nobody today can explain is how it came about that, whereas Short wanted to build a civil transport, they got a contract for a totally military aircraft which the RAF did not want, and whereas the idea of inviting others to tender was so that others should be able to compete for the same (R.6/28 military) specification, Supermarine ended up with a contract for a civil boat, which is what Short had wanted in the first place!

Moreover, whereas the Sarafand biplane had no chance whatsoever of setting new standards of performance or efficiency, the Supermarine boat could well have done just that, though it too would quickly have become obsolescent. Under chief designer Reginald Mitchell, who had already got experience with primitive forms of all-metal stressed-skin wings with the Schneider racers and F.7/30 fighter, design went ahead

rapidly on a quite impressive machine with a stressed-skin cantilever wing with a span of 174 ft and area of 4,000 sq ft. Gross weight was estimated at 75,600 lb, and with six uprated Rolls-Royce Buzzard engines of 900 hp each the cruising (not maximum) speed was estimated at 154 mph.

There are several reports which suggest that what the Air Ministry was really trying to do in funding these two big flying boats was to see whether the monoplane would be superior to the biplane with the same engines. In fact, the propulsion systems would not have been identical. Whereas the Supermarine boat was originally schemed with three tandem pairs of engines, it ultimately would have had four overwing nacelles, two tandem inboard and two single tractor engines outboard. A closer look reveals an absence of radiators. This was a time when many experts thought the next generation of Rolls-Royce engines would be steam-cooled. The water would be allowed to boil on entering the cooling passages inside the engine, the returned steam then being converted back into water in condensers. Unlike ordinary water radiators, the condensers could be aerodynam-

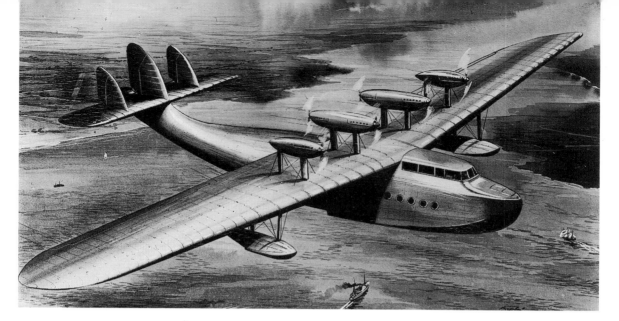

ically flush with the exterior shape of the aircraft, and could even be a stress-bearing part of the structure. In the huge Supermarine boat it was proposed to make most of the wing structure of stainless steel, except for fabric covering aft of the main spar. The whole D-nose of the wing, entirely of corrugated stainless, was to form the giant condensers for the steam bringing waste heat from the engines.

In fighters the steam-cooled engine eventually proved to be a non-starter, partly because of supposed vulnerability of big condensers to battle damage and partly because in combat manoeuvres the steam and water tended to swap places, with disastrous effects on the efficiency of the cooling circuit! Neither of these problems applied in the case of a civil transport, so I am at a loss to explain why, in late 1931, this potentially very important Supermarine boat was cancelled. Beverley Shenstone, who arrived as a Supermarine designer just as the hull was being framed, said it was because of 'the inevitable wave of economy'. Certainly 1931 was hardly a vintage year. It was the depth of the depression, and the Labour government refused even to fund a British entry in the Schneider Trophy race. Maybe when Lady Houston came along with £100,000 for that purpose they thought Supermarine had better have their big boat

cancelled so that they could concentrate on the S.6B Schneider seaplane? Rolls-Royce never built a steam-cooled Buzzard.

For the record, the well-shaped hull carried the wing without a pylon. Structure would have been all light alloy except for the planing bottom, which was stainless steel. Supermarine was very proud of the fact that 'The operating quarters for the crew are totally enclosed. Pilots are situated high up with an excellent view ... Accommodation is for 40 passengers. Detachable bunks are provided so that 20 passengers have sleeping accommodation.' This was a time when any British vehicle bigger than a bicycle had to have passengers segregated into classes. So First Class got a bunk, and Steerage didn't! Incidentally, note that the artist appears to have given the boat a tail gun position.

In 1931 the wing was by far the biggest (in area) ever built in Britain. It was naturally thought that it ought to be strength-tested, which in those days meant static testing only; fatigue had never been thought of. There was no money for a test wing, so Supermarine designed and built a one-third scale wing in the same materials, complete with the stainless nose condensers, and subjected it to a thorough test programme. Of course, true to the form followed to this day by British Airways with non-American aircraft, Imperial Airways never expressed an interest in this big boat. To an outside observer it might have seemed strange that Short should have wanted to make a com-

merical transport flying boat but were paid to make an unwanted military one which accomplished nothing, and that, because of this contract, rival Supermarine were paid to make a really good civil boat which was cancelled just before completion. But then nobody should ever look for common sense in the relationship between the British government and the aircraft industry.

27 Tupolev ANT-16, 22, 26 and 28

Earlier entries have described how the large and growing firm of Hugo Junkers pioneered all-metal aircraft in a somewhat primitive form. Salient characteristics of these aircraft were a deep cantilever monoplane wing and an external skin of corrugated Duralumin. Inside the wing, around the periphery of the profile, were from four to nine spar booms of drawn steel tube, each terminating in a root fixture held by a giant bolt on a hemispherical locating face on the root rib on the side of the fuselage. These booms were joined top and bottom by a riveted and occasionally welded metal trelliswork, the spars themselves being Warren girders.

This form of construction opened the way to truly giant aircraft, but in defeated Ger-

many Junkers did not have the opportunity to build any. To circumvent the Allied restrictions he opened factories at Linhamm in Sweden and at Fili, north of Moscow. The Fili factory built only fairly small aircraft, but the Soviet AGOS brigade studied the Junkers construction carefully, and V.M. Petlyakov quickly became the world leader in the technique. Using Kolchug (Duralumin) alloy, Petlyakov managed the wing design of the ANT-4 twin-engined aircraft of 97 ft span flown on 26 November 1925, which led to the mass-produced TB-1 bomber. Next came the superb ANT-6 four-

The MK-1 (ANT-22) at anchor. The hulls were almost 50 ft apart. (Via Malcolm Passingham)

engined aircraft of 133 ft (later 137 ft) span, first flown on 22 December 1930.

I very nearly put the ANT-6 into this book. For one thing, 818 were built, nearly all being heavy bombers designated TB-3, a few being G-2 transports or ANT-6A Arctic exploration transports. We in the West were so ignorant that, when we began to study Soviet aircraft in World War 2 we compared the TB-3 with the Lancaster and B-17 (which, incidentally, were much smaller) and thought the Soviet aircraft evidence of backwardness. In fact the TB-3's opposite numbers in the RAF and the US Army Air Corps were fabric-covered biplanes. A further reason for including the ANT-6 series is that they were used by Vakhmistrov for his most impressive Zvyeno (Link) experiments in which fighters were carried aloft on or under a large aircaft and released in flight. In one experiment the TB-3 took off with an I-5 fighter above each outer wing and an I-16 fighter under each wing. At a suitable height an I-Z fighter then hooked on to a trapeze under the fuselage. I don't know whether a joined-together formation of six aircraft counts as a 'giant'?

By 1930 the ANT (A.N. Tupolev) brigade at AGOS was committed to the creation of a series of monster aircraft that have no parallel at any other time or place. They began with the ANT-16, a direct extrapolation of the ANT-6 to a bigger size, and the ANT-22, a flying boat similar in size and

The TB-4 (ANT-16) before its first flight, with no guns or markings. (Via Malcolm Passingham)

power but with no common parts. Then came the even larger ANT-20, described separately, which led to the 20bis. At the same time work was going ahead on the colossal ANT-26 bomber and ANT-28 transport, which were never completed, and on studies for even more stupendous aircraft which, if built, would have been by far the largest aeroplanes in all history.

The two that came off the drawing board first, and into the sky, were the ANT-16 and 22. I will discuss the ANT-22 first because it was not related to the others. Tupolev had from the start produced seaplanes and flying boats, and in the early 1930s was working with the AGOS group (department of experimental construction) trying to reconcile conflicting requirements of the GVF (civil air fleet) for a large civil transport flying boat and of the VVS (air force) and AV-MF (naval air force) which wanted a basically similar machine but with even greater capabilities. The military demand, which kept being upgraded, was for an MK (*Morskoi Kreiser*, sea cruiser), to fly very long open-sea missions for reconnnaissance, but carrying bombs, torpedoes and mines. The resulting MK, the ANT-22, was first flown on 8 August 1934. It was then, apart from the Do X, the biggest and heaviest marine

The only known model of the TB-6 (ANT-26). Note the huge underwing fairings for the landing gear and, further out under the trailing edge, the underwing gun gondolas which would also have been used on the ANT-20V. (Via Malcolm Passingham)

aircraft in the world.

The ANT-22 followed the twin-hull configuration popularised by Savoia-Marchetti in Italy. Its two hulls were wide and deep, and skinned with smooth Dural, like the tail. The 167 ft 4 in wing, however, had traditional corrugated skin. The pilots sat side-by-side in a small nacelle above the leading edge. The other crew, including six gunners, were in the hulls. Six 830 hp M-34R engines were in three tandem push/pull nacelles above the wing, with the twin radiators and oil coolers in a dorsal duct above the centre of each nacelle. Gross weight, with a 13,120 lb bombload, was 73,986 lb. The twin-hulled machine had many good features, but did not go into production.

The ANT-16, built for the VVS as the TB-4, was another impressive AGOS project, designed by A.N. Tupolev's team, which remained a prototype. It was begun in March 1930 as a natural successor to the ANT-6, which was already in production as the TB-3. The ANT-16 followed established Tupolev principles, with a structure of specially formed tubing and pressings, covered with mainly corrugated Dural skin, but it was nevertheless a big step beyond the ANT-6. Linear dimensions were increased by some 35 per cent, the span of the completely cantilever wing being 177 ft 2 in. Wing area and weight were both up by roughly 100 per cent, respectively to

4,542 sq ft and 81,570 lb. As in the ANT-22 the engines comprised six 830 hp M-34, but with four mounted on the wing leading edge and two in a push/pull tandem nacelle. The crew numbered 12, when in full fighting trim, including two engineers who had access to the four wing engines. Landing gear was almost identical to that of the ANT-20, and so was the flight control system. Later an identical autopilot was installed. The pilots sat in an open cockpit, but several drawings show this to be enclosed, and that may have been the ultimate intention. Though soon surpassed by the K-7, bomb load possibly set a new record at 10 tonnes, including either 40 FAB-250 (551 lb) or 20 FAB-500. The internal bomb bays, separated by the second wing spar, were together the largest ever built at that time, each measuring 6 ft wide, 8 ft high and 8 ft 3 in long, each having powered doors. Defensive guns comprised two 20 mm cannon and 10 DA machine guns, one of the cannon being in the open cupola behind the single rudder.

Mikhail Gromov made the first flight of the ANT-16 on 3 July 1933. Though the aircraft handled reasonably well the performance was poor and, much more serious, the control forces were unacceptably high. The ailerons, in particular, were so heavy that even for ordinary routine manoeuvres the full strength of both pilots was needed. Eventually the control forces were brought down to satisfactory levels, but this monster was eventually judged to be little real advance over the mass-produced TB-3.

Back in 1929 work had been sanctioned on a far bigger aircraft still, with 12 engines and a span of 95 m (311 ft 9 in). This too was regarded as merely a stepping stone along a road which, by the late 1930s, was expected to lead to a bomber and/or transport with twin fuselages and a span of up to 200 m (656 ft). All these giant aircraft were to be similar in technology and in basic design philosophy, with built-up tubular spars and ribs and corrugated skin. All were expected to have a wing loading of about 90 kg/sq m (18.5 lb/sq ft) and to reach about 186 mph. The 200-m aircraft, however, was clearly going to need groups of engines geared to each propeller, the required power being estimated at 50,000 hp. Even today nothing, apart from the earlier Adlershof and Junkers pipe-dreams, has ever approached the 200-m bomber for wingspan, and it is certainly fair to describe such a project as never at any time or place having been a viable proposition.

The 95-m aircraft, however, was entirely practical, and it was taken to a very

advanced stage, and in two forms. The ANT-26 was a super-heavy bomber, with the designation TB-6. The ANT-28 was to be a transport, generally similar but much simpler and somewhat cruder in appearance. Both were in preliminary design as early as December 1930, when the ANT-6 first flew. It is possible that the AGOS management got permission to go ahead with these monster aircraft when the ANT-20V, the bomber version of the *Maksim Gorkii*, was cancelled in January 1933. Work went ahead fast, and TsAGI built a scale model glider with a span of 65 ft 6 in which was flown by B.N. Kudrin. Rightly, the huge ANT-26 was not just a scaled ANT-16. The wing was far bigger, but the fuselage relatively small, and the crew stayed at 12. The vast wing, of 311 ft 9 in span and with an area of about 8,611 sq ft, had a higher aspect ratio and more pointed tips. It had four spars with high-tensile steel booms and with many aspects of the structure breaking new ground. One problem was that the sheer thickness of the wing would act as a built-in headwind to propellers mounted ahead of it, and prolonged tunnel testing was done to achieve good results. As the most powerful engine available was the 900 hp M-34FRN, as also used in the ANT-20, the number needed was 12. Oddly, while Jean Alexander says these were arranged 'six of them along the wing leading edge and the rest in three tandem pairs above the wings', Václav Němeček, another noted Soviet historian,

This view of the TB-6 shows the disposition of items across the 311 ft 8 in span. (Via Nigel Eastaway)

Model of the ANT-28 transport, showing wing-compartment windows. (Via Nigel Eastaway)

says there were to be 'four on the leading edge of the wing with tractor propellers, two on the trailing edge with pusher propellers and two tandem groups on struts above the wings'. Apart from the fact that Němeček's description adds up to only 10 engines, both are at variance with the known official AGOS drawings and models. All these show four engines on the leading edge of each wing and two pairs in tandem nacelles above the wing. One of the remarkable features is how far outboard the overwing nacelles are, almost above the third engine from the fuselage on each side.

Compared with the ANT-20 the wing centre section was to be considerably wider, its span being about 128 ft. It carried the three inboard engines on each side, plus the overwing nacelles. Only the outermost engines were mounted on the long tapering outer wings. As noted, the fuselage was relatively small, overall length being a fraction under 128 ft. At the back was a typical Tupolev tail, except that it had three fins and rudders, the outer surfaces being smaller and braced by single diagonal struts which passed through the outer fins on their way to join the central fin to the tailplane. The single large tailwheel was well forward, while the four-wheel main gears, each with two pairs of wheels on tandem legs, were enclosed in large fairings into which the entire gears could retract. Up to 44,090 lb of bombs could be carried internally, the range with this load being estimated at the very low value of 620 miles. Empty weight was estimated at 110,000 lb and loaded weight 167,500 lb. Defensive armament would have comprised a 37 mm cannon in the tail, four 20 mm guns (two above the fuselage and two in streamlined gunner compartments under the trailing edge just inboard of the ailerons) and four pairs of the new fast-firing ShKAS machine guns.

While the ANT-26 would have been an amazingly impressive aircraft with great 'character', the ANT-28 transport looked very like a bigger *Maksim Gorkii*. It had a similar nose, 10 roof windows in the upper surface of each wing for the wing compartments (absent from the bomber) and plain fixed landing gears with four ANT-20 size wheels in side-by-side pairs. The fuselage would have had four integral stairways. There was no provision for bulky loads, except slung externally, but in about 1965 Tupolev said that the ANT-28 would have carried 250 troops and their equipment. Range with a payload of 55,115 lb was estimated at 2,250 miles, a tremendous contrast with the bomber. Tupolev said that Petlyakov led the ANT-28 design team and that, while termination of the huge bomber in 1936 was understandable, he thought the transport should have been continued.

28 Kalinin K-7

Konstantin Alekseyevich Kalinin was one of the first designers to become famous in the Soviet Union. He was noted for his single-engined utility transports, but in 1929 he read about the Junkers G38. He was convinced it would be possible to produce a more efficient aircraft, by making the wing large enough to carry the entire payload. In 1930 he roughed out a drawing for an aircraft with a wing big enough to seat 120 passengers or carry at least seven tonnes of cargo. Drawings survive showing 16 four-berth day/night cabins plus a buffet and large central lounge. After the discussions had reached Kremlin level Kalinin received permission to build the giant aircraft in 1931, but as a heavy bomber.

Kalinin had from the start of his career preferred wings of approximately elliptical shape. In the K-7 he extrapolated his elliptical wing to a span of 173 ft 11 in, a root chord of 34 ft 9.3 in, a centreline depth of 91.7 in and an area of 4,887 sq ft. In 1933 this was the biggest wing ever to have flown. The configuration of the aircraft was unique. Ahead of the wing projected a relatively modest forward fuselage providing accommodation for five of the crew of 11, the nose gunner having an open position and the rest all being enclosed. Along the leading edge

were six 830 hp M-34F vee-12 engines, each with an underslung ducted radiator, and a seventh identical engine was arranged as a pusher on the trailing edge at the centreline. Lost in the vastness of the wing were metal tanks for 2,008 gal of fuel. The tail was carried on twin booms, each of inverted-triangular section, spaced just over 36 ft apart — an awesome distance. Inboard of the booms, just under 23 ft apart, were twin fins and rudders, braced to the single tailplane and also joined together by a narrow horizontal aerofoil-section strut. All control surfaces were driven by large and prominent servo surfaces, which resulted in much lighter pilot control loads than in most other giant aircraft.

Under the wing, in line with the booms, were large streamlined columns and bracing struts linking the aircraft to two enormous gondolas, each 38 ft long. Most of the rest of the structure was chrome-molybdenum steel, with fabric covering (except for Dural skin over the wing centre section), but the gondolas and pylons were all Dural.

Because of its size the K-7 had to be erected in the open. The figure near the starboard wheel gondola is much nearer than the aircraft. (Robert J. Ruffle archives)

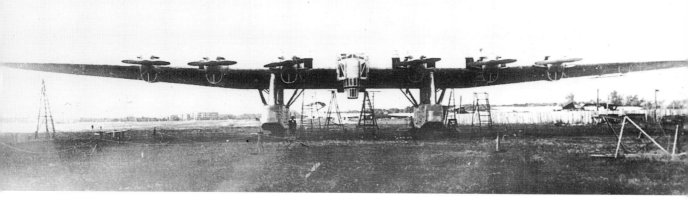

The K-7 taking off at Kharkov. (Via Malcolm Passingham)

Each housed the landing gears and two gunners. Each landing gear comprised a single front wheel and, a long way to the rear, side-by-side main wheels, all with pneumatic brakes. The crew entered though doors in each gondola, there being a ladder in the vertical rear pylon and a stairway in the inclined front one. Up to 41,887 lb of bombs could be carried, divided equally between four bays in the centre of the wing, each with two bomb doors. Defensive guns comprised a 7.62 mm ShKAS or 20 mm cannon in the nose, and in the extreme tail of each boom, and further ShKAS machine guns in the top of each boom and in the front and

rear of each gondola.

In many ways the K-7 was a very impressive aircraft, but it suffered (lethally) from the limited resources of Kalinin's design bureau, which I do not believe ever considered the need to carry out vibration and resonance testing as is today taken for granted. As soon as engine running tests were started, on 29 June 1933, it was evident that there was severe vibration, especially of the booms and tail, and that at particular engine speeds this built up in dangerous resonance. Such problems were in 1933 very difficult to solve and, though the pilots expressed a wish for geared engines driv-

Drawings showing the K-7's bomb stowage and nine gunner cockpits. (Copyright *Modellist Konstruktor* via Harry Woodman)

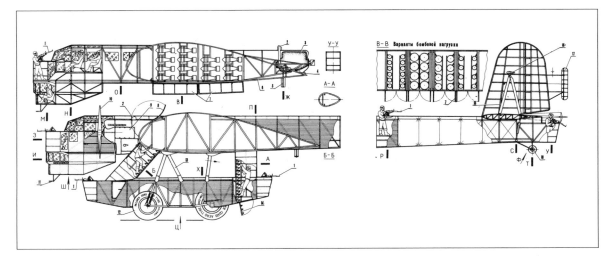

ing larger propellers, all that was done was to attach steel angle sections along the booms, partly to damp the vibration and partly for extra strength. The flight test programme opened on 11 August, the spectacular aircraft causing intense interest all over Kharkov. Sadly, on the ninth flight, on 21 November 1933, the right-hand boom broke during full-throttle tests at low level. The aircraft went straight into the ground and burned, 15 on board being killed but five (remarkably) surviving.

Kalinin was sent to a different factory, at Voronezh, where under P.I. Baranov he organised the manufacture of two improved K-7s, with stressed-skin booms of rectangular section, but in 1935 this plan was scrapped. Later poor Kalinin was arrested on trumped-up charges and shot. Like the resurgent German Luftwaffe the VVS came

to the conclusion that lots of small bombers were a better buy than a few giants. There was, however, an important difference between the reasons different countries had for building giant bombers. The Do19, Ju89, XB-15, XB-19, B-36, B-52, M-4 and Tu-20 were big in order to carry their bombs over great distances. The B-17 was big and four-engined in order to achieve unprecedented over-target height, and the B-29 was designed for both height and range. But the monsters of the Soviet Union were, so far as one can tell, mere battleships of the sky and an expression of a love of bigness. We have only estimated figures, but these indicate that neither the ANT-26 nor the K-7 would have offered a greater radius of action than the VVS already possessed. Exciting as the giants would have been, it was certainly a wise move not to build either in quantity.

29 Tupolev ANT-20 and 20bis

We have already seen how, from small beginnings and basing the technology on the work of Junkers, the design collective of A.N. Tupolev produced some of the greatest all-metal monoplanes of all time. The biggest, the ANT-26 and -28, were never completed, but I have left for this separate story the biggest that were built and flown. The

Soviet Union, the world's largest country, geographically, has always had a reputation for liking every kind of bigness. This story tells of one of the few aircraft in this book

Side profile of the ANT-20 as originally built, with spats. (Copyright *Flieger-Revue*)

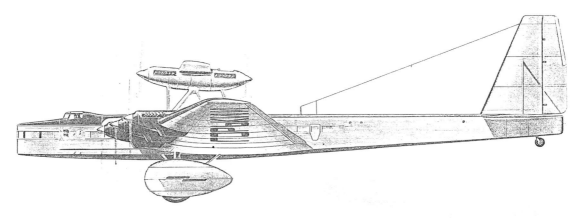

that were not only built and flown but were clearly larger than any other aeroplane in the world. Popularly known as the *Maksim Gorkii*, or MG, it was built to serve as a national flagship.

Every year the Soviet Union celebrates the start of the career of writer Aleksei Maksimovich Gorkii on 25 September 1892. For his 40th anniversary, in 1932, the President of Yurgaz, M. Ye Koltsov, launched a nationwide appeal for funds to build a giant aeroplane to be named after Gorkii and to serve as the flagship of the Maksim Gorkii *Agiteskadrilya* (propaganda squadron). The appeal raised 6 million rubles (then £2 million), and hundreds of people got in on the act in various committees and councils. Tupolev was given the task of actually designing the aircraft.

Earlier, in mid-1931, he had launched the design of a passenger version of the ANT-16 bomber, designated ANT-20. Now he simply left those drawings and started a new ANT-20, to be even larger. The original ANT-16/20 had a span of 177 ft 2 in and six 830 hp engines, four on the leading edge and

two in a push/pull tandem nacelle on top. The new ANT-20 was to have a span of just over 206 ft 8 in, and be powered by eight 900 hp engines. Tupolev, V.M. Petlyakov and A.A. Arkhangelskii knew that this stupendous and highly political aeroplane would be probably the greatest challenge they would ever have to face. The consequences of failure would be unthinkable; 1931-32 was the start of 'The Terror' in which Stalin had millions simply put to death, for trumped-up reasons. Nobody wanted to get into the slightest trouble (it didn't do Tupolev much good; the ANT-20 was a tremendous aircraft, but nonsensical reasons were still found for putting him behind bars from 1936 until 1943). But aircraft designers don't really need all that unnecessary extra worry.

Having the existing TB-4 and the original ANT-20 design as a basis speeded up work considerably, though the task was still colossal in every sense. The structure was entirely of steel or Duralumin, apart from such details as the plywood roof over the cockpit. Much of the wing structure was built up from tubes, the three spars and built-up

Left *It's 11 August 1934 and the mighty MG is about to make its last test flight at Moscow Central Aerodrome before joining the propaganda squadron. In the background are Aeroflot ANT-9s.* (Via John Stroud)

Right *An unusual view of the ANT-20, possibly taken from the fighter which usually escorted it.* (Robert J. Ruffle archives)

ribs of the inboard section generally being 2 m (79 in) apart, giving convenient compartments about 6.5 ft deep, wide and long, inside the wing for crew, fuel and other items. The gigantic wing, significantly more efficient than that of the Do X, had a root chord of about 39 ft, tapering to 36 ft where the centre section joined the outer panels just outboard of the inner engines. Root thickness/chord ratio was 20 per cent, maximum wing depth being 87 in; thickness/chord at the tip was only 10 per cent. There were no flaps, and each aileron was divided into four sections to avoid binding of the hinges due to wing flexure, the span of each aileron being nearly 70 ft. Like almost the entire aircraft, the wing was skinned in corrugated Dural.

The fuselage was made in five sections, joined at the four main longerons. This was done so that, like the wings, the fuselage could be taken from the GAZ-22 factory in sections for assembly at Moscow Central Aerodrome (today called Tushino). Cross section was 138 in wide and 98.4 in high. F-1 (the nose) had four twin and three single glass windows and was furnished as a navigator station in the extreme nose, with two seats and very full equipment, and two pairs of seats at the rear. F-1bis housed the enclosed cockpit for two pilots above, each with huge full-circle control wheels, four pairs of passenger seats below and a radio cabin to the rear. F-2, between the spars, was a 16-line telephone (intercom) exchange, and also housed the central station in the pneumatic-tube message system, secretaries and a toilet. F-3, aft of the rear spar, housed the photo library and film projector, dining area and buffet/bar, galley, storeroom, processing lab and radio racking. F-4 and -5 were not used, but the space in the inner wings was used completely. Passageways aft of the second spar led to doors to front and rear all the way to the outer engines. In front were cloakrooms, toilets and, on the right side, the main electrical room and 30 hp auxiliary generating plant. To the rear was a further photo processing room on the right and a printing press on the left. On each side, further outboard, was a six-bunk bedroom. Further out still were fuel tanks to the rear

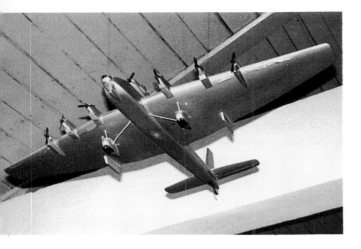

Left *Referred to in story 27, the ANT-20V bomber was never built. This model, at the VVS museum at Monino, shows the short nose, with turret and chin gondola, and gunner gondolas under the trailing edge.* (Nigel Eastaway)

Below *A beautiful photograph taken from the cockpit of the ANT-20bis. Note the completely redesigned engine installations (but the engineer's cupola was the same as in the ANT-20).* (Via John Stroud)

Right *Unfortunately, the only good photograph known of the ANT-20bis. Note the man on the cockpit roof.* (Via Malcolm Passingham)

and, in front, engineers' rooms with a streamlined 'fighter type' canopy projecting above the wing. Inboard of these canopies were six flush roof windows on each side.

Power was provided by eight 900 hp M-34FRN vee-12 engines, each driving a 13 ft 2 in two-blade metal propeller. Six were mounted on steel-tube frames far ahead of the front spar; the other two were mounted in a tandem push/pull nacelle carried on braced streamlined struts high above the fuselage, without access in flight. Radiators and oil coolers were below and to the rear of the wing engines and, grouped in pairs, above the centreline nacelle. Fuel capacity was 2,067 gal in 28 metal drums. Engines were started by a compressed-air system. The tail was typical Tupolev, who liked simple severe shapes every bit as recognisable as the curves of de Havilland. The tailplane could be driven electrically through ±5° for trimming. The rudder and elevators had inset balancing hinges and electrically driven trim tabs. Later the Soviet Union's first (two-axis) autopilot was installed. The

landing gear was again bold and simple. The tailwheel, still rare in the early 1930s, was at first castoring and later steerable. Each main unit had oleo-pneumatic shock struts with forks embracing the twin 79-in wheels fitted with four-shoe pneumatic brakes. Giant spats were fitted, but these were removed before the first flight and never replaced.

As actually built, the ANT-20 had a span of 206 ft 8½ in, length of 107 ft 11 in and wing area of 5,231 sq ft. It weighed 62,831 lb empty, and the loaded weight was 92,593 lb. Cruising speed was typically 121 mph at low level and 135 mph at 10,000 ft; service ceiling was 14,800 ft and normal range 745 miles.

Mikhail Gromov was in command on the first flight, on 17 June 1934. On the whole handling was judged excellent, and all that remained to be done was equip the interior with all the propaganda apparatus, including a 'voice from the sky' loudspeaker system and a then-unique array of electric lights under the wings for displaying slogans. The ANT-20 joined the *Agiteskadrilya* as flagship on 18 August 1934, and despite its complexity soon established an excellent record of serviceability. It began a programme of flights throughout the Soviet Union, either with a crew of eight and 72 passengers (mostly local officials and commissars being rewarded for good service) or with a crew

of 20 to 23 for air/ground propaganda. To emphasize its size it was often escorted by small aircraft, and on 18 May 1935 N.P. Blagin made an unauthorised loop in his escorting I-5 fighter around the giant's wing. He hit the ANT-20, causing not only his own death but that of the 45 on board the giant.

A planned ANT-20V bomber version (photo) was never built, the ANT-16 being succeeded by the ANT-26 as described earlier. But the crash of the *Maksim Gorkii* resulted in a huge wave of national emotion, and 35 million rubles were soon subscribed for a whole fleet of 16 replacements. The original idea was that these should be *dubler* (duplicates) of the ANT-20, each named for a revolutionary or party leader, but in the event Tupolev's arrest and other factors led to only one additional machine being ordered, and it differed in many respects. In Tupolev's absence the work was transferred to a different GAZ outside Moscow, under deputy chief designer B.A. Saukke. The aircraft was designated ANT-20bis, but it was also known by its civil registration L-760, the ANT-20 having been registered L-759.

Aerodynamically and structurally the 20bis differed little from its predecessor, though the gross weight was increased, initially from 42 tonnes to 44, and in World War 2 to a routine 45 tonnes (99,206 lb). The nose was longer, overall length (on the ground) going up to 111 ft 11 in, and the vertical tail was made broader but shorter. The availability of the 1,200 hp AM-34FRNV engine meant that the six wing engines were adequate, all accessible in flight, the centre-line tandem nacelle being eliminated. The six engines were installed in quite different nacelles, with large profiled ventral radiator ducts and internal exhaust pipes from each bank of cylinders emerging as a single pipe above the leading edge of the wing. Propellers were three-blade constant-speed, with a diameter of 11 ft 6 in. The main gears were faired in by huge spats, possibly those made for the ANT-20 but never previously flown.

Work on the ANT-20bis began in early 1938. By this time the scene had changed, the *Agiteskadrilya* was being run down, and nobody wanted a gigantic propaganda vehicle. Accordingly it was decided to complete the 20bis as a single very large passenger transport for Aeroflot. The nose cabin was enlarged, with nine wide windows all round, and the cockpit was redesigned with different windows and a better external profile, all nine crew being accommodated amidships. Normal accommodation was at first for 64 passengers, in the fuselage and wing centre section, but this was later increased. Gromov and E.I.Schwarz made the first flight on 6 May 1940. The test pro-gramme was uneventful, and within three weeks the 20bis was delivered to Aeroflot, which called it the PS-124. It began opera-tions on the route between Moscow and Mineralnye Vody. In December 1940 it was re-engined with 1,200 hp AM-35 engines,

subsequently — after the German invasion — serving as a heavy cargo transport in rear areas until on 14 December 1942 it was damaged in a heavy landing. To the pro-found regret of today's Soviet fraternity it was scrapped with 272 hr on its books.

30 Martin 130 and 156

At Christmas 1987 I had to attend a confer-ence in California, and while there I was pleased to be asked to give a talk to a very select Navy outfit called OPINTEL 1. Their HQ is on Treasure Island, in San Francisco Bay, in the hallowed buildings which once formed PanAm's base for the airline's trans-pacific route. It is not just a secure HQ but also an important museum. One display case houses one of the most perfect aircraft models I have ever seen: a Martin 130, with a span of about 6 ft. And the model has every right to be there, because from the

nearby slipway the big Martins pioneered the longest overwater route in the world. It began at 3.45 pm on 22 November 1935. Across the nation and across the globe radio listeners heard the distinctive voice of Juan Trippe say 'Captain Musick, you have your sailing orders. Cast off and depart for Manila in accordance therewith.' Edwin Musick did just that, and no other aircraft in the world could have done the same.

Obviously, I have a high opinion of the Sikorsky S-42, in the context of its time, but the Martin 130 was a whole generation bet-

Below left *Big aircraft often seem to have been pulled out sideways. This photograph was taken on 30 November 1934 as the first M-130 came out into the open.* (Glenn L. Martin via Philip Jarrett)

Right *When this photograph was taken the Martin 156 had non-standard struts bracing the starboard fin.* (Via Philip Jarrett)

ter, though only a year later. Igor Sikorsky's bunch had always been a rather strange lot who had never quite learned such things as quality control, profitability or advanced technology (there's a story that the man who formed United Aircraft, the great F.B. Rentschler, on looking at the 1933 Sikorsky balance sheet observed 'There is a limit to the contribution United can make to Russian relief'). In contrast, Glenn Martin's much bigger firm at Baltimore was run as 'a tight ship', in the hardest American manner. Nothing was left to chance, any new idea was immediately evaluated and tested, and the whole idea was to be competitive. So the difference between the S-42 and M-130 was not just of size or timing. The Martin was the result of over 35,000 hrs of testing, some in tunnels, some on structural test specimens and a lot on hydrodynamic models in

towing tanks.

A further factor, which surely ought to happen more often, was that the chief designer, William K. Ebel, was also the head of the test pilot team. Despite the unprecedented test programme the first of the three M-130s ordered by PanAm made its first flight as early as 30 December 1934. This was also very nearly the first flight of an engine destined to be made in greater quantity than any other in history: the Pratt & Whitney R-1830 Twin Wasp. We think of this 14-cylinder engine as being of 1,200 hp, but at the start of its life the take-off power was 830 hp, and that's what the M-130 got.

PanAm's requirement seemed modest enough: it wanted a boat to carry a crew of four and at least 300 lb of mail over a stage-length of 2,500 miles against a 30 mph wind. The S-42 could not do this; it could fly the sector, but without a single bag of mail. And of course the airline really wanted to carry a few passengers as well. In 1934 it was a challenging demand.

I have harped on the importance of stressed-skin construction. The M-130 was the first aircraft of its size and weight to have a truly modern stressed-skin wing. Of course the famous Martin Bomber, the Model 123, had been one of the pioneers of thin cantilever wings, but that wing had an area of 678 sq ft whereas the Model 130 wing had an area of 2,170 sq ft, and span of 130 ft. Overall length was 90 ft 11 in, and empty and loaded weights were respectively 24,611 lb and 52,252 lb, which shows a ratio that I don't believe any other civil aeroplane of the 1930s ever equalled. The enormous difference between the two figures enabled the fuel capacity to be set at 3,165 gal, nearly half of it in the capacious sponsons.

Over short ranges the big Martin could be furnished for 41 passengers, but the standard load on the long Pacific sectors was 12. One early passenger said he 'rattled around in the vast expanse of hull in a degree of comfort never known before'. Services between November 1935 and October 1936 carried mail only, but from 21 October 1936 the three Martins, named *China/Philippine/Hawaii Clipper*, operated to schedule with passengers and mail. Not only did they fly

sectors beyond the capability of any other aircraft of the pre-1939 era, but they also set levels of utilization an order of magnitude higher than anything routinely achieved in Europe. Whereas the average total flight time achieved by the equivalent British boat, the Short 'Kent' class, was 490 hr, two of the Martins almost reached 15,000 hr, the last 4,700 of which were in wartime service with the US Navy. Sadly *China Clipper*, the last survivor, was destroyed by hitting an unlit ship whilst landing at night in Trinidad in January 1945, back in PanAm service.

In 1937 Martin built a single example of what seemed a logical development, the Martin 156. This was restressed to empty and loaded weights of 30,414 and 63,000 lb respectively, most of the extra loaded weight coming from the increased fuel capacity of 4,260 gal. The wing was extended to a span of 157 ft, the engines were 1,000 hp Wright Cyclone G2 nine-cylinder radials, and a raised pylon at the rear of the hull carried a completely new twin-finned tail. The M-156 was intended to carry more than double the M-130's payload on the difficult SFO-Hawaii sector, and Martin believed it could fly the transpacific route with 26 passengers, but in the event the single example was bought by the Soviet Union. Here it was given the designation PS-30 and used by Aeroflot on sectors in the Soviet far east.

31 Kozlov Gigant

One of the least-known Soviet aircraft, the Gigant was one of three challenging aircraft programmes launched as practical projects at the Zhukovskii VVA (air force academy), where Sergei Grigoryevich Kozlov was a professor. By far the biggest of the three, it was a design for a bomber powered by 12 M-17F vee-12 engines each rated at 730 hp. These were to be mounted in nose-to-nose

pairs inside the wings, each pair being geared to a pylon-mounted tractor propeller above the wing. Span was 'greater than 60 m' (197 ft), and wing depth at the root was 3 m (almost 10 ft). The tail was carried on twin booms, and the short central nacelle was to house a large bombload and a crew of 18 to 22, with 15 guns firing in all directions. Wing area was about 6,500 sq ft, and loaded weight 'more than 40 tonnes' (88,180 lb). The project was launched in December 1931, but funds ran out in 1933 following the mechanical failure of the test rig for the twin-engine/propeller group.

32 Latécoère 521, 522 and 523

The factory at Toulouse of Pierre Latécoère was from 1917 a major source of all kinds of aircraft for the French airlines, navy and air force. By 1928 design work was in hand on a series of flying boats which were among the biggest of their day. The Laté 300, first flown on 17 December 1931, led to a series of 300, 301 and 302 boats which were bigger than they looked. Mainly powered by four Hispano-Suiza engines in tandem pairs, they had a span of 144 ft 5 in and wing area of 2,752 sq ft. The 301s were commercial, and the 302s flew long-range patrol missions with the Aéronavale.

In 1930 the design began of the Laté 520, to be a commercial transport flying boat for transatlantic service. It was to be powered by four 1,000 hp Hispano-Suiza 18Sbr engines each with three banks of six water-cooled cylinders. Unfortunately France decided not to contest the 1931 Schneider Trophy race, and the powerful engine was abandoned. The Latécoère designers accordingly had to make major changes, completely redesigning the wing to take six lower-powered engines (860 hp HS 12Ybrs) arranged as four tractors and two pushers. The result was the Laté 521, which made its first flight on 10 January 1935.

The impressive hull was all-metal, overall length being 104 ft. Like the old Porte hulls the lower portion and planing bottom was of much greater beam (width) than the upper deck, though the two merged into each other as they neared the commendably simple single-finned tail. Almost the whole of the lower deck was usable, though I do not believe it was ever furnished in the way envisaged. This specified a mooring compartment in the bow, then the radio/navi-

Launch of the Latécoère 521. The pusher engines are far from obvious. (Via Philip Jarrett)

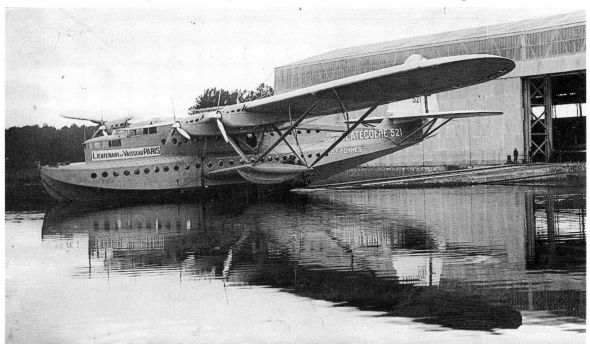

Above left *The same aircraft as shown on the previous page, much later in life, with HS12Y-37 engines and equipped as an ocean patrol aircraft for the Aéronavale.* (Via John Stroud)

Above *Nose of the only Laté 522 to be completed, seen during its wartime service with Escadrille E12.* (Via John Stroud)

gation cabin, a 20-passenger saloon, six de luxe single cabins, a 26-seat compartment, a kitchen and a baggage hold. The upper deck contained the stepped cabin for the remainder (eight) of the flight crew, with the engineers to the rear where they could reach the engines, a cabin for 18 passengers and a further baggage hold. Obviously, all 70 passengers would not have been carried, even on the less challenging South Atlantic. The wing had a metal structure and leading edge, fabric rear skin, triple-section ailerons and steel bracing struts. The span was 161 ft 9 in, and the area 3,552 sq ft. The engines drove variable-pitch propellers, by no means common in Europe in the early 1930s, and the fuel was housed in six tanks in the sponsons with the exceptional capacity of 4,905 gal, plus two 109-gal auxiliary tanks in the wings.

Named for the naval hero *Lt de Vaisseau Paris*, the huge boat emerged with a bright blue hull and engine nacelles, bearing various bold inscriptions but not its official registration, which was later to be F-NORD. Air France planned to use the 521 on the North Atlantic, flying from Biscarosse, the great terminal near Bordeaux, via Lisbon and the Azores to New York, with a crew of eight and 30 passengers. It made various demo flights before setting out in December 1935 from Dakar across the South Atlantic, via Natal in Brazil to the French West Indies. On 13 January 1936 it was at anchor at Pensacola, Florida, when a hurricane struck. Mighty seas pounded the great boat and it sank at its moorings.

It was salvaged, dismantled, returned to France and rebuilt. To increase range it was refitted with HS 12Nbr unsupercharged engines of only 650 hp, flying again on 29 May 1937. In November and December 1937 it set several world records. On one it took off at 90,390 lb and flew 3,592 miles in 34.6 hr; it set (modest) speed records round a 612-mile circuit carrying loads of 10 and 15 tonnes, and in another flight it lifted 39,683 lb to 8,520 ft and 33,069 lb to 11,509 ft. Later the 521 was re-engined with HS 12Y-37s of 970 hp and impressed into the Aéronavale, serving in the ocean patrol role with Escadrille E6 until it was demobilized in August 1940. Sadly, this great boat was destroyed when the retreating Germans blew up its hangar at Berre, near Marseilles, in August 1944.

The excellent record of the Laté 521 led to orders for three Laté 522 airliners for Air France Transatlantique and three Laté 523 long-range patrol aircraft for the Aéronavale. The three 523s had priority. They were stressed to a maximum weight of 92,594 lb, an excellent figure in view of the equipped empty weight of 45,944 lb, and the engines were 900 hp HS 12Y-27. The bow was re-designed to have a more conventional appearance, the navigators having a large compartment with windows all round, ahead of the pilots' cockpit. The number of sections of each aileron was reduced to two, and fuel capacity was slightly reduced to 4,663 gal. Armament comprised six 441 lb Type K bombs and four 904 lb Type L, all attached to rails protruding fore and aft of the sponsons, and two 1,102 lb bombs on racks attached to the wing struts. Defensive armament comprised a 25 mm AN gun in a powered dorsal turret and four 7.5 mm Darne machine-guns fired through port-holes.

The three 523s were named *Altair, Algol* and *Aldebaran*; all the biggest Aéronavale flying boats received the names of stars beginning with A. The first made its maiden flight on 20 January 1938, and all had joined Escadrille E6 before the end of that year. One was lost on 18 September 1939, a second was deliberately scuttled on 18 June 1940 at Lanvéoc-Poulmic, and the last ended its days at Dakar in August 1942.

Of the three 522s only the first was completed. Registered F-ARAP and named *Ville de Saint Pierre*, it had an airframe almost identical to the military 523s, though of course equipped for airline operation. Engines were 970 hp HS 12Y-37, and with maximum and cruising speeds of 175 and 135 mph it was the fastest of the family. The sole 522 flew on 20 April 1939 and quickly completed two round trips to New York. Then it was impressed into the Aéronavale and equipped for patrol missions at Biscarosse, beginning operational service with E12 on 10 November 1939. This aircraft was yet another blown up by the German forces before they left Berre in August 1944.

33 Junkers Ju90, 290 and 390

The Ju90 is another borderline case. A critic could ask 'Why include it, and leave out the corresponding British aircraft, the AW27 Ensign, which was similar in weight, had a little more power and was not only much longer but had 25 per cent more wing area?'

The answer is partly that, whereas the Ensign was an undistinguished aircraft, obsolete before the prototype was completed, the Ju90 was, in the words of John Stroud, 'probably the most advanced and best thought-out of all the between-the-wars

The Do19V-1, seldom illustrated with its bombardier gondola. (Dornier)

airliners'. And a further reason for its inclusion is that it was developed into the Ju290, which was bigger, and this in turn into the Ju390, which was in many respects the biggest, heaviest and most powerful landplane of the entire World War 2 era. That puts it into the decade of the 1940s, but it is sensible to treat the whole story here.

In July 1933 the RLM, the German air ministry, issued a specification for a long-range strategic bomber, often known as the Ural-bomber. Junkers and Dornier responded, the latter with the Do19. I have included a picture of the Do19 because, in the context of its times, it was one of the biggest aircraft around. Span was 114 ft 10 in. It first flew on 28 October 1936, but in 1937 the whole idea of a Luftwaffe strategic bomber force was abandoned.

The Junkers submission was the Ju89, first flown in December 1936. Compared with the Do19 this was fractionally bigger. The span was the same, but it had considerably more wing area, and was in a different class so far as weights and engine power were concerned. The first prototype, powered by 1,075 hp Jumo 211A liquid-cooled engines driving controllable-pitch propellers, set world records in lifting a load of 11,023 lb to the extraordinary altitude of 30,551 ft and 22,046 lb to 23,760 ft. Leader of the design team was Dipl-Ing Ernst Zindel. He had long since recognised that the company's traditional corrugated skin imposed both weight and drag penalties. Tunnel testing showed that the airflow directions over the skin were seldom along the corrugations but were diagonally across them.

Of course, many other manufacturers had used corrugated skins, believing Hugo Junkers when he claimed in 1923 that such skin added only 15% to the drag of a perfectly smooth wing. But in 1928 Martin Schrenk took an actual Junkers wing, of 17 per cent thickness, and by accurate momentum measures using a pitot rake, took all the figures. He then did it all again with various kinds of alternative wing skin. He found that the drag coefficient of the corrugated wing was 0.0113, fractionally worse than for 'rough wavy metal skin'. But 'smooth metal skin' turned in a figure of 0.0060. In other words the extra drag of the corrugations was not Junkers' guesstimate of 15 per cent but very nearly 100 per cent!

With the Ju60, 160 and 86 a new era of modern smooth stressed-skin construction ruled at Dessau. The Ju89 followed this, but on a bigger scale. Like the much later Me262 the Ju89 had what appeared to be a swept-back wing, and again like the 262 this was for reasons unconnected with compressibility. This wing had an area of 1,980.6 sq ft, and a complex structure with five spars, variously of plate or Warren-girder construction, with chrome-molybdenum steel tubular booms as in earlier Junkers types. Almost all the skin of the wing, fuselage and the fixed parts of the twin-finned tail were smooth Dural, flush riveted. The Junkers 'double-wing' principle was followed with the flaps, ailerons, elevators and rudders, which had corrugated skin. Huge radiators and oil coolers under the engines, with inlets on the underside, made the nacelles very deep, the inboard nacelles accommodating the large single main wheels of the tailwheel-type landing gear.

When the long-range bomber programme was abandoned in 1937 Junkers had already made plans to turn the Ju89 into a civil transport for Deutsche Luft Hansa, and it obtained permission to use the wings, 960 hp DB600A liquid-cooled inverted vee-12 engines, propellers, landing gear and tail of the third Ju89 for the first Ju90 transport. The latter naturally needed a new fuselage, and this provided excellent accommodation for 40 passengers. In the standard arrangement there were five cabins, some for smokers, each having two rectangular windows on each side and with pairs of seats facing each other across a central table on each side of the aisle. There were double doors at the back and a single door immediately behind the cockpit which folded out and down to provide a loading platform.

The first Ju90, named *der grosse Dessauer,* first flew on 28 August 1937. It was a fine-looking aircraft, the only obvious points that might be criticised being the poor fuel capacity of 814 gal (this could be increased) and use of a tailwheel landing gear with single main wheels. A more serious shortcoming was that, as the RLM informed Junkers that all high-power DB and Jumo engines were reserved for the Luftwaffe, the only immediately available engines had inadequate power. The production Ju90B-1s had 830 hp BMW 132H-1 radial engines, and though these sufficed perfectly well the aircraft never really had enough power. Two Ju90Z-2s were built for South African Airways with 1,100 hp Twin Wasps, clearly a more suitable engine, but these were not delivered because of the war.

There is great confusion over the Ju90s, even the number built being uncertain (it seems to have been 14). They cruised at just under 200 mph and were certainly the most impressive airliners to be seen at European airports in the final months of peace. After the outbreak of war some Ju90s continued to serve with Luft Hansa, but most were taken over by the Luftwaffe, many having remarkable careers. Meanwhile, Junkers at Dessau had begun further development of the Ju90 as early as spring 1937, before the

Right *Powered by the new Daimler-Benz 600 engines, the prototype Ju90 looks every inch DER GROSSE DESSAUER as it emerged from the vast Dessau factory in August 1937.* (Junkers via R.T. Riding)

Below *The Ju290V-7 was built as one of the 10 Ju90B-1 civil transports. It is seen at Dessau rebuilt as a Luftwaffe transport with Trapoklappe.* (Via Philip Jarrett)

first had flown. The Ju90S (for *schwer*, heavy) was assigned to Dipl-Ing Kraft, and such was the need for modification that about half the total Ju90 production was assigned to further development. In 1939 the entire programme was moved from Dessau to what had been the Letov factory at Prague-Letnany, Kraft becoming chief designer.

There is again extraordinary confusion over what happened. For example, the Putnam *German Aircraft of the Second World War* states that the first major rebuild was the Ju90 V-4, re-engined in early 1940 with BMW801 engines; whereas *Warplanes of the Third Reich* states 'The Ju90 V-4 was rebuilt in early 1939 with an entirely new wing in which the marked leading-edge sweepback gave place to a straight centre section with tapered outer panels. Simultaneously, enlarged and redesigned endplate vertical tail surfaces were applied to ensure adequate stability around the yawing axis with the larger, more powerful engines that it was proposed eventually to instal, and sturdier twin-wheel main undercarriage members were provided to cater for the increased operating weights'. In other words, new engines were the one thing V-4 still awaited.

V-4, which had once borne the Luft Hansa names *Schwabenland* and later *Sachsen*, also had its fuselage gutted and equipped for cargo transport. The pairs of rectangular windows were replaced by evenly spaced round portholes, and under the rear fuselage was installed a huge *Trapoklappe*, a loading ramp forming the underside of the rear fuselage which could be opened downwards under hydraulic power, raising the tail off the ground and bringing the floor to a level attitude for loading vehicles and other large loads. The '*klappe* could also be power-opened in flight for air dropping.

In 1937-39 it had been intended to re-engine the Ju90 with the BMW139, but this engine was cancelled in June 1939 in favour of the rather heavier but potentially more powerful BMW801. Accordingly, all subsequent Ju90S development aircraft were fitted

Unless a victim of gross retouching, this picture shows that the second Ju390 was flown, and was a normal transport aircraft! (Via Philip Jarrett)

with the 801, the initial version being the 1,600 hp BMW801L. With these engines came a stretch of the rear fuselage, bigger and more angular fins and rudders, long rectangular windows, various forms of armament, and an increase in span from 118 ft to 137 ft 9.5 in, giving an area of 2,192 sq ft. In 1941 the Ju90S was redesignated Ju290, and preparations were started for production at Bernburg. Subsequently no fewer than 18 versions were developed, of which nine were manufactured in modest quantities. Some were transports, while others were heavily armed ocean patrol aircraft, such as the Ju290A-8 which weighed 99,210 lb and had nine 20 mm MG151 cannon (four of them in a row of four separate dorsal turrets!) and a 13 mm MG131. The wheel turned full circle with the emergence of the Ju290B heavy bomber, which was intended to lead to the Ju290E. A comparison with the heavy bomber that started it all is interesting. The Ju89 had a maximum loaded weight of 50,266 lb and bombload of 3,520 lb. The Ju 290E was to weigh 133,380 lb and have a maximum bombload of 40,572 lb. Another contrast is the fuel capacity of the pre-war Ju90B-1 airliner of 814 gal with that of the extended-range Ju290A-5s of Luftwaffe gruppe 4/FAGr 5 which, in addition to heavy armament, carried 5,235 gal of fuel. They made numerous round trips to Manchuria carrying vital materials and other cargoes in both directions.

In 1942 Dipl-Ing Kraft proposed a further simple extension in size of the Ju290 by adding further wing/engine sections and lengthening the fuselage. In view of the apparent absence of technical risk his Prague office was authorised to go ahead with what was designated the Ju390. Orders were placed for three prototypes. The Ju390 V-1 was to be built at Dessau, as a transport. The Ju390V-2 was to be built at Bernburg, as a comprehensively equipped maritime reconnaissance aircraft. The Ju390 V-3 was to be built at Bernburg as a heavy bomber.

The Ju390 had the wings, engines and main landing gear of a Ju290, plus an extra centre section of wing added on each side with two more engines and landing gears; thus, with all gears extended, the aircraft rested on four pairs of main tyres. The span was 165 ft 1 in and wing area 2,730 sq ft. The fuselage was extended to 102 ft in the V1, subsequent examples to be variously from 110 ft to 114 ft depending on equipment. Standard loaded weight was 166,450 lb. Among the unbuilt projects was a pressurized high-altitude reconnaissance version with a span of 181 ft 8 in and area of 2,842 sq ft.

One might have thought the story of the Ju390 to be well documented, yet it seems that the Ju90/290/390 history was destined to be shot through with confusion and contradiction to the end. Until 1980 it was common knowledge that the Ju390 V-1 had been flown at Dessau in August 1943. Bearing call-sign GH+UK, it proved wholly successful, and was later used as a flight-refuelling tanker for the JU290A. It was further known that the V-2 aircraft, with call-sign RC+DA, made its first flight in October 1943. This carried the full armament of the Ju290A-4, with multiple turrets and an under-nose gondola, plus FuG200 *Hohentwiel* anti-ship radar. But in 1980 a former Junkers test pilot, who played a central role in the Ju390 test programme and says he participated in every one of the V-1 aircraft's flights, startled the world by saying that the V-1 was the only Ju390 ever to fly! According to Hans Pancherz, the Ju390 V-1 did not fly at Dessau but at Merseburg, and did not fly in August but on 21 October 1943. He also dismissed the widespread report that the V-2 aircraft had flown on one test to within a few miles of New York as pure invention. 'How could it,' he asked, 'when it never flew at all?' Well that's all very convincing, but how does Herr Panchez explain my picture, reproduced here, of the V-2 aircraft in flight? What's more, it shows RC+DA to have been a simple transport like its predecessor.

34 Boeing 294, XB-15

Part of the trouble with the puny US Army Air Corps between the wars was that it had no political muscle, and everybody on Capitol Hill in Washington hated spending money on defence and knew nothing about airplanes. To make matters worse, there were no enemies within reach except Canada and Mexico, who could hardly have been more friendly. To make matters worse still, in the early 1930s there was a thing called The Depression. Hardly a good idea in 1933 for the staff at Wright Field to dream up a requirement for a huge bomber with a range of 5,000 miles, 'capable of hitting targets in Alaska or Hawaii'.

But the requirement got drafted, and was issued on 14 April 1934 as 'A long-range airplane suitable for military purposes'. The designation allotted was XBLR-1, meaning experimental bomber long-range. Boeing and Martin competed, and in July 1935 Boeing was awarded a contract for the Model 294 design and a flying prototype XBLR-1.

Boeing did not expect suddenly to have to compete in a totally different programme for a 'Multi-engine bomber', with participating prototypes all to be at Wright Field in August 1935. An oft-told story is that 'multi-engined' had traditionally been interpreted as 'twin-engined', but that Boeing rushed ahead and built the Model 299 with four

engines. This was done not so much to make the aircraft bigger or faster but to increase the attainable over-target height. Moreover, as creating the Model 299 cost the company nearly $450,000, which was just about all Boeing had, it was an act of extreme boldness. Had the 299 been ruled out of order because it had four engines, or simply placed in any position other than first, that investment — enormous for 1935 — would have gone down the proverbial drain.

As it happened, Boeing did not need to worry. Though the first 299 soon crashed (through a pilot taking off with the controls locked) it was followed by, if memory serves, 12,730 others. They were, of course, known as B-17 Flying Fortresses, but not quite giant enough for this book.

This challenging programme rather shunted the XBLR-1 on to the sidelines, and in any case in 1935 its designation was changed to XB-15. And delay was going to happen in any case, because the huge Model 294 had been designed to use four of the Allison V-3420 double (twin vee-12) engines, each rated at 2,000 hp, and these were simply not ready. In the event, Boe-

Left *The XB-15, the Model 294, is certainly landing at Boeing Field; but why are the flaps at the take-off setting?* (Gordy Williams via Philip Jarrett)

Above right *Parked at the Army airbase at Miami's 36th Street airport in May 1944, the XB-15 is seen after being rebuilt as a very useful cargo transport.* (US Army via Philip Jarrett)

ing finished the prototype anyway, and installed the most powerful engines that were available: Pratt & Whitney R-1830-11 Twin Wasps, each of just half the take-off power of the V-3420. Obviously, it was not going to be a sparkling performer, despite having a typically American stressed-skin structure of outstanding quality, with almost the entire exterior flush-riveted.

Of course the Model 294 was a cantilever monoplane, with four tractor engines mounted ahead of the leading edge. The huge wing dominated the small fuselage. Mounted in the mid-position, its two spars formed an almost complete obstruction throughout the centre fuselage above the bomb bay, though the spar depth of 68 in not only allowed crew members to walk through, with a cautious stoop, between the massive upper and lower spar booms, but also enabled the flight engineer — a rare flight-crew species in the Army Air Corps — to inspect the back of each engine in flight. Span was 149 ft and wing area 2,780 sq ft. Behind the rear spar the unstressed aft portion of the wing was fabric covered. Flight controls were, of course, manual, but good design, inset hinges and careful use of servo and trim tabs made flying the giant quite pleasant. Normal operating crew numbered 10, the navigator and radio operator being on the main deck just behind the two pilots, between whom double doors led down to the nose where were found the bombardier and one of the five gunners,

(one normally the engineer) who manually aimed two 0.5 in and four 0.3 in guns. Bomb-load, all internal, varied up to 8,000 lb.

The big bomber abounded in new features. Each main gear had twin wheels to spread the gross weight of 70,706 lb over unpaved airfields. This gear, like the huge split flaps and several other items, was operated by an electrical system delivering raw AC at 110 volts. There were engine-driven generators, but in addition power was supplied by two petrol-engined APUs (auxiliary power units). The bombardier's station was well back from the nose, with a Plexiglas flat window in front of a ventral blister fairing. The crew operated in watches, as on a ship, those not on duty having bunks and cooking facilities. Equipment included a three-axis autopilot, and a D/F (direction finding) loop antenna directly above the radio operator's desk, opposite that of the navigator.

The sole XB-15, serial 35-277, did not make its first flight until 15 October 1937. The pilot was Eddie Allen, who later was to make the first flight of the XB-29. The big brother to the B-17, which by 1937 was already in production, it was obviously not going anywhere. It had become overtaken by events, though in 1939 it was fitted with Goodrich rubber deicers on the wings and tail and put into experimental service with the 2nd Bomb Group, bearing the code BB-89. Just before the start of World War 2 it reached 8,200 ft having taken off at a weight of well over

105,000 lb to set a record for 71,167 lb payload (more than the normal gross weight), and a payload of 4,409 lb was carried 3,107 miles at 166 mph. Maximum speed at light weight was about 194 mph.

After Pearl Harbor the XB-15, which had been languishing almost unused, was gutted of much equipment, all gun blisters and the bomb bay being removed, as well as the deicers, and fitted with the mass-produced 1,200 hp Twin Wasp. As the XC-105 cargo

aircraft 35-277 did noble work all round the Caribbean until it was sadly scrapped at Kelly Field, Texas, in early 1945. As its empty weight had been reduced from 37,709 lb to less than 34,000, and the gross weight was raised from 70,706 to 92,000 lb, the XC-105 set an excellent ratio of empty to gross weight, besides carrying loads of up to almost 30 short tons. In World War 2 I do not believe any other aircraft could do this, except perhaps for the BV238.

35 Boeing 314 and 320

With hindsight we can see that PanAm's wish in the early 1930s to fly profitable commercial services across the Pacific was at that time incapable of fulfilment. Sikorsky and Martin turned in superlative transport flying boats, but neither was capable of carrying an economic payload over sectors significantly in excess of 2,000 miles, and San Francisco (SFO)-Hawaii was 2,410 miles on a great-circle measure with perfect navigation and no headwind. The limiting factor was obviously the engine. When Pratt & Whitney and Wright were struggling to certificate an engine in the 1,000 hp class a transpacific boat would, in my opinion, have needed six or eight, and Igor Sikorsky told me his company never seriously considered more than four engines.

By 1935 things were changing. In that year PanAm began talking to Boeing. I doubt if there is anyone around today who can say if the airline was dissatisfied with its two previous flying-boat suppliers and wanted to 'teach them a lesson'. In the 1950s I often talked with Boeing's Clair Egtvedt, Wellwood Beall and Ed Wells, but never thought to ask why PanAm should have turned to yet a third company. For the record, back in 1925 Boeing had built for the Navy a flying boat able to fly SFO-Hawaii (without payload, of course), but it was hardly a recog-

nised supplier of marine aircraft and had never worked for PanAm.

Boeing had two things going for it. The crucial one was the engine. In the closing months of 1935 Wright Aeronautical at last solved serious problems which had prevented it from producing a two-row engine, bigger than the single-row Cyclone, and in November of that year the design went ahead of the R-2600, a 14-cylinder engine aimed at 1,500 hp. This was nearly double the power of the early Twin Wasps in the Martin 130. The other big factor was that the wing already developed for the XB-15 bomber was almost exactly right for the long-range commercial flying boat. So all Boeing had to do was put the wing, carrying the new R-2600 engines, on to a specially designed flying boat hull.

This sounds easy, but like so many things in Boeing's life it was a challenge on an unprecedented scale. Though the overall length of 106 ft was easily eclipsed by (for example) the Do X, I am pretty sure that for cubic capacity the hull of the Model 314 set a world record. It was divided into 11 sections by truss bulkheads, and nine of these sections housed the passenger compartments. These had different floor levels, as indicated by the seemingly crazy arrangement of the paired windows, which in most of the boats had small strip windows higher up for sleepers in bunks. The passenger accommodation varied, but was typically for 68 day or 36 sleeping passengers, one of the nine sections being a 12-seat 'lounge or recreation room' whose seats were freely available to the passengers. A staircase led to the upper deck where were found the flight crew of eight or nine, with sleeping quarters and, further aft, holds for cargo, mail and baggage.

The 152 ft wing had the same two-spar structure and split flaps as that of the XB-15, and the tail also closely followed that of the bomber. After careful study Boeing gave the Model 314 sponsons. Wingtip floats were considered to be more vulnerable, to offer at least equal drag and require extremely long struts, because the 314 not only had a very deep hull but also pronounced dihedral. In contrast, sponsons provided a convenient boarding platform as well as room for part of the enormous fuel capacity, which in the six Model 314s was 3,497 gal. The engines, right at the limit of available technology, were designated Wright 709C-14AC1. Unlike the domestic airlines, which never saw beyond the price per gallon of fuel, PanAm had taken the trouble to calculate the actual cost of operations using various kinds of fuel. At a time when Imperial Airways, like most other airlines,

was seemingly unaware that fuel PNs (performance numbers, called octane numbers if below 100) could actually go beyond 74, PanAm was already using 100-grade fuel in the Martin boats, and for the big Boeing calculated that it would pay to go even higher. Accordingly, for the first time in the world, the engine was designed for 115-PN fuel, with a compression ratio of 9.6. This was done not so much for extra power as to reduce cruising consumption. PanAm calculated that, in comparison with a 314 powered by regular Cyclone 14s with 100-PN fuel, fuel consumption would be reduced by 5 per cent. This was actually rather less than the difference in fuel price, but was more than made up by the extra payload. The propellers were HamStan constant-speed and fully feathering.

PanAm's six 314s were registered as NC-18601 to 18606. The first naturally began life as NX-18601, and because of its size it had to be put together outdoors. Boeing had each boat towed down the Duwamish River to a special dock on Elliott Bay. The first flight was on 7 June 1938, at which time the 314 was the largest production aeroplane in the world. It was clear that greater fin area

The first take-off by the 314, with single fin. (Boeing Company archives)

was needed and, after flying with the original tail replaced by a completely new tail with twin fins and rudders, the final arrangement was reached with three fins and rudders, the central surfaces being almost as big as those originally fitted. All six boats were delivered between January and June 1939. On 20 May 1939 the first-ever regular scheduled service across the North Atlantic was opened between Port Washington (New York) and Marseilles, via Lisbon, at first carrying mail only. On 28 June a regular service was opened to Foynes, in Ireland, and on 30 June the first scheduled passenger service opened to Marseilles. On 30 August NC-18602 *California Clipper* (all had Clipper names) opened a service from SFO across the Pacific to New Zealand.

No other aircraft could have flown these services profitability, but thanks to further work by Wright a little more was possible. In 1939 PanAm ordered a further six aircraft, designated 314A, and later had five of the 314s brought up to the same standard. The 314A had engines uprated from 1,500 to 1,600 hp, driving larger propellers. Gross weight increased to 84,000 lb, fuel capacity being substantially increased to 4,503 gal,

giving a range with maximum payload of 3,685 miles, at 188 mph. Among other changes was the installation of Goodrich pneumatic deicers along the leading edges. The interior accommodation was rearranged, and there were various other changes. The first 314A flew on 20 March 1941, by which time the first, second and fourth had been purchased by BOAC. These three were thus completed as G-AGBZ *Bristol*, AGCA *Berwick* and AGCB *Bangor*, respectively. They were painted in British wartime camouflage after delivery, but later *Berwick* was stripped of camouflage in order to operate the Baltimore-Bermuda service. The others followed in July 1945.

The other three 314As were requisitioned, along with a 314, by the Army Air Force, which called them C-98s. They were then handed to the Navy, which also took over the other 314s, calling the whole nine aircraft B-314s. The 12 huge Boeing boats did tremendous service, among other things carrying Churchill and Roosevelt to historic conferences. One narrowly escaped arriving at Pearl Harbor during the Japanese attack, while another, caught in New Zealand by the Japanese advance, made it

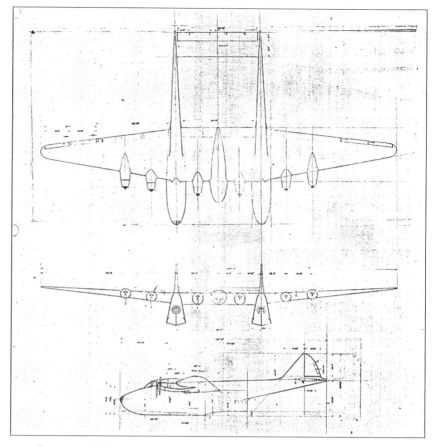

back to SFO by flying westwards around the world. Eleven of the 12 survived the war, to see further hard service with various charter operators.

In December 1935 Boeing drew various forms for a proposed large patrol flying boat for the Navy. Designated as the Type 320, this was intended to make maximum use of Type 314 parts, and in fact from the side might be mistaken for a 314. In fact, the 320 would have been a much bigger aircraft, because it was a twin-hull design with a rectangular centre section. This brought span up to 200 ft, and wing area from 2,867 to 4,379 sq ft. Overall length would have been fractionally greater at 116 ft, and of course the number of R-2600 engines would have gone up to six. Estimated gross weight was 134,000 lb. There is a kind of fundamental appeal for a 'battleship of the sky', but I am sure the Navy were right to turn this one down.

36 Douglas DC-4

From the first flight of the first DC-3 on 17 December 1935 — 32 years to the day after the first successful flight of the Wright Brothers — Douglas Aircraft never looked

The first DC-4 was an almost unique example of a fully funded and professionally engineered aircraft, designed in the closest collaboration with all the customers, getting it wrong. (Douglas Aircraft via Mike Hooks)

Inside the DC-4 mock-up on 25 January 1937. Other bunks hinged down from above, their occupants using the small roof windows. (Douglas Aircraft)

back. The worldbeating airliner had grown out of the DC-1, built for Jack Frye of TWA more than three years earlier. At the outset it had been a potentially ruinous financial gamble. By late 1935 there was no problem, but Don Douglas was not a man to sit on his hands. Before the DC-3 had flown he had gone on record to the effect that Douglas designers, notably Arthur E. Raymond, Ed Burton and Ivar Shogran, were talking with the big US airlines about four-engined airliners which could fly on any two engines and carry their passengers in pressurized comfort at high altitudes. He said 'We look forward with confidence to some solution soon'.

Clearly the risk this time was going to make the DC-1 look like peanuts. Most unusually, Douglas got the airlines to collaborate intimately in the development of the DC-4, the big new transport. For the first time a private manufacturer not only got all the chief customers to sit round the same table, and help design the aircraft, but also to help pay for it! Apart from Douglas, the mainspring behind the DC-4 was W.E. 'Bill' Patterson of United. It was he who brought in his chief competitors, and by the spring of 1936 United, American, Eastern, PanAm and TWA had all agreed to subscribe $100,000 each. But if this was unprecedented, what happened next seems almost unbelievable. By the time the DC-4 made its first flight on 7 June 1938 it had cost $992,808 for labour and engineering and $641,804 for materials and overheads. It had consumed 500,000 hours in engineering and design, and 100,000 hours of ground and lab tests. Never was a new aircraft so carefully planned, and never was a new aircraft such a disappointment. The huge prototype remained the only one of its type, and was eventually sold to Japan!

To some degree the DC-4 resembled a DC-3 scaled up. The wing was based on the same multi-spar structure, as pioneered from the Northrop Alpha via the DC-1 and -2, and this was to some degree pure luck.

Jack Northrop had no idea that such wings would give the Douglas transports fatigue lives of 60,000 hr and upwards, whereas British transports designed more than 10 years later (such as the Viking, Dove and Pembroke) had to be expensively resparred before the 7,000-hr mark. Again like the DC-3, the taper was all on the leading edge and the tips were quite pointed. Span was 138 ft 3 in and area 2,155 sq ft. The four 1,450 hp Pratt & Whitney R-2180 Twin Hornet engines were mounted in nacelles quite high on the wing and canted outwards, because they were at 90° to the leading edge. The huge fuselage had a round top and bottom but, as it was not pressurized, the sides were slightly flattened. As in the DST (Douglas Sleeper Transport), which had been the first version of the DC-3 to fly, there were rectangular windows for the day passengers and a second lot of shallow rectangular windows higher up for the night-time bunks.

The tail comprised a tailplane and elevators with dihedral and three fins and rudders. Douglas would have preferred a single fin but, said Raymond, 'She would never have got out of the door of the shop'. Boldly the landing gear was of the then extremely radical 'tricycle' type, with a steerable nosewheel and two giant main wheels mounted outboard of single legs of high-tensile steel which retracted inwards into the wings. All leading edges were protected by black rubber Goodrich pneumatic deicers. The slotted flaps, landing gears and wheel brakes were all actuated hydraulically, but the flight-control surfaces, which were all fabric-covered, were purely manual.

On the whole the DC-4 was pleasant to fly, and to ride aboard it, even before it was properly furnished, was quite an experience. Pilot control forces were normal — 'very like a DC-3', said a United captain — and to show the monster was by no means 'a dog' it took off from Cheyenne, Wyoming, 6,200 ft above sea level, with two engines at flight idle. NX18100 was certified in May 1939, and thereupon became NC18100. Painted in United livery, it began a big programme of route-proving, in the course of which it gained thousands of column-inches from scribes eager to describe the Pullman-style berths for 29 or 30 night passengers or the luxurious seating for 52 by day, hot and cold running water, fully equipped galley and even an air/ground telephone. Hardly anybody reported on the maintenance problems, high costs and questionable economics. I often discussed the story with such people as Ed Burton, Burt C. Monesmith and, once, with the great Raymond. Nobody could quite put their finger on what they did wrong. Burton said 'Obviously, we could have designed the correct DC-4 right from the start. It wasn't a case of us being overtaken by some new technology.' For whatever reason, United withdrew from its contract for the first six DC-4s, and returned NC18100 to Douglas. Late in 1939 it was sold to Japan, ostensibly for airline use. In fact the cunning Nips just wanted to get stressed-skin experience with large airframes. What they hadn't originally intended to do was make a DC-4 bomber, but that is just what happened. The result was the Nakajima G5N Shinzan. This, like the American airliner, became complex and overweight, and only six were built.

Douglas set course again, with a new DC-4. The original monster became restyled as the DC-4E, for Experimental. The new DC-4 emerged in early 1942, and though Douglas had orders for 40 all priority was given to military needs, and wartime production was completed as various C-54 Army and R5D Navy models. By this time aircraft had become bigger and more powerful and, especially as they were smaller, the production DC-4s don't rate inclusion here.

The
1940s

TAKE YOUR SEATS ON THE
5 O'CLOCK PLANE FOR CAPE TOWN

This decade was absolutely dominated by World War 2. We think of this war as having been fought by aircraft of what we might call 'normal' dimensions. Certainly, more than 99.99 per cent of the aircraft built in that period were not bigger than the Lancaster or B-17. But the odd 0.01 per cent is enough to make this the vintage decade of all time, where monster aircraft are concerned. Indeed, not only were more types of 'giant' built and flown than in any other 10-year period, but their variety was also exceptional. It embraced bombers, airliners, flying boats, assault gliders and flying wings.

Among the latter were the marvellous strategic bombers by Northrop — so uncannily similar in shape and exact wingspan to today's 'stealth' B-2 — and these were developed into new versions powered by six or eight jet engines. On the whole, however, the 1940s was the pinnacle of the giant aeroplane powered by piston engines. Perhaps surprisingly, the most powerful aeroplane of the decade, if we discount modified aircraft such as the jet-boosted B-36, was quite a small machine, the Do214. Though never completed, this would have had eight double engines totalling 32,000 hp. In contrast, the biggest aeroplane ever built, the Hughes Hercules flying boat, had only 24,000 hp.

One feature that may not be immediately obvious is that, though this was a decade of world warfare, the like of which had never been seen before and almost certainly will never be seen again, most of the aircraft that qualify for inclusion here are civil or military transports. The only major exceptions are the B-19 (used as a transport), B-35 and B-36 bombers, and the military versions of the Blohm und Voss and Dornier flying boats. Of all the transports, only the Me323 ever saw any action in the face of the enemy, so we can safely conclude that giants are not a good idea in modern warfare.

At the same time, apart from the Douglas Globemaster family, not many of of the big transport aircraft and flying boats ever did an honest day's work either. This applies to the biggest of all time, the Hughes flying boat, and also to the Shetland, the Clydesman (which never got off the drawing board), the Constitution, BZ.308, the Can-Car projects based on the Burnelli flying wing patents (ditto), the SE.200 and Potez-CAMS 161, the BV222 and 238, and the Do214 (another non-starter). The monster XC-99 of the US Air Force did earn its keep for quite a few years, though it was hardly overworked. The French Laté 631 tried to be useful but proved unreliable and so was withdrawn, and even the quite sensible Armagnac hardly made much impression on the world total of tonne-kilometres. Perhaps one could make a solitary exception in the case of the Martin Mars which, conceived as a battleship of the skies to patrol the world's oceans, really did have a long and useful career, all except one seeing arduous service. After all that, those that remained found another career as water bombers fighting forest fires. Not a bit what the designer intended!

Previous page *There was quite a spate of giant civil transports immediately after World War 2. This rather unlikely — and obviously unpressurized — jet appeared in an advertisement by the Tannoy people in the 1945-46 Jane's.*

37 Blohm und Voss BV222 and BV238

Hamburger Flugzeugbau was formed on 4 July 1934 as a subsidiary of the giant Blohm und Voss shipyard in Hamburg. It produced a succession of aircraft, almost all highly original in design and characterized by several favourite ideas of the technical director, Dr-Ing Richard Vogt. Perhaps the most outstanding of these ideas was to design the wing around a single spar in the form of a tube, the full depth of the wing, made of chrome-molybdenum steel and sealed to form the main fuel tank. Aircraft were designated by the prefix Ha, and on 31 May 1937 the company submitted to Deutsche Luft Hansa, the national airline, its Ha222 proposal for a giant passenger flying boat for use on the North and South Atlantic. Their upstart submission was preferred to the Dornier Do20 (*see Do X p.99*) and Heinkel He120, and on 19 December 1937 the airline ordered three, by now designated BV222 in consequence of the company taking the name of its parent. The BV222-V1 (first experimental example), registered D-ANTE, was rolled out from the Finkenwerder works on a trolley in August 1940 and made its first flight on 7 September.

Predictably, though the BV222 was basically a conventional stressed-skin aircraft, it did have some unusual features. The tubular spar had a diameter of 57 in, and the almost horizontal length along the untapered centre section was divided by fuel-tight bulkheads to form six compartments of 759 gal capacity each, a total of 4,554 gal. Along the front of the centre section were the six 1,000 hp Bramo Fafnir 323R-2 nine-cylinder radial engines, driving 10 ft 10 in VDM constant-speed propellers, with access in flight gained by a rather constricted catwalk just ahead of the spar. Along the trailing edge were electrically driven slotted flaps. The outer panels were tapered, as was the outer spar, though the tips were still very broad. The ailerons comprised a large inner section driven by a Flettner servo tab and a smaller outer section driven by an electric servo motor. When airspeed was insufficient for the servo tab to be effective the inner aileron was driven by stops on the outer.

The hull was one of the first to break away from traditional length/beam ratios around 5 or 6, its ratio being 8.4. Beam was only 10 ft, and though there was a pronounced vee bottom there was no flare at the chine.

The BV222 Wiking V7, fitted with the Jumo 207C opposed-piston diesels intended for the 222C series. (BV via Philip Jarrett)

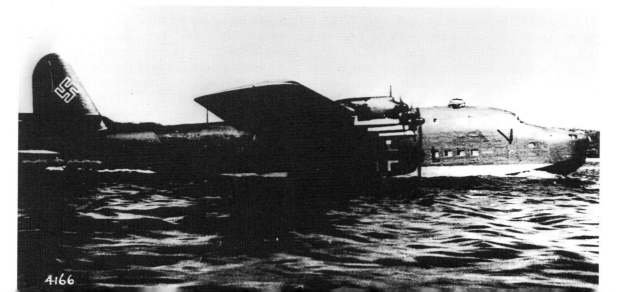

4166

Wearing factory callsign, the BV238-V1 is seen here taxiing on Lake Schaal east of Hamburg prior to first flight. (MBB via Maurice Allward)

About half-way along was the unfaired transverse step, which after further development was followed by a succession of five smaller steps downstream to improve the unstick qualities. Accommodation was on two decks, though the upper level housed only the flight crew and did not extend aft of the wing spar. All 222s had numerous long rectangular windows, though these were originally intended for civil passenger accommodation. The tail looked deceptively simple. The tailplane, mounted above the hull on the fin, had slats over its outer sections, with small fences at their inner end (later these slats were removed) and three-piece elevators, respectively driven by the pilot via a Flettner servo tab (inner), by the autopilot via an electric servo (middle) and by an electric trimming motor (outer). The rudder was driven manually, by two servo tabs. Stability afloat was provided by extremely deep but short floats, each made in two parts comprising inner and outer halves which were slowly retracted by electric motors inwards and outwards to lie flush with the underside of the wing.

No major problems appeared during flight testing, and in early 1941 D-ANTE became CC+EQ of the Luftwaffe, with an interior fitted for heavy cargo and a door added above the trailing edge on the left side wide

enough for crated aero engines. V1 remained a cargo aircraft, used on missions from northern Norway to Libya, but subsequent aircraft were configured for reconnaissance, in collaboration with U-boats, and were armed. Thus V2, first flown on 7 August 1941, had two dorsal turrets each with an MG131, four MG81s fired from side windows, and an MG81 above the bows. Under the wings were added gondolas each housing MG131s firing to the front and rear, but the 222, already marginally underpowered, became even more sluggish and the gondolas were removed.

In January 1942 the 222 was officially named *Wiking* (Viking). Aircraft V4, 5, 6 and 8 were completed as 222A-0 patrol aircraft, retaining the Fafnir R-2 but with take-off power boosted to 1,200 hp by water/methanol injection. Span was 150 ft 11 in, length 119 ft 9 in, maximum weight 100,529 lb and maximum speed 193 mph. V7 was the first of the C-series, with Jumo 207C opposed-piston two-stroke diesels, each of 1,000 hp. It had been hoped to get more range and better performance by using the

Jumo 208, of 1,500 hp, but this engine was never fully developed, and with the 207 the performance remained poor and range and endurance actually deteriorated, from 4,630 miles to 3,790, and from 33 hours to 28. Only five further boats were completed, C-09 to C-013. These were slightly longer, had underwing floats carried on struts extending the full length of the float, and armament comprising a 20 mm MG151 in each of three upper turrets, one behind the flight-deck and the others in the wing behind the outer engines, and various arrangements of hand-aimed MG81s and MG131s firing to the beam. Attrition was high, and at the end of the war only seven of the 13 survived. Of these four were destroyed, two flew to the USA, and one came to England where my father was interested to have a flight in it at Calshot where he was translating the manuals.

The BV222 certainly rates inclusion in this book, but to a timescale only a little later Blohm und Voss laid down a production line of a second type of flying boat some 75 per cent heavier! This was the BV238, which remained unknown to British intelligence until after the war, first appearing (as a German drawing) in the official British recognition journal in July 1945! The BV238 was in some ways the greatest giant of the wartime period, but its early history is slightly confused. In 1940 the RLM was seeking proposals for a replacement for the BV138 as a long-range sea reconnaissance and transport aircraft, the requirement for which grew progressively more demanding. At the same time, Vogt's team was working on a project for a truly colossal transatlantic flying boat for Luft Hansa, the Blohm und Voss P200. This was to carry 120 sleeping passengers 5,344 miles, and to be powered by eight 2,500 hp Jumo 223 box-form (four crankshaft) 48-cylinder diesel engines arranged along a 279-ft wing. This challenging project was taken a long way before, in January 1941, the RLM requested that it be shelved in order to concentrate on a smaller

aircraft to serve multiple (mainly military) roles.

This new aircraft was the BV238. It had been started in November 1940 by further upgrading of the BV138 replacement specification, the span to be just under 174 ft, the maximum gross weight 164,242 lb and the engines four Jumo 223. Notable features of this design were the hull length/beam ratio of 10 (surpassing even the figure of 8.4 of the BV 222) and the wing loading of 82 lb/sq ft, which compared with about 28 (for example) for the BV138. During the summer of 1941 the design made considerable progress until late July when, as Vogt had long expected, the Jumo 223 was admitted to be many years off. A fall-back design with six engines had already been started, and this was somewhat larger, the span being increased to 189 ft 5 in, wing area to 3,737 sq ft and overall length to 142 ft 3 in. Fortunately the proportionate increase in wing area was greater than the increase in weight, the latter eventually reaching 198,460 lb, or in overload condition 100 tonnes (220,459 lb). In about the first week of October 1941 the company received a contract for four BV238s, the first three being BV238A-0s with six 1,900 hp Daimler-Benz DB 603G liquid-cooled engines and the fourth being the first B-0 with BMW801 14-cylinder radials (the choice was expected to be the 2,000 hp BMW801E).

Once the design really got under way in late 1940 it was decided to base it as far as possible on the BV222, though of course no parts were common. The wing was built up on a tubular spar (visible in an accompanying drawing) of about 65 in diameter, subdivided into fuel and oil tanks as detailed later. Compared with the BV222 the wing was more attractive and efficient, with a centre section of higher aspect ratio and greater taper on the outer panels to give more pointed tips. The enormous electrically operated slotted flaps were in one piece, but the use of divided ailerons was repeated, one tab-driven and the other powered. The tail likewise followed BV222 philosophy, though the elevators were simplified by omitting the trimming portion. This left two inner and two outer sections, though most existing drawings show each elevator as one piece.

The enormous hull was typically Teutonic in its uncompromising severity of line, the great vertical depth, narrow beam (11 ft 8 in) and bluff nose imparting to the 238 an almost box-like character. As the diagram shows, there were two full-length decks, the lower deck, even in V1, being strengthened to carry heavy cargo loads taken on board through the nose. The extreme bow contained left and right doors which when open made it easy for personnel to move in or out. These doors were themselves hinged to large side doors hinged about 13 ft further back. When opened fully, under hydraulic power, these provided unobstructed access for items up to almost 9 ft high and 11 ft wide to be loaded or driven on board. The interior was completely unobstructed, and in a pure transport role could carry a maximum (short-range) load of 77,160 lb. There were four doors around the lower deck, that on the left side ahead of the wing being another wide cargo door, with a personnel door mounted within it. The upper level was occupied by flight crew, which in the basic armed version numbered 10, with six off-duty bunks, and various items of equipment including all radio and large ammunition magazines.

The first three boats were to be powered by the DB603G, each mounted on long cantilever truss frameworks ahead of the main spar. Coolant radiators and oil coolers were combined in extremely large square matrix blocks housed in fixed ducts under the engines, airflow being controlled by exit flaps. Propellers were three-blade VDM with a diameter of just over 12 ft. Tankage varied from 5,345 gal for rough-sea take-offs, through 7,039 gal for normal operations, and up to a maximum of 10,779 gal in the overload condition. The latter was restricted to sheltered water, and normally also required the use of four ATO (assisted take-off) rockets of 3,307 lb thrust each. Unlike the BV222 the stabilizing floats were one-piece, very short (the same length as the chord of their struts) and electrically retracted inwards. A photograph shows the floats coming up after take-off, the pilot having flicked the switch near the start of the run in order that the 40 secs needed to complete the cycle should be completed before reaching the

Stabilizing floats retract with painful slowness as the massive BV238 gets airborne. (MBB via Maurice Allward)

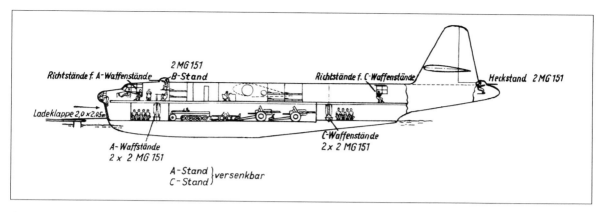

Richtstände f. A-Waffenstände
2 MG 151
B-Stand
Richtstände f. C-Waffenstände
Heckstand 2 MG 151
Ladeklappe 2,0 x 2,05m
A-Waffstände
2 x 2 MG 151
C-Waffenstände
2 x 2 MG 151
A-Stand ⎫ versenkbar
C-Stand ⎭

floats-extended speed limit of 220 km/h (137 mph).

Because of the size of the project, assistance was provided by Société d'Aviation Louis Breguet at Villacoublay and 'Weser' Flugzeugbau, while a group in Prague was assigned the task of making a wooden model of the BV238 to a scale of 1:3.75. This was to explore the water handling but, as has often been the case, it was useless because it did not fly until September 1944, whereas the full-scale aircraft began flying in April 1944! This unarmed first prototype, BV238-V1, in fact had DB603A engines, of 1,750 hp, but was otherwise closely representative of the production 238A series. It bore radio callsign RO+EZ and was based at the Schaal See (lake), where it had been assembled after trucking the parts about 40 miles from the Finkenwerder (Hamburg) factory. Flight trials went well, Vogt's outstanding flight-control system again needing very little modification. The work enjoyed only a low priority, and much of the final months of 1944 were spent discussing the fitting of armament, which was to be fitted from the start on V2 and subsequent BV238s. The basic armament varied. The company drawing reproduced here was dated 1.1.42, but by 1943 the standard fit was planned to be a nose turret with four MG131 each with no fewer than 1,800˙ rounds per gun, a similar turret in the tail, two more (with 900 rounds per gun) in the aft ends of fairings projecting aft of the wing, two

Dated 1 January 1942, this works drawing shows planned armament (but not the trailing-edge turrets) and cargo accommodation for the production BV238. (BV via Philip Jarrett)

20mm MG151 (each with no less than 1,400 rounds) in the forward dorsal turret, and four pairs of MG131 each with 500 rounds per gun firing to the beam, two of these pairs being on each side of the hull. Internal wing bays were to house 20 SC250 bombs of 551 lb plus six 110 lb flares, while external loads could include four SC1000 (2,205 lb) bombs, four Hs 293 missiles or four LD1200 (2,645 lb) torpedoes. Adding the wing turrets increased the span to 197 ft 5 in, and wing area to 3,877 sq ft.

In late 1941 Blohm und Voss had proposed a BV238 Land, for use as either a heavy bomber or a transport. The planing bottom was to be replaced by a conventional fuselage with a twin-wheel nose gear and a 12-wheel main gear with three twin-tyred wheels in a row on each side taking over 90 per cent of the weight and retracting into the fuselage. Near the extremity of each centre section was a tall outrigger gear, retracting inwards, to provide stability on the ground. In front of and behind the main-gear bay were large bomb bays for up to 44,090 lb of bombs, the range with this load being 4,350 miles. As the bomb bays were below the floor they did not interfere with the alternative carriage of up to 88,183 lb of cargo.

In 1942 four examples of the landplane were ordered as the BV250.

Despite all the other pressures on those involved, to say nothing of the virtual wiping off the map of Hamburg itself, by July 1944 the BV238-V2 was not only complete but also painted in the 'Weser' works at Einswarden; the V3 was about three-quarters complete at Finkenwerder, V4 and V5 were visible as major components, and even three BV250s were also in the pre-

assembly stage. At this point the RLM ordered an immediate cessation of work, all emphasis now switching to fighters. Thus, when on 4 May 1945 British troops entered the Blohm und Voss factory there was little to see of these true giants. On the same day, 40 miles to the east, riding at anchor, BV238-V1 was noticed by free-ranging P-51Ds. With only four days to go to the end of the war it was sunk by 'fifty-calibre' fire, only the wing showing above the water.

38 Ju322 *Mammut* and Me321/323 *Gigant*

In October 1940, for obvious reasons, the German Führer decided to postpone the planned invasion of the British Isles. But it was merely a postponement; he intended to take over Britain once he had conquered the Soviet Union. With a bit more time to think it was belatedly realised that, to subdue the British defences in the initial assault from the sky, transport aircraft would have to be provided capable of carrying heavy equipment. All the Luftwaffe actually pos-

sessed in quantity was the relatively puny Ju52/3m, hardly able to carry more than 17 troops or such loads as motorcycles or fuel drums. Accordingly, on 17 October, the RLM issued an urgent requirement for a giant assault glider, able to carry 20 tonnes (44,090 lb), such as 100 armed troops, or a PzKW IV tank, an assault gun and ammunition or an 88 mm gun and its towing vehicle. The outline requirement was sent to just two companies. Messerschmitt, which had made many types of wooden aircraft, was told to use welded steel-tube construction with fabric covering. Junkers, perhaps the only major firm never to have made a wooden aeroplane, were instructed to build their gliders out of that material! Just 14 days were allowed for the submission of completed designs, with all calculations, plus the suggested manufacturing plan for the first 100 gliders.

From the start it seemed to Junkers a case for their all-wing ideas. The special team at Merseburg assigned the task thought in terms resembling a Burnelli or even a Spanloader (*entries 44 and 80*), with the biggest possible wing and vestigial fuselage and tail. A group under Technical Director Heinrich Hertel had previously drawn EF94 (*Entwick-*

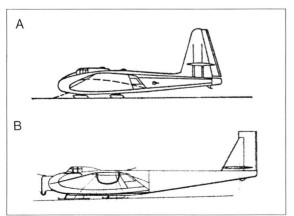

Side views to the same scale of the Junkers EF94 (A) and Ju322 Mammut *(B). (Junkers)*

lungsflugzeug, development aircraft), and this was the starting point. This design was slightly enlarged, to have a span of 203 ft 5 in and area of 6,850 sq ft, much larger than the wing of any other wartime aircraft. The rear fuselage was lengthened, to give over-all length of 86 ft, so that the tail could be reduced in size. (When Udet saw it he rightly thought the glider would be un-stable.) The assigned 8-series number was 322, and Junkers called it the *Mammut* (mammoth).

Curiously, one report speaks of 'electric servo boosters' for the flight controls. There was no obvious source of electric power (stored compressed air was used to lower the flaps for landing) and the control sur-faces themselves had full-length servo tabs. The top of the wing was horizontal, giving barely adequate ground clearance at the tips, which were protected by steel half-hoop skids. All loads were carried in the thick box-like centre section, with access via two up-ward hinged and jettisonable doors which formed the entire central leading edge. Just outboard of these doors was a projecting cupola for a gunner with an MG15 or MG131, and with a wheel underneath to prevent nosing-over. A third gunner was

above the rear fuselage. Underneath were four sprung landing skids, which on takeoff were to rest on a specially designed trolley. During World War 2 the Germans spent more effort unsuccessfully playing about with take-off trolleys than anyone else at any other time in history. That for the *Mammut* was true to form, causing considerable difficulty.

Difficulty was also experienced in loading a tank. A special ramp had been devised, but the tank pitched forward when it reached the top and crashed through the glider's floor, which had to be strengthened, adding about 8,800 lb to the structure. This played a part in cutting the payload from the stipulated 44,092 lb to a mere 26,455 lb. The author could never see why the lead-ing edge was not made to hinge downwards, forming a self-contained ramp which would be immediately available before takeoff and after landing. But what was a mere detail. More serious were the anticipated handling qualities, and the fact that nobody had thought to provide a suitable tug.

Eventually the first of the 100 *Mammuts* was coupled up behind the Ju90-V7 (*see Ju90*) in early April 1941. The lightly loaded combination just got airborne at the very end of the available run (it is said to have been the glider which was last to get airborne, but in every heavy-glider take-off I have witnessed the problem is the more heavily loaded tug), but that was just the start of the problems. First, the huge trolley disintegrated when it hit the ground; at least that was better than rebounding and hitting the glider. Second, as predicted, the *Mammut's* fin proved totally inadequate and the glider weathercocked violently, yawing from side to side. Third, the glider pilot let the monster rise higher than the Ju90, pulling up the latter's tail. At the last moment the glider cast off. The Ju90 just avoided going into the ground, and the glider stopped yawing and made a smooth landing without damage. But that was the end of the programme. The 100 *Mammuts* and a large amount of related wood was sawn up for use as fuel. This was also the end of the dream of Hugo Junkers, 30 years earlier, of building efficient all-wing aircraft. I don't know why they didn't just enlarge the fin.

In contrast, the rival Messerschmitt programme was about as successful as it could possibly have been, though even that is not staying a great deal. Perhaps its greatest accomplishment is that in the space of 14 weeks the Messerschmitt special team assigned to the task at Leipheim, under Dipl-Ing Josef Fröhlich, had completed the basic feasibility study, the complete project design, the detailed engineering design and stressing, the prototype construction, and all plans for making 100 production machines (a quantity almost immediately increased to 200). Thus, on 25 February 1941, Karl Baur made the first flight in the first Me321 *Gigant*, with 11 more in final assembly, 62 more part completed and most of the parts for the remaining 126 gathered in the Leipheim factory! This was surely a feat rarely equalled in aircraft construction, bearing in mind the *Gigant's* enormous size.

Everything possible was done to achieve a simple low-risk aircraft. The wing, of 180 ft 5 in span and 3,229 sq ft area, was based on a central box structure made up entirely of welded steel tubes, structurally divided into a centre section with slotted flaps, and outer panels, with dihedral, carrying horn-balanced ailerons with Flettner tabs and electric servo motors. A single strut of drawn steel tube braced the wing on each side to the fuselage, which was again made of welded steel tubes, and was much bigger in front of the wing than behind. The entire nose comprised giant left and right doors which hinged open for unobstructed access. Strong transverse girders supported a floor adequate for tanks or any other dense load, the hold offering an unobstructed volume of 3,814 cu ft measuring 36 ft long, 124 in wide and 130 in high. Above the hold was the box housing the cockpit for the single pilot, who had to climb a long ladder up the wall of the hold. The tail was almost all wood, the entire assembly being pivoted to the rear fuselage and driven hydraulically over a range +2.5°/−5°. Apart from the tail the only substantial wooden parts were the secondary formers of the fuselage, over which the fabric covering was stretched, and the leading edge of the wing. The glider was designed to land on four wheel skids, and to take off from a jettisonable dolly attached to these skids with two swivelling Bf109 mainwheels in front and two Ju90 mainwheels at the rear.

From the start the Messerschmitt *Gigant* was a success, almost the only urgent modification being to double the width of the cockpit so that two pilots could share the heavy control forces. Unlike the rival Ju322 the Me321 really could carry the design payload of 44,092 lb, and by inserting a series of panels forming a second deck it was possible to carry not the specified 100 troops but 200. On the other hand there were basic problems. An obvious one was lack of tugs. The Ju90 used for initial flight tests was very marginal, even with an unloaded glider, and was certainly not worth building purely as a tug for the *Gigant*. After some thought the answer appeared in the form of the He111Z, Z from *Zwilling* or twin, comprising a pair of He111H bombers joined to a common centre wing with a fifth engine. While this was being produced the best answer was thought to be the Troika-Schlepp, comprising a V-formation of three Bf110 fighters pulling on separate cables. The result was dangerous, hair-raising and often catastrophic, and the use of four, six or, most often, eight ATO (assisted take-off) rockets attached under the *Gigant's* wings caused further disfurther disasters. Most fundamental of all was the fact that, while giant gliders were fine for bringing heavy equipment in a single violent assault on enemy territory, they were highly unsuited to sustained use over a long period in supplying an established battlefront as in the Soviet Union and North Africa. They demanded large numbers of tugs, could not readily be moved once they had landed, blocked airfields and then, if they did reach their destination, had to be prepared for towing back again.

The answer was obvious: fit the Me321 with engines. Following prolonged study, which involved considerable (mostly fairly

detailed) redesign, the Leipheim team was authorised in late 1941 to begin converting two gliders into powered aircraft. The engine picked was the French Gnome-Rhône 14N 48/49, rated at 1,140 hp, a major factor in its choice being that large numbers of complete cowled engines and propellers already existed in the Bloch 175 multirole bomber in production for the Luftwaffe. One prototype, to lead to an aircraft designated Me323C was to have four engines. With these it needed a tug for a full-load take-off but could subsequently cast off and fly to its destination, thereafter flying back without payload without needing a tug for the take-off. The other prototype was to lead to the Me323D, with six engines. With this power it was calculated that the aircraft could be regarded as a self-sufficient transport, able to make full-load take-offs by itself. Predictably, in view of the experience with the Troika-Schleppe, it was the six-engined 323D that went into production.

Compared with the 321, the 323D differed most markedly in having the six engines, those on the left wing driving clockwise as

The Me323V-2, the first of the Gigants *to have six engines.* (MBB via Mike Hooks)

seen from the front and the remainder driving anticlockwise. The usual propeller was a three-blade variable-pitch Chauvière, but some versions had Ratier propellers and the D-2 a Heine wooden propeller with two fixed-pitch blades. The landing gear was, of course, completely new, comprising a long box on each side fairing in a row of five wheels, there being a pair of smaller wheels at the front completely separate from a row of three bigger wheels at the rear, all mounted on sprung levers and fitted with pneumatic brakes. On the ground, normally loaded, the 323 *Gigant* (the name was retained) sat with its tailskid on the ground and the nose tilted up, which made loading and unloading somewhat more difficult, the sill height being about 5 ft. During landing at a forward airstrip it was possible to pull up by dropping a plough-like hook from the rear fuselage. Between the two inner engine nacelles on each side was a compartment in the leading edge for an engineer who could manage fuel, synchronization and, to some degree, attend to faults. British intelligence reports gave the fuel capacity as 12 self-sealing cells of 195.75 gal

each in the wing behind the cockpit, but in fact the true figure was only six of these tanks. Two more could exceptionally be carried in the rear of the cargo hold.

Whereas the Me321B-1, the standard production glider, had an empty weight of 26,896 lb, the empty Me323D-2 weighed no less than 61,700 lb, or more than a fully loaded Lancaster. The respective payloads were: 321, up to 60,000 lb; 323, typically only 21,500 lb. Maximum and cruising speeds for a 323D-2 were typically 135 and 100 mph, the range at maximum weight being about 465 miles. All this sounds like a rather limited aircraft, but in fact the 323 was a very remarkable achievement. The Allies had no aircraft able to carry such heavy or bulky loads, and the 198 production Me323 *Gigant* airlifters made a significant contribution to the German army in the front line in both the Eastern and Mediterranean theatres. There were many versions, a few having far more power (such as six Jumo 211 or even

Loading an 88 mm gun into an Me323D-1. Note 'Bloch' on one of the engine covers. (Via R.T. Riding)

BMW801 engines) and the E-2 being fitted with heavy defensive firepower including rifle-calibre MG15s and MG81s, 13 mm MG131s and two 20 mm MG151 cannon in low-drag turrets above the outer wings. One aircraft, the 323E-2/WT, was a veritable flying fortress with 11 MG151 cannon and four or five MG131s.

Most *Gigants*, however, were easy meat, and in both the theatres in which they served they were shot down in large numbers. Of the 198 production Me323s it is known that 99 were shot down, and very few of the remainder survived to VE-Day. Not least of the *Gigant's* claims to fame is that, after being assisted off the ground by an He111Z, one Me323 dropped an experimental bomb weighing 39,021 lb. Unfortunately the *Gigant* had been structurally damaged in a US strafing attack on its airfield and it broke up in the air, the failures starting before the giant bomb was released. The film of the whole sequence was lost in Nazi Germany's death throes.

39 Douglas B-19

The B-19, rare among Douglas aircraft of its day in not having a name, is one of the few entries in this book that really was the biggest in the world. As we have seen, some (probably impractical) projects were even bigger, but among aircraft built and flown the B-19 has a particular niche in that, throughout World War 2, it had the biggest span of any aeroplane in the world. In 1942 the Mars just beat it in power, and in 1944 the BV238 beat it in power and weight, but the span of the B-19 remained unrivalled. Moreover, while the German fly-

Inside the specially built hangar at Santa Monica in January 1941. The XB-19 was yet another monster that had to travel out sideways. (Douglas Aircraft)

ing boat was an ungraceful brute, the big Douglas was a lovely example of the aircraft designer's art.

Her design stemmed from the Project A specification issued in 1934 by the Army Air Corps Air Materiel Division for a bomber able to support troops in Alaska, Hawaii or Panama. We met this specification in the entry on the Boeing XB-15, and noted that it called for a bombload of 2,000 lb to be carried at 200 mph for a distance of 5,000 miles. This was a very formidable challenge, at a

time when few aircraft could carry such a load further than 1,000 miles. There was no problem with the airframe. Though British fabric-covered biplanes would have been complete non-starters, American stressed-skin monoplanes were fully equal to the challenge, as both the XB-15 and XB-19 showed. The problem lay in the engines. An XB-19 with four 3,500 hp Wasp Majors would have been 'quite some airplane' (Douglas said in 1949 when told the monster would be scrapped). But this engine

came along just a decade too late.

Indeed, in 1935, when Douglas began project studies to meet the demand, the most powerful engine was just nudging 1,000 hp. Boeing went ahead, and though they designed the XB-15 for more power, this aircraft never did have engines of much over 1,000 hp each. Douglas aimed far higher. With the concurrence of the Army staff at Wright Field, the design team at Santa Monica — led by Sky (real name Schuyler) Kleinhans, later important on the post-war DC-7 and 8 — planned the biggest aeroplane in the world, with the designation XBLR-2. It was to have 'six engines of not less than 2,000 hp each', and it was expected that these would be available ready for a first flight not later than 1939. The design really got under way in 1936, the selected engine being the Wright R-3350 Duplex Cyclone, also known as the Cyclone 18. The design was accepted in 1938, but with only four engines. Douglas received an order for 'One bombardment ship, number 1938-471'. The designation was then changed to XB-19.

Structurally the XB-19 was superb, and one would have to look quite closely to see that it was a design of the 1930s and not the 1980s. Virtually all external skin was joggled,

for a perfect fit between plates, and flush riveted. Like the DC-3 and original DC-4 the wing had multiple spars, pointed tips and all taper on the leading edge. The ailerons and split flaps were each divided into inboard and outboard sections to avoid problems due to the flexure of the very long surfaces (a complete aileron or flap had a span of nearly 50 ft). All flight-control surfaces were manual, and it was no small achievement to make the XB-19 adequately manoeuvrable with acceptable pilot control forces. As originally built the engines were four 2,000 hp Wright R-3350-5 Duplex Cyclones, and it was a case of the XB-15 repeating itself: the giant was obviously underpowered.

In fact the wing area of 4,492 sq ft was considerably less than that of the ANT-20, reflecting the extremely efficient Douglas wing of 10.1 aspect ratio. What made the bomber underpowered was its weight. With the required fuel capacity of 9,160 gal, by a long way a world record at the time (*but see the Laté 631, p.171*), the maximum weight was no less than 164,000 lb, or almost exactly double the empty weight of 82,253 lb. This resulted in the completely unacceptable power loading of 20.5, which resulted in

Above left *Out of doors, but still lacking a few items, such as No. 2 propeller and the forward dorsal turret. Note the Bostons and A-20s.* (Douglas Aircraft)

Left *This photograph is believed to have been taken on the first flight, which almost began disastrously.* (Douglas Aircraft)

Right *The cockpit of the XB-19, with suitably enormous throttle levers and trim wheels.* (Douglas Aircraft)

sluggish acceleration at take-off and a long run. Maximum speed was originally 209 mph, cruising speed 170-186 mph, service ceiling a remarkably good 22,000 ft, and landing speed allegedly as low as 69 mph.

Other data include span of 212 ft, length of 132 ft and height of 42 ft 9 in. Typical of the era was the design of the main landing gears, each with a single gigantic wheel and tyre carried on a single leg on the inside of the wheel. The gear retracted hydraulically inwards into the wing, with no doors, in exactly the same way as the main gears of the prototype DC-4. The single-wheel nose gear retracted backwards into a long bay closed by twin doors. There was normal provision for a crew of 10. One or two were engineers, who had inflight access to the engines. The engineer compartment looked cluttered, whereas the capacious flightdeck

Left *Servicing one of the Allison V-3420-11 24-cylinder double engines which replaced the R-3350s in 1943. The propeller is a Curtiss Electric. Designation became XB-19A. (Douglas Aircraft)*

Below *Probably the last photograph taken of the XB-19A, at Davis-Monthan just prior to scrapping. (Douglas Aircraft)*

seemed quite spartan (certainly by the standards of the 1950s), notable features being the length of the throttle levers and the clarity with which exact trimmer positions were displayed. In action up to eight of the crew could act as gunners, manning a 37 mm cannon in the upper part of the nose, a 37 mm in the forward dorsal turret, in the manual installation under the rudder twin 0.5 in, in the rear dorsal turret a 0.5 in, in a beam window on each side a 0.5 in and in further left and right beam windows, twin 0.3 in. The media had a field day inventing XB-19 bomb loads, but the actual figures were impressive enough, and far in excess of the requirement. The heaviest of the dozens of possible loads of bombs and other stores totalled 37,100 lb, and this could be carried 2,000 miles. With maximum fuel and about 1,500 lb of bombs the ultimate range was in excess of 7,000 miles.

Douglas built a huge new hangar in which to erect the B-19. The company also took out insurance at Lloyds for the full value of £250,000 in return for a premium of £20,000 for the first minute of flight. In the event, for various reasons (such as intense pressure of other work) No 8471 did not fly until 27 June 1941, long after the time when it was seen to be an obsolescent 'one-off'. In command on that flight was Army Air Corps chief test pilot Maj Stanley M. Ulmstead. On take-off he pulled back on the big wheel. Nothing happened, so he pulled back further. Suddenly he got a response: the nose rose, and went on rising to an alarming angle. Gen Mark Bradley said 'He damn near lost the airplane'. Ulmstead learned very quickly that the B-19 thought a bit before responding. The media subsequently wrote that the XB-19 had been built 'as a flying laboratory', or 'to provide data on very large airplanes' or 'as a flying battleship to revolutionize the state of the art in strategic bombing'. In fact, it was simply planned as a huge strategic bomber which during its design and construction was overtaken by the rapid pace of new technology.

It never served with a combat unit and did only a limited amount of research into any aspect of bombing or gunnery, though it did help to develop the R-3350 engine. In 1942 the XB-19 was painted olive drab all over. Very soon it was pressed into use as a transport, with R-3350-11 engines. In March 1943 the aircraft was given a complete rework, being equipped as the XB-19A cargo carrier, with totally new engine installations housing 2,600 hp Allison V-3420-11s driving four-blade Curtiss Electric propellers. These engines comprised two of the familiar V-1710 vee-12 engines geared to a common propeller shaft. They made a tremendous difference to performance, especially to full-load take-off and climb. After the war 8471 languished, and was scrapped at Davis-Monthan in 1949.

40 Potez-CAMS 161

In the final years of peace before World War 2 the French industry developed three totally different types of flying boat which, though not quite the biggest things in the sky, were not far short of it. Even today researchers in France are still piecing together bits of the story, which involves quite a lot of cloak-and-dagger stuff after the French capitulation. The second and third to fly, the Laté 631 and SE200, were products of the south, but the CAMS 161 was designed and built at the long-established seaplane works at Sartrouville, on the Seine in the northwest suburbs of Paris. All three were basically fine aircraft, born into a world of political turmoil that prevented them from

fulfilling their objectives.

All were designed to meet the same requirement, issued by the Ministère de l'Air on 12 March 1936. For many years Air France had built up commercial services based at Biscarosse, on the Bay of Biscay southwest of Bordeaux. From here the route extended in acceptable stages south to the coast of West Africa and then across the South Atlantic. But Air France naturally wanted to conquer the North Atlantic, hence this challenging specification: a range of 6,000 km (3,728 miles) against a constant headwind of 60 km/h; ability to take off in 1 m (40 in) of water; cruising speed not less than 250 km/h (186 mph); accommodation for a crew of six, with bunks for off-duty members, plus full sleeping accommodation for 20 passengers; six engines, with maximum accessibility in flight; and gross weight between 30 and 40 tonnes. A year later it was considered that this did not aim high enough, and sleeping accommodation was demanded for 40 passengers, the weight limit being raised to 70 tonnes. With the concurrence of Air France the Potez-CAMS was built to the original specification, which explains why the others took a little longer. But even this first machine was impressive. Unlike its rivals only a single CAMS 161 was ordered, named *Picardie*, in January 1937.

The unquestioned team leader was Maurice Hurel, who had headed the CAMS research effort since 1923, and was also chief test pilot. Like all big flying boats, the 161's aerodynamic tunnel testing had to be supplemented by hydrodynamic trials in a towing tank. In 1936 engineer Arsandaux had recommended the use of a flying scale model to prove the flying characteristics of all very large aircraft, and Hurel agreed. As a result, a scale model designated CAMS 160 was built, powered by four 40 hp Train 4A-01 four-cylinder engines. This had all the grace, and even a little of the majesty, of the full-size machine, and it first flew on 20 June 1938.

When World War 2 began in September 1939 the 161 was nowhere near being completed. Construction was then held up by a decree of 3 March 1939 which included it in a list of commercial transport flying boats suitable for conversion into military aircraft for the Aéronavale. Urgent design effort converted the almost completed hull into that of a patrol aircraft, with four 20 mm cannon in side turrets at front and rear and with small circular portholes along the sides. To free the Sartrouville factory for mass-production of the Arsenal VG30 fighter, on 23 February 1940 the hull, wings and tail were taken by road to the SNCAN factory at Pointe du Hoc, Le Havre (Potez-CAMS having been absorbed into the nationalized Nord group under the law of 13 November 1936). Then came the Armistice of 25 June

Left *Launch of the CAMS 161 on 20 March 1941, with engineer Lambert standing in the bow port. Sartrouville is just north-west of Paris.* (Potez via Aérospatiale)

Right *The first take-off, from a short straight stretch of the Seine, a year to the day after the 161 was launched; the pilot was Maurice Hurel.* (Via Malcolm Passingham)

and all work was abandoned. Later that year the German authorities permitted the components to be returned to Sartrouville, which was judged a little less vulnerable to RAF bombing.

Here work proceeded rapidly, despite reconversion back into a transport, with turrets eliminated and the portholes replaced by passenger windows. By February 1941 the 161 was complete, painted in the regulation Vichy black and orange on the upper surfaces, nose and tail, and with no insignia save tricolour stripes on the rudders. Engine runs began a month later, but orders were then received to repaint the boat in Luftwaffe markings, with industry call sign VE+WW. In this condition it was launched on to the Seine on 20 March 1941. There followed more than a year, partly occupied in ground testing and modification and partly in wrangling. On 20 October 1941 the German authorities gave permission for the 161 to fly into the Unoccupied Zone so that it could join the other giants in flight test at the Etang de Berre, near Marseilles. A flavour of the times is provided by Luftwaffe pressure for testing to be at Biscarosse, in the Occupied Zone, by the refusal of Breguet to let the 161 be housed in its hangar at Berre, and the cautious suggestion by M Rouze, the Président of SNCAN, to his chief pilot, Robert Letierce, that he should indeed fly to the Unoccupied Zone: North Africa!

Such thoughts tended to govern who might be entrusted to fly the great boat. Eventually it was agreed Hurel was the natural choice and, with insufficient fuel to fly to North Africa (but certainly enough to reach England, were it not for the Luftwaffe escort), he made the much-delayed first flight from the wooded stretch of the Seine near the Sartrouville factory on 20 March 1942, accompanied by engineers Lantz, Vaubourdolle and Lambert.

Of course, the structure was all-metal stressed-skin, as were the other big boats. Span was 151 ft and wing area 2,829 sq ft. The wing comprised a rectangular centre section, with slotted flaps driven hydraulically to 40°, and tapered outer panels with four-section ailerons interlinked with leading-edge slats. There was 4° dihedral from the root, and the wing was strut-braced at the line of the middle engines. The twin-finned tail likewise had dihedral and was strut-braced. The engines were six Hispano-Suiza 12Y-36 liquid-cooled vee-12s, each of 920 hp and with 1,100 available for take-off. Each drove a Ratier electrically controlled three-blade propeller of 12 ft 10 in diameter. The engines were handed: 1, 2 and 3, right-hand rotation, the others left. The coolant radiators could be retracted electrically into the nacelles or lowered any desired amount into the slipstream. Five tanks in the lower part of the hull, and small ones behind the engines, held 5,845 gal of fuel, and there were equally impressive supplies of oil and cooling water. The flight engineer could reach all engines by lying on an electric trolley which ran on rails inside the leading edge. As was not uncommon at the time, the six substantial throttle levers were pivoted to the roof of the cockpit. An unusual feature was that the stabilizing floats, each nearly 22 ft long, retracted hydraulically behind the outer engines.

By the time the big boat flew, agreement had at last been reached on its future home. It was to go to Marignane, another base on the shore of the Berre lake, and accordingly it flew there on 24 March 1942. On the 29th it was agreed that the Caquot hangar, normally reserved for Air France, should be allotted to it. Free from German authority the 161 retained its colour scheme of grey, orange and black, but lost its German markings, instead carrying civil registration F-BAGV and bold tricolour stripes diagonally on wings and fuselage and vertically on the rudders. It proved an excellent aircraft, smooth and easy to fly, even at maximum weight of 94,797 lb. Maximum and cruising speeds were 220 and 181 mph, and the range was exactly the specified 6,000 km, payload varying with headwind from 5,776 to 12,080 lb. By this time no fewer than four six-engined boats were being worked on at Marignane, the others being the first Laté 631 and two SE200s, as described later.

On 11 November 1942 Germany invaded what had been Unoccupied France. Once more the CAMS 161 came under German control, and though for a time the occupying power permitted Cdt Bonnot and Lts Husson and Pierret to oversee the test programme it was not long before things changed. At first it was suggested that all the giant French boats should be hired by Deutsche Luft Hansa, but predictably there was prolonged argument and an interruption to flying. In April 1943 all the aircraft in the previously Unoccupied Zone were ordered to be painted with German insig-

nia, and where the big boats were concerned the call sign was based on the aircraft's designation and prototype number. The result for the Potez-CAMS was thus 16+11 (161 No 1). In January 1943 it had been planned to move all of them to a heavy-seaplane base at Amphion, on Lake Geneva, but this plan fell through. Further delay was caused by the death of the assigned test pilot, Yves Lantz, testing a Sartrouville-built Do24.

He was replaced by Charley Descamps, a Potez pilot since 1935. He flew to Marignane in August 1943, but the desultory flying continued to be done by the official test crew under L.V. Husson until Descamps took over on 29 September. On 9 December it was announced that the 161 had been officially 'seized' and would be transferred to Germany. One of many legends concerning the aircraft is that it was destroyed by Allied bombing at Friedrichshafen, together with a Laté 631 and an SE200. In fact it never went there, but it did almost get destroyed in an attack on 10 March 1944 by 30 Lancasters on Marignane. Accordingly, in early April two Luftwaffe officers arrived (by train): Oblt Busse and Fdw Uwe Petersen, test pilot from the Erprobungsstelle at Travemünde. After familiarizing themselves with the complex aircraft, assisted on each flight by engineers Vaubourdolle and Allarie, and with 25 French workers also on board to reduce the likelihood of sabotage, the 161 was ferried on 20 April to Travemünde, escorted by fighters. Slight problems with an engine were then rectified before, the next day, the big boat was flown east to its final destination, the naval air base at Bug on the island of Rügen.

Among other things the 161 was studied for a bold attack on New York. This would have involved fitting a Bf109G on top, Mistel-fashion, a take-off from Biscarosse and a refuelling in mid-Atlantic from a U-boat! The scheme was not abandoned until 21 August 1944. Soon afterwards the US Army Air Force solved the problem of what to do with this fine aircraft. Returning from Berlin on 18 September Cadet Yellow section of the 357th Fighter Squadron (Lts Drew, Rogers and Travis) noticed the monster — which was not under its customary camouflage nets — from 13,000 ft. They took their P-51Ds down to sea level and destroyed it, recording the strafing kill as a BV222.

41 Martin 170 Mars

The late 1930s were a period of high international tension which, among other things, resulted in vast numbers of aircraft being ordered, often in an atmosphere of near-panic, to try to build up strength. Predictably, many of the types ordered proved to be either unacceptable designs or even fundamentally ill thought-out. Among the latter were large flying boats, such as the Shetland, BV222 and 238, Do214, the six-engined French boats and the Martin Mars. None accomplished much, and some that had been planned as giant ocean patrollers never flew a single combat mission. But the Mars did find useful employment as a transport.

Except for the French boats all these types were conceived as maritime reconnaissance bombers, and the reason for their huge size was so that they would have the greatest possible range and endurance. Today, when twin-jet widebodies can easily carry 50-ton payloads 5,000 miles, it is hard for us to comprehend the desperate struggle fought by the designers 50 years ago to get a range even half as long. The brochure figure for range of the US Navy versions of the Liberator — about the longest-ranged aircraft then in service anywhere — was 2,750 miles. The big Coronado four-engined flying boat could carry its bomb load 1,370 miles (this is range, the radius of action being less than half as much). So we can see that it was no small challenge when in early 1938 the US Navy asked for a patrol bomber with a range as near to 5,000 miles as possible. This obviously meant a giant aircraft, and it was taken

The XPB2M-1 photographed off the Eastern seaboard on 15 July 1942. (Glenn L. Martin via Philip Jarrett)

It's 21 July 1945, and Hawaii Mars, *the first JRM, is launched bedecked with Navy signal flags. She flew on the same day.* (Via John Stroud)

for granted at the outset that, because of the take-off and landing run needed, it would be a flying boat.

Martin immediately set about planning the Model 170 as a conventional single-hull machine, with four of the powerful Duplex Cyclone engines mounted on the leading edge of the tapered high wing. Because of the sheer size of the aircraft there was no need for a pylon, as in the PBY, or a kinked gull wing, as in Martin's PBM. The wing was beautiful, as one might have expected from a company with so much stressed-skin experience. Leading and trailing edges were straight from the root to the almost pointed tips, dihedral was only that caused by the taper in depth, and the aspect ratio was no less than 10.9, so that even with a span of exactly 200 ft the area was only 3,683 sq ft. Features included two main spars, ailerons which extended right to the tips, and extremely large slotted flaps with hydraulic actuation. The hull was almost a scaled version of that of the PBM Mariner, though the sides were vertical. The tail again resembled that of the PBM in that the horizontal surfaces had dihedral, so that the oval fins and rudders, attached at 90°, were tilted inwards.

Remarkably, almost all fuel was housed in six integral tanks in the bottom of the hull, each with a capacity of 1,665 gal. Auxiliary tanks in the huge but otherwise empty wings brought the total capacity up to 11,008 gal, which I believe was a world record when the Model 170 was built. The engines fitted were R-3350-18, each rated at 2,200 hp and driving Curtiss Electric three-blade propellers with a diameter of 16 ft 6 in. Little was ever disclosed about armament, but the design load of bombs, mines or similar stores was 24,000 lb, and provision was made for six gun positions including power-driven turrets at the nose and tail identical to those used on PBMs. Empty and gross weights were 75,573 lb and 144,000 lb, overall length was 112 ft 9 in, crew complement 11, and maximum and cruising speeds 221 and 149 mph.

The single Model 170 was ordered on 23 August 1938, with designation XPB2M-1 and Navy Bureau No 1520. The huge boat was launched from the Middle River, Baltimore, plant on 5 November 1941, and at this time it was certainly the most powerful aeroplane ever built, by a short head over the B-19, and the fuselage was the most capacious. One of the last things to be settled was to fit fixed wingtip floats, each attached by a vee of broad aerofoil-profile struts. Armament was not fitted. Even then the first flight was delayed until 3 July 1942 by the loss of a propeller blade during ground running, which not only pierced the hull but also resulted in the engine catching fire and eventually falling into the water.

By the time flight testing started, the Navy regretted the money spent on what obviously was not going to be a reconnaissance bomber. The XPB2M had no armour, self-sealing tanks or any other of the equipment, such as radar, which World War 2 had shown to be essential. On the other hand it probably had greater lifting power than any other aircraft in the world. During 1943 No 1520 was converted as far as possible into a transport. Though it was very much a compromise, the result was still a flying boat of impressive capabilities. She re-emerged in December 1943 in wartime Sea Blue and White, with turrets faired over and a totally rebuilt interior. Redesignated XPB2M-1R, she was handed to a Navy crew who loaded her with 13,000 lb of cargo and, taking off at 148,500 lb, flew non-stop 4,375 miles to Natal (Recife), Brazil. No other aircraft in the world could have done this.

As a result, in 1944 the Navy ordered 20 purpose-designed JRM-1 Mars transports, to be shared equally between Naval Air Transport Service squadrons VR-1 (Norfolk, Virginia) and VR-2 (Alameda, California). Numbered 76819-76838, they were almost totally redesigned structurally, apart from the wing, with unobstructing frames instead of bulkheads, strong tie-down floors with steel skid tracks, rollers and ball mats, an overhead travelling crane with 5,000 lb capacity, and carefully arranged loading doors and hatches. The tail was redesigned with a single fin and rudder which increased height from 34 ft 6 in to 44 ft 7 in. The engines were 2,300 hp R-3350-8, driving four-blade Curtiss propellers, and among many other changes was an increase in cargo capacity from 2,970 cu ft in the −1R to 4,010 cu ft, mainly by redesigning the

structure but partly by extending the bow forwards and the rear step about 4 ft aft.

The first JRM-1, named *Hawaii Mars*, was flown on 21 July 1945. Finished in Midnight Blue all over, it looked the capable transport that it was, but unfortunately — through no fault of the aircraft — it foundered on 5 August after what was officially called a 'semi-controlled landing'. Thus, the first to join VR-2, in February 1946, was *Marshall Mars*. By this time the war was over, the Navy had cut back the 20 boats to five, and abandoned plans to use JRMs on the Atlantic with VR-1 (which had been looking forward to flying to Europe non-stop, which was more than any USAAF transport could do). By autumn 1946 the *Marianas* and *Philippine Mars* were in service, and in 1947

Today two of the noble Martins are still serving, but as fire bombers: C-FLYJ Marianas Mars, seen here in action, and FLYK Philippine Mars. (Via Mike Hooks)

the four boats flew 7,900 hr with VR-2, carrying everything from 20-ton coral crushers to admirals and their families.

Martin never built the numerous planned post-war civil versions, all to be powered by the Pratt & Whitney Wasp Major engine, but the Navy did agree to this engine being installed in the last boat, 76824. Designated JRM-2, this aircraft flew in July 1947 and then spent an intensive year testing before, after flying the 4,290 miles non-stop from Hawaii, she was formally christened *Caroline Mars* at Chicago on 25 August 1948. Empty and gross weights were, respectively, 80,311 lb and 165,000 lb. The 3,000 hp R-4360-4 engines enabled payload on the Alameda-Hawaii run to be almost doubled, to 38,000-40,000 lb, and cruising speed was increased to 173 mph. Not to be outdone, *Marshall Mars* flew from Alameda to San Diego on 19 May 1949 carrying 301 Navy personnel and her crew of seven, which I am sure was a world record. Just a week later the USAF received the XC-99, described later but, surprisingly, never went for a 'most people' record.

Normal load for a JRM was 132 troops and equipment or 84 stretcher patients plus nine medical attendants, though during the Korean war 100 casualties was a common load. In 1949-50 the four JRM-1s were brought up to JRM-2 standard, with minor differences, being redesignated JRM-3. The XPB2M-1R, which for years had been called *The Old Lady*, was scrapped. In 1950 *Marshall Mars* was lost due to a fuel leak and explosion, but without any injuries. The remaining four boats were withdrawn from 1956 and sold for scrap. Fortunately, Forest Industrial Flying Tankers saw possibilities, and the first was converted into a water bomber by Fairey Aviation at Victoria, British Columbia, in 1958-60. The 6,000-gal water tanks could be replenished in a low run over a lake or sea inlet, and dumped in various ways through side doors. This aircraft crashed into trees during a drop on a fire, and a second was destroyed at its moorings by a hurricane. This leaves just two, which to this day — as C-FLYK and FLYL — have fought fires using part of the original fuel tankage for the extinguishant, dumped through bottom doors. Yet again, not remotely like anything the designer intended.

42 SNCASE SE200

Second of the great flying boats to be accepted by the French Air Ministry as likely to meet the specification of March 1936 (*see Potez-CAMS 161*), the SE200 was originally designed by Lioré et Olivier. This famous company had designed two outstanding commercial transport flying boats during the 1930s, and its design staff at Vitrolles (Marignane suburb) expected to produce the eventual winner for the company which in June 1937 was formed as Air France Transatlantique.

As explained (*Potez-CAMS*) the original specification called for a flying boat with six engines to carry 20 sleeping passengers across the North Atlantic. Lioré et Olivier came up with a design with a gross weight of 92,593 lb powered by either GR14N or Wright R-1820 Cyclone radial engines of 1,100 hp each. When the requirement was upgraded to sleep 40 passengers the design had to be slightly enlarged and completely restressed to operate at a weight of 149,912 lb, a figure later slightly increased. The engines were changed to the Wright Cyclone 14, the same GR-2600 as selected for the Laté 631. Work went ahead as the LeO H.49 Amphitrite, and in late 1937 two prototypes

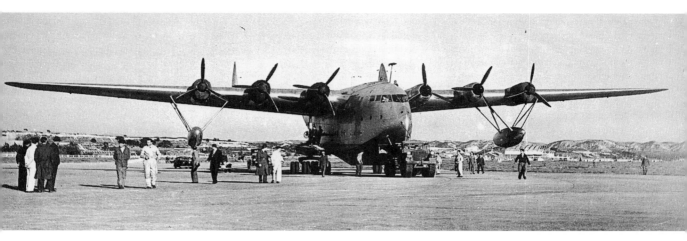

The war is over, the sun is shining and the only surviving SE200 is pulled from the Marignane factory — on 2 April 1946 far from repaired — for her first flight. The engines were GR14Rs. (SCA via John Stroud)

were ordered. However, under the 1936 law for the nationalization of all defence industries, Lioré et Olivier was absorbed into the national SNCASE (Société Nationale de Constructions Aéronautiques de Sud-Est). The H.49 was redesignated as the SE200.

A mock-up of the forward fuselage, inboard wing and engine was displayed at the Paris Salon of 1939 (bearing the name *Rochambeau*, an 18th century general). By this time the engines for both aircraft had been imported, and major components of aircraft 01 were being assembled at Marignane, on the Etang de Berre. The collapse of France led to a temporary cessation of work, but as Vitrolles/Marignane was in the Unoccupied Zone it was possible in early 1941 to get Vichy permission for a resumption. At about this time an order was placed for two further SE200s, to the same standard as the first. Eventually, painted with the regulation tricolour bands on wings, hull and rudders, and with the registration F-BAHE, aircraft 01 was flown on 18 August 1942.

Though it looked pugnacious, rather than graceful like the Laté 631, the SE200 was perhaps the most impressive of the three big French boats. The fuselage, or hull, was fractionally shorter than that of the 631, at 135 ft 8 in, but its cross-section and therefore internal volume were considerably larger. This big cross-section made it possible to

have two full-length decks. The upper deck contained the cockpit in the extreme nose. Jacques Lecarme, who was not only chief engineer but also headed the test pilot team, and was at the controls on the first flight, told the author that he had been impressed by the Short S.23 'Empire' boat, and had come to the conclusion that a flightdeck right at the front could offer reduced drag, a better all-round view and better use of the available hull volume. All engine and propeller controls were hung from the roof, so there was no obstructing console between the pilots. It was thus simple to walk down a few steps under the instrument panel to open the hatch in the extreme bows for mooring the craft. There was a further rather cramped mooring position in the tail. Unlike the rival boats, the upper deck not only included the usual crew rest provisions but also extended aft of the wing to provide additional passenger accommodation. Each main-deck cabin provided seats for four passengers by day and berths for all four at night, and had a close pair of windows, as in the Boeing 314. The two main doors were

F-BAIY proceeds towards Berre Lake, surrounded and followed by a crowd of well-wishers. Fuselage volume was a little more than double that of a Sunderland. (SCA via John Stroud)

on the lower deck, on the right side at the front and at the extreme rear on the left side, each in a vestibule leading up or down to the two decks. Though never fully furnished there is little doubt the SE200 could have carried 32 sleeping passengers on the North Atlantic, and probably the stipulated 40. On shorter ranges 70 were specified, in a volume which in a modern airliner would seat about 200!

The huge left and right wings were each manufactured as a single unit, joined on the sides of the hull to a massive bridge structure. Span was 171 ft 3 in, wing area 3,660 sq ft, and almost all of the sharp taper was on the trailing edge. On each side were three sections of hydraulically driven slotted flap and a two-piece aileron which, like the tail controls, was hydraulically boosted and also linked to an autopilot. The three engines on each wing were slightly canted outwards to be at right angles to the leading edge. Ratier electrically controlled feathering (and later reversing) propellers were fitted, the diameter being 14 ft 1 in. A total of 7,919 gal of fuel could be carried in bag tanks in the main wing box, all of it inboard of the outer engines. It was intended to fit thermal deicing, though this was absent from aircraft 01.

The tail had twin fins and rudders mounted on the tips of a tailplane which had dihedral, though nothing like as much as the Laté 631. The shape of the vertical surfaces was almost identical to that of the prototypes of the LeO 45 bomber. Unlike that much smaller aircraft, the big flying boat's tail seems to have been right from the start, instead of being the subject of endless changes. Unlike the two rival boats the SE200 had fixed stabilizing floats, though these were mounted directly under the outer engines and Lecarme said it had been their intention later to make them retractable.

On 11 November 1942 the Germans occupied the whole of France. In April 1943 the German authorities gave notice that they would seize the SE200 and Laté 631 (the 161 was taken later). The French sent a delegation to Wiesbaden to argue that the commercial character of these boats precluded them from being seized as war material, only to be told that the Germans attached 'great importance to these flying boats with a long radius of action'. From 7 January 1944 sentries guarded the boats day and night to prevent attack by the Maquis. On 15 January came a final order stating that 'every aircraft manufactured in France during the Armistice period is considered war material'.

F-BAHE by this time had been painted in German markings, with call sign 20+01 (200 No 1). A German crew arrived on 16 January and, after what must have been a very hurried conversion course, ferried the monster on the following day with fighter escort to the base at Friedrichshafen, on the Bodensee. On the following day, the 18th, a French meeting announced that it was terminating discussion of the fate of the SE200, which in view of the circumstances seemed reasonable. The Germans planned to put the big boat into service with 3/KG200, Haupt Theodor Queens being placed in charge of a ZBV (special missions unit) to carry out operations requiring very long-range aircraft. This unit, at staffel strength had one or two Ju290s, but these lacked the range of the French flying boats.

RAF Bomber Command put paid to the notion. On 10 March 1944 a small force of Lancasters made a precision attack on Marignane during which SE200 02, which had German markings and code 20+02, was completely destroyed before it had flown. The 03 and 04 boats were in the factory, only just beginning final assembly, and they were damaged. A little over a month later another Lancaster force raided Friedrichshafen. In this attack SE200 01 was also destroyed, along with Laté 631 No 01.

After the liberation SNCASE came under the technical direction of André Vautier. He surveyed the damaged parts of boat 03 and recommended that it be completed. No 04 was abandoned, though it was to have been the first with retractable floats. To save now-scarce dollars 03 was fitted with 1,600 hp Gnome-Rhône 14R 26/27 engines, and it differed from its predecessors in many details. Empty and gross weights were 72,191 and 158,730 lb, an excellent ratio, and range with full payload was 3,766 miles at 190 mph. Part of the funding came from the Defence Ministry, so 03 bore military roundels as well as civil registration F-BAIY. It was first flown on 2 April 1946. Though a thoroughly satisfactory aircraft, the decision was taken not to pursue the programme any further.

SNCASE President Georges Hereil did, however, sanction the design of a completely new and even bigger flying boat, to be powered by turboprops and to weigh 140 tonnes. A one-third scale model, the SE1210, was flown in 1949. This had a span of 68 ft 7 in and was powered by four 300 hp Renault engines. Wisely, the full-scale machine was not built.

43 Latécoère 631

Longest, and perhaps the best-looking, of the trio of big French flying boats of the wartime period, the Latécoère 631 was the only one to be continued as a programme after the war. It even entered revenue service, but it was dogged by misfortune and after several had been lost the remainder were withdrawn. They were nevertheless beautiful aircraft, and deserved the backing of a strong and technically capable company. Instead Pierre Latécoère had progressively ceased to exert a competitive driving force, and when he died in early 1944 M Moine took over merely to see the 631 programme through. I believe the resources were inadequate to tackle the serious problems that were encountered.

The requirements of the Air Ministry specification of March 1936 were outlined in the story of the Potez-CAMS 161. SIAL — Société Industrielle d'Aviation Latécoère — put in a submission, discovered the

Laté No 02 seen on test in 1945. Later in the year this aircraft suffered a propeller failure which killed two passengers. (SCA via John Stroud)

requirement had been significantly upgraded and so put in a second proposal, the Type 631. Together with the rival LeO H.49 (*See SNCASE SE200 p.168*) this was accepted in July 1938, a single prototype being ordered. At an unknown pre-war date a second was also ordered. Design and construction, under MM Jarry and Moine, went ahead with all speed, though at that time the small Toulouse design office was still working on the 521/523 (*see earlier*) and on the 611 long-range reconnaissance flying boat, itself no mean project.

War further interrupted the 631 programme. Moreover, Gnome-Rhône failed to develop the intended engine, the 1,500 hp GR18L, but the company managed to redesign the 631 to take the Wright Cyclone 14, at first in the same 1,300 hp form as used in the first Boeing 314. In 1939 Latécoère imported six engines, little knowing that it would then be cut off for five years from any more. By late 1941 many major parts for both the 01 and 02 aircraft were nearing completion. The company had been in the habit of transporting parts of its large flying boats to Biscarosse for assembly, but this was now just inside the Occupied Zone. Accordingly, the parts for 01 were instead taken to the Marignane airbase on the eastern shore of the great Etang (lake) de Berre, not far from Marseilles. Here test pilots Pierre Grespy and Prévost, with a crew of five, made the

first flight on 4 November 1942.

Of course, the 631 was a modern stressed-skin aircraft, and with flying boats as big as this there was no problem in mounting the wing on top of the hull and still having the propellers sufficiently clear of the sea. The wing was made as a centre section of the same width as the hull, two inner wings and two outers, though taper and dihedral were uniform throughout. Span was 188 ft 5 in, and area 3,768 sq ft. Each wing tapered equally on the leading and trailing edges to elliptical tips, and there were no bracing struts. The shapely hull was 142 ft 7 in long, and though the original design weight was 66 tonnes the production 631 weighed 75 tonnes (165,344 lb), at which the draught was 70 in. There were two decks, the upper including all flight crew positions as well as a cabin for crew rest. For guidance when manoeuvring on the water, and for mooring, doors could be opened in the bows and in the extreme tail. The tail itself was what the French call Type U, with twin fins and rudders carried entirely above the tailplane, which had dihedral. In fact the military Type 611 had been redesigned in 1936 to have an almost identical tail, so this was almost a known quantity before the first flight.

Another almost known quantity, again because of the 611, was the stabilizing float, retracting electrically to be housed behind the outer engines, though in the case of the

631 most of the retracted float was enclosed by hinged doors. On the 01 boat all engines rotated in the same direction, driving Ratier electric propellers of 14 ft 1 in diameter. To conform to the specification, access to all engines could be gained by riding on a trolley along the leading edge. Remarkably, fuel was housed in integral tanks — I believe these were the first in Europe? — three in each wing inter-spar box, total capacity being 10,999 gal. I am sure this was, next to the Mars, a world record. Each wing had hydraulically positioned Fowler flaps and two-section ailerons which, like the tail controls, were boosted by a servo command system.

In conformity with all French civil aircraft at this time No 01 was painted with the diagonal tricolour bands across the wings (four bands) and across the front and rear fuselage, with vertical stripes on the rudders. Registration was F-BAHG. The aircraft completed 40 hrs of ground running and 50 hrs of flight, but on 11 November 1942, just a week after the first flight, the whole of France was occupied. In April 1943 F-BAHG was repainted in the regulation grey and orange, with black nose and tail, for a Vichy civil aircraft, together with German insignia and the radio code 63+11 (631 No 1). On 22 January 1944, following long arguments, 63+11 was flown with a fighter escort to Friedrichshafen, on the Bodensee in Ger-

Laté 631 No 04 taking off down Southampton Water, past Netley Royal Victoria Hospital. This aircraft was not named. Sadly, it joined the list of 631s that crashed. (Temple Press via Philip Jarrett).

many. On 27 April 1944 it was destroyed there by Lancasters.

All the major structural parts for Laté 631 No 02 had been completed by the summer of 1942, but no engines could be imported. Amazingly, though the Germans knew that a second machine had been ordered, all the parts were hidden in the forests around Toulouse, remaining undiscovered even when the region was occupied by German troops in November 1942. During 1942 the Vichy government ordered aircraft 03 and 04. Very shortly after VE-Day (8 May 1945) a further seven aircraft were ordered, but there is confusion over this. I was told by M Moine that, discounting the first two prototypes, 'nine series aircraft were built, the first six for Air France'. This tallies with Latécoère archives, which describe 11 aircraft as having been ordered altogether. But there is no doubt that, if No 11 was ever completed (which is most unlikely), it was never flown.

Once the German forces had left the Toulouse region in September 1944 the parts of 631 No 02 were gathered together, sent to Biscarosse and the aircraft completed with all speed, six new R-2600-A5B engines of 1,600 hp each being imported from the USA. The propellers remained Ratier three-bladers, Type 1892. During the war it was reported in Britain that the Vichy government was to name the first two 631s *Maréchal Pétain* and *Amiral Lartigue*, but in fact 02 was the first to receive a name, and (the war being over) the name was *Lionel de Marnier*; registration was F-BANT. This aircraft first flew on 6 March 1945.

In October 1945 02 made a publicity tour of South America. On 31 October, during a flight from Rio to Buenos Aires, a fatigue crack in the light-alloy hub of No 2 propeller finally ruptured, releasing a blade. This blade knocked out engine No 3 and then penetrated the hull in an almost perpendicular attitude, causing a gash about 7 ft high. It then killed a Brazilian journalist and mortally injured a French cameraman before coming to rest on the far side in a baggage hold. Engine 3 was a complete mess, and No 2 was hanging on its mounts but still rotating and causing severe vibrations. Capt Moulignié skilfully put 02 down on a lake, despite three of the servo-command pipes being severed. Eventually engines 2 and 7 were swapped over so that the boat could take off on four engines and fly to Montevideo for full repairs. Asking about this horrific incident some years later, a friend of mine was told 'We've cured the problem; we removed that row of seats!'

Despite this, Air France did take delivery of three of the giant boats, 03 F-BANU, named *Guillaumet*, 04 F-BDRA and 06 F-BDRC. These were the first 631s to be fully furnished, for 46 sleeping passengers. Powered by 1,900 hp R-2600-C14BB engines, they cruised at 199 mph and with a gentle headwind took 10 hr 40 min on the 1,990-mile South Atlantic crossing. Passengers went by train to Biscarosse and then flew in the giant *hexamoteur* via Port Etienne to Fort de France in the Antilles. Services began on 5 July 1947. Like many flying boats of the period the 631s were lavish in the space devoted to bars, kitchens, smoking rooms and individual toilets for each cabin! Can you wonder that some older passengers, queueing for a toilet in a modern wide-body, wonder if we really make progress?

On 21 February 1948 aircraft 07, F-BDRD, which had been assembled at the Le Havre factory, crashed into the Channel soon after leaving on its delivery to Biscarosse. The cause was never fully understood, but as a severe snow blizzard was in progress, and the 631 had no deicing equipment, it was thought the weather might have been a factor. The unfortunate factory manager was even brought to trial, it being thought that he might have been in some way negligent, but of course nobody could prove a case against him. As for the Air France boat 06, on 1 August 1948 this simply vanished in mid-Atlantic, with over 50 on board. Nobody had the slightest idea what happened, and for a time all 631s were grounded. Air France stopped 631 services permanently.

Eventually SEMAF (Société d'Exploitation du Matériel Aéronautique Française) was formed in January 1949 to operate the remaining boats on long-distance cargo services to Africa, Indo-China and South America. The No 08 aircraft F-BDRE was used in a gruelling and dangerous test programme involving 500 hr of flight in which every effort was made to fatigue the engine/propeller groups. This finally produced a régime in which different engines were held either at 50 rpm above or 50 rpm below the nominal cruise setting, each régime being varied every two minutes. On 28 March 1950 aircraft 04, BDRA, took-off in fine weather from Arcachon, near Biscarosse, to test this routine, and within a very short time dived into the Bay of Biscay off Cap Ferret. This triggered off a further investigation whose final report looked at least an inch thick. I won't go into detail, but it was discovered, and proved in a Chalais-Meudon wind tunnel, that engine vibrations could be multiplied by resonance in the outer wing which, over a period, reacted with aileron flutter to cause structural failure. I failed to see how all this could have happened without its being obvious to all on board.

It was decided to mount a salvage operation, and most of BDRA was recovered, but no light was shed on the sequence of events. SEMAF was dissolved. Nevertheless, it looked as if the Achilles heel of the 631 was now understood, and as 08 had by late 1950 flown just over 600 hours exploring the symptoms, it was considered worth carrying out a major rebuild to eliminate the problem, and also convert 08 into a more effective freighter. New outer wings and ailerons were designed, with different aileron mass distribution and a modified control system. Just behind the wing a cargo door was inserted, 99 in high and 63 in wide, the floor strengthened, lifting tackle added and the interior cleared to provide 6,360 cu ft of space for a load of 20 tons for 1,860 miles or 22 tons for 1,553 miles. The C14BB engines (some documents say R-2600-20, but that is a military designation) were geared at 16:7 to modified Ratier reverse-pitch propellers. Painted in the livery of Compagnie France-Hydro, the almost rebuilt 631 made a round trip Biscarosse-Saigon-Berre, completed on 15 April 1952, under the command of M Demouveaux, a CFH director. No 08 then went to Cameroun, where in 15 months it carried 3,300 tons of cotton from Lake Lèrè, in the north, to Douala, carrying fuel and other cargo on the return trips, often calling at Fort Lamy.

Charles E. Brown snapped the busy port of South-ampton — nearest ship, the liner Orontes *— as F-BDRA flew past in take-off configuration. Flaps had to be retracted before raising the floats. (Via R.T. Riding)*

In 1954 it was decided to modify the six remaining boats for use by CFH, and in 1955 No 02, which had had the original propeller accident, was rebuilt to the same standard as 08. But it was not to be. On 10 September 1955 No 08, flown by Cdt Demouveaux, crashed in north Cameroun, in the region of Sambolabo. At this point the general feeling was 'enough is enough'.

44 CCF B-1000 and B-2000B

Most readers will be familiar with the lifelong struggle of Vincent Justus Burnelli to see his lifting-body aircraft replace the traditional kind. His idea was that the fuselage should have the shape of a segment of a giant wing, with chord equal to the

length of the aircraft. Later he toned this down and carried the tail on slim beams, while sticking to the basic idea of the lifting body. One of the obvious shortcomings was that such a fuselage is unsuitable for pressurization, unless a few tons of re-

inforcement are added to tie together a 'quilted' top and bottom. The basic difficulty was that, like many things in life, you win some and you lose some. The Burnelli had many attractive features, but it had at least as many drawbacks, so the world never adopted the idea. Perhaps we are now moving even beyond Burnelli's layout, with the Spanloader cargo aircraft described later. Sadly, Burnelli increasingly felt (possibly with some justification) that he was the victim of political chicanery which persistently suppressed the superiority of his ideas.

Some of the last Burnelli designs were very large projects designed at the Canadian Car & Foundry Co's Cancargo Aircraft Division at Montreal. Cancargo had a capable designer in Charles Villiers, and one

Burnelli-type aircraft, the much smaller CBY-3 Loadmaster, was actually built and flown in 1945, enjoying a good career. But the giants were on the drawing board in 1942. The B-1000 was a commercial transport, with a span of 220 ft, wing area of 4,499 sq ft, and empty and gross weights of 120,000 and 220,000 lb, respectively. Engines were to be eight 2,500 hp Allison V-3420 (each comprising two V-1710 engines joined by a common gearbox), geared in pairs so that 5,000 hp was available for each 21 ft propeller. It was to carry 135 passengers and baggage 4,500 miles at 220 mph.

The B-2000B was the final form of the bomber version. For some reason this had 1 ft added to each wingtip, but (apart from being a bomber, carrying bombs and

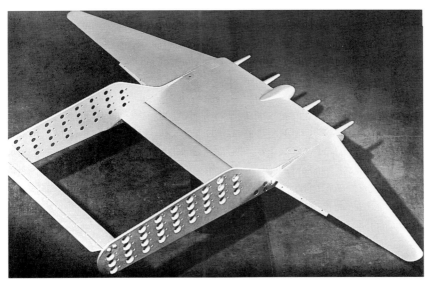

Above *Head-on view of a model of the B-1000. Burnelli claimed it offered 'less drag than the best conventional plane, and 1.5 times the floor area and volume'. Burnelli via R.T. Riding)*

Left *The wind-tunnel model of the B-1000 used to establish comparative figures with traditional aircraft in a report by Dr Max Munk of 3 July 1943. (Burnelli via R.T. Riding)*

bristling with turrets) the chief difference was that its tail was carried on two booms of traditional type, to provide mountings for two dorsal, two ventral and two tail turrets. (The B-1000 had a later arrangement in which the wing was extended even further aft so that the triple-finned tail could be mounted directly on it). The B-2000B was to carry a 40,000-lb bombload 4,000 miles, even when burdened by seven turrets each with twin 20mm cannon. It was submitted to compete against the Northrop XB-35 and Convair XB-36. Either Burnelli's figures were optimistic nonsense, or the Army Air Force ought to have considered it a little more seriously than they did.

45 Dornier Do214

The trouble with the Do214 is that it was never completed and flown. Reading the specification confirms that it would have been an impressive aircraft, but it is only when you start plotting its numbers on a graph that the surprising fact emerges that it would have had twice as much installed horsepower as it should have had!

We left the Dornier *Grossraumflugschiffe* (huge flying boat) story with the unbuilt Do20, a kind of modernised Do X of 1936. We now pick it up again in 1938, with Claude Dornier getting a positive reaction from both the RLM and Luft Hansa to his proposal that he should build a giant flying boat, bigger and much heavier than the BV222, for passenger operations on the North Atlantic. He always liked tandem engines, and so he proposed to use eight engines of 4,000 hp each, four tractors and four pushers. Dornier was confident a 4,000 hp engine would become available in time, even if it meant doubling up two engines on one reduction gear and propeller.

The programme went ahead with the RLM 8-series number Do214. At first it bore company project number P93, specifying the carriage of 36 sleeping passengers for 6,000 km (3,728 miles), such as Lisbon-New York,

Model of the civil Do214. (Dornier)

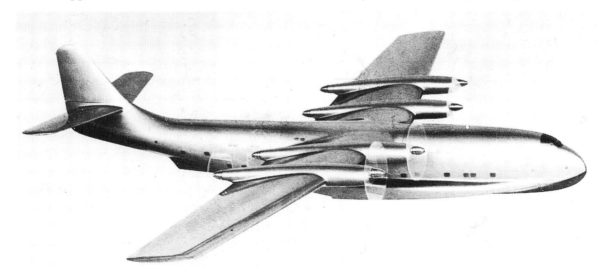

at 249 mph, the boat weighing 100 tonnes. A firm go-ahead came in June 1939, and tunnel and tank testing followed. A one-fifth scale model was made by Hütter & Schempp-Hirth, the span being 39 ft 5 in; it was designated Göttingen Gö8. Hull construction began in August 1939, but in early 1939 the RLM had decreed that so big a project must have military uses. Accordingly the Do214 was recast with six variants: P192-07, the baseline transport, with range reduced to 1,552 miles with a payload of 28 tonnes or 320 armed troops; P192-08, ambulance, range 2,205 miles with 93 stretchers and 100 sitting patients; P192-03, assault transport with 31-tonne payload; P192-06, fuel transport, 31-tonne load carried in special tanks; P-192-05, mine transport and layer, 25 tonne load; P192-04, U-boat supplier.

Dornier published a detailed description of the Do214, but I will let the illustrations do most of the talking. One interesting feature was the way lateral stability on the water was to be ensured by streamlined sponsons in the form of a bulge extending most of the length of the hull. Dornier called them beads. Apart from the fact they had flat bottoms these almost resembled the protective outer hull of early battleships! Each wingtip formed a sealed float, not normally to enter the water. Flight controls were metal-skinned, fitted with full-span tabs and signalled electrically. The eight engines were to be Daimler-Benz double units, the prototype to have the DB606 (as used in early He177s) and production boats to have the DB613A (3,500 hp) or 613C (4,000 hp), each comprising two DB603G inverted vee-12 engines geared to a common four-blade VDM propeller of 16 ft 5 in diameter. Integral tanks in the bottom of the hull, between frames 20/23 and 26/45, were to house

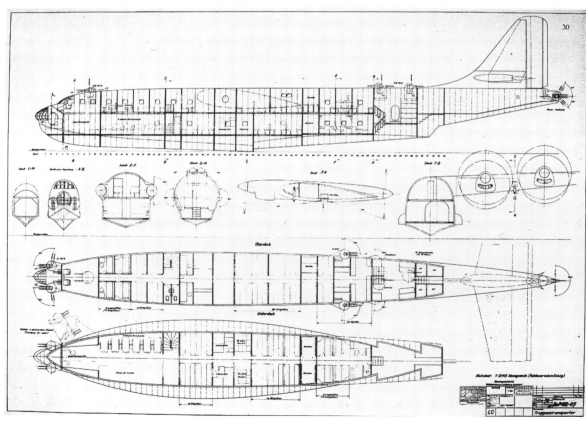

15,068 gal of fuel. In the tanker role tanks above the floor would have carried a further 14,518 gal — awesome figures for 1939-40.

Span would have been 196 ft 10 in, and wing area 5,382 sq ft. Length of the civil version (project of 10 July 1942) would have been 169 ft 3½ in, that of the military 192-07 being about 175 ft. Gross weight would have varied slightly, the civil version weighing 145 tonnes (319,665 lb). Maximum speed was estimated at 304mph. The crew would have numbered 12 for the civil boat and 15 for the military 192-07, eight of the latter being gunners. The tail turret would have had three MG151/20 cannon, and the seven other turrets two each. In most of the military versions the entire bows, with left and right twin-cannon turrets, would have hinged round to the right to open the interior for loading.

Dornier had a deep emotional attachment to giant flying boats. Prof Dornier told me in the early 1950s how sad his team were when, in late 1943, the RLM decided the manpower should be diverted to more immediate war-winning projects. He said 'The 214 represented the pinnacle of the design of large flying boats. It would still be a valid proposition today, but of course with turbo-propeller engines.'

46 Short Shetland

In 1938 both Saunders-Roe Ltd (Saro) at East Cowes, and Short Brothers at Rochester were studying the next generation of large flying boats. Saro had just received a contract for a big machine for long-range reconnaissance, and Short was awarded a similar contract not long afterwards. In 1940 the specification was revised (upwards, of course) in R.14/40. To save manpower the two firms, previously rivals, were asked to collaborate on one design. This was given the Short designation S.35, and named

Shetland. In parallel the S.36 was studied as a long-range landplane bomber, but this never got off the drawing board. Like its predecessors at the two companies the S.35 was to have a high wing of sheet-web Alclad construction carrying four 2,500 hp Bristol Centaurus sleeve-valve radial engines.

Saro was assigned the task of designing and making the wing and engine installations. Of course the design was all-metal, with a cantilever wing mounted high on the deep hull. Overall design control was exercised by Short at Rochester, under Chief Designer Arthur Gouge. He had, in fact, worked closely with his opposite number at Saunders-Roe, Henry Knowler, but in 1943 left Short to become Vice-Chairman of the Cowes company. Right at the start Rochester had to sort out the basic shape, getting the wing in the right place so that one strong frame could bear the loads both from the main wing box and from the step in the underside of the hull. The wing had a span of 150 ft 4 in and area of 2,400 sq ft. It was given all its taper on the leading edge, which slightly eased the problem of correctly locating the engines, fuel and bombs in order to get the CG in the right place. To achieve this the engines were moved well outboard of the hull. To facilitate production the airframe was divided into handy sections, easily worked on in the shop and, in the case of the wing, sent by road from the Isle of Wight.

The bluff-nosed hull had a length of 110 ft and a depth of about 20 ft. The main step was a faired curve, and because of the upredictability of hydrodynamic flows the planing bottom was tested in model form on the Saro A.37 Shrimp, a little four-engined flying boat which had been built in 1939 as a scale model of another big boat that was never built. The results were encouraging, and in fact the S.35 was more or less right from the start. All control surfaces were fully manual, driven via geared tabs and with fabric covering. Earlier Short aircraft had had round-topped Gouge flaps of

impressive chord, but the S.35 was given more efficient slotted flaps. Oddly, these were of constant chord, notwithstanding the sharp taper of the wing, and as in previous Short types they were driven electrically.

The main wing box structure was well forward, the rear of the torsion box being at 25 per cent chord. Left and right boxes were joined by the fuselage frames, which for this purpose were reinforced by massive steel booms, the joints having 3-in diameter pins. In the rear of the inner wings were welded Elektron (magnesium alloy) tanks for 2,928 gal of fuel, and a further 2,681 gal was housed between the wings in the top of the hull. Hardly anything was inside the wing box except an 80-gal oil tank behind each engine. The latter were Centaurus VII, with carburettor intakes above and oil coolers below, and single exhaust pipes. The propellers were DH Hydromatic four-bladers, with a diameter of 16 ft. At first these had large spinners, soon removed.

Offensive armament was to comprise up to 4,000 lb of bombs, mines or depth charges carried in 12 wing cells, six on each side, behind the inner nacelles. The planned defensive armament was nose, dorsal and tail turrets, each with twin 0.5 in guns. Though of Frazer-Nash type, these turrets were driven electrically, and the power demand for maximum-rate elevation and traverse was large. Almost all other auxiliary power services on board were electric also, and after some argument it was decided to generate 28V DC in a Rotol plant in an insulated compartment under the flightdeck. Two 60-hp petrol engines drove 20 kW generators. Today big jets have alternators with short-term ratings 10 times as high as this, but in World War 2 a total of 40 kW was impressive. The advantage of a self-contained 'power station' was that, even with the boat moored, current could be generated to load heavy weapons, run bilge pumps, cook meals, heat the interior or charge the batteries. Electro-thermal deicing of the leading edges was also discussed, but in the end a Dunlop fluid system was adopted.

As the war progressed, it became apparent that the Shetlands were going to join the long list of British aircraft that nobody wanted. Virtually all these aircraft ended up as rather inefficient transports, and the huge flying boat joined them. The planned weapon bays, gun turrets and ASV Mk VIc radar were never installed, and instead of Coastal white/grey DX166 emerged on to the Medway on 24 October 1944 in regular camouflage. Empty and gross weights were 75,860 and 125,000 lb. One of the few attractive things was the totally glazed flightdeck, which had working stations for five plus two rest bunks. The pilots could look back across the wings and tail if necessary. On the first flight, on 14 December, the chief test pilots of the two companies were in charge, John Lankester Parker in the left-hand seat and Geoffrey Tyson on the right. Parker, soon to retire, said the control forces were 'nothing like as heavy as on some of the old flying boats'. Maximum speed was 263 mph. Soon afterwards DX166 was partly con-

verted into a proper transport, in all-silver finish, and taken on RAF charge at the MAEE, Felixstowe. Here, before dawn on 28 January 1946, it was burned out at its moorings because someone forgot to open the generating plant's radiator shutters.

The second Shetland was to have been DX171, but instead it was completed as the S.40 Shetland II civil transport. The hull was redesigned with a streamlined bow and stern and accommodation on two decks for 40 passengers, with sleeping facilities for 24. Typical of the times was a 'dining saloon for 12' at the rear on the upper deck and a 'gentlemen's dressing room' downstairs. The engines were civil Centaurus 660s, rated at 2,705 hp, with a cooling fan and groups of individual exhaust stacks. Inboard propellers were reversible. The fuel system was redesigned, and partly by using the weapon bays its capacity was increased to 6,112 gal, increasing loaded weight to 130,000 lb. Another major change was that the flight-control system was redesigned to incorporate Swift Synchromo electric servo units.

The first Shetland is seen here after the war when it had been stripped of its camouflage. Armament was never fitted. (Short Brothers via Mike Hooks)

These were among the earliest British power-boosted control systems, and their rack-and-pinion design today looks clumsy. I have also heard tales of blue sparks, smoke and expensive smells. Similar Synchromo links governed the engine throttles.

The Shetland II was registered G-AGVD and first flown by Tom Brooke-Smith (who succeeded Parker as Chief Test Pilot) and Harold Piper on 17 September 1947. Four years later, with only 180 hr logged, it was scrapped at Belfast. Altogether the Shetland was just one of several dozen British aircraft which were designed and built despite the absence of a customer. The original military specification was almost certainly a mistake.

Short's later civil flying boats were notorious for their profusion of different floor levels, and the No 2 Shetland maintained the tradition. (Via Mike Hooks)

The reason for a giant aircraft is usually to get greater range and endurance, yet the Shetland offered the same weapon load as a Catalina and considerably less range and endurance, despite having more than four times the installed power. Having lost the original market, there seemed no point in continuing with either machine. Short Brothers wisely made no attempt to build various pressurized developments, with compound or turboprop engines.

47 Douglas Globemaster

At the end of World War 2 the British aviation magazines were becoming quite used to receiving news of mightly new aircraft built on the other side of the Atlantic which had no counterpart in Britain. But we still harboured traditional ideas. When, after the war was over, the first picture was received of the first Globemaster, a British magazine called it the XC-74 and reported 'It may be built for the Army Air Forces, but, of course, only in very small numbers'. This was wrong on two counts. First, there was no 'XC' prototype. Second, Douglas began with a straight run of 14, and then followed with no fewer than 448 of an even bigger version, the Globemaster II!

When the United States entered the war the Douglas Santa Monica (Los Angeles) plant was about to fly the first production DC-4, commandeered along with all those on the production line behind it as an olive-drab C-54 for the AAF. But one had only to look at a map of the world to see that to win the war as quickly as possible there would be a great need for transport aircraft much bigger even than the C-54, carrying heavier and bulkier loads over greater distances. It was to help meet this need that in May 1942 design effort began on the Douglas Model 415A, an AAF order for 50 being placed almost immediately as the C-74.

With hindsight we can see that perhaps this ought to have been a high-wing aircraft, with a level floor close to the ground at so-called 'truck-bed height', with a full-width rear ramp door as on the C-130 Hercules. But a complicating factor was that PanAm was beginning to talk to Douglas about a commercial transport in the same size and power class, called the DC-7, and Douglas naturally wanted to combine the two requirements with a common basic design. From the outset this challenging programme was assigned to the huge Long Beach plant. Today this has replaced Santa Monica as the HQ of the whole Douglas empire, but in World War 2 it made aircraft, such as the C-47, A-26 and B-17, but didn't design them. To cut one's teeth on almost the biggest land-plane in the world was quite a challenge, though a handful of B-19 designers were on

hand to assist the growing Long Beach team.

From the start the configuration was that of a scaled-up DC-4, though totally different in detail and in most respects more advanced. For example, the wing had a span of 173 ft 3 in, area of 2,506 sq ft, higher aspect ratio than that of the DC-4, and a later 'laminar' aerofoil profile. Along the trailing edge were Fowler flaps, and though not strictly correct it was said 'These extend across the full span, the outer sections serving as ailerons'. The ailerons did translate aft like the flaps, and did depress to a neutral position at +25° for landing, but differed from the flaps in their geometry.

The vast tubular fuselage had a diameter of 13 ft 2 in. The team working on the DC-7 version for PanAm had to provide for full pressurization, then often called super-charging, to permit long-range cruising at 20,000 ft. The DC-7 was to provide the unprecedented sleeping accommodation for 76 passengers, or 108 by day, and along each side of the fuselage were six large pairs of windows, each pair together forming a flat oval shape as in the DC-4. The DC-7's cargo and baggage areas were to be under the floor. In the C-74 the main floor was about the same size, namely 75 ft by 11 ft 6 in, but it was a tough metal cargo floor with a 20-in grid of tiedown rings. Two electric cranes, each rated at 8,000 lb, could run on rails

The first C-74 on test over a Long Beach oilfield. The bugeye canopies seemed vaguely incongruous. (Douglas Aircraft)

Left *Inside the twin-bugeye cockpit. Note the horizon marker on the left windscreen.* (Douglas Aircraft)

Below right *Now called a Globemaster I, No. 265413 is seen on 9 May 1955 as the first to be rebuilt with a conventional cockpit.* (Douglas Aircraft)

Bottom right *C-124C Globemaster IIs in full production at Long Beach (nearest, a C-124A).* (Douglas Aircraft)

along the whole length. If they were run to the rear they could be connected to a section of floor (complete with the underside of the fuselage) designed to act as a cargo hoist, raised and lowered vertically aft of the wing. Ahead of the wing on the left side was a cargo door 11 ft wide with its own 4,500-lb hoist. Hatches admitted to the lower (underfloor) cargo deck.

The whole nose was devoted to the flight crew, which in the C-74 numbered 13 (10 or 11 more than we would have today). After considerable discussion the cockpit was given two so-called 'bug eye' canopies, one over each pilot. The crew entered via a hatch and ladder under the nose. This admitted to the lower-deck relief compartment, with six bunks. A further ladder provided access to the flightdeck. The separate transparent blisters were considerd to give a better view and less drag than conventional all-round windows. Pressurization also played a part in this seemingly odd choice, but in the case of the military transport the large cargo doors made pressurization difficult. At first Douglas merely said pressurization was 'provided for'; later it was simply ignored.

The tail was simple, and rather surprisingly the rudder and elevators were fabric-skinned, their geometry being almost a direct scale of the DC-4. The landing gears also owed something to the earlier aircraft, though the nose unit had twin wheels. All three units had single legs and retracted forwards hydraulically. The chosen engines were 3,000 hp P&W R-4360-22 Wasp Majors, each driving a 17 ft Hamilton Standard four-blade reversing propeller. The engines were mounted on steel-tube frames extending ahead of the front of the two-spar box of the wing centre section, which had a span of 101 ft 8 in. The spar box was sealed internally to form three integral tanks on each side for a total of 9,138 gal of fuel. Entry doors in the wing root and a leading-edge crawlway allowed all engines to be inspected in flight.

The 50 C-74 Globemasters were to be Douglas Nos 13913/13962, with AAF serials 42-65402/65451. In late 1944 PanAm also ordered 26 of the DC-7 version, but the airline later got cold feet about the operating costs and cancelled the contract. Ironically the airline did buy a fleet of Stratocruisers, which had the same engines but in a much smaller aircraft. Then came VJ-Day in August 1945, and military contracts were cancelled wholesale. In the circumstances Douglas was fortunate to retain the contracts for all C-74s that had reached wing/fuselage mating. This number was 14, so those from 42-65416 onwards were cancelled. The first C-74 made its first flight from Long Beach on 5 September 1945. The rest followed until early 1947. Little modification was needed, though before delivery Sperry A-12 autopilots were installed, and eventually the standard engine was made the R-4360-49, rated at 3,500 hp with water injection and driving four-blade Curtiss Electric propellers. Gross weight was increased from the original 145,000 to 165,000 lb, enabling long sectors to be flown at a pedestrian 176 kts with 55,586 lb of cargo or 125 troops or 115 stretcher casualties with attendants.

On 18 November 1949 a C-74 was the first aircraft to fly the Atlantic with more than 100 persons on board. They proved useful aircraft, but in 1947 Douglas and the newly-formed US Air Force discussed how the Globemaster's proven reliability and lifting capacity could be better used. The handicap had been the need for commonality with the civil DC-7 (which of course bore no relationship to the DC-7 built in the 1950s). Once this need was removed it was possible to fit a much bigger unpressurized double-deck fuselage on the same wing and tail. Accordingly the fifth aircraft, 265406, was completely rebuilt as the prototype YC-124 Globemaster II, making its first flight on 27 November 1949. It was an immediate success, and the type was put into production. Meanwhile, the C-74s were henceforth called

rear hoist were retained, but the body cross-section was increased to give over 10,000 cu ft of usable space. A most important modification was to redesign the forward fuselage to give a characteristic ventral bulge from the nose back to the wing. A new and much shorter nose gear was fitted well back at the lowest part of the bulge. Ahead of this were large left/right clamshell doors and folding ramps enabling large vehicles to drive straight in to the cargo hold. Later this entrance was used to carry Thor and Jupiter ballistic missiles to Europe. Payload was actually slightly reduced, to a maximum of 50,000 lb, but the space and convenience were totally different. A multi-panel upper deck could hinge down, as the two rows of windows show. With this deck in place 200 troops and their equipment could be carried. Alternative loads included 127 stretchers plus 53 sitting patients and attendants.

Douglas delivered the first C-124A in May 1950. A month later the Korean War began, and suddenly the order books lengthened. First came 204 C-124As (Model 1129A), with 3,500 hp R-4360-20WA engines. Then came an order for a tanker (Model 1182E), which was actually completed as the YC-124B. This was not tanker-equipped, but had 5,500 hp YT34 turboprops and a modified tail. Production was completed by 243 C-124C (Model 1317), ending with 52-1089. These were cleared to a weight of 194,500 lb (empty weight, 101,165 lb), and had numerous improvements. Chief among the latter were 3,800 hp R-4360-63A engines, driving 16 ft 7 in Curtiss three-blade propellers, APS-42 weather radar in a nose pimple, and high-capacity combustion heaters in wingtip pods and in the tailcone to deice the wing and tail and heat the fuselage. The improvements were retroactively fitted to most of the C-124As. I travelled from California to Lincolnshire with a Thor IRBM in a C-124C, and can only conclude that it must have been pretty grim before the heaters were fitted, especially as the trip took nearly 40 hr.

Forty years ago the interior of the C-124A was stunning. Even today it would still be useful. (Douglas Aircraft)

Globemaster Is. They continued in service, the only big change being that their characteristic bug-eyes were replaced by a conventional flightdeck roof and side windows. The first to be rebuilt, 265413, was rolled out on 9 May 1955. Surviving C-74s were retired after 1961, three being operated by Aeronaves de Panama.

Basically, the C-124 fuselage was a double-deck version of that of the C-74, though length was slightly increased (addition of radar later extended the length further, to 130 ft 5 in). The two travelling cranes and

48 Northrop B-35 and B-49

One of the truly remarkable coincidences in the history of aviation is that during World War 2 Northrop Aircraft created a fantastic all-wing bomber with a span of 172 ft, and nearly half-a-century later the same company created an even more fantastic all-wing bomber with a span of 172 ft. Today's bomber is, of course, the B-2; and though 172 ft is just as big today as it was in the past, I have omitted the B-2 from this book because in today's world it is not really a giant. Indeed, seen from the side, the wartime flying wings didn't look so big either, but when you walked around one it was breathtaking.

John K. Northrop was convinced that, if you could leave off the bits of an aeroplane that merely contribute weight and drag, such as the fuselage and tail, then a more efficient flying machine ought to result. He built and flew his first flying-wing aircraft in 1928, at first with a tractor propeller and later with a pusher. Perhaps wisely at this stage he kept a simple tail, carried on two thin booms. But on 3 July 1940 hired test pilot Vance Breese made the first, timid, test flight with the N-1M. This twin-engined machine was described by *Time* as 'like a ruptured weather-racked duck, too fatigued to tuck in its wings'. But it was the first truly all-wing aircraft ever to fly successfully. It led to faster and better successors, including one powered by a rocket and another with twin jet engines and a leading edge deliberately strengthened for slicing tails or wings off enemies!

In 1941 the need of the USAAF for a bomber able to make the round trip to Berlin, which led to the enormous B-36, also seemed like a possible opening for a very big flying wing. Basic aerodynamic calculations suggested that, at equal speed, a flying wing could fly 13 to 41 per cent further than a conventional aircraft; that it would need only 75 to 88.5 per cent as much cruise power; and that at full throttle over the tar-

In 1946 the first XB-35 seemed like something from another world, rather as the same-size, same-make B-2 does today. Here it actually has four contraprops, all working! (Northrop Aircraft)

get it would either fly 7 to 18 per cent faster for equal power or else need only 60 to 81.5 per cent as much power. Another advantage was that the wing loading of a typical flying-wing bomber could be around 40 lb/sq ft, compared with 70 to 100 lb/sq ft for conventional bombers, and this meant higher ceiling and probably better manoeuvrability, especially at great heights. Almost the only drawback was that the flying wing found it more difficult to fit very powerful high-lift flaps. This was more than countered by the lower wing loading, and moreover Northrop did overcome the problem.

Of course, even during a war a customer as capable and as accountable as the US Army has to be very sure of what it is doing, especially when large sums of taxpayers' money are involved. The number of people who studied the notion of a flying-wing super-bomber at Wright Field alone exceeded 100 — exceptional for those days — and a powerful team also grew at the Northrop plant at Hawthorne, Los Angeles. It was September 1941 when Northrop submitted its preliminary bomber proposal, and the more the Wright Field Engineering Division looked at it, the more promising it seemed. Detail design began in February 1942, the full-scale mock-up — almost unbelievable, to anyone seeing it for the first time — was agreed in July, and an order was placed for a single XB-35 prototype. Northrop had no spare productive capacity, so the first production order, for 200 B-35s, was placed with Martin. The Baltimore firm was also asked to assist with detail design, especially of the engine installation, and further design work was farmed out by Martin to Otis Elevator in New York (no, they didn't fit a lift inside the aircraft!).

It proved to be a gigantic task, and like the rival B-36 the B-35 missed the war. After VJ-Day Gen H.H. Arnold, USAAF Chief of Staff, announced the existence of the amazing bomber and added that Northrop would build 14 YB-35 development aircraft. He did not disclose the Martin production order,

nor the fact that this had been summarily cancelled. Henceforth the B-35 project was right back in the Northrop works, where there were other distractions such as the F-15 photo aircraft, the XP-79 twin-jet fighter, the X-4 tailless research aircraft, the C-125 STOL transport and, above all, the F-89 jet night-fighter. And the mighty bomber not only posed as many problems as ever but now had a proposed jet-propelled successor, the YB-49!

Thanks partly to the work done by Martin and Otis the XB was completed ahead of its Convair rival. It had come out into the open at Hawthorne in July 1945, to be completed in the sunshine. On 25 June 1946 Max Stanley made the 44-min first flight, assisted by co-pilot Fred Bretcher and engineer Orva H. Douglas. They accomplished more than the set objectives, and landed at Muroc where the XB-35 was subsequently based. The only place to write the USAAF serial, 42-13603, was on the outer sides of the outboard propeller-shaft fairings. Constructor's number was N-1486.

The vast wing had an NACA laminar profile, with quite a small leading-edge radius and almost symmetrical profile. Span was 172 ft, area 4,000 sq ft, leading edge sweep 28 degrees and centreline chord 37 ft 6 in. At the tip were Northrop's patented Decelerons, hydraulically driven double-split surfaces rather like those used as airbrakes on today's Grumman Intruder and Sukhoi Su-25 but used also as ailerons to enable the flying wing to make turns without slip or skid. Inboard of these were hydraulically boosted elevons, serving as both elevators and ailerons. Inboard of the outer engines were powerful split flaps. Built into the outer leading edges were large fixed slots, normally covered by doors which opened as the stall was approached.

Though many of the development problems encountered were entirely novel, all were solved within the original timescale except one. This one was late delivery of the 18-ft Hamilton Standard eight-blade coun-

ter-rotating propellers and the associated drive gearboxes. When they did arrive they caused more trouble than everything else combined. The engines comprised two R-4360-17 and two R-4360-21, all rated at 3,000 hp. They were installed inside the main wing torsion box, driving the propellers via long shafts. All air was taken in via long but shallow inlets along the leading edge, which led into ducts serving the main cooling flows, the engine induction trunks, oil coolers and other services.

Normal crew numbered 15, including three gunners. The latter were to control the turrets, remotely sighted and powered electrically. At first twin-20 mm barbettes were specified, but this scheme was changed to a total of 20 guns of 0.5 in calibre, in seven turrets, with quadruple guns in the fore and aft turrets above and below the centreline and twin installations above and below the outer wings. Part of the armament control system was installed in the first XB, but the turrets were simulated by metal blisters. Most of the crew were housed near the centreline, the pressurized region extending aft into a vestigial 'rear fuselage' extending behind the trailing edge in the tail turret and along engineer inspection passages to the outer engines. At the front was a large Plexiglas bubble over the tandem pilots, to the left of centre, and a glazed portion of leading edge on the right side of the centreline for the navigator and bombardier. Behind were six bunks for off-duty crew. On each side were bays devoted to bombs (10,000 lb for 10,000 miles, with 15 per cent fuel reserve) and landing gear. The single nosewheel folded to the left, and the twin-wheel main gears retracted rearwards. Operation was electric, and great care was taken to ensure the most perfect exterior finish over the whole wing.

As mentioned, the main problem was the propellers. The first aircraft was actually completed with a six-blade contraprop on No 1 engine, but this was not meant to be permanent. Another feature that could have been troublesome was that, to avoid discharging white-hot exhaust on to the highly stressed roots of the propeller blades all exhaust was ducted forwards, mixed with fresh air and discharged from eight blisters under the leading edge. So severe were the propeller problems that all three of the piston-engine bombers actually to fly were eventually fitted with simpler four-blade single-rotation propellers. Though these had increased diameter they were unable to translate all the shaft power into thrust, and performance suffered. For example, maximum speed fell from 391 to 365 mph, and service ceiling fell from 40,500 to about 36,000 ft. Northrop and the USAAF had no doubt that single-rotation propellers had to be an interim measure.

In any case, on 1 June 1945 the USAAF had approved a bold recommendation by Northrop that two of the eight (originally 15) YB-35s should be completed with eight jet engines instead of the troublesome piston engines and propellers. In the 1945 state of the art this meant a drastic reduction in range, but the benefits included troublefree operation, higher top speed and generally better all-round performance. So only the first YB-35 (42-102366) was completed with piston engines, flying on 15 May 1948. Long before this, both the jet-powered wings had flown. Designated YB-49, the first (42-102367) flew on 21 October 1947, and the second (numbered consecutively) followed on 13 January 1948.

These were even more remarkable than their predecessors. This is despite the fact that their engines were by modern standards primitive, being among the earliest axial turbojets produced outside Germany. Designated General Electric TG-180, and intially rated at 3,750 lb thrust, they were quickly replaced by production Allison J35-A-15s rated at 4,000 lb thrust, though these were basically the same engine, handed to Allison for series production. Almost the same engine was used in the first P-86 Sabre and B-47 Stratojet. Each group of four engines fitted neatly into a fraction of the space previously occupied by two Wasp Majors, fed with air from a redesigned duct system from the leading-edge inlets. Because of the absence of the huge propellers and their shaft fairings it was necessary to add four fixed fins, bracketing the quadruple jet nozzles on each side. Each fin was almost symmetrical above and below the trailing edge, and was continued ahead above the

wing in the form of a long but shallow fence, exactly like the ECM dispensers on a MiG-29. These fences exerted a major beneficial effect on the air flowing across the top of the wing, which in the absence of propellers tended to spread out towards the tips.

Even with the four fins it was found that in most flight conditions the damping of yaw (directional) oscillations was inadequate, making accurate bombing impossible. Accordingly the YB-49s were fitted with one of the world's first yaw dampers, called a yaw-stabilization system (and known to the test crews as Little Herbert). It was a product of Minneapolis-Honeywell, which was one of the few companies already experienced in the challenging field of avionics. With this system engaged the all-wing aircraft became an extremely stable bombing platform, and it could carry a 16,000 lb bomb load. The rest of the airframe was almost unchanged, though fuel capacity was reduced (gross weight fell from 209,000 to 196,193 lb) unless an overload weight of 220,000 lb was accepted. In the latter case it was possible to carry 30,000 lb of bombs and 90,000 lb of fuel, sufficient for a still-air range of 5,400 miles. Maximum speed was 493 mph.

There was only one major accident in the whole programme, and that occurred on the very last flight in the Air Force Phase 2 Acceptance Tests on 5 June 1948. The aircraft was the No 2 YB-49, and the flight comprised dives with CG at the forward limit. On the final dive the design limits were exceeded, and the outer wings separated symmetrically from the centre section, which dropped like a stone. In command was Capt Glen Edwards, who did not get out, and Muroc was subsequently renamed in his memory.

The YB-49 was known to be such a clean aircraft that it picked up speed very quickly in a dive, and without using the outboard Decelerons it took a very long time to slow down. The accident was ascribed to too sharp a pull-out at beyond 'red line' indicated airspeed. The Northrop bomber continued to be highly regarded. Gen Roger M. Ramey, Commander of the US 8th AF, called it 'The fastest bomber I have ever flown — a fine ship with a real future'. In July 1948 the Air Force ordered 30 modified reconnaissance bombers designated RB-49A, with only six internal engines and two more slung underneath in the newly fashionable pods. This made a lot more space available for fuel, and with its tremendous altitude capability and a fantastic array of reconnaissance sensors the RB-49A looked a sure winner. But the Air Force hit on the lunatic idea of getting 29 of the 30 made by the deadly rival, Convair at Fort Worth!

In November 1948 Northrop was further charged with rebuilding the 10 remaining YB-35s as RB-35Bs, yet another new configuration with only six engines of a more powerful type, the 5,600 lb Allison J35-A-19. Two of these were to be in underslung pods, so that only four needed to be internal, making still more space available for fuel. Within very few weeks Northrop had nine of the giant wings in a row, those at the back having four projecting prop-shaft fairings and those at the front having four fins with new jet bays between them. Northrop also received a contract to convert one YB-35 (42-102376, ship N-1496) as a special test aircraft designated YRB-49A. Yet another conversion was N-1498, a YB-35 rebuilt with four internal engines, two podded engines and two of Northrop's own XT37 Turbodyne 10,000 hp turboprops driving pusher propellers.

Northrop had a super product, demonstrated by a flight in early 1949 by No 1 YB-49 from Edwards to Washington at 511 mph. The Air Force announced that the flying wings were 'by far the longest-ranged jet aircraft in the world'. But Northrop didn't have enough political clout. In January 1949 the Air Force cancelled the agreement with Convair (which Convair was eager to avoid implementing) and also the RB-35B programme, putting the money into older-generation RB-36 and B-50 bombers. On 28 October 1949 the Air Force cancelled everything else, except the single YRB-49A. This flew on 4 May 1950, and predictably proved an outstanding aircraft. Empty and normal gross weights were respectively 88,500 and 206,000 lb, and range was 9,000 miles. The increased cabin pressure of 7.5 lb/sq in made it a comfortable aircraft at 43,000 ft, and it was stuffed with advanced cameras and radars. Sadly, by this time the Air Force had — I think shortsightedly — lost interest. In early 1951 the YRB was put into 'dead storage' at Ontario International, and scrapped two years later. Nobody then had the slightest idea Northrop would later build 172-ft flying wings for the same air force costing a reputed $600,000,000 each.

This view of 42-102367 shows the upper and lower fins, which replaced the stabilizing side area of the XB-35's propellers. All three pictures were taken over Edwards, in those days called Muroc dry lake. (Northrop Aircraft via Mike Hooks)

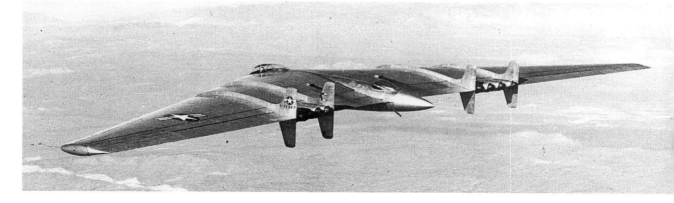

49 Convair B-36

Stories about this giant bomber abound. 'We don't have a clock on the flight deck, we use a calendar...It's like standing in the bay window and flying your house...It's an airborne Hilton hotel...' There is documented evidence that on one trip a B-36 had 4,000 cases of Scotch stashed away in an odd corner, and on another a Nash Rambler car. And to hear one pass overhead at high altitude on a quiet night was unforgettable. Many people have heard a Tu-20 or Antonov 22, whose rumbling propellers can be heard for many miles. The B-36 sounded like that, plus (in later versions) the roar of jets. To round off the reminiscences, the Hollywood film *Strategic Air Command* had a worried June Allyson waiting at the ramp gate for her shiny new husband, who was 'just being shown one take-off and landing'; she was still there about three days later.

On 11 April 1941 the USAAC asked for proposals for a bomber able to deliver a bomb load of 10,000 lb to a target 5,000 miles away and return. Such an aircraft was expected to be needed in order to bomb Berlin after the defeat of the United Kingdom. Douglas and Northrop made unofficial submissions, as a result of which Northrop's proposal for a flying-wing bomber seemed promising enough to receive support, as explained in the preceding story. The official competition was against Boeing, and Convair's formal submission of the Type 37

was made on 6 October 1941. On 15 November the company received a $15 million contract covering all costs in designing and building two prototypes, the first to be delivered in May 1944. The designation assigned was XB-36.

All work was centred at the San Diego plant of Consolidated Vultee Aircraft. Here under 'Mac' Laddon a powerful team of design engineers included Harry A. Sutton, Vice-President Engineering; Dick Sebold, Chief of Engineering; and Herbert W. Hinkley, Project Engineer on the Model 37. Unfortunately, the whole of the company's technical staff was over-extended, and to make matters far worse the XB-36 project had a priority way below the B-24, XB-32 and even the PBY. At first it was schemed with four pairs of tandem push/pull engines, but promised availability of the 3,000 hp Pratt & Whitney R-4360 Wasp Major enabled the number of engines to be reduced to six, and to avoid turbulent slipstream over the huge wing it was decided to instal these as pushers. This novel layout also was calculated to improve overall propulsive efficiency, and the fact that it made inflight access to the engines difficult was not regarded as serious.

The mighty wing eventually matured with an NACA 63 type laminar profile, and in order to get the CG in the right place the wing was slightly swept, the trailing-edge

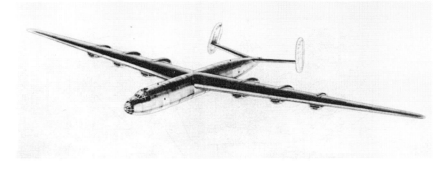

First artist's impression of the Model 37, dated February 1942. (Consolidated Vultee)

Above *The prototype XB-36 parked at Carswell AFB next to a B-29.* (Consolidated Vultee via Philip Jarrett)

Right *A pleasing portrait of the same aircraft on flight test.* (Consolidated Vultee via Philip Jarrett)

angle being 3 degrees back. Structurally there were two main spars, and the depth at the root was about 7 ft 6 in. The six massive engines were cantilevered on welded steel-tube trusses off the back of the main wing box. Under the wing were flattened-oval (almost slit) intakes giving perfect ram recovery. Each engine had two, the large upper inlet admitting cooling air (boosted by an engine-driven fan) and air to the carburettor (in Dash-53 engines, fuel injection pump equipped, direct to the cylinders). The smaller lower inlet fed air to the oil cooler and turbocharger, with branches to the intercooler and various accessories. In 1943 the inlets were moved up to the leading edge. The huge air trunks running across each wing divided it into four sections. In most versions the wing box between the air trunks was sealed to form three huge integral tanks on each side, the capacity in later versions being 3,509 gal inboard, 3,402 between the next pair of ducts and 1,884 outboard, giving a total of 17,590 gal, certainly a world record for the time. The final version added fuel in the outer wings.

The Curtiss Electric propellers were among the largest ever used. Each had feathering and reversing capability, and three hollow steel blades, with a diameter of 19 ft. The cooling air and engine exhausts were discharged immediately upstream of the spinners, intercooler airflow coming out of flush grilles in the top of the wing. All propellers had right-hand rotation.

The fuselage was a giant tube, containing pressurized crew compartments in the nose, rear fuselage and for the tail gunner. The front and rear compartments were linked by an 85 ft tube along which crew members could travel lying face-up on a trolley, pulling themselves along by an overhead rope. Despite its size, the volume being almost 18,000 cu ft, almost every scrap of space in the fuselage was put to good use, though the XB-36 was not representative of production aircraft. The original design had a twin-finned tail but — as in the case of the smaller XB-32, which consistently stole the available development engineers — this was eventually rejected in favour of a single-finned tail. In the case of the B-36 the change took place before the prototype was built. The leading edges of all tail surfaces, like those of the wings, were deiced by combustion heaters feeding hot air through the double skin.

All flight controls were manually operated via geared servo tabs. In the B-19 such a system had worked well, once the surfaces had been accurately balanced, but the B-36 was to fly approximately twice as fast and twice as high, and the test pilots, at least, were rather concerned at hitting the right point between inadequacy and overbalance. The geared tabs and trim tabs occupied almost the entire trailing edge of each surface. The ailerons were especially long, occupying the entire trailing edge outboard of the outer engines. Between the engines and the fuselage were three sections of slotted flap on each side, driven by electric motors via spanwise shafting and irreversible screw-jacks.

Two features of the prototype destined to change were the cockpit and main landing gear. The latter comprised a single wheel carrying a multi-ply tyre 110 in in diameter and 36 in wide. These were said at the time to be the biggest wheels ever used on an aircraft, and I believe this to have been true. The wheel was carried on the outer side of a giant single oleo strut, braced at the top to attachments on the aft face of the wing box and retracted inwards hydraulically to lie inside the wing root between the structural box and the flap. The twin-wheel nose gear was small by comparison, having hydraulic steering and retracting forwards to lie under the cockpit floor. Immediately in front of it was the boarding ladder, crew members climbing up from the wheel bay through a hatch into the pressurized area. The two pilots sat side-by-side in a capacious cockpit covered by a giant multi-paned transparent roof faired into the fuselage downstream. The nose was also made up of multiple Plexiglas panels, but most of the interior of the XB-36 was devoted to instrumentation.

As explained, low priority and many other things delayed the programme for more than two years. One of the factors was that in August 1942 the entire programme had been moved from San Diego to the vast government plant outside Fort Worth. In August 1944 an order was placed for 100 of the giant bombers, though it looked probable that none would be delivered before the end of the war. It was particularly galling to the B-36 team that a prime cause of delay was the B-32, which in the event (though it did see active service) was to play almost no part in the war and be withdrawn from service the moment the war was over, whereas the B-36 was assured of a role in the post-war bomber force. Indeed, it was the termination at the war's end of the B-24 and B-32 programmes that at last released the engineers needed to complete the XB-36.

The R-4360-35 engines began to arrive in November 1945, and the propellers soon afterwards. Project engineer Henry Growald was so keen to make sure the propellers were not held up that he asked that they should be consigned to him personally. Late one night 24 huge crates were offloaded at his house!

At the eleventh hour further delay was caused during ground running of the engines. The flaps had been designed with magnesium structure and fabric covering, and as soon as the engines were opened up to high power the flaps began to break up, with pieces flying into the propellers. The flaps were redesigned to be aluminium alloy throughout. At last the assigned test pilots, Beryl A. Erickson and G. S. Green, were able to begin taxi trials on 21 July 1946, followed up by a very successful first flight on 8 August. Bearing only national insignia and USAAF serial 42-13570, the huge aircraft looked graceful but, like the Comet 1, somewhat marred by the clumsy main gears.

The next aircraft to fly, on 28 August 1947, was the first of 22 production aircraft designated B-36A. Because it was needed so urgently it was completed ahead of the second prototype, the YB-36 (213571). This did not fly until 4 December 1947, and it differed from the XB chiefly in having a distinctive new bulged roof over the forward crew compartment. This made the interior much lighter and more congenial, increased space and, above all, gave the pilots a much better all-round view. Only the top panel was aluminium, and this had an observation dome, chiefly for astronavigation, in the centre. This roof was standard on all subsequent aircraft. The YB had something approaching the production arrangement of internal work stations for the crew of 10 or 11, plus a relief crew of five. It included a

redesigned and lengthened nose, with a gun turret above the nose compartment, but the aircraft was unarmed. Later the YB was given the production-type landing gear, becoming the YB-36A.

This landing gear was first fitted to the batch of B-36As, the first of which preceded the YB. The single main wheels were each replaced by a bogie, with four wheels of 56 in diameter, improved disc brakes and other advantages. When the first B-36A (44-92004) rolled out it was one of the first aircraft ever seen with bogie main gears in the modern manner. Each unit had a vertical main oleo pivoted to the centre of the bogie beam, a radius rod at the front, snubber shock strut at the rear and side bracing struts which 'broke' during the retraction cycle. The latter was unchanged, apart from the addition of small blisters above the wing to accommodate the retracted inboard rear wheels.

The 22 A-models were initially unarmed and used for training by the newly formed USAF Strategic Air Command. They were officially given the name Peacemaker, though it was seldom used. Next came 73 B-36Bs (44-92026 et seq), powered by the

One can almost hear the snarling growl of 44-92033, the eighth B-36B. (USAF SAC via Mike Hooks)

3,500 hp R-4360-41 and with full armament and operational equipment. The original planned armament, for which structural provision had been made in the XB, was five 37 mm cannon and 10 0.5 in guns. This was completely changed to a total of 16 cannon of 20 mm calibre in eight turrets. Those in the nose and tail were remotely controlled, but were sighted directly by adjacent gunners. The six fuselage turrets, comprising left and right pairs above the front and rear and under the rear, were doubly complex. First, they were normally retracted, and faired under large doors which could slide open like bomb doors to allow the turrets to be raised or lowered clear of the fuselage to fire in all directions above or below. Second, each turret was remotely controlled by a gunner in a Plexiglas bubble sighting station, control being passed from one gunner to another automatically.

The B-36B could carry the design bombload of 72,000 lb, in two front and two rear bomb bays with a capacity of 12,300 cu ft. With maximum bombs and fuel the service ceiling was still no less than 42,500 ft. Indeed, on 29 January 1949 a B-36B dropped two giant 42,000-lb bombs, one from 35,000 and the other from 40,000 ft, and later ver-

sions were cleared to carry this 84,000 lb load routinely. The B also introduced the K-1A radar bombing system, the rotating antenna causing a large blister aft of the nose gear, the radio compass causing a small blister ahead of the nose gear.

Convair had intended to go on to build a B-36C with six turbo-compound versions of the R-4360 in tractor nacelles, but these were cancelled and built as the last 34 Bs. So the next model was the B-36D, first flown on 26 March 1949 in the form of a converted B. This was a crucial development. Strategic Air Command (SAC), and especially the B-36, had been under attack by the Navy and by Congress for consuming funds said to be needed for giant carriers and naval aviation. There was also the enduring threat of the Northrop flying wings. With the B-36D Convair ensured that the Fort Worth plant would continue to build the main 'big stick' of what had become known as the nuclear deterrent.

It looked like previous versions except for the obvious addition of two pairs of turbojets under the outer wings. These were added to boost over-target height to 45,000 ft and speed to 435 mph. The engines were the General Electric J47-19, each rated at 5,200 lb (sea-level static), and they were in-

stalled in twin pods, almost identical to the inboard nacelles of the B-47, except for the kinked pylon strut and the fact that the inlets could be shut off by a kind of iris diaphragm to reduce drag, because the jets were not used in cruising flight. The Dash-19 had to have starting and ignition systems able to work at over 40,000 ft. Their fuel was 115/145 grade petrol drawn from the main tanks. Gross weight was 358,000 lb. Convair made over 400 further changes in the D, many of them associated with the switch to the K-3A radar bomb/nav system and the APG-41A gunlaying radar. Another change was the fitting of snap-action folding bomb doors instead of a slower-acting sliding pattern. Production totalled 22 (49-2647/2668), and 64 of the B-models were rebuilt to the D standard. The RB-36D was a strategic reconnaissance version with two of the four bomb bays occupied by a huge installation of 14 cameras, the crew being increased to 22. Convair built 17 (49-2686/2702), and seven B-36Bs were converted to this standard. A further 21 B-36As plus the YB-36A followed, but these rebuilds were given the designation RB-36E.

Next came 34 B-36Fs, starting with 49-2669. The main difference was the installa-tion of R-4360-53 engines, fitted with direct fuel injection and rated at 3,800 hp. The corresponding recon version was the RB-36F, of which 24 were built (49-2703 et seq). These had additional fuel capacity which replaced the space in the unused pair of bomb bays. The GRB-36Fs were modified to carry a fighter in the FICON (fighter conveyor) programme. Back in 1948 the stubby McDonnell XF-85 Goblin had been designed as a jet fighter small enough to fold up and be carried inside the B-36 bomb bay and released to protect the bomber over enemy territory. This was eventually abandoned as too hazardous, but prolonged testing with the F-84E, F-84F and finally the GRF-84F photo-recon aircraft actually led to operational service in 1955, followed in 1956 by the RF-84K.

To compete with the Boeing B-52, Convair built two YB-36Gs (49-2676 and 2684), subsequently redesignated as YB-60s. These were fitted with a huge swept wing carrying eight Pratt & Whitney J57 turbojets, as noted later. Convair pointed out the cost and maintenance advantages of using a proven aircraft as a basis, but the Air Force picked the all-new Boeing.

By the 1950s the huge and rather slow

B-36 might have been thought vulnerable, but in fact the B-36H sustained an unbroken run of 83 new aircraft, starting with 50-1083. This differed only in having an improved crew layout in the forward fuselage and various equipment changes, including later radar. No fewer than 73 examples were built of the corresponding RB-36H with comprehensive electronic sensing and recording systems. One B-36H, 51-5712, was completely gutted and rebuilt as the unique NB-36H to test-fly an operating nuclear reactor in the rear fuselage. It was the operational difficulties experienced with this aircraft that did much to kill the proposed WS-125 NPB (nuclear-powered bomber), which might otherwise have brought forth a totally different species of 'giant'. The final model, the B-36J, had extra 1,193-gal fuel tankage in each outer wing, bringing maximum weight up to 410,000 lb, for many years the all-time record weight for any aeroplane. The main gears were strengthened, but some of the 33 examples built had all but the tail guns removed, reducing the crew to nine and the weight to about 398,000 lb, which restored most of the lost over-target height.

Altogether the B-36 was a truly staggering achievement. It seems surprising that so obviously important an aircraft should have limped ahead, starved of support, at a crucial time in a nation's history, and then raced ahead after peace came. It is even more surprising that, in a time of parsimonious defence funding, no fewer than 385 of the costly monsters should have come off the production line.

In fact Convair made one more aircraft, based on the same wing, engines, tail and landing gear. The XC-99 (43-52436) was a transport built for the USAF and first flown in November 1947. It had one of the biggest fuselages ever seen, with a volume of just on 30,000 cu ft. It remained a San Diego project, and was completed there with single-wheel main gears, not getting bogie-type units for another two years. There were two decks, the lower comprising 40-ft usable sections ahead of and behind the wing, and the upper having a straight run of 158 ft from the impressive flightdeck in the extreme nose right back to the tail. Loads could comprise 101,000 lb of cargo, 400 troops or an amazing 300 stretcher casualties. Pressurization was installed but seldom used. The XC never lost its experimental status, and never received J47 jet pods, though it spent eight years in routine 'special service', from Kelly AFB. In 1954 it was structurally modified to permit gross weight to be increased from 265,000 to 320,000 lb, and C-124 type weather radar was fitted. It was retired in 1957.

Data for the B-36 include: span 230 ft; wing area 4,772 sq ft; length (typical) 162 ft 1 in (XC-99, 182 ft 6 in); height 46 ft 8 in; empty weight (B) 140,640 lb, (J) 171,035 lb; maximum weight (prototype) 278,000 lb, (B) 328,000 lb, (J) 410,000 lb; typical mission, 10,000 lb bombload for range of 6,800 miles.

50 Lockheed Constitution

The company founded by the Loughead (pronounced in Scottish style 'Loch-heed') brothers was a typical US success story, once Bob Gross and his colleagues had rescued it during the depression. In February 1934 it moved up to two engines and all-metal stressed-skin construction with the Model 10 Electra. But it was still a small outfit, and when on the first flight Marshall Headle couldn't get the Electra's gear down Lockheed thought they'd go bankrupt. Gradually they built bigger and faster aircraft, and in much greater numbers, catapulted into the big time by a British order for 200 Hud-

The XR6O-1 looked good and was a fine performer, though it could have used more power. This is the No. 1 aircraft. (Lockheed Aircraft via R.T. Riding)

sons in June 1938. A year later work began on what became the famous Constellation, initially for TWA, and this 'Queen of the Skies' — as it was dubbed — only just missed getting into this book. PanAm had an interest in the launch of the Constellation, and in April 1942, almost a year before the first Connie made its maiden flight, PanAm told the US Navy it needed an even bigger transport to enable it to fly heavy Navy cargoes all over the world.

In the end the two aircraft were ordered and operated by the Navy. The contract was signed in May 1942 for two Lockheed XR6O-1 Constitutions, with BuAer numbers 85163 and 85164. Lockheed called them Model 89, the Connie having been the Model 49. As these were to be Navy aircraft, PanAm's Juan Trippe soon afterwards ordered a very similar aircraft from Douglas as the DC-7 (see Globemaster). Like Douglas, Lockheed chose to build a conventional low-wing machine with tricycle landing gear and, despite the towering height needed, a single fin. Both firms chose the same engine: the 3,000 hp Pratt & Whitney R-4360 28-cylinder 'corncob' radial, in Lockheed's case driving enormous Curtiss Electric propellers, with four reversing blades and a diameter of no less than 19 ft 2 in. Maximum weight was 184,000 lb.

Thanks to the Constellation most parts of the Model 89 were merely the same as on the earlier aircraft but bigger. The project engineer was 'Dick' Pulver, and the head of the design team was Willis Hawkins, assisted by Harry Jansen and Ray Warner. Their names are mentioned because the Model 89 is still remembered by old-timers as one gigantic programme where almost everything went right first time. The 189 ft 1 in wing, with an area of 3,610 sq ft, was basically scaled from that of the Model 49, though it had machined skin panels of the type not used on Connies until the Model 1649 of 1956. In the beautifully efficient wing box were four tanks, two on each side, for 8,326 gal of fuel. The rectangular flaps were in one section on each wing. Running out on six steel tracks, they were among the biggest Fowler flaps of all time. Operation was hydraulic, with emergency electrical or manual drive. They achieved a lift coefficient of 3.55, giving the monster a stalling speed of only 72 kts.

Flight controls were straightforward, each surface again being in one section. All were hydraulically boosted, this being the first aircraft to have triplex flight-control circuits so designed, at least in theory, that control would be retained even with any two rendered inoperative. The first drawing of the Model 89 showed a Connie-type triple tail unit, but by 1942 it was realised that a single fin is more efficient. As a result Lockheed had to add Building 309 to the Burbank plant to accommodate the 'six-storey high' tail of the new monster. The actual height was 50 ft 5 in, more than double the 23 ft of a Connie and almost certainly a world record until the Hughes Hercules came along. All leading edges had double skins fed with hot deicing air from heat exchangers in the engine exhaust systems.

These heat exchangers were downstream of the two General Electric turbosuperchargers fitted to each engine. The latter were of the R-4360-22W type, W signifying water injection which on take-off could be used to boost power to 3,500 hp. Each complete powerplant, with ventral ducted oil cooler, aft oil tank, General Electric CH-9 turbo and intercooler, was interchangeable with the others and could be removed and replaced in an hour. The whole lot could be serviced in flight. The doors into the wings led from a series of room-like hydraulic and electrical centres on the lower deck, just like we have on widebodies today. The wing walkways also gave access to various acccessories, and to the complete retracted main landing gears. The latter had two long shock struts in tandem, each carrying twin wheels, the struts being independent. Each unit retracted inwards, big rectangular doors closing to present an unblemished wing undersurface. The steerable nose gear retracted forwards.

Lockheed used a bit of poetic licence in ignoring the matter of floor strength when they said the Constitution's fuselage 'could hold the biggest railroad Pullman car ever built, plus the biggest boxcar, plus the biggest flatcar, and still have room left over for a passenger bus'. Not only this, but the whole double-deck accommodation was pressurized to 4.67 lb/sq in, resulting in what can either be called a 'double bubble' or a figure-8 cross section. Apart from the much smaller XC-97 I believe the giant Lockheed was the first double-bubble ever built. The capacious flightdeck was rather like a bigger edition of that on the Connie. Behind was the flight engineer, facing what seemed to be hundreds of dials. The normal flight crew numbered 12, including two flight orderlies who among other things ran the big galley behind the flightdeck. Of course there were rest bunks and toilets, but the rest of the upper deck later had 92 troop seats, arranged 3 + 2, an unprecedented number. They boarded via the nose-gear bay or a door on the left behind the wing, thence ascending two spiral staircases. The lower deck was usually for freight, but it could if necessary take another 76 passengers, 41 ahead of the wing and 35 behind. Bob Gross told me that about two weeks too late chief engineer Hall Hibberd came up with a drawing showing how the nose could open with clamshell doors for loading cargo the full cross section of the lower deck.

The first Constitution was pulled out of Building 309 on 21 August 1946, but it then had months of final systems work and testing to be completed. At last, watched by most of the workforce, No 85163 became airborne after a run of only 1,820 ft (a lift coefficient of over 3 is really something!). At the controls were Joe Towle and co-pilot Tony Levier, with three flight engineers. This first trip landed by arrangement at Muroc, later named Edwards AFB, where Towle said he had been unable to tell when they had actually touched down. This became such a problem they had a cockpit caption added saying: AIRPLANE ON GROUND, illuminated by a microswitch on a main leg. One day this failed. Roy Wimmer was concentrating on landing when Towle pointed to the ASI — which read something like 45 — and said 'Seldom flies much at this speed, may as well use the brakes'. There were a few other hairy moments caused by all the clever systems. On Wimmer's first check ride Engines 3 and 4 confused the water-injection control, which incorporated a safety device which shut off fuel if the water, for any reason, failed to be injected at high power. When Wimmer pulled back after take-off the two right engines quit, this safety device having been triggered. The one fault of an otherwise splendid aircraft was that it was underpowered, and with two engines out on one side there was a crisis. Wimmer was looking for 'somewhere to put it' when power was restored. Yet another memorable occasion had the aircraft performing strange manoeuvres without any input from the pilots. Eventually a keen Navy air mechanic was found in the electrical centre, going through the system with a mighty manual in one hand and various tools in the other!

By the end of the war PanAm had switched to the DC-7, and later cancelled this as well. No more Constitutions were needed, but the two that did exist lost their X prefix, and one made the formal induction into Navy service at Alameda on 2 February 1949*. A parade was held, during which 180 bluejackets formed up and marched on board. Then a Jeep drove in at the lower deck side cargo door. Rear-Adm Lynde McCormick welcomed the newcomer, after which it took off in a blast of white smoke from six ATO (assisted take-off) rockets clipped above the wing roots. Subsequently the giant Lockheeds did all that was required of them, often taking off at over their authorised weight of 184,000 lb. A typical cruising speed was 286 mph. During the Korean War they mostly shuttled between Hawaii and Moffett Field, but spares were hard to find and in 1955 the Navy sold the monsters for a combined price of $98,000. All they really needed was four 5,500 hp Pratt & Whitney T34 turboprops, and I never did understand why, instead of fitting them to the Constitutions, the Navy fitted these engines to a pair of R7V-2 Super Connies, which couldn't make full use of so much power!

Lockheed's Navy letter O was often confused with a zero, so from 1950 all Lockheed aircraft were redesignated with the V previously used by the Vega division. Thus the Constitution became the R6V.

The Fowler flaps needed no prominent track fairings, and the turbosuperchargers discharged straight back from the rear of each nacelle. (Lockheed Aircraft via R.T. Riding)

51 Hughes H-4 Hercules

Though it was unkindly dubbed 'The Spruce Goose' by the US media, and for their own purposes was made to appear a misuse of taxpayers' money by hostile Congressmen, the Hercules was in fact one of the greatest achievements in the history of aviation. It was conceived with the highest patriotic objectives, the greater part of the costs were borne by Howard Hughes himself, and it was — so far as anyone can judge — a thoroughly sound aircraft, in both design and manufacture. It also happens to be, in many important respects, the biggest aeroplane ever to fly. One has only to glance at its place on the tables at the end of this book to see just how big it really was — and is, because it still exists.

In May 1942 U-boats were sending war supplies to the bottom of the ocean at an alarming rate. Shipping tycoon Henry J. Kaiser suggested that a good answer would be 5,000 gigantic flying boats — a huge fleet of 'unsinkable Liberty ships'. He immediately produced a brochure depicting a twin-hulled flying boat with what seemed to be the same number of decks and portholes as an ocean liner. He got little but polite encouragement in Washington, but his idea struck sparks from Howard Hughes, the unique billionaire who, though one of the world's leaders of the oil drilling industry, a famous film producer, a man with deep engineering knowledge of advanced aircraft and certainly one of the greatest pilots of all time, was often dismissed as 'a playboy'. He met Kaiser and formed Kaiser-Hughes Aircraft. Throughout the summer of 1942, in between making the Hollywood epic *The Outlaw*, Hughes directed the design of the HK-1 flying boat, which was handled by his design staff at Culver City. In November a contract was signed with the DPC (Defense Plant Corporation) in the sum of $18 million, under which Kaiser-Hughes (KH) would

supply two HK-1 aircraft and a static-test airframe. The two flight aircraft were to be ready in 20 and 25 months, but K-H did not warrant that the task could be done for $18 million.

From that point the project had, perhaps inevitably, good and bad features. The good feature was the aircraft itself, as described here. The bad features stemmed from the fact that there was nobody able to manage the work professionally. For example, it would have been sensible, for a very modest sum, to carry out the entire operation at a purpose-designed building at a suitable coastal site. Instead Hughes built what was probably the biggest wooden building of all time, measuring 750 ft by 265 ft by 100 ft high, where only a single set of HK-1 components were manufactured. These were then taken by road 28 miles to an assembly site on Terminal Island which Hughes personally leased from the City of Long Beach

Not a slave ship but HK-1 'Cargo arrangement G', for 350 stretcher patients. The drawing was dated 15 October 1943. (Hughes Aircraft via John Stroud)

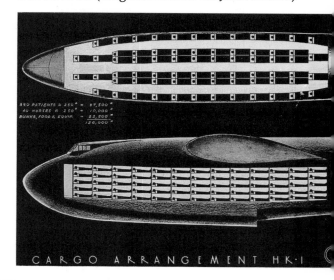

for 40 years, in later years at $40,000 annually.

Thus, from the beginning nobody bothered to adhere to the terms of the contract and the No 2 boat and static-test airframe were never really started. There was never a customer in the true sense, and two years into the programme it was obvious that the HK-1 would be far too late to influence the war. The DPC and the US military lost interest, the contract was cut to one aircraft and the DPC said the $18 million was meant to include all the plant and facilities. Hughes and Kaiser had their predictable row, the joint corporation was dissolved and a year later, in 1945, the whole programme was declared surplus to national requirements. That should have been that, but Hughes had that streak of determination which often overcomes common sense. He promised himself that his biggest aeroplane should never be thought a failure, or the kind of sick joke conjured up by the 'Spruce Goose' appellation. At his own expense Hughes Aircraft completed what had now been redesignated the Hughes-4, and he was determined to fly it, to silence his critics.

The basic design could hardly have been more straightforward. Instead of two hulls Hughes used just one, and like all the rest of the mighty airframe it consumed hardly any metal or other war-critical material. The ruling material was birch, cut by large bandsaws and glued and pinned in multiple laminations; when the glue had set, the pins were pulled out again, saving a total of eight tons. The entire skin was resin-bonded birch ply made in hot dies by the Duramold process originally patented by Col V. E. Clark and used in an earlier form by Jack Northrop on the fuselage of the Lockheed Vega. The left and right wings were each made in one piece, butt-jointed on the centreline and recessed into the top of the hull. The latter had a completely unobstructed interior 25 ft wide and 30 ft high. The main floor was stressed to accept point loads of 125 lb/sq in, and could have carried

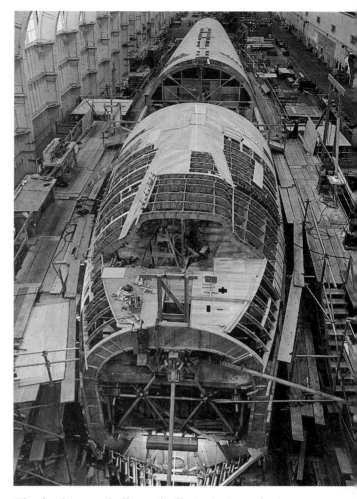

The fuselage, or hull, gradually took shape during 1944 inside the vast wooden building at Culver City. (Hughes Aircraft via John Stroud)

a single compact load of 50 tons (but the only Hercules built had no doors for bulky cargo). Seats could have been added for 700 troops. Under the floor were 18 watertight compartments, any 12 of which could be flooded without sinking the monster. Some, between frames 16 and 36, housed 14 aluminium tanks of 833 gal each, a total of 11,662 gal. A stairway led to the upper deck, which extended from the beautifully appointed cockpit back to the main spar.

It's 4 April 1945 and the hull is approaching completion. One gets an idea of the effort involved from the mass of temporary staging and support structures (20 vices and cramps can be counted), all done under artificial light. Any mistake could severely damage the hull. (Hughes Aircraft via John Stroud)

Towards the rear on the left side were up to 33 seats (the number varied), together with a conference table and flight-test instrumentation. The cockpit had giant windows extending down to the level of the pilot's thighs, and even lower in front to give a view of the sea directly in front of the bows.

Each slotted flap was hinged on five pivots about 6 ft below the wing. The single fin had the almost unbelievable root chord of 53 ft, and net area of 1,699 sq ft. About one-third of the way up it carried the tailplane, whose span was 113 ft 6 in. The enormous ailerons, elevators and rudder were each a single surface, but fitted with twin tabs and driven by hydraulic boosters. The latter were originally inside the hull, driving via cables, but Hughes found there was unacceptable delay in the system; a pilot input demand was eventually followed by 'surging, and then an aggravated response'. He had the whole

system redesigned in 1947 so that each booster drove the surface directly.

Tandem tractor/pusher engines were never considered. After much study, the power plant picked in October 1942 comprised eight Pratt & Whitney R-4360 Wasp Major engines (those fitted were related to the 3,000 hp R-4360-4). These, and the Hamilton Standard propellers, were GFE (government-furnished equipment). Each propeller had four blades and a diameter of 17 ft 2 in, and the four innermost units had reverse-pitch capability for braking and manoeuvring on the water. Among the few metal structures were the enormous welded steel-tube cantilevers, almost 25 ft long, needed to carry the stresses from each 7,000-lb powerplant group back to the front spar. Of course, there was inflight access to all engines, the wing catwalk having 9 ft headroom.

The hull length/beam ratio is difficult to calculate, because the rearmost 90 ft of hull was downstream of the aft step, and at rest nearly all of it was out of the water. If this is included the ratio is about 10; if not it comes out at about 7. The planing bottom had one large and deep oblique main step, the vee bottom tapering to a point not far behind. The stabilizing floats, for some reason called pontoons, had excellent aerodynamic form, with a small step right at the rear, and were fixed in place on extremely broad cantilever struts.

As already noted, from 1945 Hughes was determined to finish the whole job at his own expense. During construction some of the workers wore soft slippers while the rest worked in their socks. The lower part of the hull was filled with big rubber balloons, not so much to catch falling workers as to avoid damage caused by hammers, wrenches or anything else falling perhaps 30 feet. On 11 June 1946 over 2,000 people were involved in moving the main components to the dry dock at Long Beach. Here large cranes and surveying methods were used to put everything together, the fin (bringing the height to 79 ft 4 in) needing a calm day. When the

Above *The wings being readied for the 28-mile trip to Long Beach in summer 1946. Both floats can also be seen.* (Via R.T. Riding)

Below *Now it's 6 August 1947 and the engines and propellers are fitted; but there's still a lot to be done.* (Via Philip Jarrett)

main airframe was complete, in August, every square inch of skin was given a coat of wood filler, a coat of sealer, a layer of rice paper (applied before the sealer dried), two coats of yacht varnish and a top coat of aluminium-pigmented varnish. By October the engines, propellers and most systems had been installed.

Hughes then spent a year testing and tinkering. In 1947 he was not outwardly concerned that a powerful Congressional committee, headed by Sen Owen Brewster, was minutely studying every large government contract it could find, using all the time-honoured methods of harassing witnesses and tapping telephone lines (and anything else one could think of) to try to find a whiff of scandal to help the Republicans win the coming Presidential election. Hughes was perhaps their favourite target, notwithstanding the fact that even a cursory audit showed that Hughes himself spent on the Hercules twice the $18 million received, about half of which had in any case gone to Mr Kaiser. One result was that clubs sprang up to try to make Hughes the next US President, while Mr Brewster failed even to win his state primary.

By late October 1947 not even Hughes could find anything to fault. Bearing experimental civil registration NX37602, the Hercules was floated by flooding the dock, large air bags being tied under the outboard 'pontoons'. All was ready on 1 November, but the weather was bad. At last, on 2 November 1947, the air bags were removed and Hughes made two fast taxi runs, both showing such beautiful control that the wings were exactly level, both floats brushing the tops of the waves. At about 1.40 pm Hughes made a third run. Distant newsmen saw what looked like eight explosions: the white bursts were vapour behind the propellers biting the moist air at full power. In what seemed like no time the majestic boat was riding on the step. Then Hughes lifted her off and flew for a little over a mile across LA harbour, at about 30 ft at 94 mph. After each

run, including the short hop, Hughes was ecstatic. He was far too deeply ingrained an engineer to adopt a false 'sales pitch'. He was all agog to start the test programme in earnest, and immediately began planning the schedule with George Haldemann of CAA's Region Six.

Alas, it was not to be. Hughes was far too busy making movies, trying to run TWA, trying to run RKO Radio Pictures, keeping one eye on the vast oil business and another on the way Hughes Aircraft was growing up. During the war it had been a lusty infant but one frowned upon by the generals. By 1950 the company had been catapulted into the very forefront of the most high-tech business of the age: fighter radars, computerized fire-control systems, and the entire first generation of air-to-air missiles. Hughes

Left *Today the Hercules still holds the all-time record not only for wing span but also for height (79 ft 4 in). (Via R.T. Riding)*

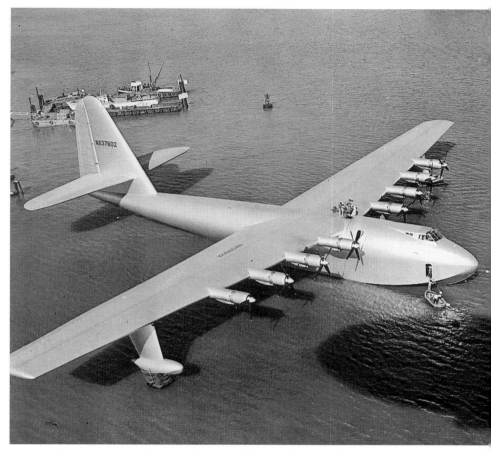

Right *Now it's 1 November 1947 and the huge wooden flying boat is all ready to go. Hughes is among the group near the top hatch. She was to fly next day, but we've seen that picture! (Via Philip Jarrett)*

never forgot about the giant boat, but never did get around to the increasingly 'Herculean' task of getting her airworthy again.

Indeed, by May 1951 the Hercules had been re-engined with 3,500 hp R-4360-TSB-3G engines, with electrically signalled controls. The boat itself was housed on a swivelling cradle inside a permanent metal building, but in September 1953 the sea broke in and caused an alleged $3.5 million worth of damage. Over the years oil drilling, the very business that underpinned the Hughes fortune, had caused widespread subsidence on Terminal Island, and it was soon obvious that the Hercules hangar was sinking slowly into the sea. Everything about the Hercules is big, and things can't be rushed, but in late 1980 the monster was stripped of her engines, cautiously put on

her original cradle, with fresh flotation bags under the pontoons, and floated out into LA harbour once more. Then she was towed to a new location beside RMS *Queen Mary*, on firm ground above sea level and protected by a stone breakwater. Here a beautiful permanent home was built around her, and N37602 (I don't know how she lost the X) has been repainted glossy white and polished as bright as a new pin. She is the one giant from the past that anyone can go and visit.

For the record, her span is 320 ft, wing area 11,430 sq ft, length 218 ft 7 in; equipped empty weight 262,000 lb, design gross weight 400,000 lb; estimated maximum speed 218 mph, and calculated range 3,500 miles with 130,000 lb payload, cruising at 175 mph.

52 Blackburn Clydesman

Today the industry has probably grown up, and the aviation press along with it, but when I joined *Flight* magazine in 1951 it was considered perfectly normal for us to devote a lot of space to detailed descriptions of wonderful aircraft that had no customer and virtually no chance of ever getting anywhere. If the project looked really exciting we would run a full description, even if the company had produced nothing but a brochure.

Some years earlier, in 1945, brochures were coming out by the truckload describing beautiful new civil aircraft. The manufacturers had prospered during the six years of war, but didn't want to be left behind in the rush for civil orders, which were clearly not going to be forthcoming in the numbers they were used to. One company whose future looked rather bleak was Blackburn Aircraft, which during the war had done little to be proud of. It had made Sunderlands, Barracudas and Swordfish under licence, and taken the entire period of the war to bring the Firebrand to the stage at which the Royal Navy could describe it in terms which I had better not repeat here (I have the

report). Much later the company was to achieve the near-impossible: thanks to engineers such as Barry Laight and Roy Boot it won one of the most far-seeing requirements ever issued and gave us the Buccaneer, one of the most misunderstood and undervalued aircraft of all time (except by the chaps who fly it).

Towards the end of the war, however, Blackburn urgently felt it ought to launch a major civil project, and it thought the obvious thing to attempt was a large transport flying boat. At this time the Shetland was being turned into a passenger aircraft, and Saunders-Roe was in the early stages of designing the Princess. Despite this, Blackburn's chief seaplane designer, Maj J. D. Rennie (whom we met in the Fury story), spent most of his time in late 1944 scheming a huge commercial flying boat in the traditional manner. In March 1945 a large brochure was issued (the accompanying Blackburn press release getting Maj Rennie's initials wrong). We were told almost every

Three-view of the Clydesman. (Blackburn Aircraft)

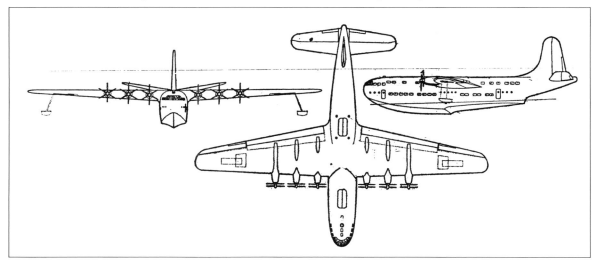

detail of a six-engined machine with designation B-49 and named Clydesman, because it would have been built at the company's works at Dumbarton, on the Clyde. There was just one small omission: though the drawings clearly showed that the engines were turboprops, driving contra-rotating propellers and with jetpipes projecting above the rear of the wings, not a word was said about the engines, and it was clear that nobody knew what these might be. The best choice, by pure coincidence, would have been the Rolls-Royce Clyde.

For the record, span, length and wing area were 202 ft, 148 ft and 5,000 sq ft, gross weight was 310,000 lb and payload to be 160 passengers plus 30,400 lb of cargo for 2,500 miles, cruising at 269 mph, or 45 sleeping passengers and 15,125 lb cargo for 4,375 miles, cruising at 280 mph. As the drawings show, huge rectangular windows were envisaged, despite the fact the hull was to be (probably quite mildly) pressurized to permit operation at 15,000 ft. There was probably nothing wrong with the concept, beyond the fact that the company's arguments cut no ice with the airlines.

53 Breda-Zappata BZ.308

One of the lesser-known aircraft in this book that actually got built, the BZ.308 suffered from its location and times. Filippo Zappata, one of the most distinguished Italian designers (he put the Z in such famous CANT aircraft as the Z.501, 506 and 1007), designed the BZ.308 before the war. It was intended simply as a large passenger or cargo aircraft, but by the time construction of a prototype became possible, in 1945, Zappata had thought of further versions.

Among these were a pressurized variant, a much heavier transport able to fly the North Atlantic, and a twin-float version. For the moment he was content to build the original design.

This got under way at Milan in 1946, was

If the war hadn't got in the way the BZ.308 might have flown (with different engines) in about 1942. (Breda via Mike Hooks)

halted by the Allied Control Commission in January 1947 and finally led to a roll-out in the late spring of 1948, the first flight being in August. I don't need to say a great deal about the 308, which just about rates inclusion here because of its size in relation to other pre-war aircraft. Span was 138 ft 2 in, wing area 2,224 sq ft, length 110 ft, gross weight 88,185 lb (a later version would have weighed 101,411 lb) and normal seating for 55 passengers. The engines were Bristol Centaurus, and strangely all contemporary reports rate these at 1,750 hp, but Bristol actually supplied Mk 568 engines rated at 2,550 hp. These were more powerful than the engines originally planned, and Zappata would have liked to move the engines further apart. Unable to do this, he had to use

fighter-type 12 ft 9 in five-blade Rotol propellers, and even then their discs overlapped!

The single prototype was quite a good performer, and the Italian certification authorities recorded a maximum cruising speed, at maximum weight, of 357 mph. The estimated service ceiling was 32,800 ft, but of course without oxygen and pressurization this was academic. Fuel capacity was 3,740 gal, which was probably enough to make the 308 a useful transport, but Zappata wisely saw that what was basically an outdated design had no chance against the Connie and DC-6, and Breda's precarious financial situation made it impossible to go any further.

54 Breguet Deux Ponts

This is another of the marginal giants. I never considered including the DC-6B (though that was more than twice as powerful as its DC-4E ancestor, which I did include), but how about an aeroplane which in effect has two DC-6B fuselages one above

the other, yet has exactly the same four engines? Louis Breguet, a member of the famous family of clockmakers, founded his company in 1911. It survived even the nationalization law of 1936, German occupation and British bombing, and in 1949 this

Driving an AMX13 light tank, with turret reversed, into a Br763 Deux Ponts. (Soc L. Breguet via R.T. Riding)

quite modest firm built five completely new prototypes, whilst for good measure working on four other types! Pity we have progressed today to the point where the planemakers are so colossal they never do anything new at all.

One of the new prototypes, flown on 15 February 1949, was the Type 76-1. This was to lead to a family known collectively as the Breguet Deux Ponts (two decks). The prototype was powered by four 1,600 hp Gnome-Rhône 14R engines, but production aircraft were powered by 2,400 hp Pratt & Whitney Double Wasps. The civil Br.763 had R-2800-CA18 engines and the military Br.765 the R-2800-CB16, in each case driving a HamStan reversing propeller. The Deux Ponts was a well-engineered all-metal machine, with hydraulic slotted flaps and landing gear, and a tail with three fins and two (upper/lower) pairs of rudders. The span of 141 ft 0.5 in and MTO weight of 113,759 lb were not really exceptional, but how about the fuselage cross section: width 10 ft 10 in and depth 16 ft 5 in? Air France operated 12 Deux Ponts with 48 passengers downstairs and 59 upstairs, though 135 could be carried. The Armée de l'Air called the military version the Sahara, and this not only carried 146 armed troops or 85 stretcher casualties and attendants but paradropped then-record loads of six tonnes (13,228 lb) and carried many other loads including AMX 13 light tanks. When Air France retired its last 763 in 1972 they were freighters called by the name Universal.

55 Sud-Est 2010 Armagnac

We have already met the French national group SNCASE in the story of the SE200. During World War 2 its numerous factories managed to avoid too much production for the Germans, but completed large numbers of LeO 45 bombers for the Vichy government, and also began production of what began life as the Bloch 161 four-engined airliner, became the SO161 and ended up as the SE161 Languedoc. Under André Vautier design also began on a big transatlantic landplane, the SE1000. This was soon replaced by the SE2000, to be powered by four 2,100 hp Gnome-Rhône 18R engines. A firm go-ahead was received in 1945, but by this time progress in the USA had made the 2000 appear inadequate. After urgent discussion the decision was taken to scale it up to match the Pratt & Whitney R-4360 Wasp Major engine, which was available for export, and also to make the fuselage pressurized.

The result was the SE2010 Armagnac, the prototype of which, F-WAVA, made its first flight at Toulouse-Blagnac on 2 April 1949. Bearing in mind the shattered state of the French industry in 1945 this aircraft was an impressive achievement. The wing, of NACA 23017 at the root, thinning off to 23010 at the tip, had a span of 160 ft 7 in and area of 2,536 sq ft. Outboard of the engines the leading edge was hinged, and aft of the torsion box were large slotted flaps. Flight controls were manual, statically and dynamically balanced. The engines were R-4360-B13, rated at 3,500 hp with water injection, fed from eight wing tanks with a capacity of 6,908 gal. The propellers were Curtiss Electric four-bladers, of 15 ft 2 in diameter. This was just 3 in less than the diameter of the circular-section fuselage, which was pressurized to about 4 lb/sq in (8,200 ft at 20,000 ft). All leading edges had thermal deicing. The landing gear had twin-wheel main units hydraulically retracting forwards. The nose unit had a single wheel, and though contemporary descriptions all said it retracted backwards it actually went

forwards, the wheel lying in the very tip of the nose where there was a third door covering the front of the bay.

From the start the Armagnac — like the Languedoc, named from a region of France, but in this case a much smaller region west of the SE2010's birthplace — was a pretty sound aeroplane, looked at purely from the engineering viewpoint. By the start of 1950 SNCASE were working on an order for 15 series aircraft, eight of them for Air France, but after evaluating the prototype the airline eventually declined to accept the type at all. It claimed that the Armagnac was uneconomic. I have seen this explained on the basis that the fat fuselage was designed for three tiers of bunks, and that when sleeping accommodation became unfashionable

An idea of the size of the Armagnac can be gained from the relative smallness of the R-4360 Wasp Majors. (SNCASE via Mike Hooks)

the fuselage was far too deep for a single layer of seats. That may be so, but normal accommodation was for 84, with high-density seating for 160, which is a lot more than Stratocruisers carried with the same engines. In the end, after a brief try with Transports Aériens Intercontinentaux, seven Armagnacs toiled mightily on the long run to the war in Indo-China in 1953-55 with the specially formed airline SAGETA. One aircraft, the SE2060, flight tested the impressive Vulcain turbojet.

56 Bristol 167 Brabazon

One has to take a deep breath before beginning this story, because, like the Princess, it tells how the work of the designers and engineers, almost all of it outstanding, was brought to nothing by programme management, by the customer, that was nothing short of disastrous. This was a time when

inept British politicians had somehow failed to notice that aeroplanes are products. Like any other products they have to have a customer. During World War 2, when there was no limit to the demand for aircraft, it had been a good idea to create a Ministry of Aircraft Production to try to get aircraft built quicker. After the war was finally won, the MAP was merely renamed the MoS, Ministry of Supply. This was a wonderful idea. As it was interposed between the manufacturers and the customers it could spend billions ordering things that it thought might be wanted — or, then again, might not.

This particular story began in the darkest days of the war, in August 1941, with the issue of B.8/41, a specification for a heavy bomber to carry a 10,000-lb load over the awesome range of 4,000 miles at 300 mph. Amazingly, this was sent to only the three firms already building four-engined bombers, one of the responses being Arthur Gouge's S.36, which was basically a landplane Shetland. In 1942 the Bristol Aeroplane Company was busy with the Buckingham medium bomber, with an initial order for 580, but the British and American Chiefs of Staff agreed that the USAAF should handle day bombing and the Buckingham became redundant. This left a hole in the Bristol design office, and Capt R. N. Liptrot at the Ministry asked Technical Direc-

tor Leslie Frise if he would like a design study contract for a bomber to carry 80,000 lb to Berlin. This was a rough translation of the requirement that led to the American B-36. This was at first a free and easy exercise, though pressure to use Bristol engines (Centaurus or Orion radials) buried in the wing made the wing very deep, and upper and lower four-cannon turrets as in the Bristol B.1/39 made the fuselage portly. The project became known as 'the 100-ton bomber'.

It was clear to the project team that a high priority had to be placed on reducing drag. Traditional designs, such as the lumpy Bristol 159 (a large bomber that was never built), simply could not meet the range requirement. On the other hand, truly advanced aircraft, even with a wing deep enough to accommodate the eight engines

Three-view of the Bristol 100-ton bomber, showing fields of fire from the cannon turrets. (Via Sir Archibald Russell)

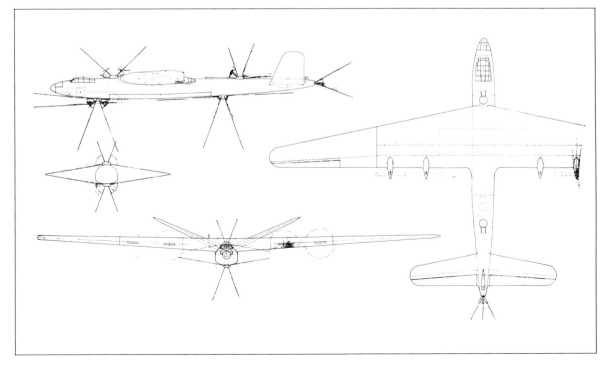

inside it, promised to carry the stipulated bombload for 5,000 miles or even slightly more. No Type Number was raised, but Frise, Russell and a growing team arrived by November 1942 at an impressively futuristic design with a span of 225 ft and area of 5,000 sq ft. Such a wing could accommodate more than enough fuel, even allowing for large parts of it being occupied by the powerplants and their various duct systems. To increase efficiency it was decided to use pusher propellers, and the final arrangement was for the pairs of Centaurus sleeve-valve radial engines to be mounted diagonally, inside the main torsion box of the wing, fed with air ducted in from the leading edge and driving through long shafts passing through the rear spar. Altogether, very much like the B-36.

The diagonal installation brought the two shafts together at the main combining and reduction gearbox, from which concentric shafts extended back through fairings aft of the trailing edge to drive a Rotol contra-rotating propeller with six blades and a diameter of 16 ft. Wind-tunnel tests refined the idea, with each wing having just two 'letter box' slit inlets in the leading edge, each of which immediately divided into two to feed one pair of engines. As with all giant aircraft, it was easy to arrange for inflight inspection of the engines. Integral tanks were studied, but lacking experience and being naturally cautious the team chose to use flexible cells, capacity being 11,700 gal. A little later it was realised that gearing two piston engines to a single shaft system is mechanically very undesirable. Even with two 18-cylinder engines the sequence and exact timing of the firing strokes would inevitably overload the gearteeth, and in any case it would not be easy to start the two engines of each pair simultaneously. Accordingly, the obvious solution was adopted of making one engine of each pair drive the front propeller and the other engine the rear propeller, each half of the powerplant being entirely independent.

The bomber's main crew compartment in the front resembled that of the Bristol 159. At the back a tapering rear fuselage carried one of the new vee-type 'butterfly' tails, again adopted for minimum drag. The aircraft would have been unpressurized, and the defensive armament would have comprised 12 20 mm cannon in dorsal, ventral and tail turrets, but in the event it was never ordered. I think it is fair to believe that the war would have been over before it would have got into action, though it might have avoided the RAF having to borrow B-29s in 1950!

Having been appointed as the ultimate in dynamic Ministers of Aircraft Production in the desperate days of May 1940, Lord Beaverbrook reckoned by late 1942 he could resign (he became Lord Privy Seal). Before he went, he asked that a special committee should be formed to recommend what types of civil transport aircraft should be developed for use after the war. This startling example of farsightedness led to many important aircraft, though unfortunately nearly all failed, for one reason or another, to carve out any share of the world market, the exceptions being the Viscount and Dove. And the chief designers invited to the first meeting, on 23 December 1942, did not include most of those who had experience of civil aircraft. Nobody would have dreamed of inviting Miles, but Bristol was also absent. Both firms soon heard about the committee, and Frise at once visited BOAC to seek their views on large long-range aircraft. Liptrot told the committee the huge Bristol bomber could provide the basis for the first aircraft on the list, to fly non-stop to New York.

The committee, chaired by Lord Brabazon, met again on 14 January 1943. This time both Bristol and Miles were represented. The latter were regarded as a tiny bunch of upstarts, not really to be taken seriously, but since 1936 George Miles had been working

on what he called the Miles X. This, like the Burnelli, was intended to shape the fuselage to obtain useful lift, and in Miles' case the chief feature was that the fuselage was blended into the wing, as is done in modern air-combat fighters. By 1943 Miles had taken the concept to the point where he arrived at the Brabazon Committee with a detailed brochure for the M.26, to be powered by eight 3,000 hp Rolls-Royce Pennine X-24 sleeve-valve engines driving tractor contraprops. These powerful but flat engines fitted inside a very thin wing. With a span of 150 ft and gross weight of 165,000 lb, the M.26 was calculated to fly the North Atlantic (3,650 miles still-air range) with 50 passengers at 350 mph. Predictably, nobody took any interest, and on 11 March 1943 it was announced that the Bristol company was to be invited to design what had become known as the Brabazon I transport. Some time later George Miles discovered that, in their extremely pessimistic evaluation of the M.26, the Ministry had assumed the use of Griffon engines, not Pennines, which completely destroyed the capabilities of the aircraft. Don Brown told me 'Our little team at Reading naturally felt that, yet again, it was "jobs for the boys", and we were not one of the ruling clique'.

My own feeling is that Miles was well out of it. As it was, Bristol was at first told to order materials for two prototypes with the 'intention' — whatever that means — that 10 production aircraft would also be ordered. Nobody said who wanted them. The aircraft received Type Number 167, and the name Brabazon became official, although he had merely been the chairman of the committee. By March 1946, when the design was well advanced and construction of the first aircraft was in progress, Bristol received a definitive contract for four Brabazons, a single Mk I to Specification 2/44 (Bristol No 12759) to fly in April 1947, and three Mk IIs to Specification 2/46 to follow in 1948. The Mk IIs were to be powered by turboprops.

Of course, to say this schedule was ridiculously optimistic is an understatement. After prolonged and angry arguments a new dual-carriageway bypass was closed and half a village destroyed to extend and strengthen the Filton runway, while a gigantic new assembly hall was built specifically for this aircraft. The 8,176 ft runway is nice to have, but was certainly never needed by the Bristol 167, and the huge building proved inconvenient for most of the things it has subsequently been used for. Building the Brabazon became a kind of national enterprise, and from time to time pictures would be released showing bits of airframe making what seemed to be very slow progress. At last the outwardly complete monster came out for engine runs in December 1948. It was then given Service markings and serial VX206, and then civil registration G-AGPW and a Union flag on the fin — but, of course, no nice row of symbols of customer airlines — before newly appointed Chief Test Pilot Bill Pegg made a completely successful first flight on 4 September 1949.

Despite the appearance of a beautiful Bristol advertisement in 1946 showing a direct civil version of the original bomber, complete with pusher propellers and butterfly tail, the configuration finally adopted — after considering aborted full-flap landings — had tractor propellers and a conventional tail. The powerplant, on which a lot of work had been done, did not differ greatly except that the engines were civil Centaurus XX of 2,650 hp, installed ahead of the wing box, much closer to the propellers than would have been the case with a pusher installation, with leading-edge ram inlets on each side of the propeller shaft and exits for hot air and exhaust under the wing. The propellers were those originally developed for the bomber, but slightly modified for tractor operation by swapping over the front and rear blades.

From the outset it was clear that the fuselage would have to be pressurized. Britain had practically no experience of pressurized fuselages, having produced only small capsules for research aircraft, and to pressurize what would obviously be one of the biggest fuselages in the world was no joke. It seemed odd to me that BOAC should be able to lay down the law regarding the passenger accommodation without actually showing any interest in buying the aircraft. The airline said passengers needed 270 cu ft of space each, and an 8,000 ft interior at a cruising height of 35,000 ft. To try to meet

On early flight test, with black lines as camera and photo-theodolite targets. (Charles E. Brown via Philip Jarrett)

*Black lines removed, the Brab looks shiny and new as Pegg accurately brushes the grass on arrival at Heathrow on 25 July 1951. Any engine noise was swamped by the impressive deep rumble from the propellers. (*Flight *via R.T. Riding)*

these requirements the Type 167 was originally planned with a fuselage of 25 ft diameter, with two decks, but this was cut back in 1945 to 20 ft and finally to 16 ft 9 in. As for pressurization, though the fuselage was designed for it, it was never installed, the aircraft being used mainly at low level with nothing inside but test instrumentation and, lost at the back, triple passenger seats. The fuselage was 177 ft long, and its cross-section was a perfect circle. At front and rear the low floor left a vast open space unused above the passengers, almost like being in a cathedral, while above the very thick wing the headroom was somewhat constricted. The difference in levels showed externally from the windows. But riding in the giant was impressive, even quite low and slow, as I discovered in July 1951.

As in the case of the wartime bomber, tremendous efforts were made to reduce drag and structure weight. Skin gauges and stringer sizes were precisely controlled, the shanks of rivets were trimmed, and massive longerons and spar booms were replaced by large numbers of light stringers. The wing, though very deep, had a low-drag 'laminar'

profile, and great care was taken to keep the skin exactly to the desired contour. Mr Frise told me that there was no doubt the buried engines reduced drag, though he said they had never been able to ascertain exactly how much. One has only to look at the aircraft to appreciate its beautiful lines, and because of its size it was possible to fit a capacious cockpit into what looked like a pointed nose.

The wing span was 230 ft, root chord 31 ft and area 5,317 sq ft. It seemed strange that Frise, having invented the excellent aileron that bears his name, should have been content on this gigantic aircraft to use simple plain flaps. Driven hydraulically, these were in eight sections, six on the 100-ft-span centre section and two on the more sharply tapered outer panels, which had just 2-degree dihedral. In the wing box, outboard of the engines, were the bag tanks for 13,600 gal of fuel, even more than in the bomber. The tail looked good in side elevation or plan, but somehow the horizontal and vertical tails clashed when seen together. Tailplane span was 75 ft, and its area of 1,103 sq ft was not far short of that of a Lancaster wing. The towering fin brought the height of the parked aircraft to fractionally over 50 ft. All flight control surfaces were metalskinned, and fully powered by duplicate tandem units, each served by its own hydraulic system. This seemed the prudent answer to a big and partly unknown design requirement. Perhaps the most striking and unhappy feature of the Mk I aircraft was that each surface carried a gigantic mass balance, behind a fairing on the fixed surface. These prominent excrescences — surely a strange addition to surfaces driven by irreversible power units — were intended to be replaced by something better.

All leading edges were deiced by hot air supplied by combustion heaters, two in the wings and one, fed by a ram inlet which marred the beautiful curve of the fin, in the tail. The Brab sat commendably close to the ground. So-called tricycle landing gear was still a novelty in Britain, though Bristol had boldly specified it on the unbuilt 159. The Brab's main units were, like the legs of an elephant, short and massive, each bearing two Dunlop Compacta wheels carrying twin tyres. The diameter was only 64 in, yet surprisingly (because the wing was much deeper than this) the rectangular doors incorporated large blisters. Retraction was hydraulic, forwards, and the brakes were pneumatic. The twin-wheel nose gear was hydraulically steerable, and retracted to the rear.

In view of the slow progress, the last two aircraft were cancelled in 1950, before much work had been done on them, but the second Brabazon, the first Mk II, was continued. Like the Mk I, this kept being improved in the light of new knowledge or new ideas, but in general it retained the same airframe modified to accommodate

four Bristol Coupled Proteus turboprops. The aircraft was Bristol No 12870, and it was intended to be MoS serial VX343 or civil G-AIML. Span was unchanged, but the modified engine installation increased wing area to 5,422 sq ft, and to increase tip clearance the outer panels were given 4-degree dihedral. Addition of radar was to increase length to 178 ft 10 in.

Under Chief Engineer Frank Owner, Bristol's Engine Division had planned the Proteus as a very advanced turboprop in which mechanical complexity was accepted in order to achieve high power and good economy. The basic engine was to weigh 3,050 lb and produce 3,200 hp plus 800 lb of jet thrust. Its two initial applications were both giants, the Brabazon and the Saro Princess. In both aircraft the engine was to be installed inside the wing, air being rammed in through the leading edge and ducted to the engine inlets which were towards the rear. The air then travelled forwards through the compressors and, after a second 180 degree turn, back through the combustion chambers and turbines, and thence out through the jetpipes, which in both aircraft emerged above the rear part of the wing. The Coupled Proteus was even more complex, because here two Proteus power sections, lying parallel side-by-side, put their power into a single shaft driving a massive gearbox from which coaxial shafts extended forwards to drive the propellers. There was a primary gearbox on the front of each engine with a ratio of 3.2 and the final gearbox had a ratio of 3.7, so that the overall ratio was 11.9.

Each Coupled Proteus weighed no less than 7,730 lb — and that was Bristol's own figure, who were unhappy about it. In his biography, which I wrote, Sir Stanley Hooker recalled:

Frank Owner was capable of acting like an ostrich and putting his head in the sand, though he must have known the day of reckoning would come when the giant Brabazon

The view passengers were never to see (but the author did). Flying from Heathrow on 25 July 1951, with the now-demolished art-deco Hoover factory just in view behind the wing. (E.C. Webb via R.T. Riding)

II and Princess would need their engines. Meanwhile, this abysmal engine sank ever deeper in the morass, failing its compressor blades, turbine blades, bearings and many other parts, even at totally inadequate powers well below 2,000 hp. One day we were walking across for lunch and he said 'You know, Stanley, when we designed the Proteus I decided we should make the engine with the lowest specific fuel consumption in the world, regardless of its weight and bulk. So far we have achieved the weight and bulk!'

Thus, even though the Brabazon II was years late, it still looked like arriving at the end of the runway with nothing to drive the propellers, which in this aircraft were to be reversing eight-blade units, though retaining the same 16-ft diameter. There were also many other changes to be developed. The wings were redesigned to incorporate integral fuel tanks of over 16,000 gal capacity,

increasing the gross weight from 290,000 to 330,000 lb, with top-hat stringers instead of Z-section. Then everyone got cold feet and decided to use bag tanks anyway. Another change was to use new main landing gears, with four-wheel bogies, each wheel having twin tyres for a total of eight on each leg. The cabin was this time to be fully pressurized, and to the greater differential of 8.2 lb/sq in, to give an 8,000 ft interior at 40,000 ft. Partly because of this the passenger windows were reduced in size, though they remained rectangular. Perhaps the biggest change of all, apart from the engines, was that the flight controls were to be manually driven via trailing-edge servo tabs, this scheme having been shown surprisingly effective in research for the Britannia. This required the trailing edges to be straight. Hydraulic boost was to be provided in the prototype — it was hoped, as a temporary insurance.

During 1952, when the Mk II was still nowhere near completion, various things happened to kill off the entire project. First, progress had been so slow the basic concept had been overtaken by events, and would have no chance of competing against long-range jets. Second, the same job could now be done by smaller and more cost/effective aircraft, such as Bristol's own Britannia. Third, the politicians had got cold feet about the cost, the seemingly never-ending development delays and the increasing lack

of interest on the part of either BOAC or the RAF. Fourth, 400 hr of flying with the Brabazon I had not only shown up structural trouble with the propeller mounts and gearboxes (which did not necessarily read across to the Mk II) but had indicated that the fatigue-free life of the main structure might be only 5,000 hr, which of course was totally unacceptable. Fifth, and the real killer, the Air Registration Board insisted on the Brabazon II being able to fly at cruising speed through severe vertical atmospheric gusts. Great efforts were made to develop a gust-alleviation system, driving the ailerons symmetrically at 60 degrees per second, but it was thought simpler in the end to give up. Both aircraft were scrapped in 1953.

The
1950s

After World War 2 Britain spent what were by contemporary standards very large sums on the Brabazon and Princess, even though these had no customers, but otherwise showed little interest in nationally funded advances in aircraft technology. In the sharpest contrast, other countries worked as fast as possible to put into the sky swept-wing fighters and bombers and supersonic research aircraft. The so-called Cold War increasingly promoted high defence spending, further accelerated by the outbreak of the Korean War in 1950.

Thus the 1950s were a decade of sustained aeronautical effort, with continuing rapid development in aerodynamics, structures, propulsion and systems. Quite suddenly the flying boat became a very rare species, mainly because of the availability everywhere of large paved runways and the dramatically better reliability of gas-turbine engines. Thus, several aircraft first flown in the 1950s, including one in this book — Tu-20/95/142 — have spent their lives over the world's oceans even though they cannot land there. It also seems strange that it was not until 1954 that all the obvious attributes of a heavy airlifter, such as a flat level floor at truck-bed height, an unobstructed interior and a full-section ramp door (if possible at the front as well as at the back) should have been combined in one aircraft. This aircraft, the C-130, is not a giant, but we find two in the same class in this decade, and several more later.

Despite the severe problems, the attractions of a supersonic bomber were so great that the first in this category were flown in this decade. They assisted in the development of supersonic transports in the 1960s. Aircraft in these classes tend to look enormous in side view and tiny from head-on. After much thought I decided to include the Myasishchyev 50 and a brief mention of the Avro 730.

On the whole, however, this is a thin period compared with the amazing profusion of the 1940s. The launch of both Sputnik 1 and the first ICBMs (intercontinental ballistic missiles) triggered off both a reduction of interest in large bombers and a large-scale transfer of funds from seemingly outdated aircraft to missiles and spacecraft. Nobody would expect to find any of the latter in this book, but I might comment that the biggest space launch vehicles make most of our supposed giant aircraft look like tiddlers. For example, the Saturn V which took men to the Moon in 1969 had a height of 364 ft and a lift-off mass of about 6,423,000 lb, while today's Soviet *Energiya* with strap-on boosters thinks nothing of accelerating up from our planet at 7,884,000 lb — the weight of 10 loaded 747s. And of course, their propulsive horsepower runs into tens of millions.

Previous page *Two of the 'designs that got away' were the Handley Page HP.97 and, with tip tanks, HP.111. They were planned as the double-deck commercial jetliners based on the Victor bomber, the HP.97 being based on the Sapphire-engined Mk 1 and the 111 on the Conway-engined Mk 2. Technically they rated 100 per cent; politically they scored zero. (Via Mike Hooks)*

57 Boeing B-52

I believe it was after a formal dinner that a SAC officer got to his feet and opened his speech by describing the bomber that formed the backbone of the Command. He said 'Its engines have the power of 100 locomotives. It contains 1,000 miles of wire, and the metal in a B-52 would fill 20,000 trash cans. And when I open those eight throttles on take-off and charge down the runway it's like 100 locomotives were towing 20,000 trash cans on the end of 1,000 miles of wire.'

I still can't think of this without laughing, but it underscores the way these noble aircraft have become 'a legend in their own lifetime'. The original project studies dated from 1946. The requirement, similar to that of 1941 which led to the B-36, was to carry 10,000 lb of bombs (or, rather, a single 10,000 lb nuclear weapon) over a radius of 5,000 miles. This was the tough part, and only propeller aircraft had any hope of getting near it. Neither the 450 mph speed nor the 40,000 ft ceiling was a problem, but it was going to mean a big aeroplane. Boeing had started

with the Model 462, with an unswept wing of 225 ft span carrying six 5,500 hp Wright XT35 Typhoon turboprops, but soon switched to Model 464s which became progressively smaller, more swept and more attractive, but relying heavily on air refuelling. On Thursday 21 October 1948 a top Boeing team arrived at the Van Cleve Hotel in Dayton, Ohio, to present a pile of proposal documents on the 464-35 to Col Pete Warden, of the Bombardment Branch in the Air Research and Development Command at Wright Field. It so happened that Warden had just had his ear bent by Waldemar Voigt, who in Hitler's Germany had been the first designer of swept-wing fighters. Voigt urged Warden not to accept any turboprop, but to push for a jet and rely on the development, in the short term, of superior turbojets with reduced fuel consumption. The Boeing team were all to become famous: Ed Wells, George Schairer, Maynard Pennell, Harold Withington, Art Carlsen and George Blumenthal. Warden hardly glanced at the huge proposal, but asked if they could fairly

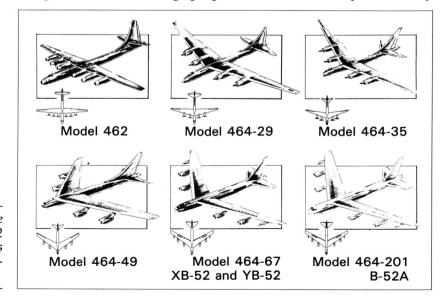

Major milestones in the development of the B-52 design. The small plan views are to scale. (Boeing Company Archives)

Model 462   Model 464-29   Model 464-35

Model 464-49   Model 464-67 XB-52 and YB-52   Model 464-201 B-52A quickly come back with a proposal for a jet.

Normally this would take weeks; today the pre-feasibility study might take 10 years, and the original team's children might design the actual prototype. In 1948 things were different. The six men locked themselves in their hotel room and never stopped work for four nights and three days, except that on the Saturday Pennell went to a hobby shop and bought material with which he made an accurate and detailed model of the big jet, mounted on a desk stand. During the Sunday a public stenographer produced fair typed copies, which together with all the drawings were bound into large binders marked SECRET. The team was back in Warden's office at eight on the Monday morning. The resulting Boeing 464-49 was just what the USAF had been looking for. It needed only minor changes to become the 464-67 which, in March 1949, was the basis for a Phase II contract, involving two flight articles, the XB-52 (Boeing No 16248, AF serial 49-230) and the YB-52 (No 16249, 49-231). They were built at the original

Boeing plant in Seattle, from where the XB was moved under cover of night, and shrouded in acres of white cloth, to the new Flight Test Building on Boeing Field on 29 November 1951. The XB then underwent a major rework to bring in later ideas which were already incorporated in the YB. This emerged on 15 March 1952, and made a very successful first flight on 15 April, crewed by Chief Test Pilot A. M. 'Tex' Johnston and Lt-Col Guy M. Townsend. They departed from schedule and worked through many parts of the future flight-test programme before landing at the bomber's test base, Larson AFB, at Moses Lake.

The new bomber had the same span of 185 ft as several earlier turboprop studies, but sweep was increased to 35 degrees and area from 2,600 to 4,000 sq ft. The wing had

---

Possibly the B-52 with lowest drag, and also the most graceful, the YB is seen here in 1952 against the favourite background of Boeing photographers. (Boeing Airplane Co)

a new profile, deeper than that of the B-47 jet bomber, yet despite this the wing proved amazingly flexible. With the aircraft parked the tips moved down (typically) 9 ft when the tanks were filled. In cruising flight the wings flexed up and down, in rough air sometimes violently, and the static test wing was bent 10 ft down and 22 ft up at each tip! Inflight flexure was slightly damped by the engines, eight massive Pratt & Whitney J57s, installed wholly outside the airframe in four twin pods respectively 34 ft 2in and 60 ft 0 in from the aircraft centreline. In these first two B-52s the engines were YJ57-P-3s each rated at 8,700 lb. Each double pod weighed over five tons.

Boeing was one of the first companies to use the Fowler flap — surely the best ever designed — and tradition was continued with the B-52. The huge flap sections, inboard and outboard of the gap necessitated by the jets from the inboard engines, were each driven by two irreversible screwjacks rotated by a dual hydraulic motor in the fuselage. In common with many other great

Boeing aircraft, powered flight controls were avoided where possible. In most flight regimes roll was handled by small 'flipper' ailerons in the gap between the flaps, driven manually by trailing-edge spoilers. These were supplemented by seven sections of serrated-edge spoiler above each wing, ahead of the outer flaps, each section having its own jack. The spoilers could be opened symmetrically to serve as airbrakes (when, incidentally, the little ailerons became much more effective). They could also be opened asymmetrically following any engine failure.

From early in the 464 studies Boeing decided to sit the aircraft on four landing-gear trucks on the fuselage, the narrow track of 11 ft 4 in needing outrigger gears near the wingtips. All units were arranged to retract hydraulically, the outriggers inwards into the

52-8716 was the last of the 27 RB-52Bs, with provision for a pressurized manned reconnaissance pod in the bomb bay. Note the tail armament. (Boeing Airplane Co)

wing and the main trucks diagonally inwards into bays in the fuselage, the left-hand trucks going forwards and the right ones to the rear. The front pair of trucks incorporated hydraulic steering, and all four could if necessary be slewed up to 20 degrees to left or right prior to making a cross-wind landing (which helped a lot, as you had to keep the wings level).

Though nothing like as demanding as a B-47, plenty of skill was needed to land a B-52 absolutely level in pitch so that all eight main wheels hit together. On take-off there was no way the pilots could rotate the aircraft about the rear wheels, so the mighty wing was set at no less than 8 degrees incidence to give a positive climb-out with the fuselage horizontal or even slightly nosedown. To anyone unused to it, this was unnerving, giving the sensation of being in some enormous VTO or lift. The wing root, no less than 15 per cent thick, had the thickest part swept forward to reach almost to the top of the box-like fuselage. In the upper part of the fuselage were a row of six huge flexible fuel tanks, and seven more in the wing. The resulting capacity of 32,362 gal was by a wide margin a world record, and not far short of twice that of a B-36. It meant that even the YB at first flight could weigh a maximum of 405,000 lb, though it actually took off at about 300,000.

The point has already been made that asymmetric thrust was handled by the spoilers. Indeed, throughout its career the B-52 has needed careful handling with one or more engines out, and at light weights the engines must not be used asymmetrically at high power or uncontrollable roll and structural damage is likely to result. Thus, in real trouble, with one complete pod inoperative, you have to get your landing right first time. This is despite the enormous vertical tail, which brought the height to 48 ft 4 in. In comparison the full height rudder looked like a mere tab on the fin, though it did have servo tabs of its own to drive it. So that the giant could enter hangars the

vertical tail power-hinged to the right. The horizontal tail likewise looked like a broad slab with tabs, but was in fact a tailplane with manual servo-tab driven elevators. For trimming, the main surface could be driven by a huge Acme-thread screwjack which stalled only under a load of 158,000 lb, and in early B-52s the tailplane could also be cranked by the rear gunner through a 200:1 gearbox. Of course, in the XB and YB there was no armanent, and the two pilots sat as in the B-47 in tandem staggered cockpits. This was well liked, and offered minimum drag, but after Generals LeMay and Griswold had sat in a Valiant at Wisley they decided the traditional side-by-side arrangement was better. But one thing they thought little about — until later — was the most unusual auxiliary power system.

After some sales pressure by AiResearch and others, Boeing decided not to hang the alternators, generators and pumps on the engines, where it appeared they might cause bulges in the pods. Instead the high-pressure compressors of the engines were tapped to provide bleed air at 250 lb/sq in pressure and 400 degrees C (750 degrees F, a bright orange-red heat) which was piped through carefully lagged ducts to air turbines in various parts of the fuselage. The little turbines shrieked and hissed at up to 90,000 rpm, geared down to all the accessories, putting out powers that ranged from tens of horsepower up to over 1,000. These miniature power stations drove everything, right down to the cabin air systems, water-injection pumps and deicing.

First flown on 2 October 1952, the XB-52 still differed in numerous respects, two external ones being the three spoiler sections per wing and absence of ailerons. During 1953 many modifications were made, but on the whole development went well. In particular, the manual flight controls and unusual secondary power system proved satisfactory. On 5 August 1954 the first of three B-52As joined the flight programme. These aircraft had 9,000-lb J57-9W engines, the side-by-side cockpit and provision for flight refuelling by the Boeing boom method, the receptacle being in the top of the fuselage just behind the cockpit. They had Boeing model number 464-201-0. Next followed 23 B-52Bs and 27 RB-52Bs, the latter having provision for a pressurized box in the bomb bay housing two operators and four large cameras. These were full production aircraft, powered by the J57-19W or -29W rated at 12,100 lb, and with full combat equipment including a tail barbette with twin 20-mm cannon aimed by a gunner in a pressure cabin aided by the A-3A radar fire control and a periscopic optical sight. Gross weight was set at 420,000 lb, including up to about 24,000 lb of bombs aimed by the MA-6A nav/bombing system which weighed three tons and included the ASB-4 radar under the nose. Like the A, the B carried injection water in the rear fuselage and 1,665 gal of fuel in two jettisonable tanks under the outer wings. Empty weight of a typical B was 169,300 lb.

The B-52B was cleared for combat duty on 29 June 1955, on the last day of the promised (1955) Fiscal Year. Deliveries had already begun to the 4017th Combat Crew Training Squadron and the 93rd Bomb Wing, both at Castle AFB. As so often happens, the troubles start when aircraft get into service, and for the next two years there was plenty of trouble with the B-52. There were many causes, but by far the most important was the pneumatic secondary power system which had caused numerous inflight fires, turbine-wheel explosions and several lost aircraft. Everyone worked round the clock looking for fixes.

Next came 35 B-52Cs (464-201-6) with no less than 2,500 gal in each enormous drop tank, raising gross weight to 450,000 lb. Another major change was a more advanced nav/bomb system, while the 350 gal of injection water was moved to tanks in the wing roots. From early in the run the Cs had a totally new tail armament with four 0.5-in guns, and were delivered with their under-

I couldn't resist including this, to emphasize the fact — ignored in almost every book and article on the B-52 — that 53-373, like nearly all other B-52Bs and RBs, had twin 20 mm cannon at the back. The A-3A system also included an impressive radar. (HQ 93rd Air Base Group, USAF)

sides painted in anti-radiation white. By this time a general intensification of the Cold War and fear of Soviet bombers had caused massive acceleration of plans to build KC-135 tankers, and combined with a flood of orders for the commercial 707 (at the time thought a giant, but not really one for this book) the Seattle and Renton plants became overloaded, so B-52 production was progressively switched to Wichita. The first model built in Kansas was the B-52D (464-201-7).

GIANTS OF THE SKY

Last of the line, the B-52H with TF33 engines and many other upgrades. This one is 60-0008, and equipment has been changed or added every few days for years. There's a long way to go yet. (Mike Hooks)

This differed only in details from the C, and while Wichita built 69 Seattle built 101.

Next came 100 E-models (464-259), 42 from Seattle and 58 from Wichita. These introduced another totally new nav/bombing system, and indeed from this point onwards the B-52 story became increasingly one of modification and updating, particularly in the matter of avionics. The first E flew on 3 October 1957, and by this time both plants were turning out B-52s at such a rate that the average price for an E was only $6.08 million, which today might just about pay for the nine IBM computers and displays that were in the E's ASQ-38(V) system. The final model made at Seattle was the F (464-260). Seattle made 44 and Wichita 45, the first flying on 6 May 1958. Few of the changes showed, though the engine pods did look different. They housed the J57-43W (or WA or WB) engines, rated at 13,750 lb, with steel blading changed to titanium and incidentally all made not by Pratt & Whitney but by Ford Motor at East Wacker Drive, Chicago. The engine could have fitted into the original pod, but in fact the installation was completely redesigned. Instead of looking simple, with just a big hole at the front for each engine, three smaller inlets appeared, plus a big bulge on the lower left side (lower right as seen from the front). Chin inlets served the oil coolers, and the third inlet provided ram air to cool the massive package of a 40-kVA alternator and its Sundstrand hydraulic constant-speed

drive which was responsible for the bulge. At last all the network of 750° piping and air-turbine drives were eliminated. Another change in the F was to put the injection water in the leading edge at each engine pylon strut, which is where it should have been put in the first place.

Eliminating the hot pipes allowed Boeing to do something else it had wanted to do for years. The B-52G (464-253), made only at Wichita, had the main wing boxes sealed to form integral tanks, reducing empty weight and increasing fuel capacity. The sealing process involved a 15-man skin-diving team inspecting every nook and cranny inside the tanks and also cutting away surplus sealant. The new fuel capacity was 38,827 gal. This enabled the huge drop tanks to be replaced by smaller fixed external tanks of only 583 gal each, giving a total of 39,993 gal. Gross weight climbed to 'over 488,000 lb' despite a total structural redesign which took about 10,000 lb of dead weight out of the airframe. The most prominent changes were to cut down the vertical tail by nearly 8 ft, the spoilers having proved able to deal with engine asymmetry, to use powered tail controls and eliminate the ailerons, and to move the gunner into the forward pressurized crew compartment, leaving the unchanged rear barbette to be managed by the new ASG-15 fire-control system.

It had been expected that the G would complete the run at 603 aircraft, but in fact additional Gs were ordered, to a total of 193, and then yet a further model, the H (464-261). Wichita built 102, the first flying on 6 March 1961 and the last being rolled out on 22 June 1962. The H introduced a further total structural rework to enable these giant bombers to operate at low level, though normally at quite low speeds and, except in real wartime, about 100 tons below their gross weight of 505,000 lb, or 566,000 lb after flight refuelling. The visible changes were that the pods again looked different, for they now housed the new Pratt & Whitney TF33 turbofan, rated at 17,000 lb and needing no injection water, and the tail armament was a single 20 mm M61 'Gatling gun' with ASG-21 fire control. While the 'wet wing' of the B-52G had increased the high-altitude range from 7,370 miles to 8,406, the new fan engines of the H extended it to 10,130. In fact in June 1962 a B-52H flew from Seymour Johnson AFB to Bermuda, Greenland, Alaska, California, Florida and back to Seymour Johnson to set a world closed-circuit distance record of 11,337 miles which stood for nearly 25 years.

This is still only half the story of the B-52. I do not propose to dwell on the bomber's various weapons, defensive and offensive avionics, structural troubles at low level, gruelling missions in South East Asia carrying huge loads of conventional bombs and ongoing service in new roles into the 1990s, including use as a carrier of special test aircraft or special test engines. These things can be read in many places. Today, parked at a major airport, a Buff (politely translated as 'the big ugly fat fella') would not look particularly big, and because it is so close to the ground the wide-bodies would tower over it. But everyone would treat it with the greatest reverence.

58 Convair YB-60

Convair Fort Worth Division received the USAF contract to build two prototypes of this bomber on 15 March 1951. It was a prudent move, to guard against any serious

The first of the two YB-60s. Not a lot of the B-36 was left. (Consolidated Vultee via R.T. Riding)

difficulty with the all-new B-52. The YB-60 was basically a jet version of the B-36, but it actually turned out to be almost a fresh design, though portions of the fuselage were very similar to its predecessor. The engines were the same as those of the B-52: eight 8,700-lb thrust Pratt & Whitney YJ57-P-3 turbojets hung below and ahead of the wing in twin pods. The wing, of course, was almost completely new, swept at 35 degrees and with area increased but span reduced (to 206 ft). Fuel capacity was considerably increased, even over that of the B-36, and gross weight rose to 445,000 lb, requiring strengthened main landing gear. Armament would have been simplified, probably to just a tail turret, though there was a pressurized rear fuselage section with lateral sighting blisters. Not including the nose instrument boom the length was increased to 171 ft, and height over the swept tail to 50 ft.

Convair produced the two aircraft with amazing rapidity, having the first (YB-60-1-CF) ready for its engines in eight months. It flew on 18 April 1952, three days after the YB-52. The serial numbers, 49-2676 and -2684, were taken out of production B-36F blocks, and the YB-60 was originally designated YB-36G. In the event the B-52 did all it was meant to, and the production B-60 was not needed. The two YBs were the largest jet aircraft until the Lockheed C-5A of 1968.

59 Saunders-Roe SR.45 Princess

The Princess was the biggest aircraft ever built in Britain, and there is not the slightest chance we shall ever build anything bigger (though fortunately we share in making the wings for the Airbus A330 and A340 which are broadly similar in size and will do a very much bigger job for the airlines). The Princess was also the last member of that great class of passenger flying boats. They had sleeping cabins, smoking rooms, dining rooms, dressing rooms (separately, of course, for ladies and gentlemen) and sometimes promenade decks with potted palms. We could have all this today, and the fare to Australia might be £8,000. Instead we have ten-abreast seating, can fly to Australia non-stop at 550 mph and it costs £800 (less if you shop around). I don't regret the change.

We have seen in the story of the Brabazon how Britain farsightedly, at Christmas 1942, formed a committee to consider what civil transport aircraft should be built after the war. They made no recommendations regarding flying boats, and even in 1942 such aircraft were beginning to look just a tiny bit uncertain, emerging as they would into a post-war world where every major city would have a big paved runway nearby. Previously, civil transports in the very largest sizes tended to be flying boats because huge landplanes could not conveniently use the tiny fields of soft grass that so often served as airports. Once airborne, the landplane tended to have a lighter airframe and to fly faster, because it could have a low wing, an almost perfectly streamlined fuselage, engines untroubled by waves and spray, and no need for a planing bottom or either underwing floats or sponsons. There was ample scope for argument, and several respected designers said that above a particular size or weight — 100,000 lb was often cited — flying boats could be made as aerodynamically efficient as landplanes. What hardly anyone appeared to look at was the appalling record of accidents with flying boats, usually whilst alighting. Thus, in the first decade with US trunk carriers DC-3 casualties (flying round the clock)

amounted to just under 2 per cent, whereas the corresponding figure for the Short Empire boats (flying mainly by day) was 55 per cent.

As noted in the story of the Shetland, in 1943 Arthur (later Sir Arthur) Gouge left Short Brothers and became Vice-Chairman of Saunders-Roe Ltd, a smaller firm based at East Cowes on the Isle of Wight. Saro's managing director was Capt E. D. Clarke, and Chief Designer Henry Knowler. The company had studied a large civil flying boat before the war, and in early 1940 flew a small-scale model of it, the Saro Model 37 Shrimp. Even during the war the Shrimp and various tank models were used to help refine the design of a big commercial boat, which by 1944 had begun to firm up as a 100-passenger machine powered by six Centaurus or Eagle engines. However, even as he was initialling the final drawings Knowler was realising he had to tear them up. A future airline boat would have to have gas-turbine engines and be pressurized.

Development of the turboprop opened up new vistas of power. Even the earliest and most primitive examples offered power beyond anything attainable with piston engines. The Armstrong Siddeley Python

The first SR.45 rolled majestically into the water at Cowes at midnight on Wednesday 20 August 1952. She was a brilliant example of aircraft engineering, and deserved better project management. (Via R.T. Riding)

was soon to go into production at 4,110 hp and the equally primitive Rolls-Royce Clyde was running soon after the war at 4,543 hp, so the future looked bright. By early 1945 Knowler had produced a proposal brochure and drawing for a completely new and larger aircraft, the SR.45. This was to weigh 120 tons and have a 220-ft wing carrying six 5,000 hp engines. Lacking such engines he proposed coupled pairs of Rolls-Royce Tweeds, but these were cancelled. After studying pushers, whose propellers suffered from spray, it was decided to mount the engines conventionally ahead of the wing. The hull was to be 146 ft long and to have a double-bubble cross section 16 ft wide and 24 ft high, pressurized to 8 lb/sq in. Not only was this one of the biggest fuselages in the world, exceeded only by the XC-99 (marginally) and Hughes Hercules, but this pressure differential had never before been attempted. Patented floats were devised, mounted well in from the tip and retracting inwards so that the outer side of the float formed the unblemished underside of the wing. Another patented idea was an automatic docking system. Knowler records:

In consultation with the post-war MCA (Ministry of Civil Aviation) and BOAC, who were to be the operators, the design was finalised and the order to go ahead given in 1947. This was for three Princess flying boats. In the process of design, steadily increasing range, load and equipment requirements caused the weight to rise from 268,000 to over 300,000 lb. This aircraft also required the design of completely new installations and equipment, none of which was then available.

The actual order, placed by the Ministry of Supply in May 1946, was for three boats at an all-in price of £2.8 million, then a very large sum. Various press releases made it clear that the contracting authority was not the MoS but the MCA, while the future use of the boats by BOAC, or perhaps British South American Airways, was assumed in only the vaguest way. One statement announced that they would carry 105 passengers, 'some in private two-berth cabins',

the 3,450 miles from London to New York against a 90 mph headwind. No attempt was made to implement any of the schemes for a marine airport near London. At the 1947 SBAC show visitors marvelled at the SR.45's centre-section bridge, linking the left and right wing boxes. It was by far the most massive chunk of aircraft structure ever built in Europe (or, possibly, anywhere) at that time, with parts squeezed out by James Booth's new 12,000-ton press and partly hand-forged as in shipyards. Indeed, building the Princesses seemed to have a lot in common with shipbuilding, but overlain with the very latest high technology. After all, this was the fastest propeller aircraft, the biggest metal aircraft, the biggest pressurized aircraft and the biggest gas-turbine aircraft, and it was quite a challenge.

In January 1948 the seemingly ignored matter of engines was answered, and

G-ALUN did a lot of her flying somewhere near the Isle of Wight. It is typical of Britain that, having spent all the money, nothing was done to fit good engines when these (very quickly) became available. (British Hovercraft via Mike Hooks)

nobody had any inkling of what horrors were to come. Like the Brabazon II the Princess was to be powered by the Bristol Proteus, supposedly each rated at 3,500 hp. The growth in weight of the Princess meant that not six but 10 engines would be needed, arranged in four coupled pairs, as in the Brab II, plus two singles outboard. Saro had to redesign the entire wing to accommodate the powerplants internally, all fed from ram inlets in the leading edge with ducts taking the air round to plenum chambers surrounding the rear part of each engine, or each pair. Jetpipes went straight back through the wing to plain nozzles above the front of the flaps. The complex drive systems of both the single and coupled engines were as briefly outlined in the Brabazon story, though in the Princess the propellers were by de Havilland. Each unit had four blades, at first of solid Duralumin; it was planned to replace these with hollow steel blades. Diameter was 16 ft 6 in, all blades had electric deicing, and the eight-blade contraprops on the outer coupled engines had 120 degree pitch range for braking and water manoeuvring.

The wing was made in five units: a centre section of 30 ft 9 in chord integral with the hull, two slightly tapered inner wings containing the engines, and two outer panels quite sharply tapered on the leading edge. Unlike the Brabazon the laminar profile was quite thin, the maximum thickness at the root being only 64 in. Though an access tunnel was provided into each wing it was not expected that anyone would attend to the engines in flight, as in the days of piston engines. Structurally the wing had two massive sheet web spars, the torsion box between the outer coupled engines and the hull being sealed to form a total of four huge integral tanks with a capacity of 14,580 gal of kerosine. On the trailing edge were three sections of slotted flap on each side, driven electrically. The leading edge was deiced by hot air taken from heat exchangers in the jetpipes of the outer engines. To deice the tail

a ram inlet in the fin leading edge served a cockpit-controlled combustion heater.

The flight-control system was one of the biggest challenges, and Saro, in partnership with Boulton Paul Aircraft (BPA), created a system of remarkable capability. It began, of course, in the splendid flightdeck, which instead of being well back in a hemispherical nose, ended up right in the bows, more than 20 ft above the water, where both pilots had a perfect view right down to the great ship's waterline. Pilot input demands travelled by cable to three basically similar electro-hydraulic power units, one in the top of the hull for the ailerons and two inside the rear upper pressure dome for the tail surfaces. Each unit consisted of two identical torque converters driving through a differential gearbox, so that failure of either portion merely halved the output speed. The motors were driven by the DC electrical system, which most unusually was not at 28V but at 120, and were each rated at 7.5 hp. They were geared down to variable-delivery hydraulic pumps whose stroke, and thus output, was normally zero, though the motors ran at full speed continuously. Receipt of a pilot demand displaced the pump swashplate and made the pump start working, at a rate proportional to the demand. This drove a hydraulic motor which, via long rotating shafts, joints, gearboxes and finally irreversible screwjacks, drove the surface. Again for redundancy, each surface was split. Each aileron was in four sections, the elevators two each and the rudder three, each section having its own screwjack drive. Chief Test Pilot Geoffrey Tyson helped develop the system, using a Sunderland, and considered it satisfactory long before he flew the Princess. Saro and BPA never did develop the q-feel system they wanted, making force feedback proportional to airspeed (or the square of indicated airspeed, to be more precise), nor did they complete modifying the system to have electrical signalling to power units adjacent to the surfaces.

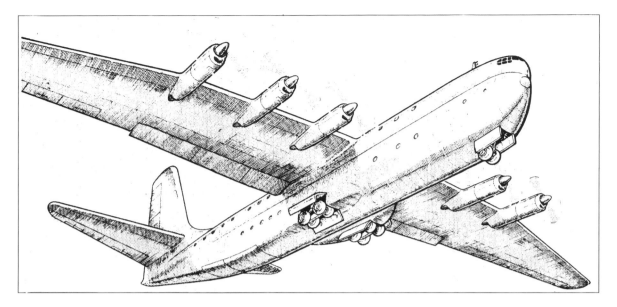

Maker's brochure drawing of the P.199 Princess land-plane. It was intended for civil use; a military airlifter would have needed about 28 wheels. (Saunders-Roe via R.O. Lyon)

With such a gigantic double-deck hull, every bit of it pressurized except for the planing bottom, very large flows of heated and pressurized air were needed, and it was not thought that turboprops could supply this without running into problems with turbine temperature and other factors. Accordingly each inboard Coupled Proteus was connected through a four-stage gearbox, with automatic gear-change, to a large two-stage centrifugal compressor solely for supercharging the fuselage. Overall length was 148 ft, slightly up on the first estimate. Another dimension that changed was the span, because at quite a late stage, in early 1949 (after the original first-flight date) it was decided to redesign the stabilizing floats to retract outwards, Catalina fashion, to form the wingtips. When these were in the up position they increased the span from 210 ft 6 in to 219 ft 6 in. Wing area was 5,250 sq ft. Empty and gross weights finally came out to about 184,000 lb and 330,000 lb. The height of 55 ft 9 in was, at the time, second only to the Hughes Hercules.

With hindsight it is clear that the Princess, like the Brabazon, was running a race. Too much delay and it might as well never have been started. And this is — probably predict-

ably — what did happen. The awful Proteus 600 took so long that, far from flying in early 1949, the first Princess did not even get its first engine until 14 February 1951. At last, painted like the Brabazon with a Union Jack and registration G-ALUN, it made a majestic first flight on 22 August 1952. Tyson was, on the whole, well pleased with his monster charge, but the engine remained a disaster. To quote Sir Stanley Hooker:

It was a nightmare to attend Saro's progress meetings at Cowes...Until we were able to demonstrate in 1953 that we had a totally different animal in the Proteus 3 I felt stretched to exhaustion...The Ministry and BOAC were beginning to realise by this time that to carry the world's air travellers you needed a modernised DC-6B, not a Princess. So the second and third Princesses never flew. I must say what a spectacular sight the giant boat was as it soared across the Farnborough air show with all ten engines running; but, as it passed into the distance, I breathed a prayer of relief and grabbed a stiff double whisky.

I won't repeat here the agonizing and rather pointless succession of non-decisions that followed 1952. Work on Nos 2 and 3 Princesses, which were structurally complete, was suspended in January 1953, and they were put into cocoons at Calshot. G-ALUN continued to do a little flying, confirming a cruising speed at 25,000 ft of 360 mph on the 2,400 hp (or thereabouts) she was getting from each engine. As Hooker's new Proteus 3, over 1,000 lb lighter and a better engine in every way, was about to go into production at 4,445 hp, they would have made quite a difference. But, while showing no interest in the Princess, Sir Miles Thomas of BOAC said he was buying 60 Bristol BE.25 Orion turboprops, each of potentially 8,000 hp. Several people, including Ministers, said the Princess would be resurrected in 1957 with six BE.25s. All work stopped in May 1954, and G-ALUN was cocooned at Cowes.

Obviously, all the Princess wanted was a good engine, and there were several projects for fitting BE.25s or 6,000 ehp Rolls-Royce Tynes. A very long shot in 1956 was the P.193, called a Combat Information Centre, but what we today call an AWACS. The engines would have been six BE.25s, and the APS-20E radar would have looked through antennas in the nose, a dorsal blister and the tail. There were also tanker and transport versions of the 193. More unexpected was the P.199 of 1957. Powered by six Tynes, this would have been a landplane. The rounded wingtips reduced area to 5,140 sq ft, but otherwise dimensions and weights were very close to the flying boat. It was intended to barge or float the landplane from Cowes to 'a suitable airfield'. One of the last projects based on the Princess was the P.213 of 1958-59. A lot of work was done on this, because it interested the US Navy. A nuclear reactor was to be installed, and the favoured schemes were a direct-cycle system with 15,000 hp T57 turboprops (Pratt & Whitney collaborated in studies) or two indirect-cycle schemes, one with a pressurized-water reactor. Several versions were investigated, one having two Princess hulls on a 310-ft wing and a weight of about 950,000 lb.

The last idea of all was to use the Princesses as carriers of space boosters for NASA. This finally fell through in May 1966, an on 12 April 1967 the last of these great aircraft went on her last sad journey to a breaker's yard in Southampton.

60 Tupolev Tu-95, 114 and 142

The Soviet design bureau of Andrei Nikolayevich Tupolev has already figured prominently in these pages, and it continues to this day to be responsible for some of the world's largest and most powerful aircraft. It was the OKB chosen in 1944 to produce a Soviet copy of the B-29 Superfortress, and this aircraft, the Tu-4, was the starting point for a series of developments which led, via the Tu-70 and 75 transports and Tu-80 bomber, to the Tu-85, a considerably more capable bomber with piston engines of 4,300 hp each. This was abandoned in favour of an even more capable aircraft with almost the same fuselage but turboprop engines designed to produce 12,000 hp each. This impressive engine, and its associated propeller, has been the key to perhaps the most remarkable family of aircraft of modern times. Starting with a strategic bomber first flown in 1954, it encompasses aircraft for many other purposes including special cargo, passenger transport, missile carrier, all forms of strategic reconnaissance, electronic warfare, submarine communications and anti-submarine warfare. The same basic aircraft have been in production for 37 years.

As the key to the whole development, the propulsion system is worthy of some attention. It had long been common knowledge that turboprops could not efficiently be used at speeds above about 450 mph, though the United States spent a lot of effort trying to develop propellers with blades designed to operate at over Mach 1. The equally logical Soviet alternative was to see how far it would be possible to coarsen the pitch in cruising flight. With the blades almost feathered, provided they did not stall, then the propeller could rotate quite slowly yet the aircraft could reach speeds similar to those of jet aircraft. Prolonged research showed that, without losing propulsive efficiency, it would be possible to coarsen the blade pitch to a degree never previously thought possible. As a result, Tupolev's powerful team designed the Tu-85 replacement, the Tu-95, with swept wings and tail.

Whereas the Tu-85 had a design gross weight of 235,891 lb, the turboprop bomber was designed to weigh about 340,000 lb to start with, with considerable capacity for future growth. To match this, the wing was given a span of 167 ft 8 in, the leading-edge

sweep being 37 degrees inboard and 35 degrees outboard, the area being 3,342 sq ft. The leading edge remained fixed, deiced by hot air from jetpipe heat exchangers. The flaps were of the area-increasing slotted type, differing from the Fowler in not having a fixed shroud covering the retracted flap. Outboard ailerons were tabbed and hydraulically boosted, and ahead of them were later added one-piece spoilers used symmetrically or asymmetrically at all speeds. The swept tail again had hydraulically boosted surfaces, the tabbed elevators being hinged to a fixed tailplane mounted part-way up the fin, the entire tail having a lot in common with the Tu-88 (Tu-16) twin-jet bomber which ran about two years earlier in timing. A combustion heater was used to deice the tail.

The fuselage retained the B-29 cross-section, and very similar detail design of the three pressurized compartments, but overall length was about 35 ft greater even than that of the Tu-85, and because of the greater speeds and loads the material thicknesses were increased. As in the Tu-80 and 85, the

Possibly the most-photographed of all versions is the maritime surveillance/targeting platform called 'Bear-D' by NATO. This one has the extended tailcone, replacing the turret.

foward pressure cabin moved the two pilots back from the nose to an 'airline type' cockpit, the extreme glazed nose being occupied by the navigator and bomb-aimer. The defensive armament comprised 10 NR-23 cannon — each far more powerful than any contemporary gun of 20 mm calibre — in front and rear dorsal and ventral remotely controlled turrets and a manned turret in the tail. The main control stations had transparent domes above the forward fuselage and on each side at the tail, each gunner being able to take over from the others when desirable. The tandem bomb bays could each accommodate the largest thermonuclear bomb or a wide range of other stores, range with a 25,000-lb bombload being no less than 9,200 miles.

To make the whole thing possible a large team of mainly German prisoners of war, many of them former Junkers engineers and led by Dipl-Ing Ferdinand Brandner, was organised in 1947 as part of the engine KB (construction bureau) of N.D. Kuznetsov at Kuibyshyev, and told to develop the 12,000 hp engine. The result was the NK-12, certainly a landmark in gas-tubine technology, though to be fair it got its power mainly by simply being big. Of course, so challenging a project had to pass through various stages of modification, but after five years the definitive NK-12M was running at 12,000 hp in 1952. It had a single axial spool with variable inlet vanes and multiple blow-off valves, with a pressure ratio (depending on flight condition) of 9 to 13. Mass flow was 143 lb/sec. The whole engine had only one shaft, the five-stage turbine driving the compressor and the massive gearbox which split the drive to the two four-blade propellers forming the AV-60 contraprop. At first engine control was electric; in current versions it is electronic. Under all flight conditions the control maintains engine speed at a constant 8,300 rpm and propeller speed at only 750 rpm, blade pitch being varied to suit airspeed, and fuel flow being scheduled to match the power demand. Propeller

diameter in the Tupolev bombers has always been 18 ft 4 in. Blade tips were cleared to Mach 1.08, but in normal missions the whole blade is subsonic at all times.

Each engine was carried far ahead of the main wing box on a stainless-steel frame. The whole engine could be exposed by opening the hinged cowl panels, the oil cooler being underneath and the jetpipes being bifurcated to discharge on each side under the leading edge. Despite the structural challenge of the wing the decision was taken to seal the structural box to house 16,054 gal of kerosine. In subsequent versions this capacity was to be increased to 20,900 gal. The inner nacelles were grossly extended to the rear to house the main landing gears, each having a four-wheel bogie which somersaulted as the unit folded hydraulically to the rear, to lie inverted in the rear part of the nacelle projecting behind the wing. This unusual arrangement, to become a Tupolev trademark, imposed surprisingly little drag and was to be featured on many jet aircraft, even including the Tu-28 supersonic interceptor. The exceptionally tall nose gear had twin wheels with levered suspension and hydraulic steering. It too retracted backwards, into a long bay under the floor of the pressurized forward compartment.

The first flight was delayed by the engine/propeller combination. Like almost every Western high-power turboprop it was the propeller that caused the gravest problems, and in 1953 senior test pilot A. D. Perelyet was killed by the disintegrating propeller of the NK-12 installed in the No. 3 (right inner) position on a Tu-4LL flying testbed. At last the engine was cleared to power the Tu-95, and the first flight took place in the summer of 1954. No fewer than seven development aircraft appeared at the Aviation Day display at Tushino in 1955. Western reaction was one of incredulity; in a nutshell, it was 'Everyone knows that sweepback and propellers don't go together, so this huge bomber is ridiculous'. We should have remembered that Soviet aircraft are seldom ridiculous, and things in this class have to meet tough specifications. As it was, we grossly undervalued the giant, and though we gave it the impressive NATO name of 'Bear' we failed to believe Austrian engine-designer Brandner when he casually commented, on being released from the Soviet Union, that the Tupolev bomber was designed to cruise at Mach 0.85, corresponding to 560 mph at 36,000 ft. The official estimate of the US Department of Defense was a maximum speed of Mach 0.76, or 500 mph, and a maximum cruising speed (which some experts thought an exaggeration) of 450 mph.

The production bomber, called Tu-20 by the VVS (air force), entered service with the DA (long-range aviation, later restyled as the ADD) in late 1956. The production bomber had a crew of nine. Under the nose was the rotating antenna of the navigation and blind-bombing radar, while above the tail gunner's compartment was added a smaller radar to warn of targets astern and assist in aiming the various guns. The tailplane was now pivoted, driven by a screwjack for trimming purposes, the tail bumper was replaced by two small retractable wheels, and the defensive armament was simplified to six NR-23s, one pair in the tail, one pair in a retractable rear dorsal turret and the other pair in a non-retractable rear ventral turret. Several factories participated in manufacture, with assembly at Taganrog. Between 240 and 300 were built between 1955 and 1962. Later versions were built from 1968 onwards.

Early in the programme one of Tupolev's life-long colleagues, A. A. Arkhangelski (who had played a major role in such earlier giants as the ANT-6, 16, 20, 22, 26 and 28) was assigned the development of a civil passenger version. First he produced the Tu-116, better known as the Tu-114D (D for *dalnyi*, long range). Three 116s were built, the first being registered 76462 for Aeroflot and the other two going to the VVS as 7801 and 7802. They were essentially unarmed

versions of the bomber, with the entire rear fuselage pressurized and furnished for 24 or 30 passengers in 2 + 2 seats. These aircraft had plenty to do. In the mid-1950s large sums were being spent on upgrading VVS and naval AV-MF airfields, but civil airports were almost all geared to aircraft such as the Li-2 (DC-3). The Tu-116 did much pioneering work in checking out electronic aids such as ADF, NDBs and ILSs, and in verifying the ability of runways and taxiways to handle heavy aircraft. No 76462 also made several publicity flights, and these at last forced Washington to reassess the bomber. In April 1958 this aircraft flew from Moscow to Irkutsk and back non-stop, a distance of 5,282 miles, at 503 mph average.

During 1958 the Kuznetsov KB cleared the NK-12MV engine at its increased rating of 14,795 hp, and this immediately replaced the earlier engine in the bomber. Four of the first MV engines were also installed in the Tu-114, which had first flown on 3 November 1957. This was Arkhangelski's true civil counterpart of the bomber, with a totally new airline-type fuselage mounted above the wing. This fuselage had a diameter of 157½ in and length of 177 ft, and it was fully pressurized to the high differential of 8.39 lb/sq in. This required the highest-capacity environmental system ever fitted in an aircraft up to that time, and in fact despite the existence of the Boeing 707 and DC-8 the Tu-114 was, for 10 years from the date of its appearance, the biggest airliner in the world. Western visitors were rather awed by the prototype, L-5611, when it came to Paris in 1959 (though I didn't endear myself to Tupolev when, noticing the massive section of armour plate on the fuselage in the plane of the inboard propellers, I asked if he was still worried about shedding blades; he said, 'No, we are worried about the blades shedding ice', though as the blades had electric deicing I was perplexed by this).

The interior, I think the longest I had ever been in, was a never-ending vista of cabins furnished in mahogany, brass and fine lace.

The prototype Tu-114, L-5611, attended the Paris air-show in 1959. Two years later this production air-craft followed suit. Note the cabin ram-air inlet under the belly. (Via Philip Jarrett)

There was a dining saloon and various sleeping cabins, though these were absent from the high-density version which seated 220. About 30 of these monsters were built, and for 15 years they served all Aeroflot's longest intercontinental routes. Before it entered service the Tu-114 was used for several world record flights. For example, on 9 April 1960 a test crew under I. M. Sukhomlin carried a 25-tonne payload around a 5,000 km (3,107 mile) closed circuit at an average speed of 877.212 km/h (545.1 mph), which for the second time made the Washington experts think twice about the bomber. Another record was a height of just under 40,000 ft with a payload of 30 tonnes. The 114s did, in fact, have slightly less fuel than the original production bomber, at 15,754 gal.

By 1961 many small changes were indcating that the Tu-20 in service was finding new roles. A book published in Britain in 1964 said 'The Tu-20 has now been largely relegated to the roles of missile carrier and reconnaissance'. This gave a misleading impression; far from being 'relegated' the basic Tu-95 design was proving so capable that new missions kept being assigned to it, and new batches of aircraft kept being ordered. Concisely, the following are the major service variants, listed in order of the NATO reporting designations:

Bear-A The original Tu-20 free-fall bomber, of which a small number (possibly none) remained in service in 1990. All survivors have been rebuilt for other roles, while any remaining development Tu-95s are used for test programmes.

Bear-B Converted to carry giant air/surface (primarily anti-ship) cruise missile (NATO AS-3 'Kangaroo'), with long-wave (low end of I-band) guidance radar in unglazed nose, displacing navigator and bomb aimer. Most from 1962 added FR probe, with external pipe along right side. Some have air-sampling pods on underwing pylons and an Elint (electronic intelligence) blister on right side of rear fuselage.

Bear-C Similar to 'B' but configured primarily for oceanic reconnaissance and Elint, with blister on both sides of rear fuselage and often tail turret replaced by long tailcone housing electronics and antennas (the latter believed to include 8-km VLF spool); missile capability can be retained, but some have cameras/IRLS/SLAR instead.

Bear-D Widely used oceanic reconnaissance rebuild, with original nose but different chin radar, giant I-band surface search radar under former weapons bay, two Elint blisters, pods on tailplane tips, larger tail warning radar. No weapons, primary role is to find surface targets for friendly surface ships and submarines armed with anti-ship missiles. Some have extended tailcone for submarine communication.

Bear-E Simple rebuild of 'A' for multisensor reconnaissance with twin Elint blisters and bomb bay rebuilt to house six/seven cameras and IRLS/SLAR.

Bear-F Totally redesigned aircraft built as Tu-142 at Kuibyshyev from 1968. Primary role ASW. New airframe has wing with increased camber and stressed for greater weight (414,470 lb), extended forward fuselage, fully pressurized rear fuselage with crew rest and galley, sonobuoy stores and launchers (sonobuoys also dropped from rear weapons bay, which carries torpedoes, nuclear depth charges etc), I/J-band search radar further forward than radar of 'D', no Elint, nose superficially like 'A', considerably enhanced fuel capacity (basic 20,900 gal), tip pods on tailplane, added stores bay for sonobuoys in rear fuselage in place of ventral turret. New main landing gears with tyres to handle weight, requiring larger nacelles and bulged nose-gear doors. Subsequent versions include: F Mod 1, normal

Bearing no markings or numbers, save the national insignia, this Tu-126 was being escorted by F-4Bs of the US Navy. Note that the steel anti-ice armour now extends right to the top of the fuselage. (Ministry of Defence via Mike Hooks)

landing gear, chin radar removed, fewer antennas; F Mod 2, forward fuselage lengthened by a further 9 in, flightdeck structure redesigned to give pilots greater headroom and better view, FR probe angled 4 degrees down; F Mod 3, long MAD (magnetic-anomaly detection) boom added projecting to rear from fin tip, rear stores bay longer but less wide, tailplane pods removed; F Mod 4, as Mod 3 but numerous additional items including self-protection ECM thimble radome on nose, large chin package housing various sensors including a radar, and additional spiral ECM antennas facing to rear, including two on pylons under extreme tail.

Bear-G Tu-95 rebuilt as cruise-missile carrier, generally as 'Bear B' or 'C' but with original weapons bay occupied by fuel and pylons for new missiles (NATO AS-4 'Kitchen') under each inner wing. ECM thimble on nose and four ECM pods on fuselage pylons, left/right at front and left/right at rear. Extended tailcone standard.

Bear-H New production with Tu-142 airframe but with forward fuselage of original length. Internal rotary launcher for long-range cruise missiles (NATO AS-15 'Kent'), and provision for carrying four more on twin pylons under inner wings. No Elint blisters, larger and deeper nose radome, shorter fin-tip fairing, new tail turret with hemispherical mount for one twin-barrel gun rotating in bearings above and below, no other guns.

Bear-J Naval AV-MF communications plat-form with both tail and centre-fuselage VLF antennas and many other communications systems including Satcoms; airframe based on Tu-142.

A small number were also made in early 1960s of Tu-126 AWACS-type aircraft, with rotating antenna for over-the-horizon radar carried on large single pylon above rear fuselage of Tu-114-type airframe. Length with FR probe and early form of long tail-cone about 188 ft.

61 Saunders-Roe projects

As if the Princess, the supersonic rocket/jet fighters and the helicopter were not enough for a small company, Saunders-Roe must have kept quite a few people busy in the 1950s thinking of new projects. One, in fact, was specially dreamed up for a book, *Wings of Tomorrow*, by John W. R. Taylor and Maurice F. Allward, in 1952. It showed a vast flying boat, exactly like the Do214 but larger, with eight 12,500 hp engines (type unknown!) arranged in push/pull formation. The span would have been 318 ft, take-off

weight 500 tons (which in the UK means 1,120,000 lb) and the objective to carry 300 passengers and 40 tons of cargo to New York at 345 mph (and they did mean starting from the UK). The sketch shows three super-imposed pressurized lobes in the hull.

Just to avoid getting bored, in 1955 a team got on with various forms of the P.188 super-sonic reconnaissance bomber to meet specification B.192T (*see Avro 730 p. 247*). The P.188/2 would have had four formidable afterburning turbojets, but I rather liked the

This was the biggest trans-oceanic flying boat that Saunders-Roe could envisage in 1952. It resembles an enlarged Do214 with pressurization. (Saunders-Roe via Maurice Allward)

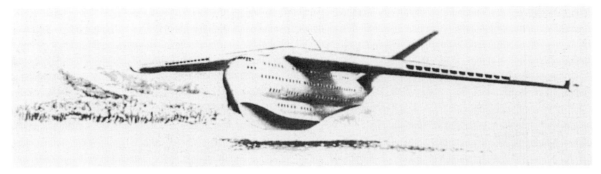

P.188/1 with 16 turbojets grouped eight above each wing. The idea was to use an advanced form of Coanda-type flap blowing, deflecting the entire mass flow of the engines. All the P.188s would have been about 196 ft long and had a take-off weight of (for example) 243,000 lb.

But surely the palm for sheer effrontery goes to the P.192, also of 1956. It's hard not to be facetious — these days, when about 200,000 people can't do the feasibility study inside 25 years — and suggest that maybe Saro thought the odd half-dozen chaps might just build this in their spare time? It wasn't much of a challenge. It only had 24

Four years later the concept of the long-range jet had become viable. The P.192 hoped to balance revenue from 1,000 passengers against the costs of 24 Conway engines. (Saunders-Roe via M.J. Brennan)

Rolls-Royce Conway turbofans grouped inside the 313 ft wing, and the hull only had four highly pressurized decks to carry the 1,000 passengers. Range 4,200 miles at 510 mph, after taking off at 1,500,000 lb. There was also a T-tailed version with 16 BE.25 Orion turboprops, but that wouldn't have been half so exciting.

62 Douglas XC-132

One of the lesser-known Douglas transports is the XC-132. This is a pity, because it would have been a giant in its day, and bigger than any subsequent Douglas actually built until right now, when it is just pipped for length by the MD-11. A heavy airlifter, it was designed to meet a USAF request of January 1951. By this time not only was it obvious that the C-124 configuration was extremely inconvenient but the Korean War had underlined the tremendous need for a giant global airlift capability. The war had also loosened the previously tight purse-strings in Washington. Accordingly the growing design team at Long Beach got to work on a totally new aircraft to the logical formula, with a

high wing, pressurized fuselage with a vast unobstructed cargo hold with a full-section rear ramp door, and multiple landing wheels retracting into blisters on the body.

It was logical to adopt turboprop propulsion, though obviously this constituted the high-risk part of the project. With four engines, about 15,000 hp was needed from each, and fortunately this was the power that Pratt & Whitney could see coming from the XT57, the turboprop derived from the JT3 (J57) turbojet. This classic engine was one of the pioneer two-spool high-compression gas turbines, and it promised to set a new standard of fuel economy. With such applications as the B-52, KC-135, B707, DC-8,

F-100, F-101, F-102, A3D, F4D and F8U the basic turbojet was clearly going to be made to deliver the goods, but for the T57 the problem areas were the extra parts, the gearbox and the HamStan B48 propeller. To this day I do not believe another such gearbox and propeller exist outside the Soviet Union. The prop, for example, had only four blades but each blade was about three feet across (see picture in *World Encyclopaedia of Aero Engines*; PSL 1989). As for the gearbox, this represented almost as much development effort as the rest of the aircraft.

Detailed design data were submitted to Air Research and Development Command in February 1954. The four T57-P-1 engines, each of 15,000 shp, were hung on a wing with 25 degrees sweep and a span of 186 ft 8 in and area of 4,201 sq ft. The whale-like fuselage had two decks, giving a cross-section like a cottage loaf, the upper deck extending from the flightdeck, through the wing to the tail, and being used for flight crew, off-duty crew, various systems and, aft of the wing, the odd 150 seats or space for extra cargo. Including the weather radar the overall length was 183 ft 10 in, and maximum weight was to be 389,500 lb. At this weight the XC-132 could have carried 137,000 lb payload for 2,530 miles or 74,700 lb for 5,180 miles. It was also envisaged as a tanker, cleared to a take-off weight of 469,225 lb, at

Above *Full-scale mock-up of the XC-132 at Douglas Long Beach.* (Douglas Aircraft)

Right *Artist's impression of a C-132 (but the slow boats actually existed).* (Douglas Aircraft)

which it could have transferred 16,279 gal of fuel at a radius of 2,475 miles from its base (what, all through one little boom?). The 132 was cancelled in 1956, along with the T57 and its propeller. Had the USAF seen Vietnam coming the 132 might have entered service.

63 Douglas C-133 Cargomaster

Though not in the same class as the XC-132, the C-133 was almost as large in overall dimensions, and just about rates as a giant in the context of its times. It is rather surprising that the same team should have worked for the same customer on the XC-132 and C-133 simultaneously. Both were heavy strategic freighters for the USAF, with identical layout. One major difference was that, whereas the XC-132's engines and propellers did not exist at the start of the programme, the C-133 was designed to use one of the first gas turbines ever designed in the United States.

Pratt & Whitney began work on the PT2 turboprop before the end of World War 2, and obtained funding for it from the Navy as the T34. Built largely of steel, it had an axial compressor, but was a single-shaft engine, the three-stage turbine having to drive both the compressor and, via the gearbox mounted in the centre of the inlet duct, the propeller. T34 engines were tested in several aircraft including the YC-124B Globemaster and R7V-2 Super Connies. Thus it was regarded as a known quantity, so Douglas Long Beach was told to go straight into production with 35 C-133As. The first flew on schedule on 23 April 1956.

It was an impressive machine, and was pretty well right from the start, except for enlarging the dorsal fin and turning the fuselage tailcone into a flat 'beaver tail'. Configuration was like a C-130 or the XC-132. The slender wings, of 179 ft 8 in span and 2,673 sq ft area, had double-slotted flaps, vortex generators running the full span of the ailerons above and below, and thermal deicing. The tail, 48 ft 3 in high, had rubber deicer boots. The fuselage had a circular cross-section giving a pressurized cargo hold over 90 ft long, with full-width access by a rear ramp door. Overall length was 157 ft 6 in, and maximum weight 255,000 lb, which could include payloads up to 100,000 lb. Later this take-off weight was increased to 282,000 lb, which was also the maximum landing weight.

The C-133A was powered by four 6,000 ehp T34-3 or 3A engines, turning Curtiss Turboelectric propellers each with three blades of 18 ft diameter. Though the aircraft could carry 200 troops, and soon set a record in climbing to 10,000 ft with a payload of 117,900 lb, the most important load soon became large ballistic missiles, and of these the Atlas ICBM was rather a tight fit, with near-zero clearance through the back doors. Accordingly the last two of the 35 aircraft were built with a redesigned back end with a ramp and four sections of clamshell door, giving plenty of room. The new doors also added 3 ft to the hold length, enabling an assembled Titan to be carried. By this time (1959) the Dash-3 engine had been replaced by the P-7W, rated at 6,000 ehp dry or 7,000 with water injection. Pratt & Whitney then came up with the Dash-9W engine, rated at 5,950 shp (6,500 ehp), or 7,600 ehp with water, and this powered a further 15 aircraft with the new rear door called C-133Bs. The 133s never got a lot of publicity, but did a fantastic job during the Vietnam war. Retired in 1971, at least three found further work later as civil freighters in South America.

In 1962 Douglas Long Beach began a

series of studies aimed at finding the optimum C-133 replacement. The first, the Model 895 or C-133X, was essentially a C-133 with a swept tail and a DC-8 wing and engines. It was soon evident that this was too much of a compromise, and that the USAF was looking for an all-new aircraft. Studies continued with the D-902 and 903, of 1963, as part of the CX-4 effort (*see Lockheed C-5 Galaxy p. 270*). The 902 with six TF33 engines in C-141 pods had a wing area of 4,600 sq ft matched to a weight of 506,000 lb, whereas the 903, with four of the new-technology Pratt & Whitney STF200A engines (forerunner of the JT9D), each rated at 30,000 lb, was able to come down to 4,180 sq ft and 467,000 lb, with almost the same fuselage. CX-4 requirements continued to grow, and by 1963-64 the D-906 had reached 606,000 lb. From here it was only a short step to the company's submissions for the C-5A

First take-off by the first C-133A on 23 April 1956. (Douglas Aircraft)

competition, the D-916 and 917, as shown in a company drawing on page 271.

64 Myasishchyev M-50

Now languishing forlornly on the grass at the VVS (Soviet air force) museum at Monino, the M-50 was another of the 1960s crop of impressive prototypes which never got into production. Work on this massive supersonic bomber began in January 1953. By this time the design effort on the 103M (M-4) subsonic strategic bomber was easing off, but V. M. Myasishchyev still had to rely on a lot of outside assistance with the M-50. Designed to cruise subsonically but to accelerate to Mach 1.85 for long distances in the neighbourhood of its target, the new aircraft also had to carry a heavy load for 6,000 km (3,730 miles).

Though capable of delivering free-fall weapons, the M-50 was planned as the original carrier of the supersonic stand-off missiles subsequently given the NATO names 'Kitchen' and 'Kingfish', each being about 36 ft long and weighing some 13,000 lb. This exerted an influence over the aircraft's layout. Moreoover, it was obvious that the M-50 had to be designed to incorporate totally new engines, avionics, accessories, and equipment of every kind. Virtually no existing hardware could be used. Completely new afterburning turbojets were developed by a team led by P. F. Zubets, who had directed the design of the AM-3 in the bureau of A. A. Mikulin. In fact the new engine had several features in common with the AM-3, but still represented a huge effort, in which the Central Institute of Aviation Motors assisted, led by G. P. Svishchyov.

In the basic design of the aircraft another famous national organization, the Central Aerodynamic and Hydrodynamic Institute, played a leading role. Over 40 aerodynamicists and design engineers from the Institute were involved, led by Prof M. V. Keldysh. More than 30 basic configurations were studied, many having canard foreplanes, both with and without a horizontal tail. The final choices rested with the team collected by V. M. Myasishchyev himself, led by L. L. Selyakov. They decided on a low-risk conventional layout which actually had much in common with the MiG-21 and Su-9, with a thin delta wing and swept slab tailplane. After rejecting two of the three preferred engine arrangements — one engine pod above each wing and another slung below at the same point, or two engines in the tail and two in underwing pods — the scheme of V. A. Fedotov and Ye. E. Ilyenko was adopted, with single underwing pods and engines attached to square-cut wingtips.

At last the first of what were intended to be several M-50s made its first flight on 27

October 1959, in the hands of N. I. Goryainov and A. S. Lipko. The engine from the Zubets bureau was not yet cleared for flight, and this first aircraft was powered by the less powerful and less economical ND-7, developed by the bureau of V. A. Dobrynin (later taken over by Koliesov). The wingtip engines were ND-7s, without afterburners, probably rated at about 24,000 lb thrust, while the underwing engines were ND-7Fs rated at 30,865 lb each with afterburner. Fuel was housed in both the upper part of the fuselage and in the extremely large but very thin integral-tank wing. Span was 121 ft 5 in, and area is given as 2,099 sq ft, though rough calculations suggest 3,000 sq ft to be nearer the mark. Thickness/chord ratio was only 3.7 per cent at the root and 3.5 near the tip. The conventional ailerons, tailplane, rudder and triple-secton slotted flaps were all powered hydraulically. Control demands were passed along an area-ruled dorsal spine from the tandem cockpits for the only two crew members (both pilots), who had ventral hatches and downward-ejecting seats. The M-50 was the first aircraft in the Soviet Union to have 'fly-by-wire' electrically signalled flight controls, though it was thought prudent to add mechanical reversionary circuits as well.

Overall length was 187 ft, and design gross weight 440,900 lb. The landing gear was particularly interesting. At rest over 60 per cent of the weight was supported by the massive four-wheel bogie rear centreline gear, the rest being taken by the two separate pairs of wheels further forward. There was room between the landing gears for the missile, recessed under the internal bomb bay. For lateral stability outrigger wheels were provided, retracting into special wing extensions just inboard of the tip engines. On take-off, as soon as the speed reached a certain level, which varied with gross weight and atmospheric density, the nose gear automatically extended to rotate the aircraft positively, to increase angle of attack and reduce field length. The M-50 is dis-

Four sooty trails follow the M-50 as it flies over Tushino on 9 July 1961, escorted by an early MiG-21 fighter. Aerodynamically they were almost brothers. (Via R.T. Riding)

played at Monino in the high-incidence position. They called it 'the galloping bicycle'.

The M-50 was packed with other interesting features, including fuel tanks immediately behind the pressure cabin, and in the extreme tail, between the tailplane power unit and the bay intended for the aft warning radar. Fuel was automatically pumped between these tanks to trim the aircraft during transonic acceleration and deceleration, as was later done with Concorde. Goryainov and Lipko noted 'good cockpit layout, visi-bility and comfort, flying uncomplicated, and controls effective throughout the flight envelope', though of course with the interim engines the design performance could not be achieved. The M-50, with '12' painted on the fuselage, flew past at the Aviation Day show at Tushino in 1961, escorted by two Ye-6T (MiG-21) development prototypes to give scale. It was described as 'a strategic missile carrier'. It never received the Zubets engines, and was eventually retired to Monino, where even the entrance hatches hang open.

65 Avro 730

I commented in the introduction to this decade that supersonic aircraft tend to be long but do not have much frontal area. Britain's only supersonic strategic reconnaissance bomber just about makes it into this book on the score of length alone.

The Avro 730 was designed to meet specification RB.156T for a reconnaissance bomber, issued in May 1954. The company had already done a lot of work on the Avro 721 to meet the 1952 B.126T requirement, and thus knew quite a bit about high-Mach flight as well as the problems of flight at both very low and very high altitudes. Preferred over Handley Page and Vickers submissions, the 730 was from the start endowed with a long needle-like body of circular cross section. There was a sharply tapered wing of low aspect ratio towards the rear, and a rectangular foreplane at the front. The engines were to be four Armstrong Siddeley P.159 afterburning turbojets mounted in superimposed pairs in pods at the wingtips, with fully variable three-shock inlets and variable convergent/divergent nozzles.

It should be stressed that the requirement was not for a subsonic aircraft with supersonic dash capability but for a supersonic-cruise aircraft. The required Mach number was 2.6, or 1,720 mph. Almost the entire air-frame was thus to be constructed in a brazed honeycomb sandwich, similar to that used for the Avro 720 mixed-power supersonic fighter but made not of light alloy but of stainless steel. The span over the engines was only 59 ft 9 in, but length was 163 ft 6 in. Wing area, measured to the nacelle centreline, was 2,000 sq ft, and thickness/chord ratio only 3 per cent. The Dowty main landing gear, mounted on the centreline, was to be a four-wheel bogie for weights up to 158,000 lb. For higher weights, four extra wheels were added, jettisoned as the aircraft became airborne. The nose gear was very similar to that of the Vulcan, while for lateral stability a small outrigger gear, with an all-metal wheel (because of the high temperature), retracted into each engine nacelle. The crew compartment, pressurized to 10.5 lb/sq in, accommodated a pilot on the left with a retractable periscope and two navigators facing aft at the rear who managed the avionics.

The chosen diagram shows one of the major avionics items, the Red Drover SLAR (sideways-looking airborne radar). This pioneer reconnaissance tool would have been based on a mighty central keel beam, made of stainless honeycomb like everything else, carrying two 50-ft antennas look-

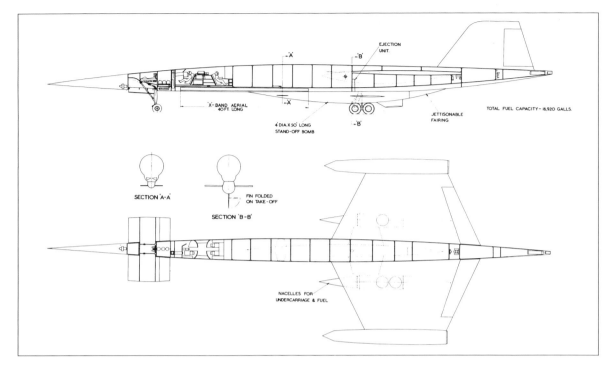

ing obliquely down to the left and right. In the diagram, which shows the biggest type of bomb the 730 was required to carry — later it became the Blue Steel cruise missile — the antennas had to be reduced in length to 40 ft. This would reduce the picture definition, but it would still have been amply good enough for blind bombing. The large weapon would, like some of the others considered, have displaced fuel. However, with the total of 16,920 gal — far more, incidentally, than in the Hughes Hercules — this aircraft of less than 60 ft span would take off at 265,900 lb, release its 18,000 lb stand-off bomb at a distance of 2,595 miles at 60,100 ft and reach a height of 70,500 ft on return.

The P.159 was a single-shaft turbojet specifically designed for cruising at high Mach numbers. Uninstalled, take-off thrust was 21,750 lb, and with the specified three-shock inlets the cruise thrust at 60,000 ft was 7,830 lb allowing for the large air bleed that was to be taken to power the air-turbine-driven accessory systems (as in the B-52). In 1956 the Avro 730 was redesigned to have an

In my view it was unbelievably shortsighted to cancel the Avro 730. Take a look at the sizes of the SLAR and stand-off bomb, and then at the fuel capacity, and then look at what we have today. Or has peace broken out? (A.V. Roe via British Aerospace)

almost delta-shaped wing carrying different engines at about mid-span. The engines were to be eight Armstrong Siddeley P.176 in nacelles very like those of the SR-71 but of almost square box-like section. Most of the remainder was unchanged, and constructed of the first of these extremely advanced aircraft was proceeding as part of a huge development and production programme when the Minister of Defence, Duncan Sandys, announced on 4 April 1957 that Britain did not need any more manned military aircraft because everything would be done by missiles. So far as I know, 34 years later we still don't have missiles that can search for strategic targets, bomb targets of opportunity or fly reconnaissance missions.

The
1960s

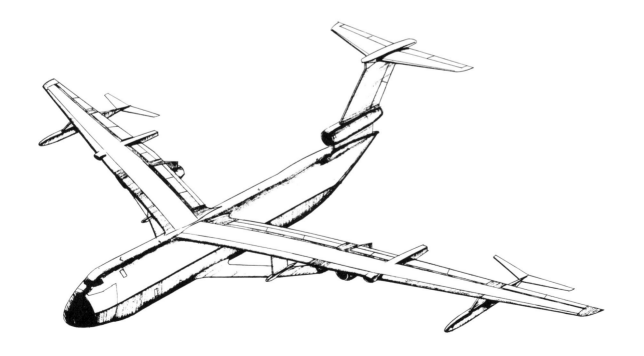

By 1960 the industry had matured. The famous designers, all 'great characters', were no longer in harness. In their place were faceless teams numbering hundreds, who were increasingly replacing sliderules and 6H chisel-point pencils (at least that's what I used) by keyboards and light pens for accessing powerful processors and graphics displays. The computer doesn't mind whether we want a span of 30 ft or 300, and if the software is totally debugged (a big if) then the answers are unfailingly correct.

By 1960 these impressive teams of engineers took it for granted that structures would be all-metal stressed skin, but new alloys were becoming available — such as aluminium-lithium, or for supersonic aircraft B-120 titanium — and there were even disturbing notions that light, strong and stiff fibres of carbon (graphite) or boron might force everyone to learn a whole new ballgame. And even in the field of propulsion designers were having to think a bit. Whereas at the start of the decade the turboprop seemed to be obsolete, the time would come — though after 1970 — when it would come back in the biggest possible way. This was despite the fact that, in the 1960s, the calculations and carefully described 1935-36 patents of Sir Frank Whittle would actually percolate into the closed minds of the experts.

Whittle pointed out that the turbojet, imparting violent acceleration to a relatively small jet, was fine for aircraft that flew fast enough to match the jet velocity. For most subsonic aircraft this jet velocity was too high. In Sir Frank's words:

The propulsive efficiency would be only about 50 per cent, as compared with about 80 per cent for a propeller at much lower speeds, so

I cast about for ways to improve on this. I wanted to 'gear down the jet', to convert a low-mass high-velocity jet into a high-mass low-velocity jet. The obvious way to do this was to use an additional turbine to extract energy from the jet and use this energy to drive a low-pressure compressor or fan capable of 'breathing' far more air than the jet engine itself . . .
I filed a patent application for this arrangement in March 1936.

Of course, because we have so many experts and are so good at aero engines, we made a complete pig's ear of it. Metrovick began making turbofans, so the Ministry instructed them to stop making aero engines altogether. Much later Rolls-Royce made the Conway with the pointless bypass ratio of 0.3!

In March 1959 Don Brown, a super engineer/pilot who went from Miles to Power Jets, wrote an article about Whittle's patents in which he expressed astonishment that not one turbofan was in service anywhere. He need not have worried. The moment Whittle's patents expired the American JT3D and CJ-805-23 replaced turbojets on the world's airlines, and by 1963 US engine builders were busy with much bigger engines with bypass ratios from 5 to 8 which made possible the C-5 Galaxy and 747. Such engines today dominate the propulsion of giant aircraft.

Previous page *Called a Long-term Technology Transport, Long Range, this study by Lockheed has a fuselage based on that of the C-5A, flown in 1968. The rest of it would make use of much later aerodynamics and structures in order to fly further — maybe 40 per cent further — on each gallon of fuel. Note the braced wing with an aspect ratio of 20 fitted with active tip controls to eliminate the effect of gusts.*

66 WS-125A (NPB)

In the years immediately following World War 2 many new technologies were affecting aircraft design. Most countries, including Britain, could do no more than study the possibilities and undertake low-cost research, but in the United States funds were made available for some of the most exciting projects in the history of aviation. One, the so-called CPB, is described later (*North American XB-70 Valkyrie p. 255*). Its partner was the NPB, standing for nuclear-powered bomber. This was launched as Weapon System 125A in 1954, but more than three years earlier major back-up programmes had been initiated. All involved very large aircraft.

Of course, colossal research and development programmes were necessary in order to produce engines drawing their heat energy not from burning conventional fuel but from a nuclear reactor. For aircraft use the reactor had to be as small and light as possible, for the required power output. This inevitably meant a core that could run at very high temperature, such as 1,370°C (2,500°F), which in turn meant many problems in design, materials and mechanical integrity. The light weight precluded the usual few hundred tons of concrete shielding, which in turn meant that after each flight the cores would have to be downloaded into a deep pit under each aircraft, closed by a heavy lead door like a missile silo. Before each flight a mobile crane, with nuclear shielding for the operator, would then have to hoist the core back into position in such a way that all the control wires, white-hot pipe connections and every other connection were all made automatically.

Of course, an NPB would tend to be heavy, cumbersome, slow and ponderous in comparison with a conventional aircraft. It

Models to the same scale of the J79 afterburning turbojet, engine of the F-4, F-104 and many other aircraft, with the monster nuclear X-211, with reactor amidships. (General Electric via Pilot Press)

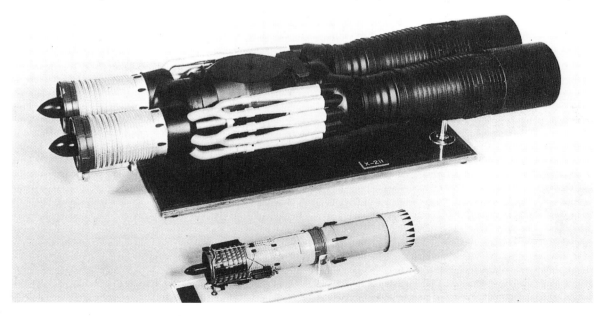

Released for publication on 28 July 1960, this artist's impression shows one version of the Convair NX-2. The underwing engines burned kerosine. (Convair via Pilot Press)

would also tend to be extremely expensive both to develop and to operate, and to suffer a much greater defect rate and need more maintenance per flight hour. Its one advantage would be that its flight endurance, and hence range, would be limited only by the fortitude of the crew. Thus, it could approach any target on Earth from any direction. In early 1951 the USAF defined an NPB as 'a military necessity'. Even though it repeatedly commented that no actual requirement for such an aircraft had been substantiated, it insisted that it was essential to develop an NPB in case it should be needed.

Such a development programme involved several phases. First, to help determine the problems associated with an operating reactor in an aircraft, a quite small nuclear reactor, with a thermal output of 1 Megawatt, was designed for installation in the aft bomb bay of B-36H No 51-5712, turning it into the NB-36H. Special provisions were made for storing and testing the reactor in a pit at the Fort Worth airfield, and for hoisting it into the NB-36H without direct human assistance. Aft of the reactor were large ram-air inlets on each side serving heat exchangers which disposed of the reactor's heat at full

power. (Of course the reactor was not used to power any part of the aircraft.) Ahead of it were large looms of test instrumentation and nine tanks filled with water to stop most of the harmful neutrons and other radiation. Then came a lead shield at the rear of the pressurized nose compartment for a crew of five. The crew compartment, with shield, weighed 12 tons. Even the entry hatch, on top (where radiation could hardly be a problem at all), was so heavy it was powered hydraulically. The NB-36H made 47 flights between September 1955 and March 1957.

The next stage was to build a testbed aircraft to fly actual candidate propulsion systems. General Electric worked on a direct-cycle system in which the compressors of the turbojets would deliver air to the reactor, from where it would emerge at what might be called 'white heat' to be ducted back through the turbines (driving the compressors) and out through the jetpipes. General Electric actually ran a test rig in which a reactor drove two J47 engines, but the definitive NPB engine was the X-211, comprising a pair of monster J87 turbojets with the normal combustion chambers replaced by a reactor. The twin-engine package was 41 ft long, and with chemically fuelled afterburners in operation achieved a thrust in January 1961 of 27,370 lb from each unit, or 54,740 lb total. The bomber was expected to have two X-211s. In contrast, Pratt & Whitney worked on an indirect-cycle engine. The core was first both cooled and moderated by supercritical water, heated to quite a modest temperature (816°C, 1,500°F) but maintained in the liquid state by being kept at 5,000 lb/sq in pressure. Liquid sodium or lithium then carried the heat away to a secondary heat exchanger where liquid NaK (sodium/potassium alloy) carried the heat to the J91 (JTN9) turbojets.

Because of its apparent greater simplicity and higher output the General Electric system was front runner, with the indirect cycle as a back-stop. Convair was teamed with General Electric, and Lockheed with Pratt & Whitney, though many other contractors were involved. In the meantime, to help prove the operating system, Convair was to build the testbed, designated X-6. This was to be based on either the B-36H or the YB-60, the eight-jet derivative of the B-36 which had lost in competition with the B-52. In the event the choice fell on the B-36, and in February 1951 Convair was contracted to rebuild two B-36H aircraft to X-6 configuration. Each was to fly the P-1 nuclear powerplant, comprising a huge drum-like reactor mounted above two X-211 engines, as described above, connected by octopus-like ducts at front and rear. Ground testing was to begin in 1954 and the first flight was scheduled for 1957, but the programme never supported these developments.

Meanwhile, Convair, Lockheed, Boeing and others were busy studying NPBs to meet the WS-125A requirement. Several were published, including the Convair NX-2. This tailless canard had control surfaces on the wingtips looking like modern winglets. In the form illustrated, chemically fuelled engines were hung under the wings to augment power on take-off, for providing power during the landing (the reactor being then inoperative for safety reasons) and for rapid adjustments of inflight power. Span and length might each have been about 190 ft, and take-off and landing weights 620,000 and 600,000 lb, respectively. But nobody found an answer to the radiation hazard posed by an NPB crash.

67 Short Belfast

Most readers would probably consider the Belfast not really a giant in the modern context. I have included it merely because it does have a large fuselage cross-section. This is a perfect circle, because the aircraft is pressurized, but it was a circle drawn to enclose a 12 ft square, because the original design was for carrying cargo. Much later, however, the same fuselage was considered for carrying passengers on two decks.

I won't go into much detail on the history, except to comment that it is a typical example of the way we do things in Britain. The original idea was that, to save money, the new heavy airlift freighter for the RAF, the Britannic, should be based on the Bristol Britannia, but of course with a high wing on a new fuselage. The Air Staff went along with the idea, and the initial plan was to build 30 SC.5 Britannics, other versions coming along later. What actually happened was that Short's aircraft turned out to be a totally new design, needing approximately three times the planned develop-

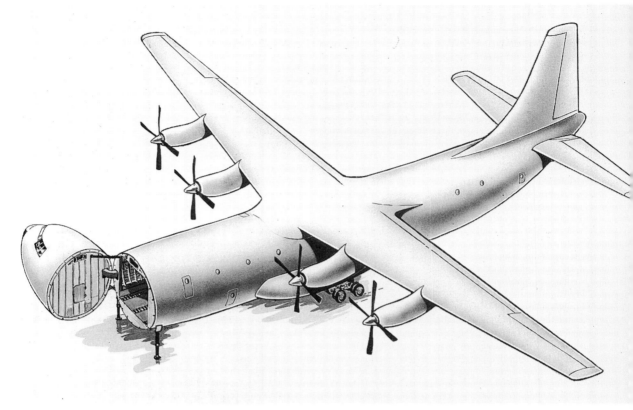

Above *Never built, the swing-nose civil Belfast was to carry 100,000 lb from London to New York. (Short Brothers via Mike Hooks)*

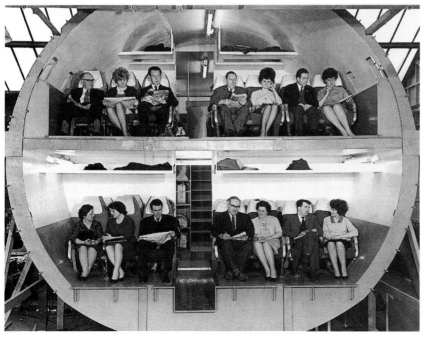

Left *Mock-up of the Short SC.5/10A, the 'airbus' Belfast to carry 284 people. (Short Brothers via Mike Hooks)*

ment effort, and we built just 10 of them. I don't mean to criticise the aircraft, which was ultimately named for the city it came from rather than Britannic, but to criticise the programme. One can't help looking wistfully at Lockheed-Georgia which, in two years less than it took to turn the Britannia into the Belfast, designed the C-141 Star-Lifter from scratch and delivered 284 of them.

To be fair, after all the painstaking development, and curing an excessive drag problem, the Belfast was not at all a bad aeroplane. Unlike the C-130 and C-141, its cargo hold was not too constrictive for bulky loads. Whereas the US freighters have an available cross-section approximately 10 ft wide by 9 ft high, the Belfast's hold is just over 16 ft wide by 13 ft 5 in high, and this makes quite a difference. Available volume is 11,000 cu ft. It is this ability to carry outsize cargoes, at modest costs and using often quite poor airstrips, that has made the Belfast a very useful vehicle. Looked at objectively, the political management was (of course) sheer nonsense. The aircraft was

created to fly Blue Streak and Titan missiles and their bulky associated ground equipment between the UK or USA and Australia. We never had such missiles, so we never needed the Belfast. The RAF said it would buy 30, actually bought 10 and put them up for sale after only eight years. But that's beside the point; British taxpayers seldom hear about such things.

The 10 Belfasts operated almost flawlessly, despite quite considerable complexity which included the avionics required for fully automatic landings in blind conditions. When they came up for sale they attracted a lot of civil interest, and eventually, after a great deal more development in order to get civil certification (the unspoken inference being that the RAF are happy to fly unsafe aeroplanes) three entered service with TAC Heavylift in March 1980. But the version which passengers might have thought a giant was the unbuilt SC.5/31, with a swinging nose. It could have carried 60,000 lb on the lower deck and 141 passengers upstairs, or, as an 'airbus', 284 passengers on both decks.

68 North American XB-70 Valkyrie

If I wanted to give reviewers a controversial quote I could say the B-70 was an American equivalent to the Brabazon. Like the British transport this strategic bomber was designed to meet an almost impossibly difficult specification, and many years later — despite overwhelming efforts by thousands of dedicated people — was judged a good thing to cancel. This did not in any way reflect on the excellence of the prototype which emerged into the California sunshine on 11 May 1964. Painted brilliant white all over, the first of two XB-70 flight articles was in almost every way the greatest aeroplane ever built up to that time. It was certainly the heaviest, noisiest, most powerful,

most costly and, except for the much smaller X-15s dropped from parent aircraft, the fastest. It only just missed also having the longest range. One has only to comment that the root *chord* of the wing was 110 ft (getting on for double the length of a Lancaster) to see that this was no ordinary bomber.

In an earlier story it was noted that in 1951 the USAF had begun preliminary studies for two future manned strategic delivery systems: Weapon System 110A for a CPB (chemically powered bomber) and WS-125A for an NPB (nuclear). Very soon it was also to begin work on three more gigantic weapon systems, 104A which became the

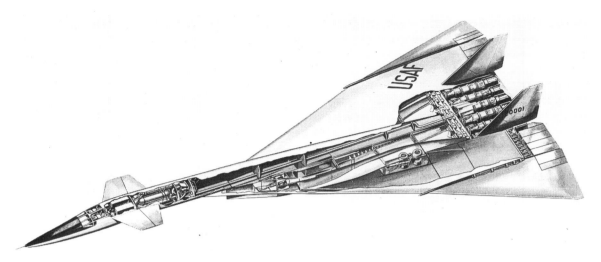

Maker's simple cutaway of the XB-70 No. 1, showing avionics racks and water tanks up front, the sweep of the inlet duct past the cooled MLG bay, the accessory gearboxes above the front of the engines, and the battery of dual power units driving the elevons. (NAA via R.T. Riding)

Navaho intercontinental cruise missile, and 107A and 107A-II which became, respectively, the Atlas and Titan ICBMs (intercontinental ballistic missiles). All were to cost much more than any previous weapon systems, and not even the USAF could afford all of them. In the event, only the two ICBMs were to go into service.

The term 'chemically powered' meant 'not nuclear'. In other words, a CPB's engines obtained their heat by burning fuel in the atmosphere's oxygen. Obviously the B-52 is a CPB, but in the early 1950s the term also embraced what by 1955 were being called 'Zip fuels'. These promised to release more heat energy per unit mass or volume than ordinary hydrocarbon fuels, such as kerosene. This extra energy appeared well worth the very much greater cost in order to achieve the desired flight performance. What was this performance? In 1951 the B-52 was about to fly, to accomplish SAC strategic missions at Mach numbers up to 0.9, and the B-58 was in full development, able to cruise at Mach 2 but with an unrefuelled range of only 5,125 miles. WS-110A broadly asked for B-52 range and bombload, combined with 'as high a speed as possible', whilst operating from the same runways. 'As high a speed' was taken to mean certainly well over Mach 1 and if possible over Mach 2, but this speed was needed only for a

1,000-mile dash across hostile territory.

After much prior study, requests for WS-110A were issued by the Air Research and Development Command in February 1955. Six companies responded on 13 July 1955, and the following 11 November Boeing and North American Aviation were awarded Phase I contracts. It was then very difficult to build any kind of supersonic aircraft able to fly long distances or carry loads. With the pioneer B-58, Convair cheated by carrying the weapon load and much of the fuel in a giant external pod, so that on the return trip the aircraft was significantly smaller. For the more challenging WS-110A, NAA went even further. Its Phase I submission, made in October 1956, was for a huge canard delta bomber which, in the final 1,000 miles of the outward trip, would jettison two outer wings, previously connected by hinges, each of 80 ft span and carrying a fuel pod almost as big as a B-47 fuselage. At take-off the span was to be about 260 ft, and gross weight nearly 750,000 lb, 380,000 of which comprised the outboard fuel pods. When the redoubtable SAC Commander, Curtis LeMay, was shown this he removed his cigar and growled 'Hell, this isn't an airplane, it's a three-ship formation!'

Boeing did no better, and both manufacturers retired to do more thinking. One area were there was less scope for manoeuvre was the engine. It could at a pinch be a variable-cycle engine, and the USAF was already funding the Wright J67/RJ55 for the Republic XF-103, an interceptor to fly at Mach 3.7 (2,446 mph). Today we recognise that the VC engine is the best answer for future supersonic-cruise aircraft — that's a provocative statement in view of the YF-22/23 competition — but in the mid-1950s it was quite tough enough producing a supersonic turbojet. The two favoured candidates were the Allison J89 and Pratt & Whitney J91, the latter being (in one version) part of the Pratt & Whitney propulsion system for a nuclear-powered bomber. As has often happened, crafty General Electric came from behind and in May 1957 was awarded a contract for the engine for two potentially enormous future USAF programmes, the WS-202 interceptor, won by NAA as the XF-108 Rapier, and the WS-110A CPB. The engine was designated the J93, and it resembled an advanced and enlarged J79, with a single variable-stator compressor spool. The plan was initially to use Zip fuel in both the engine itself and in the afterburner, and in 1956 the Department of Defense authorised the Air Force to build a huge plant, to be managed by Olin Mathieson Corporation, to produce about 10,000 lb per day of ethyl borane, the selected Zip product. The Navy built a parallel facility. In the course of very troubled development Zip was eliminated from the engine, but in the J93-5, the planned engine for the CPB, it was retained in the afterburner, giving a maximum thrust of 31,000 lb (static, at sea level). After more problems and arguments the entire Zip programme was eliminated in 1959, leaving

the bomber with the J93-3, burning almost normal fuel (actually various forms of JP-6, with additives), reducing thrust to 27,200 lb. The new bomber was to need six, the most powerful engines in the world in the 1950s.

In 1953 the National Advisory Committee for Aeronautics had come up with the Area Rule, which explained how to design aeroplanes for minimum transonic and supersonic drag. In March 1956 the NACA issued a classified report entitled *Aircraft Configurations Developing High Lift/drag Ratios at Supersonic Speeds*. This was Manna from Heaven. The report was authored by Alfred J. Eggers and Clarence A. Syvertson. It described how a supersonic air vehicle, cruising at between Mach 3 and Mach 5, could be so shaped as to make favourable use of the pressure distribution created around it by its own shockwave field. Briefly, it said the body should be a long, slender delta wing with a flat top but a half-body underneath. One popular report tried to get the concept across by saying such an aircraft could 'climb atop its own shockwave much as a speedboat rises on its step'. Eggers, who was suddenly struck by the idea as he was mowing his lawn, called it 'compression lift'. Later, after the NACA had become NASA, the vast research organization collaborated with NAA in shaping the WS-110A bomber.

NAA began tunnel testing new compression-lift shapes immediately, and discovered that the potential gains were enormous. Peak L/D (ratio of lift to drag) was increased by 22 per cent, and reached at a smaller angle of attack, while for the much lower angles as used in cruising flight the improvement exceeded 100 per cent. Suddenly the way could be seen not only to building a bomber to meet all the demands, but even to build one that could cruise at full speed (over Mach 3, or 2,000 mph) all the way. Dr H.L. Dryden of NASA said 'A strange and wonderful thing has happened, as if the pieces of a jigsaw were falling into place'. The term for such an aircraft today is a 'supercruiser'.

As a result, in July 1957 the USAF cancelled NAA's huge WS-104 (SM-64) Navaho system, and this doubtless played some part in the fact that on 23 December of that year the WS-110A programme was awarded to the same company. On 6 February 1958 the aircraft was designated the B-70, and on 3 July 1958 the name Valkyrie was chosen after a SAC-wide competition. NAA assigned the company model number NA-378, and on 4 October 1961, after the design had been virtually completed, the USAF ordered one test airframe and three flight articles. The latter comprised two XB-70s, actually completed as XB-70As, numbers 62-001 and 62-207, and one XB-70B, 62-208. The XB-70B was cancelled in May 1964.

There followed seven years of often acrimonious argument. The debate should have centred on whether the B-70 promised to be the right kind of bomber, but instead it was fanned to white heat by ignorant people who, in a nutshell, said 'Now we've invented the ICBM we don't need bombers'. This was very much like the foolish argument put forward by the British Ministry of Defence (which extended to fighters as well). The main problem was that the XB-70 had been designed to escape interception by flying faster and higher than any other conventional aircraft, and by 1962 Defense Secretary McNamara was forced to admit 'the speed and altitude of the B-70, in itself, would no longer be a significant advantage. It has not been designed for the use of air-to-surface missiles, and in a low-altitude mission it must fly at subsonic speeds ... It would be more vulnerable on the ground than hardened missiles, and it does not lend itself to airborne-alert measures.' He was presenting just one aspect of a multi-faceted argument.

Later in that year the USAF decided the planned force of 200 B-70s was a mistake, and it switched to requesting 150 RS-70s, RS meaning reconnaissance/strike. By this time the first two aircraft were structurally complete, though No 20001 was to spend almost

two further years curing various problems before it could be cleared for flight. Whether the task could have been speeded up, had the B-70 remained a top-priority programme, is doubtful. The most intractable fault was that when the gigantic fuel-system rig was heated to 290°C (554°F) and subjected to flight loads the JP-6 fuel vapour billowed away in clouds from millions of microscopic holes in the welded joints. At last, on the date given at the beginning, the monster aircraft was rolled out, but the No 5 tank was even then unusable, and it was to remain so.

The startling shape of the B-70 speaks for itself. Overall length was 196 ft 1 in. The long fuselage, totally above the wing and almost totally in front of it, stretched forward some 80 ft without sagging, about 25 ft above the ground. About halfway along were giant powered canards which, like 69 per cent of the structure, was made as a knife-edged brazed honeycomb sandwich of a new stainless steel called PH 15-7Mo. There were over 100 of these stainless honeycomb panels, each of which had to be hot-creep formed at 1,200°F or deep-freeze formed at −100°F. Ahead of the canard was a door, higher off the ground than any previous aircraft door, admitting to the side-by-side cockpit. In a bomber there would have been two more crew just behind, but in 20001 there were just the two pilots, each in a rocket seat which, as it left the aircraft, would have enclosed its occupant in a protective capsule stabilized by long telescopic booms at the rear. The pilots looked ahead through three large flat windows which in Mach 3 cruising flight were pivoted up to form a smooth contour with a vizor extending almost to the nose. Nearer to the pilots was a row of inner windscreen panes which carried the cabin pressure.

At the rear the oval-section fuselage, made of titanium alloy, was sealed to form integral tanks. Huge areas of wing were likewise sealed, and (including the stubborn No 5 tank) the total capacity of 43,646 gal of JP-6 weighed very much more than the empty weight of some 205,000 lb. Gross weight was 550,000 lb Skinned entirely in the fabulous mirror-like sheets of stainless honeycomb, the wing was an almost perfect delta with a leading-edge angle of 65.5° (and really sharp). Though span was a mere 105 ft, the area was 6,297 sq ft. But, unlike other wings, this one was structurally divided at about two-thirds of the semi-span on each side. The resulting giant triangular tip was mounted on hinges incorporating hydraulic drives of colossal power which, ignoring the enormous aerodynamic loads, could rotate the outer wings down to either 25° or, for Mach 3, to 65°. At 65° the wings really 'boxed in' the high-pressure field under the rest of the wing to increase lift without increasing drag. On the trailing edge were a total of eight inboard elevons, four on each side, and four outers. These handled almost all flight manoeuvre demands, and could also serve as flaps for landing, the foreplane hinged flaps then being fully down to can-

cel out the trim change. The main canard was used primarily as a trimming surface in cruising flight, working in conjunction with the elevons to achieve minimum drag caused by offset surfaces. Above the rear of the fixed wing were two large fully powered rudders, with no fins, which were not normally used with all engines operative.

The six J93-3 engines were installed in the rear part of an engine box the like of which had never been seen before, and perhaps not since. The box was specially shaped to enhance compression lift, the depth being a constant 7 ft but the width varying from only about 18 ft at the inlet to 37 ft about 30 ft further back. Overall length of the engine box was 110 ft; in other words it started and finished at the edges of the wing root. At the front was a left/right flow divider like the bow of a supersonic battleship, downstream of which were various perforated walls, doors and other moving parts, mostly bigger than you could get into an average room. Hamilton Standard had the

For sheer concentrated thrust the XB-70 had no equal. (NAA via R.T. Riding)

Ship No. 1 landing at Edwards after its first trip to Mach 3 on 24 October 1965. (Via Philip Jarrett)

mighty task of making the complex automatically scheduled system work. At the back was the row of six afterburner nozzles, more concentrated power than ever seen before.

The landing gear was relatively conventional, though the bays housing the retracted gears in the outer sides of the engine box had to be cooled. The onboard refrigeration, incidentally, had a capacity 15 times greater than in any previous aircraft, and the heat exchangers dumped excess heat into water tanks which occupied half the fuselage volume between the foreplane and engine inlet. Cleveland Pneumatic took the odd decision to add a small fifth wheel to each main bogie to serve as an anti-skid reference. These gears retracted straight backwards, the bogie turning inwards to lie on its side. The nose unit likewise went backwards to lie between the mass of doors and movable walls at the upstream end of the inlet ducts. Secondary power was under the overall system management of Sundstrand. Each engine drove a 60-kVA brushless alternator, the total number of electrically powered services exceeding 600. The hydraulics were all-metal, even includ-

ing the O-seals, and filled with 260 gal of a new fluid called Oronite 70. Total hydraulic horsepower could be nine times the total installed engine power of the first Ilya Mouromets, and among other devices served 85 linear actuators and 44 hydraulic motors.

Right up to roll-out, not only did storms rage in Washington on whether B-70s or RS-70s were needed, but hundreds of often small but significant changes kept being made to this 'leading edge' aeroplane. Many concerned new materials, which kept being qualified and thus became available to do a better job at the minimum ruling B-70 temperature of 244°C (470°F). Many more concerned the details of the 14,880 lb of flight-test instrumentation. At last, as noted, 20001 was pulled outdoors with its vizor up, wings at 25° and a black 'radome' painted on. Ground testing continued, and it was not until 21 September 1964 that Al White and Col Joe Cotton rotated at 183 kts and made the 30-mile delivery flight from Palm-dale to Edwards. In the course of this brief trip the main gears refused to retract, one engine overspeeded and was shut down and the brake system (despite the fifth wheel) malfunctioned, locking the two left rear main tyres, which not unnaturally blew, with clouds of smoke and loud reports, but at least the triple 28 ft drag chutes deployed properly. Subsequently the flight pro-gramme was impressive, even if Cotton did liken it to 'driving a Greyhound bus at 200 miles an hour round the track at Indian-apolis'. One minor task was deciding where the pilot should look ahead on landing, because the main gears were 110 ft behind him and 44 ft lower.

The No 2 aircraft, with radar, a totally new form of engine instrumentation and control, stellar-inertial navigation and about 30 other new subsystems, joined in flying from 17 July 1965. On 19 May 1966, on its 39th flight, 20207 began to show what the B-70 was all about by holding Mach 3.08 for 33 min dur-ing a 2,700-mile run over eight states in the NASA sonic-boom programme. A little later, on 8 June, 20207 was booked for a simple 'clean-up' mission to round off a few tasks before completing Phase I testing, and because of the small work-load it was thought it would be a good opportunity for Maj Carl S. Cross to have his familiarization ride. GE had arranged that, at the end of the mission, the B-70 would be formated on by a T-38, F-4, F-5 and F-104 (why no A-5, T-2 or B-58?), while a Learjet (also GE-engined) took pictures. Just as the job was

finished Joe Walker, one of the world's most experienced supersonic pilots and long-time 'king' of the X-15 programme, tucked his F-104 much too close to the B-70's right wing. Suddenly it was gripped in the vast pressure field round the 25° downturned wingtip. In the twinkling of an eye it was whipped round the tip, rolled inverted and slammed in across the top of the B-70's wing, carry-ing away most of the two rudders. The almost-demolished F-104 exploded in a fire-ball, but the B-70 just kept on. Then, with slow majesty, it began to yaw and roll. With no yaw stability it progressively departed from the flight envelope and broke up. White ejected, but Cross never even initiated the ejection sequence. The ensuing politi-cal storm was enormous and unjust, and to this day makes it harder for writers and photographers to obtain USAF collabo-ration.

For nearly three further years the No 1 air-craft continued to fly extremely valuable research programmes, sometimes obtaining data that no other aircraft could have col-lected. Sadly, perhaps, much of it was in support of the SST programme, which as described later came to nothing. But the SST still lived when, on 4 February 1969, Fitzhugh Fulton and Lt-Col Ted Sturmthal completed Mission 83. They recorded 'Sub-sonic cruise 0.91, ILAF and exciter-vane data, 33,000 ft. Landed Dayton, Ohio.' The unexpected landing place is the home of the Air Force Museum, where the white triangle is one of the biggest exhibits.

69 Antonov An-22 *Antei*

Having developed a truly fantastic long-range propulsion system in the NK-12 turbo-prop and (especially) the associated AV-60 propeller, it is remarkable that the Soviet Union has not made more use of it. Apart

from the Tupolev Tu-95/142 family and close relatives, its only other application is to power this heavy strategic freighter. This could have been produced 10 years earlier than it was, but delaying factors included

Thanks to its unique propulsion system the prototype An-22 Antei *offered new capabilities in long-range heavy transport.* (Philip Jarrett)

the difficulty of agreeing on the requirement, the acceptance of rail transport for almost all parts of giant ICBMs and space launch vehicles to the assembly plants and on to the launch centres, and also the limited number of airfields where large airlifters were both needed and could be accepted. Put another way, there were many major military airbases with superb paved runways and taxiways, but the places where heavy transport was needed tended to be small strips on boggy tundra, with an iron-hard surface in winter that could cut tyres to ribbons.

In 1962 it was agreed that something had to be done, and the obvious OKB (experimental construction bureau) to do it was that of O.K. Antonov at Kiev. Within a year a detailed requirement had been agreed between Aeroflot (the civil operator) and the VTA (military transport aviation). The cross section of the cargo hold was agreed at 14 ft 5.3 in square, the final available length being 108 ft 3 in. After much agonizing, Antonov himself decided not to pressurize the whole volume but to provide a pressure bulkhead with two doors to seal off the front fuselage. This is arranged for 29 or 29 passengers, ahead of which is the flightdeck with stations for five or six including a navigator compartment in the nose. In the prototype this had a fully glazed front, but the produc-

tion An-22 has a weather radar in the nose and a huge mapping radar in the chin position, the navigator having windows in the space between the two. The main cargo hold, for payloads up to 80 tonnes (176,350 lb), has rails along each side for two electric travelling gantry cranes each rated at 22,046 lb, and two winches each with a pull of 5,511 lb. The forward rear door lowers to any desired position either to truck-bed height or to form a ramp, while the aft rear door hinges upward to provide clearance for the highest loads or vehicles, and also to provide (on its external side) extra sections of rail for the cranes. The cargo floor is titanium with a non-slip surface.

A remarkable feature of the An-22 is the relatively small size of the unswept wing, which has an area of 3,714 sq ft. At maximum weight of 551,160 lb this results in the formidable wing loading of 148.5 lb/sq ft. Of typical Antonov gull-wing form, with progressively greater anhedral from root to tip (which almost disappears in cruising flight at normal weights, as the wing flexes upwards), the wing has a fixed leading edge but double-slotted flaps so effective that full-load take-off and landing runs are only 4,260 and 2,620 ft, respectively. Ailerons, elevators and four sections of rudder are all driven manually by Flettner tabs. Noteworthy features of the tail are the twin-fin layout (today unusual), the small overall size, the big anti-flutter fairings on top of the fins and the precarious way the fins are mounted by their trailing edge on the leading edge of the tailplane. The engines are completely under-slung, and unlike the Tupolev aircraft with this engine have single jetpipes containing large heat exchangers, the cross flow being supplied by a ram inlet on the underside of the nacelle. The hot air deices the wing and is also fed to the landing-gear fairings to serve the cabin environmental system. Though of the AV-60 series, the eight-blade contra-rotating propellers are larger than the 60N, the diameter being 20 ft 4 in.

The wing box forms integral tankage for about 12,290 gal of fuel. The two main-spar frames in the fuselage, which like many other parts are massive machined forgings using a 75,000-tonne press, are used to mount the main landing gear. This com-prises three tandem pairs of levered-suspen-sion wheels on each side. Tyre pressure can be adjusted in flight. The enormous fairings

Two views of SSSR-09329 arriving at the 1988 Farn-borough airshow. It had come from the Antonov OKB in Kiev with a spare engine for an An-124. (Mike Hooks)

which accommodate the retracted gears each incorporate a personnel door and also house the APUs, cabin-air system, refuelling couplings and other items. Overall dimen-sions of the An-22 include a span of 211 ft 4 in, length of 190 ft and height of just over 41 ft 1 in. The name, Antheus in English, is that of the giant son of Poseidon and Gaia.

Antonov was very pleased with the way the An-22 turned out, the prototype (SSSR-46191) making a successful first flight as early as 27 February 1965. This aircraft had NK-12MV engines and AV-60N propellers, a fully glazed nose and a simple map-ping/weather radar in the right main-gear

blister. There was nothing else of note except an HF wire antenna along the top of the forward fuselage, VHF and UHF rods and blades underneath, a retractable landing lamp under the glazed nosecap, taxi lamp on the steerable nose gear and duplicated venturis, total-temperature thermistors and ice-detector probes. The production An-22 has 15,000 hp NK-12MA engines, and a redesigned nose. It had been intended to build 30 per year, including a stretched double-deck passenger version seating 724. In the event production was completed in 1974 at only 100, of which about 60 are in current use. One is modified for carrying the wings of production An-124 (and 225) aircraft from the manufacturing plant named for Valery Chkalov at Tashkent to the assembly works at Kiev. A small central fin is

added, and the wings are carried singly (left or right An-124 wings each weigh about 51,000 lb) on pivoting links which prevent body flexure stresses being transmitted to the wing mounted externally above the fuselage. Another *Antei* was used by the Antonov OKB to bring a replacement engine to an An-124 at the 1988 Farnborough airshow.

Like the giant turboprop Tupolevs the *Antei* has engines automatically controlled to hold a constant 8,300 rpm, the electric subsystem then being used to vary fuel flow and propeller pitch to give the desired power at any airspeed from zero to the maximum of 460 mph. In the air the huge slow-turning propellers put out a very low-frequency rumble which is absolutely distinctive and can be heard for miles.

70 Aero Spacelines Super Guppy

In World War 2 the B-29 was on many counts a giant, certainly on such grounds as weight and installed power, though as bombers carry very dense payloads they do not need particularly large fuselages. But towards the end of the war Boeing produced a transport version, and I remember my amazement and disbelief when I saw the size of the upper lobe that was added on top of the existing B-29 fuselage to produce the familiar C-97 or B-377 Stratocruiser. In fact its diameter was a mere 11 ft, compared with 9.4 ft for the original, but it absolutely dominated the new transport version. I wondered how such a huge bluff-nosed brute could be so fast.

Eventually I was to learn that air flows in funny ways, and that huge bluff-nosed brutes, such as today's widebodies, can be every bit as fast as slim pointy-nosed ones. One of the men with practical experience of all this was A.M. 'Tex' Johnston, for many years Boeing's Chief Engineering Test Pilot.

On several occasions I was privileged to steer him through various places in London's West End that I would never have visited by myself, and on the last of these sorties he told me of his plan to fit a C-97 Stratocruiser with an enormous new fuselage to enable it to carry sections of the giant space launch vehicles then being developed for NASA. I asked him about the aerodynamics. To me merely adding a giant fuselage seemed a likely recipe for disaster, but Tex said 'We do have a good design team.'

They gave the job to On Mark Engineering, of Van Nuys, who did it by stages. First, a Stratocruiser was lengthened aft of the wing by 16 ft 8 in and test flown. Then the seemingly huge new upper lobe was added with an internal diameter of 19ft 9 in. This was tailored to the envisaged payload, the Douglas-built S-IV stage of the original Saturn I vehicle. This big fuselage was flown, and the final modification was to

remove the original upper lobe from inside, and also provide a bolted joint immediately aft of the wing so that the entire rear fuselage could be removed for loading an S-IV. Called the B-377PG Pregnant Guppy, the aircraft, N1024V, flew in its final form on 16 May 1963, and received FAA Supplemental approval two months later. It immediately went into service under contract to NASA.

Tex's company was called Aero Spacelines. It not only did a very professional job but did it without any external funding. I think if I had been asked I would have said that to slap such a huge body on a tired old Stratocruiser was tempting providence, and that it would prove virtually uncontrollable (assuming it could ever accelerate to V_2). So I was, for the third time, unprepared for what happened next. The mid-1960s were a time when the colossal Saturn V launcher was coming into production ready for the 1969 Moon flights, and Boeing, Lockheed and Douglas were all planning enormous new 'widebody' airliners. Tex had the incredible idea of putting a body on a Strato-

Arrival on the apron at Toulouse St. Martin of the front fuselage of the 51st A320 and the nose of the 461st A300/310 in November 1988. The three fuselage diameters explain why the Super Guppy is in this book. (Airbus Industrie)

cruiser into which you could load the S-IVB, the third stage of the Saturn V, and major airframe parts of widebodies, such as wings and sections of fuselage.

Not surprisingly the aircraft was called the B-377SG Super Guppy. It was not so much a modification as building a new aeroplane using parts of others. The prototype, N1038V, used the wing, flightdeck and forward fuselage of one of the two YC-97J turboprop testbeds powered by 5,700 shp Pratt & Whitney T34-P-7 engines. Parts were then added from four Stratocruisers or C-97s. When the bits had all been put together, eight months from the start, and flown on 31 August 1965, the Supper Guppy had a wing extended to 156 ft 3 in, an overall length increased by 30 ft 10 in to 141 ft 3 in, and a gigantic upper lobe able to accommodate loads with a diameter of 25 ft, and an internal volume of 49,790 cu ft! Against this the original tail looked miniscule, so I was relieved to see that the SG was fitted with a new tail of improved shape, the fin actually projecting above the top line of the fuselage.

In 1965 Aero Spacelines was purchased by Unexcelled Inc, which decided that they would do future conversions themselves, which was tough for On Mark. The firm was moved to exclusive Santa Barbara, where work was put in hand on one prototype and, later, two production Mini Guppies, with bodies able to take loads up to 18 ft diameter. Alongside them two production Model 201 Super Guppies were built, at first registered N211AS and N212AS. Though very like the prototype, the production aircraft were considerably refined, and powered by the Allison 501-D22C rated with water injection at 4,912 shp and driving HamStan propellers with four extremely broad blades. The fully engineered fuselage was built from scratch, there being no trace of a lower lobe. Instead the vast upper portion tapers off with flat sides to a small radius along the centreline underneath, the

floor being inserted just above the wing where the internal width is 13 ft. The huge nose, dwarfing the flightdeck, is hinged on the left. To open it, two struts are extended vertically down to support the front of the main fuselage, and an auxiliary gear is extended vertically down just to the right of the centreline at the extreme rear of the nose section. The nose gear is steered to the correct angle to the left, and the quick-disconnects made of the main longerons and all the auxiliary services, flight controls and other pipe and cable connections. Then the power drive to the two small wheels on the auxiliary gear is switched on, and these wheels gently drive the nose round through 110°. There are personnel doors, with integral airstairs, at front and rear of the fuselage on the right side. The production Model 201 is a little bigger than the prototype, span being 156 ft 8 in and length 143 ft 10 in. The interior, which can be lightly pressurized, holds the maximum 25 ft 6 in diameter for 32 ft, and overall available

F-GEAI, newest of the Airbus fleet. Almost certainly two more will have to be built. (Airbus Industrie)

length is 111 ft 6 in. Empty and MTO weights are 101,929 lb and 170,000 lb, so with a maximum cargo load of 52,925 lb there's not much margin nor fuel.

Ironically, though the SGs were initially used for DC-10 and TriStar production, by far the most important user has been Boeing's growing competitor, Airbus Industrie. There is no way the Airbus programmes could have been managed without aircraft of this class. Both the production SGs were bought by Airbus, becoming F-BTGV and F-BPPA. Subsequently they have purred and thundered between Chester, Bremen, Hamburg, St Nazaire, Bristol and Madrid and the assembly centre at Toulouse. Later they will take A321 components to assembly at Hamburg. The heaviest loads have always been the A300B wing boxes, the two forming the ship-set for one aircraft being flown together. The wings have to be carried tips at the rear, and this brings the CG much further forward than anyone would like. I respect the pilots, because they are quite used to carrying these wings. With both pilots hauling

hard back the nose gear still hits the runway first, but not quite hard enough to break anything. The nose gears are now of B707 type, which helps. I don't know what will happen when the much bigger wings for the A330 and 340 have to be carried.

Certainly Airbus Industrie's need for Guppies has never ceased to grow. By 1979 the two aircraft could no longer cope. Aero Spacelines had become Tracor, no longer making aeroplanes, but they sold Airbus the drawings and rights to the Model 201, and in 1982-83 Airbus received two more freshly built by Aéromaritime/UTA at Le Bourget, registered F-BDSG and F-GEAI. In fact, for many years Aéromaritime carried out the entire trucking operation between the factories of the Airbus partners, but in the summer of 1989 Airbus brought the whole job 'in house'. Without doubt two more Super Guppies will have to be built, stretched even further to carry tomorrow's even bigger and heavier wings; or maybe they'll go piggyback on An-225s?

71 BAC VC 10 projects

I have often said there's very little wrong with the British aircraft industry except the politicians and British Airways (or, in the time we are talking about, BOAC). Faced by BOAC with a ridiculous specification — build a rival to the 707 six years later but handicapped by having to take off in only half the length of runway — Vickers-Armstrongs produced an outstanding aircraft in the VC10, and an even better one in the Super VC10. BOAC did its best to make life difficult by injecting massive changes in the size of the aircraft and the number they wanted, but at last they got a fleet of both versions, tailored precisely to their own misguided requirements. They were popular with passengers, pilots and engineering staff and,

despite the severe short-field handicap, actually showed higher utilization and better economics than the 707, and made the biggest profits in BOAC. Ignoring this, the airline vociferously told the world the VC10 was a lousy aeroplane, pretty well ensuring that nobody would buy it. Chairman Sir Matthew Slattery said to the Parliamentary Estimates Committee (for example) 'The original VC10 order could not by any stretch of the imagination be considered a commercial decision...the decision to buy the Super VC10 was done under pressure from the Ministry to complete the formation of British Aircraft Corporation.' In 1963 the next Chairman, Sir Giles Guthrie, said he 'wanted to cancel the 30 Super VC10s and

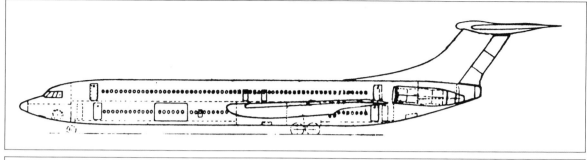

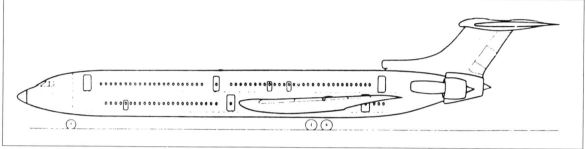

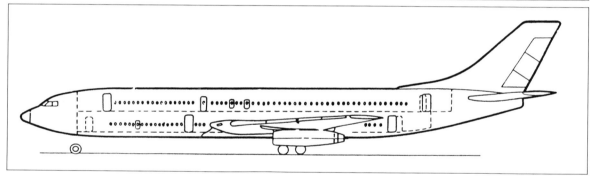

buy more 707s. . .' Meanwhile, true to form, the British popular press kept up a stream of articles pointing out what a useless aeroplane the VC10 was (try *The Economist* for 25 April 1964, for example).

What on earth could BAC do? Having produced a world-beater they couldn't sell, they could either lay everybody off or try to develop it. With Sir George Edwards around, nobody was going to call it quits, and an interesting series of 'Super Super VC10s' followed. They began with fairly modest stretches, roughly back to what the Super VC10 would have been if BOAC had not ordered it made smaller. Then BAC did a lot of research, supported by the RAE

Top *The Super VC10 300 for PanAm was closely related to the DB264 (double bubble, 264 seats). (BAC via John Stroud)*

Centre *The DB295 was to be powered by RB.178-14 aft-fan engines. (BAC via John Stroud)*

Bottom *With this further stretch BAC switched to underwing engines. (BAC via John Stroud)*

Farnborough and the National Physical Laboratory, which showed prospects of a drag reduction of 10 per cent even in various forms of double-deck developments. The newspapers said PanAm was 'about to buy the 707-820'. Boeing never did build a stretched 707, but PanAm was indeed interested in a bigger vehicle than the 707-320 and actually sent a team to Weybridge to discuss 'Hyper VC10s'. At the same time, in February 1965, Rolls-Royce began to talk about the RB.178, its first big fan engine, with a high bypass ratio and a thrust of 25,000 to 35,000 lb, depending on what the customer wanted.

So, while the first general-arrangement drawing here shows an early suggestion for PanAm, the Model 1180 seating 249 on two decks and the 1181 seating 273, the next drawing shows a slightly stretched aircraft

This drawing, dated 4 May 1964, was entitled '450-seat passenger aircraft based on Standard VC10'. Perhaps Grahame-White would have liked it! (BAC via John Stroud)

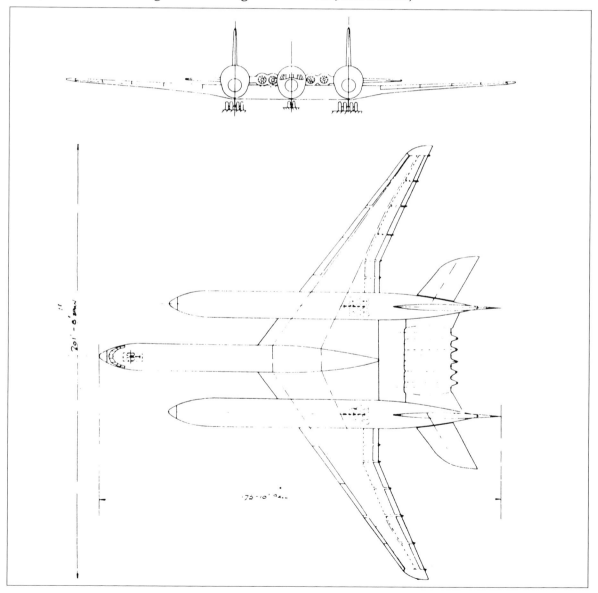

seating 295, and powered by three RB.178-14s in the proposed aft-fan version. Note that the middle engine needs only a small air inlet at the base of the fin, to feed the core, the huge fan airflow having a separate inlet around the fuselage. Next comes a further-developed aircraft looking rather like a presumptuous 737. Underwing engines meant a major redesign, and ruled out high-bypass engines, so the choice would have been 'Super Conways', each of 26,000 lb thrust, with reversers above and below. Typical seating would have been 318. BAC even did studies to see if there were any problems in passengers boarding or disembarking through an upper-level jetway loading bridge and at ground level simultaneously.

Well, if two decks might have posed passenger-handling problems, how about three fuselages? The last project here, dated 4 May 1964, would have had just that, the three bodies being mounted on a wing based closely on that of the Super VC10 but with a new centre section. Between the two

tails (with low-mounted outboard tailplanes) were the six Rolls-Royce Medway turbofans forming a kind of central tailplane. At that time the Medway was running at 17,500 lb, but Rolls said they could develop it to 23,000 lb. Sir Matthew Slattery even said he looked forward to 'seeing a VC10 with this engine, which promises ten per cent lower fuel consumption'. Of course even the three-pronged VC10 came in different versions, but the one shown would have seated (typical mixed-class) 450, had a span of 201 ft 6 in, a length of 175 ft 10 in, distance between outer fuselages of 50 ft and MTO weight estimated at 675,000 lb.

Of course, it all came to nothing. BAC said it needed a lot of launch money from the Government. The Government asked BOAC if they wanted a big aeroplane, and Sir Giles said, and I quote, 'We can make no decision about big-capacity subsonic equipment until BAC can tell us definitely if they are going to build an aircraft of this type.' So BAC said 'We will, if you order it.' So Sir Giles said. . .

72 CX-HLS and the Lockheed C-5 Galaxy

For many years the biggest American transport aircraft, civil and military, have been produced by Boeing, Douglas and Lockheed. After the cancellation of the C-132 in 1956 the next major event was the 1960 SOR-182 requirement for a turbofan-engined multirole transport for USAF Military Airlift Command, won by Lockheed with the C-141 StarLifter. An extremely useful aircraft, this was modest in size and constricted by a hold cross-section the same size as a C-130, so in its original form it seldom was able to pack in as much cargo as its weight limits permitted (bags of lead shot would have been just dandy). But nobody seemed to

want another giant like the C-99, Constitution or C-132.

In fact, the Navy have not bought any more big transports at all, but in 1962 the Air Force did what I hope our own RAF does (though we never hear about such things): look ahead. If the RAF did look ahead I'm surprised they bought three different V-bombers, or ordered both Swift and Hunter in quantity (so that the Swift was in production in two factories), or bought the Belfast or Whitworth Gloster 681 and many other things, but these are digressions. Back in 1960 the USAF was looking 30 years ahead in Project Forecast. Under

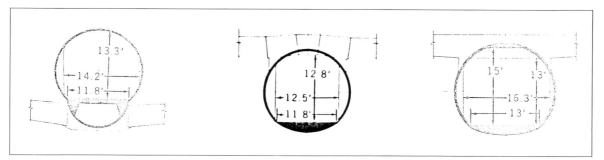

brilliant Gen Bernard Schriever, who had previously masterminded the entire ICBM programme, AF Systems Command asked the US industry for data by the truckload. One of the principal segments of such data concerned the way the world's biggest logistics transport should be designed. Called the CX-4, the Air Force outlined the requirement as being in the 600,000 lb category, and suggested it should be a jet. At a stroke, this opened the way to the kind of engine that

Side elevation from the general-arrangement drawing of the final Douglas submission, the D-916. (McDonnell Douglas)

CX-HLS studies involved examining the cargo-carrying ability, loading problems, structure weight and aerodynamic drag of more than 2,000 body cross sections, by Boeing, Douglas, Lockheed and the USAF. Here are three from Douglas: 1, Model D-890; 2, Model D-895; 3, and clearly superior, D-900. (McDonnell Douglas)

carries the world's population on intercontinental journeys today: the high bypass ratio (HBPR) turbofan. Such engines would have happened anyway, but this project spurred the idea on.

We don't seem to manage aviation well in Britain. In 1936 Whittle had patented the

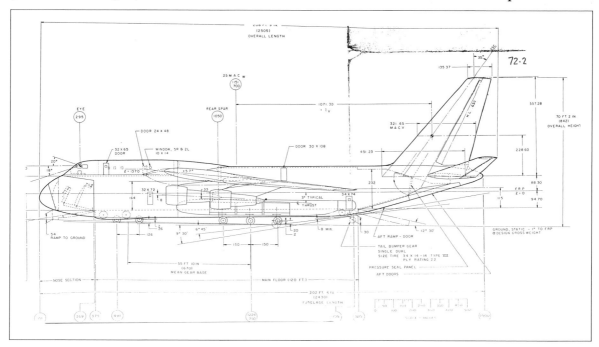

turbofan and outlined the optimum bypass ratio for different applications, ranging up to ratios of 5 or more for long range at speeds not over 500 kts. But nobody did anything about it except Metrovick, who produced an HBPR turbofan and even a propfan, so it was told by the Ministry to stop making aircraft engines. Nothing then happened until 1952, when Rolls-Royce began work on the Conway. This was aimed at a bypass ratio of about 1, but in order to squeeze it inside the wing of the Victor the BPR was cut back to 0.3, which made it merely a complicated sort of turbojet. We totally failed to cash in on our world lead in the turbofan, and we let Whittle's (Power Jets) patent on such engines lapse just as the US fan engines came into production.

Thanks to Project Forecast the US engine companies were paid to look far ahead and explain how a CX-4 should be powered. Such things are not done on the basis of the personal hunches of a few top engineers. The two companies most directly competing for what might eventually be a very large engine contract were General Electric and Pratt & Whitney. Both assigned roughly 600 engineers, aerodynamicists, analysts, mathematicians and other staff to get the

answers. Many models and test rigs were built, and a great deal of preliminary design work was done on what was clearly going to be a totally new kind of pylon-mounted pod. For the first time since the enforced stopping of Metrovick, aircraft engines with a BPR of from 3 to 8 were being discussed. This means a slim, very hot and high-pressure core driving a huge fan (either on the front or at the back) to provide the thrust, the core merely providing the shaft power and a very small amount of residual thrust. Like so many things in aviation, both the engine and the pod were thrusting into the unknown.

CX-4 studies by the aircraft companies tended all to look more or less alike, the only real difference being that some people suggested four engines in the 40,000 lb class while others suggested six in the 25,000 to 30,000 lb bracket. Of course, everyone studied all possible layouts, but all suggestions had a pressurized fuselage of about

Right *The one unanimously picked by the Air Force: the Boeing.* (Boeing Company Archives)

Below *First take-off by the one the Air Force actually got, the Lockheed.* (Via Mike Hooks)

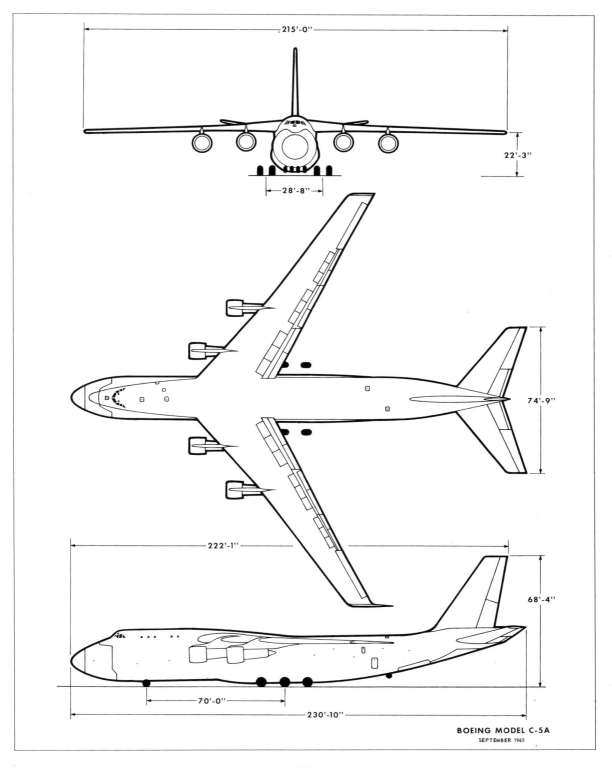

215'-0"

22'-3"

28'-8"

74'-9"

222'-1"

68'-4"

70'-0"

230'-10"

BOEING MODEL C-5A
SEPTEMBER 1965

20 ft diameter, with multi-wheel main landing gears retracting into bulges external to the pressurized structure, and full-section access at both ends. At the back there was no alternative to a powered ramp door, up which a main battle tank could drive and which could be opened in flight for heavy dropping. The nose, however, could swing sideways or (with or without the cockpit) hinge upwards.

When all the data were in they were digested at Systems Command and in the Pentagon. The mass of knowledge enabled the Air Force to write a detailed (1,560-page) specification for a CX-HLS (cargo experimental, heavy logistic system). This time it was for real; the Air Force would buy the winner. The basic requirement was to carry a cargo load of 125,000 lb for 8,000 miles or 250,000 lb over shorter distances, and to take off from an 8,000-ft runway and land on an unpaved airstrip only 4,000 ft in length. Just this part of the specification alone was to prove not merely demanding but, in the mid-1960s, beyond the state of the art (which was just what the CX-4 studies had sought to avoid). Following the preliminary design competition in May 1964 the Air Force awarded engineering design contracts to Boeing, Douglas and Lockheed for the aircraft, which was designated the C-5A and named the Galaxy, and to General Electric and Pratt & Whitney for the engine.

By this time the aircraft had grown well into the 700,000 lb class, but it had been decided to use four engines rather than six. In my view this called for an engine in the 50,000-55,000 lb class, as now used in the 747, which does not have to meet such severe field-length requirements. But the engines stayed in the 40,000 lb category, and while Pratt & Whitney offered the JT9D (*see Boeing 747 p.277*), General Electric offered a seemingly even more advanced engine with several remarkable features: a bypass ratio of no less than 8, a unique '1.5-stage' fan handling an airflow of 1,549 lb/s, an overall pressure ratio of 25, and a turbine inlet temperature of 1,371°C. The Air Force was impressed, but insisted that General Electric must demonstrate these features in an engine. Accordingly the GE1/6 was built as a two-thirds (linear) scale demonstrator, giving a thrust of 15,830 lb at the promised specific fuel consumption of the full-size engine (0.336, an unprecedented figure). General Electric went flat out to win the contract, not only tooling up to build the definitive engine in quantity, a massive calculated risk, but quickly producing 50 copies of a 90-volume proposal. Three days before the deadline the Air Force asked for many extra volumes filled with specific information for the evaluation teams. When in April 1965 it was time for the oral presentations General Electric sent down the whole 'first eleven' including Gerhard Neumann and Jack Parker. Such total commitment paid off, and in October 1965 General Electric won its biggest-ever single contract, for TF39 engines worth $459,055,000. In December 1965 the first engine went on test.

It wasn't quite the same with the C-5A aircraft. The submissions from the three giant competing companies were all similar to their CX-4 proposals, the chief difference being that the Air Force now asked for an extended upper deck which changed the fuselage cross section from a circle to a two-lobe pear-shape. All three candidate aircraft were similar in size, layout and configuration, and of course offered with either engine. Taking the Boeing C-5A as the baseline, the only significant differences were that Douglas continued to prefer a sideways-opening nose, and its final submissions, the D-916 and 917, were the result of seven years of refinement. I am including a side elevation of the 916 because many readers may not have seen what company general-arrangement drawings look like. MACV means the mean aerodynamic chord of the vertical tail, and FRP means the fuselage reference plane; dimensions are in inches. This proposal would have been slightly lighter than the Lockheed with an operating weight of 313,640 lb and a MTO weight of 716,000, but its interior width of 24 ft 6 in was appreciably greater. Lockheed proposed a T-tail (incidentally, with a remarkably small horizontal tail). The Lockheed GL-500-13-7 was also bigger than its rivals.

The SSB (Source Selection Board) was the most powerful ever convened in the Air Force, and it included two major-generals and two brigadier-generals. After a tremendous amount of deliberation the SSB sent to Washington its unanimous preference for Boeing. But this was an odd time, when the people in Washington appeared to go out of their way to ignore the findings of the Air Force's detailed and painstaking evaluations. A year previously another SSB, having sifted through six tons of proposals and supporting data on the F-111, unanimously picked Boeing, so the contract was awarded to the other firm, General Dynamics. Now the politicians noted that Boeing's C-5A was the unanimous preference, so they awarded the contract to Lockheed. Why? Well, the fact that Richard Russell, Chairman of the Senate Armed Services Committee and the most powerful of all Congressmen, was

the senator from Georgia may not have been entirely unconnected.

The contract, at a target price of $1,951 million for 115 aircraft, was awarded in October 1965. The design was virtually complete by August 1966. Lockheed farmed out various parts. For example, the complete wing went to Avco Aerostructures, and the entire tail to LTV. But Avco merely made the inner, centre and outer wing to Lockheed's design, and Lockheed did not do the design but farmed this out to a company formed in a matter of days in England by hundreds of designers thrown out of work by the British government's cancellation of all new British military projects. They were gathered in an office block in Southall, west of London, and undertook the almost impossible task of meeting the weight targets under intense pressure. History was to show they ought not to have been forced to achieve an impossibility.

The wing had a 25° sweep, a span of 222 ft 8.5 in and area of 6,200 sq ft. Inside the wing box was sealed to form 12 integral tanks housing 40,801 gal of fuel. Overall length was 247 ft 10 in. The fuselage was

C-5A interior, 1969, taken from about Fuselage Station 1850. (USAF)

Its crews would say the C-5B is 'a pretty good air-plane'. (Mike Hooks)

divided into a main cargo deck with a length (including the rear ramp) of 144 ft 7 in, width of 19ft and height of 13 ft 6 in, giving a usable volume of 34,795 cu ft, an upper deck forward (flight crew and systems) of 2,010 cu ft and an upper deck aft (76 troop seats) of 6,020 cu ft, the whole being pressurized to 8.2 lb/sq in. The high-lift system comprised six sections of Fowler flap and seven sections of leading-edge slat on each side, the slats opening or closing as the flaps moved through the 40 per cent position. Ailerons, spoilers, rudders (2) and elevators (4) were fully powered, and trimming was by the irreversibly driven tailplane. The latter, like the rear ramp and doors, was driven by a hydraulic screwjack, but the nose was cranked up by a hydraulic motor on the fuselage geared down to an output pinion engaging with a curved rack on the nose. Each engine nacelle incorporated inwards suction relief doors around the fan cowl to admit sufficient air on take-off, and a fan reverser of the translating-cowl type. To meet the rough-field requirement there were four nosewheels all in a line, and four main gears each with a six-wheel bogie having two wheels in front and two pairs at the rear. MTO weight was 728,000 lb, or, with a restriction to 2.25 g, 764,500 lb.

Leo Sullivan had a good first flight from the Marietta plant on 30 June 1968. But by this time many factors were conspiring to hurt the programme, including a nationwide defence-procurement boom that extended lead-times and inflated costs, many vendor problems and delays, numerous design or operational deficiencies and, especially serious, failure of the main wing static-test article at 125 per cent in July 1969, nowhere near the value necessary for the target fatigue life of 30,000 hr. Urgent fixes were put in hand, and the C-5A was restricted to only 712,500 lb and 2 g. Even so, wing life was calculated to be a mere 8,000 hr. The soaring costs eventually became public, and though it pushed up unit costs even further the Air Force decided to cut back from six squadrons to four, buying only 81 aircraft instead of 115. Like the F-111 the C-5A became the butt of any writer or broadcaster in the media with not much else to do, and one self-appointed critic wrote a major book, *The C-5A Scandal, a $5 billion boondoggle by the military-industrial complex.* In such books nobody can ever be toiling day and night to the best of his ability; they all have to be wicked people against whom the taxpayer has to be protected.

Deliveries began in December 1969, since when the C-5As have each flown about 700 hr a year with the 60th MAW (Military Airlift Wing) at Travis and the 436th at Dover. During their first decade many things were done to reduce wing bending moment and eke out fatigue life. This indicated that Military Airlift Command could continue flying its C-5As until about 1976-80 (depending on date of original delivery); then the main wing box, including the central structure inside the fuselage, would have to be replaced. Lockheed started a 28-month design phase in January 1976, followed by 11½ years of work fitting new wing boxes to the 77 aircraft in service. The entire box was redesigned to lower stress levels and using new alloys with higher fracture toughness and corrosion resistance. Avco (today Textron) Aerostructures was again the manufacturer of the wings. After reassembly each C-5A had a new wing box, painted in Europe 1 camouflage, while the 'feathers' (slats, flaps and other leading and trailing parts) were white like the rest of the aircraft. The programme was completed in summer 1987, by which time all C-5As were repainted in Europe 1. Capability and life were transformed, and (for example) on 17 December 1984 one aircraft lifted a payload of 245,731 lb to 6,561 ft (2,000 m), having taken off at 920,836 lb. This would have been unthinkable with the original wing.

In 1979 a supposed shortfall in national airlift capability was to be met by a new airlifter, the CX. This was won by McDonnell Douglas with the C-17, an excellent aircraft of DC-10 size. But Lockheed pushed hard for a further buy of updated and troublefree C-5Ns (N for new), while the US Senate voted in favour of the Air Force buying used 747s. Eventually the inability of the 747 to carry an M-1 tank and many other loads led to a go-ahead on a further batch of C-5s, while the C-17 was put on hold. Eventually McDonnell Douglas got their go-ahead, but so did Lockheed, with an order for 50 C-5Bs. These look identical to an updated C-5A but incorporate every new feature, and the TF39-1C engine rated at up to 43,000 lb. It is a measure of how much extra strength had to be built into the Galaxy wing to note that, whereas the original OWE (operating weight empty) was 325,244 lb, the figure for today's C-5A and C-5B is 374,000 lb. And, whereas MTO weight was (2.25 g) 764,500 lb, today's figure is 840,000 lb, with flight refuelling cleared to bring the inflight weight up to 920,000 lb. This should have enabled payload to go up to 291,000 lb, but in fact the limit is 261,000 lb, the range then being 3,434 miles.

There's an old proverb about spoiling the ship for a ha'porth of tar. Lockheed and the Air Force were never short of tar, but if only there hadn't been such pressure to (1) pare 8,000 lb of metal out of the main wing box to keep within a purely notional target structure weight, and (2) do it all in a great hurry, then billions would have been saved and everyone would have been spared years of strife and extra work.

73 Boeing 747

The Boeing 747 — at least its popular name Jumbo Jet — is probably known to more of the world's population than any other aircraft. It is the world's greatest people-carrier. And it will go on shifting the world's popu- lation for as far ahead as anyone can see, because — unless someone with an incredibly persuasive tongue emerges in the Soviet Union — there does not seem to be much chance of the 747 ever having a rival.

Yet, at the beginning, it was yet another case of Boeing girding its loins and launching a programme that risked much more than the net worth of the company. Some of the greatest Boeing people, including George Schairer, Maynard Pennell, Jack Steiner, Joe Sutter, Tex Boullioun and today's Phil Condit, have told me, in effect 'We ought never to have attempted it on our own'. I believe the bumblebee's wing loading is so high that it cannot take off, but it is too stupid to know this, so it just goes ahead and flies. The birth of the 747 was like this. Now Boeing cry all the way to the bank.

There's no point in regurgitating the history of the 747, pointing out the detailed differences between about 200 sub-variants. Instead I would like to give an overview, and pay tribute to a noble aeroplane. Incidentally, I'm glad Boeing never built some of the early project studies; I wouldn't have felt the same about them, for they were positively ugly.

Of course, if Boeing hadn't built the 747, such a vehicle would long ago have been created by someone else. It all stemmed from the availability of the giant HBPR (high bypass ratio) fan engine, for which the world really has the USAF to thank. As noted in the preceding story, such engines were produced for the USAF CX-HLS competition in 1962-66. Boeing fought hard to win this competition, submitting its 4,272-page proposal on 14 September 1964. They were good pages, and the Boeing C-5A was the unanimous choice of the USAF. But politics count for far more than such trivial factors as who has the best aircraft, and Sen Richard Russell of Georgia had even more clout than Sen Henry Jackson of Washington.

To say this was a blow to Boeing is an understatement, but a month before the

---

Boeing found it difficult to decide on the 747's fuselage cross-section: a, November 1965; b, December 1965; c, February 1966, the solution chosen; d, the freight and tourist passenger 747 compared with the previous biggest. (Boeing Company Archives)

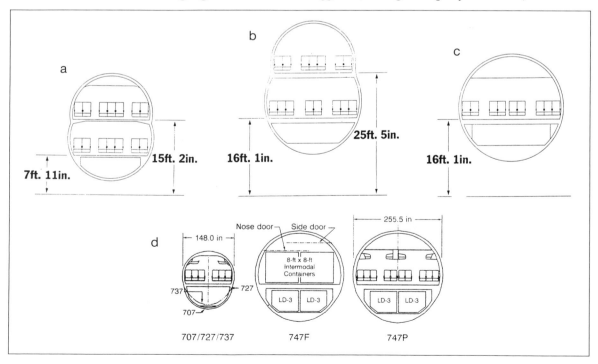

blow fell, in August 1965, Boeing had established a group of design engineers to work on a commercial jetliner in the same general size class as the C-5A and using the same engines. The prospect was awesome. At a time when the 707 was the biggest, heaviest and most powerful commercial transport, the aim was to build something twice as big, twice as heavy and more than twice as powerful. The spin-off problems were also considerable. A 747 (the obvious next number in Boeing's series) would demand a complete rethink of airport gates, lounges, servicing facilities, passenger handling and even car-parking. Almost the only thing that could stay the same was the runway, providing it was strong enough.

Before doing much, Boeing talked to customers. These included most of the leading intercontinental airlines, but by far the most important was PanAm. This was the only customer likely to place a launch order; others would initially be scared even to follow. But Juan Trippe who, in October 1955 at the stroke of a pen, had launched both the 707 and DC-8, was still in command of PanAm and intensely interested in the next giant plateau in air transport. Indeed, he

Some of the ones that didn't get built, with the one that did (white top). At the rear, double deckers; lower left, the 'ant-eater'; lower right, almost the final form but with close-spaced engines and an aft cockpit. (Boeing Company Archives)

and both Donald Douglas and Boeing's Bill Allen had often discussed what to do.

In April 1965 Douglas had decided on a major stretch of the DC-8. The resulting Super Sixty series had sold well from the start, and could have been countered by a super-stretched 707. But it had cut no ice with PanAm, and it was obvious that the stretched DC-8 was not really the next generation but a prolongation of the existing one. In any case, some old-timers remembered how Boeing's new-technology 247 of 1933 had been stopped in its tracks by Douglas's bigger and better DC-2. There was no point in stretching the 707. Boeing had to use the new giant fan engines, to obtain significantly better fuel economy, and incidentally much less noise. The question was, did the airlines want two, three or four engines, in other words did they want 200, 300 or 400 seats?

Trippe instinctively picked the biggest, and so did all the other airlines canvassed. This meant an airliner of C-5A size, but hardly any portions of Boeing's excellent C-5A proposal could be used, except possibly for the tail, engine pods and some systems. Even the wing would have to be started afresh, because for the 747 cruising speed mattered more than short field length. The wing never varied greatly from the final shape, with no less than 37.5° sweep at the quarter-chord line and a ruling thickness of 7.8 to 8 per cent. This wing was planned for a cruise at Mach 0.88 and can actually fly on the 747 at 0.92, but in practice, since 'the Fuel Crisis', is cruised at 0.82. In 1990 Boeing was seeking ways to finance a new wing that could actually be cruised at 0.89, which makes about an hour's difference on, say, London to Hong Kong.

While dealing with the wing, it should be noted that this vital component incorporated innovations, as they had done in several earlier Boeings. The classic 707 formula was continued, with outboard ailerons, used only at low speeds, partnered by small 'all-speed' inboard ailerons between the inner and outer flaps in the wake of the inboard engines. The flaps were triple slotted, as on the 727, but these ones were enormous. And the leading edge had three sections of Kruger flap inboard, swinging down from the underside of the wing (but, oddly, not coming anywhere near the root) and variable-camber flaps between the engine pylons and from there to the tip. These flaps looked like slats, but as they extended under power they were designed to bend into a curve giving optimum lift. Usually structural deformation is something the designer tries to avoid!

There was never much argument about how to design the tail or where to put the engines, but the fuselage was something else. I doubt if any other civil transport, except possibly the Il-86, has been the subject of such prolonged thought on how to arrange the payload. A photograph shows some of the configurations that were left after Boeing had thrown out the more bizarre ideas, including side-by-side tubes and giant flattened ovals. I should emphasize that — notwithstanding the amazing fact that 10 years earlier the 367-80 (707 prototype), KC-135 tanker and commercial 707 had all had quite different body cross-sections — the cross-section of the fuselage is something the would-be designer of a commercial transport simply has to get right. Once settled, any alteration would be extremely costly, and would disrupt production very seriously.

Having said that, I'm going to stick my neck out and say that, with the 747, Boeing got it wrong. It came about like this.

With a cabin pressure differential of 8.9 lb/sq in you can have any cross-section you like, provided it's a perfect circle. But if you draw a huge circle and then draw in the floor you either have far too much under-floor cargo space or a vast empty space over the passenger's heads. If you instead go for a double-deck layout, with superimposed intermeshing circles, things are much better. Boeing soon found that all the most efficient configurations were double-deckers. Some lacked underfloor cargo/baggage capacity. Around 1965 the airlines were just bringing in a range of standard underfloor cargo/baggage containers, the largest being the LD3, which weighs about 2,500 lb loaded. Eventually a good cross-section was reached with space under the big lower deck for two LD3s back-to-back.

I'm personally not enamoured of the double-deck 747s, though I can see no reason why a good-looking version could not have been produced. But Trippe was enraptured by 'The Flying Double Decker', and at the end of 1965 confidently expected his 747 to be built that way. But then Boe-

ing found a large spanner was being cast into the works. As explained in the next story, another Boeing team was working hard to submit a giant Mach 2.7 SST to the FAA, and there seemed every reason to believe that SSTs would gradually — or not so gradually — take over the long-haul passenger market. That meant the 747s would be relegated to being freighters. If this were so, the fuselage cross-section would have to be dictated by containers rather than by people.

Air cargo is either packed on a pallet 8 ft wide or into a container with a cross-section 8 ft square. Boeing could hardly invent a new set of internationally agreed unit load dimensions, and the double-deck 747s could hardly have been more wrong. They could carry a single row of loads, with masses of unused space, but were unable to carry two rows abreast. After considerable agonizing a new shape was drawn: a circle of 21 ft 4 in (6.5 m) diameter. Then the floor was added at such a height that two rows of LD3s could fit underneath and two rows of 8 ft × 8 ft containers on top. (Other wide-bodies carry the LD3s except, oddly, the 767,

Above left *The very first 747, N7470, on test wearing the logos of 28 famous airlines.* (Boeing Company)

Right *Inside an economy-class section of the furnishing mock-up on 30 September 1968. The passengers are Boeing office staff, who usually do get to eat things dispensed by the steward-esses, who are professional models (occasionally they are real, lent by customer airlines).* (Boeing Company)

which was made a few inches too narrow.) Thus, though the single-deck solution gives a passenger cabin wider (20 ft 1 in) than any double-decker arrangement, it was not adopted because of any thoughts of passenger appeal but in order to carry standard box containers side-by-side above the floor.

Switching to a single deck reduced passenger capacity, did little to reduce aerodynamic drag and resulted in lots of empty space (take away the interior trim and you could have 13 ft headroom). Today's 747 is a pretty good vehicle, but one can't help noticing that the SST never really happened, not many 747s are cargo aircraft and for the past 20 years Boeing has been wondering how to get back to a double-deck layout, starting with a super-wide lower deck. It is doubly ironic that, in early 1966, Boeing should have had to ponder on how to kill its customer's fixation on the double-deck aircraft. I find it hard to believe that Boeing went out of its way to build a cabin mock-up approached by a shaky staircase. Trippe, nearing 70, is reputed to have lost his enthusiasm for the idea as he neared the 25 ft level. Frankly, I don't get it; Trippe was no fool, and would have known that passengers would board via an enclosed jetway. As for vertigo looking down from a 25 ft 5 in floor, people on the *QE2* don't mind leaning over a rail at about 80 ft but, according to legend, that is how Boeing sold PanAm on the single deck.

Having at last got the cross-section, it would have seemed reasonable to stick the cockpit on the front, as in all the other widebodies. But Boeing's belief that, perhaps in the short term, all 747s would end up as freighters again dictated a different solution. If you are going to spend your life loading and unloading cargo containers, you want to do it straight through the nose. Boeing even looked at the other end, and studied C-5A arrangements, but wisely took no action here. If you load through the nose, the nose either hinges up, or opens to one side, or is split down the centre and opens

to left and right. Whichever arrangement is adopted, it helps if the flightdeck — Boeing call it the cab section — is further back, above the main deck. One model was made with a cab in the nose. To allow the nose to hinge up above it, the cockpit was put not in the obvious place but low down in front of the underfloor area. It looked silly, and was at once called 'the Ant-eater'. The inevitable answer was to put the cockpit in a bump on top — which, according to the old joke, enables the pilots to sit on their wallets. Totally unexpectedly, this little bump is today enabling Boeing to get back in stages to a very imperfect double-deck layout.

In almost all other respects the 747 was conventional. The cockpit was arranged for two pilots and an engineer (who increasingly was himself a type-rated pilot), with one or two jump seats. As for the space behind, Boeing produced beautiful artwork showing bars, lounges, playrooms, perhaps even a swimming pool or barbershop, but Trippe simply said 'Seats', and got 32. A spiral staircase gave access. He asked about giving the First Class passengers windows round the nose, but Boeing held up its corporate hands in horror and said this would cost 700 lb (no big deal, in my view), so even with an expensive ticket you can't get the view enjoyed by the navigator in the old Russian jetliners!

Among the other things that needed a bit of discussion were the spacing of the engines and the design of the main landing gear. The final choice, not necessarily the best, was to space the engines out very widely, which makes the wing lighter. Engine failure is today so rare that the severe asymmetry of an outboard failure is not a worry. From the start Pratt & Whitney, like Boeing a loser in the C-5A programme, worked as engine supplier for the 747, a choice eminently acceptable to PanAm. Its JTF14 matured by 1966 as the JT9D, with a brochure thrust of 43,500 lb and — unlike General Electric's C-5A engine — designed with community noise levels in mind. The

engine first ran in December 1966, and flew in 1968 on a B-52. Boeing had to solve extremely difficult engineering problems in designing the nacelle for minimum drag, with a reverser for the supersonic fan airflow and a spoiler for the slim core jet. The MLG (main landing gear) has often been seen on the world's TV screens. The two pairs of four-wheel bogies are broadly similar, one pair folding inwards and the other forwards.

The fuselage has radar at one end and the APU at the other. There are five doors along each side, though it is usual to use only those forward of the wing. There is a door on each side of the upper deck, but flight crew invariably use the forward main door. And on 9 February 1969 Jack Waddell climbed the spiral staircase of N7470 and prepared for the first flight. Previously, at Boeing Field in Seattle (which is not the same airfield as Renton), Waddell had climbed a much taller ladder to a cockpit mounted 32 ft high on a frame of steel girders, riding on a geometrically correct version of the 747 landing gears. This helped solve several problems. But N7470 was three months late, and the JT9D-1 was not giving even the initial promised 42,000 lb. This was a problem, because the gross weight of the 747 had inexorably climbed from 650,000 lb to 680,000 lb (at April 1966) and then to 710,000 lb. But the 747 flew beautifully, even if there was a flap malfunction which made Waddell fly cautiously and keep the gear

Emperor Ashoka was a 747-237B in Air-India's distinctive styling. Through no fault of the aircraft it exploded and fell into the sea about three miles from Bombay on 1 January 1978. (Boeing Company)

and flaps extended.

This first flight had taken off from Paine Field, home of the still-unfinished 747 assembly plant which has often been described as (in volume terms) the world's largest building. It finished at Boeing Field, where the flight-test and certification programme was based. Boeing had announced the 747 on 13 April 1966, stating that PanAm would buy 25 costing, with spares, $525 million. This was not a firm go-ahead, and Trippe is reputed to have bet Bill Allen $10 million that Boeing would not have launched the full go-ahead by August of that year. I have never discovered if this was a personal bet; Trippe may have had that much cash, but I'm sure Allen didn't, even though he was a lawyer! Anyway, Allen won, because in July Lufthansa and Japan Air Lines bought three 747s each, and Boeing fired the starting gun on the 25th of that month. If anyone had had time to think what they were doing they'd never have slept at night (they were also doing the SST).

At first orders came quickly, exceeding 150 before first flight. Then a terrible recession set in, traffic actually fell, Boeing almost ran out of money trying to develop the 737, 747 and SST, and Pratt & Whitney had severe problems with the JT9D. PanAm's aircraft were numbered from N731PA. At last, five weeks late, N735PA began to taxi at JFK bound for London on the first service on a bitterly cold 21 January 1970. A JT9D played up, and it was almost another eight hours before the first scheduled service actually departed with N733PA. One of the problems was starting the engines in a crosswind, which caused severe airflow distortion and overheating. A more intractable problem was ovalizing of the casings, especially around the turbine, causing gas leakage, blade rubbing and a severe loss in power and soaring fuel consumption. Pratt & Whitney was having severe problems with other installed engines at this time, notably in the F-111A, yet so far as I know they still do not have an installations centre resembling that of Rolls-Royce at Hucknall. The eventual cure was to design a massive Y-frame to pick up the engine at three points. I recall PanAm's Vice-President Service, Harold Graham, saying 'Next summer, in August 1970, we'll be despatching eight 747s between 6.30 and 8 pm every evening'. What actually happened was that they despatched the odd one or two, while back at the Everett plant 21 newly completed monsters had concrete blocks hung on the pylons to stop them tipping on to their tails.

This was the hard time when Boeing laid off what seemed to be about half the working population of Seattle (employment sank from 103,450 to barely 37,000), and someone stuck up the famous placard LAST ONE OUT PLEASE TURN OFF THE LIGHTS.

From then, it got much better. The JT9D, basically a massively tough engine, gradually got well, and with water injection gave 45,000 and then 48,000 lb. General Electric's CF6 and the Rolls-Royce RB211-524 gave airlines more choice, and for more than 10 years the standard model was the 747-200 in various forms, weighing up to 833,000 lb and with engines rated at up to 56,700 lb. All early 747s were built as PIs (passenger but with insurance provisions for easy conversion, as expected, into freighters). When the SST was cancelled the PI provisions were omitted, and for two years most people forgot about the all-cargo 747. Instead Japan bought the 747SR to carry 550 passengers over shorter (2,300 mile) ranges, while the USAF signed for special versions designated E-4B and VC-137.

The first variant to look different was the 747SP, standing for Special Performance. First flown in 1975, this was aimed at long

N747SP was — you guessed — the first 747SP. It eventually went to PanAm as N530PA and was later sold to United as N140UA. (Boeing Company)

Registration N401PW gives a clue to whose engines power the first 747-400, first flown on 29 April 1988. (Boeing Company)

but thin routes, in which distances are great but traffic moderate. The obvious answer is a different aircraft, but Boeing thought it worth redesigning the 747 with a gross weight well below 700,000 lb, a body 47 ft shorter, a larger tail with a double-hinged rudder, simple pivoted single-slotted flaps and many other expensive changes, including an airframe restressed for the lower weights. SPs typically seat 288-332, and though they have lower aircraft-mile costs than the full-size versions their seat-mile costs are higher. Boeing sold 46, ending in July 1982.

Boeing had meant to slot cargo and combi aircraft into the Everett line from No 31 onwards, but the severe weight growth ate into payload and eroded the attraction of cargo versions. Growing engine power restored the lost payload, and the first 747-200F flew in November 1971 as the 180th off the line. Registered D-ABYE, it immediately entered service with Lufthansa carrying 100 tons of cargo on the round trip between Frankfurt and New York every day of the year. Whereas the 100- series freighter conversions have a big side door aft of the wing, the true -200F has no passenger windows and an upward hinged nose, as noted.

Boeing tried hard to sell it to the USAF. Seaboard World was the first customer for -200Fs equipped to carry 14 standard ISO containers each 8 ft × 8 ft × 20 ft.

In June 1980 Boeing announced the SUD (stretched upper deck) option, in which the 'top floor' is extended 23 ft 4 in towards the tail, typically increasing seating there from 32 to 69. The steep slope of the walls gives upstairs passengers a better view of the clouds than of the ground. Rather surprisingly after so many years, Boeing discovered that replacing the spiral stairs by an ordinary straight flight, at the rear of the upper deck, would add another seven seats. It also discovered that the long upper deck — which if anything improves appearance — increases high-speed cruise from 0.84 to 0.85. Several customers elected to have their aircraft modified — for example KLM has a fleet of General Electric engined aircraft called -206B/SU — while new examples are designated 747-300.

In May 1985 Boeing announced the 747-

400. This looks like a -300 with winglets, but in fact it is a big advance in several respects. Whereas the -300 had the same '833k' maximum weight as the later -200s, the -400 goes up to a valuable 873k (873,000 lb). This is matched with engines in the 60,000 lb class, a wing stretched at the tips (with the winglets span is increased from 195 ft 8 in to 211 ft), digital avionics, a two-pilot flightdeck with six of the biggest (8 in square) displays, carbon brakes, aluminium-lithium alloys and many other updates. The first -400 flew on 29 April 1988, and two years later Boeing had sold 284. Whereas PanAm paid $21m for each of the first 747s, today's -400 (the only model on offer) costs about seven times as much, hence my comment about crying all the way to the bank. By May 1990 Boeing had taken orders for 1,007 of 'The Big Ones', made up of 205 -100s, 46 SPs, 391 -200s, 81 -300s and the first 284 -400s. With no competition, I can't see why they should not take orders for another 1,007 in due course.

These stories inevitably tend to get bogged down in technicalities, so that you can lose the wonder and romance of these big aeroplanes. I'll finish with the words of a retired 747 captain, from *Flying* for April 1988:

Seven years after setting brakes in Fat Al for the last time, I was back in that lofty cockpit looking down a long runway, conscious of the muted rumble of idling JT9Ds, awaiting clearance to roll...'Checklist complete, captain', said the engineer. I took a final glance at the killer items: trim, flaps, fuel, spoilers, flight controls, pitot heat. This old habit takes 10 seconds, and is cheap insurance.

'Cleared for take-off' said the tower. I eased the thrust levers off the stops, waited for the rpm to stabilize, then worked the levers forward until max power stood on the gauges. The huge Pratts growled and we moved, all

375 tons of airplane, fuel, passengers and freight, and accelerated — far too slowly it seemed. You sit way up there and seem to be doing 50 when airspeed confirms 100. Remembering that, I regarded the remaining runway without apprehension...

That's how the world's peoples are brought together. Whatever would we do without it?

It is interesting to note that the 747-400 has extra span plus winglets. Any aerodynamicist will tell you that you get far more extra lift by adding to the span than by adding winglets. The difference is about 2.5 to 1. But with very large aircraft extra span accentuates what may already be a severe problem. This is that commercial jets must fit the spacing of the gates at airports. Many thousands of gates around the world are spaced at the 150 ft span of the 707 and DC-8, and this also matched the L-1011-1 TriStar and DC-10-10. Later versions of these trijets were a squeeze, and the 747, at nearly 196 ft, required many gates to be respaced. This is very costly, because it means moving lounges, jetway loading bridges, baggage conveyors, pilot guidance systems and, not least, underground air, water, electric and fuel supplies. Even today many 747s have no place to go. Alan Mulally of Boeing told me in late 1990 he had just seen 47 Jumbos at Tokyo Narita, of which over 30 were out on the apron, their passengers having to use a bus. This is exerting an influence on the size of future aircraft. Mulally told me the 767-X (777) is being given hinge-up wingtips because its intended span of 197 ft worries a few key launch customers. The folded span will be 156 ft. He said 'One day we will have to put a new wing on the 747. This will take the span to at least 240 ft, so we may as well get used to folding wings right now.' An even bigger successor to the 747 seems out of the question.

Since
1970

The fact that this section covers two decades already and looks ahead to year 2000 underscores the fact that today we have more and more people seemingly doing less and less. I have selected seven stories to tell, the near misses including the Il-86/96, MD-11 and A330/340. These are all good stories and impressive aircraft, but, coming after the C-5 and 747, they hardly rate. What qualifies as a giant has tended to get, if not bigger, at least heavier and more powerful all the way through this book, and with reluctance I didn't feel these aircraft were what we would call giants today. So that leaves a single entry in the 30-year period, an entry describing work done by a team at Kiev, capital of the Ukraine, one of the republics of the Soviet Union. You'll drive them up the wall if you say 'Russia'!

Now one entry covering a 30-year period doesn't stack up too well against the 10-year periods that have gone before. I suppose the answer is that today the project, evaluation, feasibility study, parametric analysis and mathematical modelling and simulation teams have grown so enormous, and are assisted by such vast data-processing networks, that 10 or 20 years can go by without anything seeping through for the designers and engineers actually to create. By the time anything does get through to the design stage either it's obsolete or the political situation has changed and it's no longer appropriate. It makes you think. Are we really going to be flying 747s in another half-century?

What have we got at the end of the book? Well, the LH$_2$ (liquid hydrogen fuel) aeroplane has for 20 years been regarded as highly desirable, bound to come eventually and a fine thing for the nations to collaborate on, but unfortunately a total non-starter. That's precisely how it will be viewed in 2010, but 100 years on will be a different story. As for the Spanloader, well I was foolish enough to take out a Provisional Patent on it in 1963. This action didn't cost much, and I did it just to feel better, fully recognising that nothing would happen for (I thought) at least another 10 years. What I didn't expect was that nothing would happen for another 30 years. Like LH$_2$ the Spanloader seems a natural development that is bound to come in time. Who knows? Maybe some of our grandchildren might actually see it. But you can't rush things.

Previous page *NASA and US manufacturers have carefully studied the slew-wing (and flown a small version). At both subsonic and supersonic Mach numbers it seems to have a lot to offer. This '300-seater' is a model by Boeing. Lockheed have gone even better with a single slew wing joining two fuselages!* (Via Mike Hooks)

74 Douglas C-6

In 1967 Douglas Aircraft, having lost the C-5A contract to Lockheed and the giant commercial widebody to Boeing, began to investigate the prospects for a minimum-cost commercial cargo carrier. It was obvious that, not having to undertake heavy dropping, nor meet the requirement of loading at both ends, the best configuration would have a low wing and be fairly similar to that of an enlarged 747. In 1968 the C-6A and C-6B were the subject of marketing brochures as part of the D-974 study. The height of the fuselage off the ground was greater than ideal, but dictated by tail clearance on rotation. Some studies had various forms of nose loading, while others had tails that swung sideways or upwards, the fin lying over the fuselage. The C-6A and 6B were both to be in the 1.2 million lb class, with a cargo payload of 412,000 lb. Engines would have been a future promised uprated JT9D or an equivalent 50,000-lb engine from General Electric such as the CF6-50. Unfortunately there was no way Douglas could work off the large development cost on the very small number that the market appeared

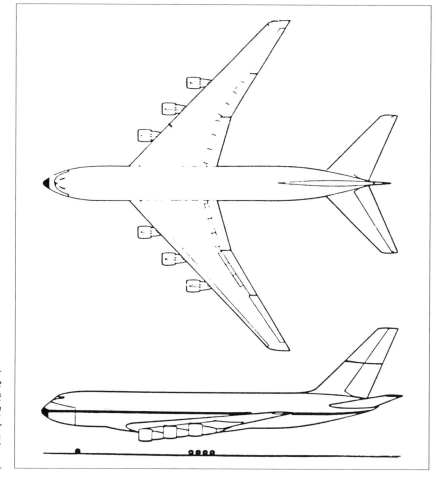

These two views show the Douglas C-6A. Such aircraft would be the conventional alternative to the Spanloader concepts. (McDonnell Douglas)

to need, and a very high unit price would have negated the objective of low ton-mile costs. Douglas wisely launched the DC-10 instead. The C-6B design is of interest in being the tallest in this book.

75 Boeing SST

Different aircraft qualify as giants in different ways. The HAPP (*see p.296*) is of interest because of its span, whereas its gross weight is no more than that of a Cessna lightplane. An SST (supersonic transport) tends to merit inclusion on the grounds of its length. After much agonising I decided to omit Concorde, which despite a length of 204 ft is rather too lithe and graceful to be a giant; and it is the subject of numerous books. I could hardly leave out Concorde and put in the Tu-144, though the Soviet aircraft is bigger; but the US SSTs were bigger still. The reason for the great length of such aircraft is that for acceptable drag at high supersonic Mach numbers you need an extremely high fineness ratio, in other words for a given body cross section you have to have a lot of length. Put another way, an SST with a length of 100 ft (like a 737) would have a cross section that would just allow two seats abreast. For a length of 200 ft (rather like a 747 or MD-11) you can get two double seats abreast, as in Concorde. To get accommodation like a wide-body you would need a fuselage length of about 1,100 ft, and it's not really on!

Unlike the modest target set with Concorde, the US SST design competition, which closed in January 1964, aimed at a cruising speed initially set at Mach 3, or 2,000 mph, but subsequently down-graded to Mach 2.7, or 1,800 mph. This gives better propulsive efficiency than Concorde's Mach 2, through greater air compression in the engine inlets, but it poses many problems of which one is that it is no longer possible to use traditional light alloys. Instead the structure has to be titanium and stainless

steel, in order to retain adequate strength at the temperatures at which the airframe soaks in cruising flight. I need hardly add that the problems of the aerodynamics, structure, propulsion and systems of any SST are numerous and very formidable, and the winning US design was no exception. No company on Earth has more technical strength and dedication than the winner,

I doubt if any aircraft has ever progressed through such drastic stages in redesign as the Boeing SST. For a company as powerful as Boeing to be so uncertain underscores the magnitude of the problems. (Boeing Company Archives)

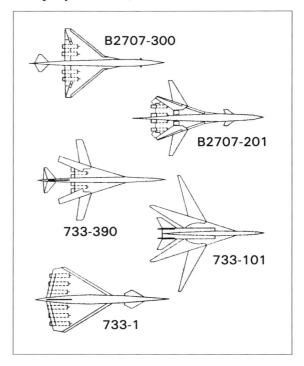

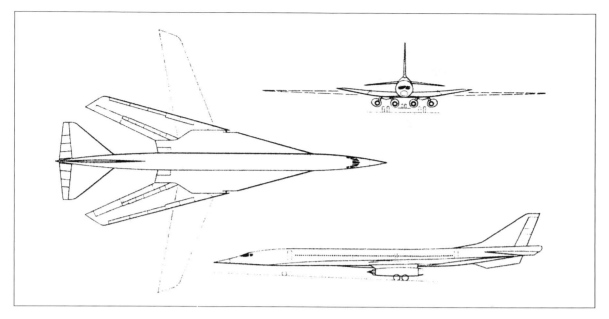

Boeing, and yet they found it was repeatedly a case of 'back to the drawing board'.

Boeing had been studying SSTs, on and off, since 1952. The design the company submitted for the 1964 competition was the Model 733. Unlike the Lockheed and North American rivals the Boeing 733 had been altered to have a variable-sweep wing. It was the biggest variable-sweep wing then considered, and it was one more element of risk to add to the mainly titanium structure, complex systems, and need for 60,000 hr of reliable fatigue-free operation. The fixed inner wing had a rounded leading edge extending along the lower forward fuselage almost to the nose, the main portion having a leading edge swept at 74° and with radius rapidly reduced to match that of the pivoting outer section. The latter generally resembled the wing of the 727, with slats, flaps, spoilers and ailerons. This wing would be set at 20° for take-off and landing, but moved back to 40° during the climb, to 66° for supersonic acceleration and 74° in cruising flight.

Basic data for the three generations of Boeing SST can be found on page 296. The 733 would have had its four engine pods,

Three-view of one of the intermediate forms of Model 733, basically a 733-390 plus refinements. (Boeing Company Archives)

each with a fully variable inlet and nozzle, hung side-by-side under the fixed inboard wing. The pylons on each side were to be splayed out to give even spacing between the engines, with the four-wheel bogie main gears retracted forwards between then, the bogie rotating to lie flat in the wing. The area-ruled fuselage would have had a circular section of 137 in maximum diameter, curving up towards the tail. The latter would have had a swept upper fin with four sections of rudder, a large ventral fin, and a delta horizontal surface pivoted to the fuselage and carrying no fewer than four sections of elevator on each side. Though the double-slotted flaps on the outer wings were naturally usable only at 20° sweep, split flaps under the fixed inner wing could be used as airbrakes at any time. Of course, the US SST requirement was purely for a passenger carrier, capable of non-stop operation on the North Atlantic, and able to fit into existing traffic patterns and airports.

So great was the effort, development cost and financial risk of the SST and its engine that, uniquely, the US Government agreed that it should be a national project, funded with Government money and administered by the FAA. By the time Phase II of the competition was reached, in September 1966, the field had narrowed to two. Boeing's remaining rival was the Lockheed CL-823, a tailless delta. Boeing very much wanted to win the SST programme, and was concerned that in some respects the Lockheed might prove superior. Apart from being superficially simpler it had a far bigger wing (just over 8,370 sq ft), a droop-snoot nose for good view ahead near airports, and a design cruising Mach number of 3. Boeing decided it had to rethink its design, and in later 1965 recast it completely. Redesignated as the Type 2707, it was appreciably bigger than the 733 (see data). By this time the General Electric GE4 was way out in front as the likely engine, and after coming through several phases of study and project design was firming up at almost double the original target thrust. This matched the increase in MTO weight of 58 per cent. But the airframe was not merely enlarged. Boeing-Wichita's work on the TFX (F-111) programme (in which they had been the preferred choice of the USAF over the company awarded the contract) had emphasized the advantages of a particular form of variable-sweep wing which, in the fully aft position, butted up against a large delta horizontal tail, turning the entire aircraft (in effect) into a tailless delta. Accordingly the 2707 was redesigned along these lines, and the engines were moved from under the inner wing to a unique position under the large horizontal tail. The resulting rearwards shift of CG was matched by an extension of the forward fuselage which put the nose 90 ft in front of the wing roots! This area-ruled fuselage was easily the longest ever designed.

Of course, in aircraft design one change tends to trigger off several others. The increase in weight demanded the use of four four-wheel bogie main gears, but the relocation of the engines made retraction geometry somewhat easier (though nobody liked the disturbed airflow caused by the bogies retracting and extending close in front of the inboard engines). Another change completed by 1966 was to fit a droop-snoot nose, and to keep the tip clear of the ground it had to hinge at two places, the front 15 ft (with radar) remaining horizontal at all times. After much discussion it was decided that the tailplane, plus engines, should be fixed, leaving just four sections of powered elevon between and outboard of the engines. This appeared to give inadequate

Artist's impression of the Lockheed CL-823 of 1965, very like a 222 ft Concorde. (Lockheed-California via Mike Hooks)

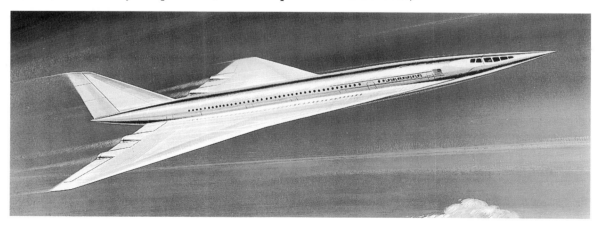

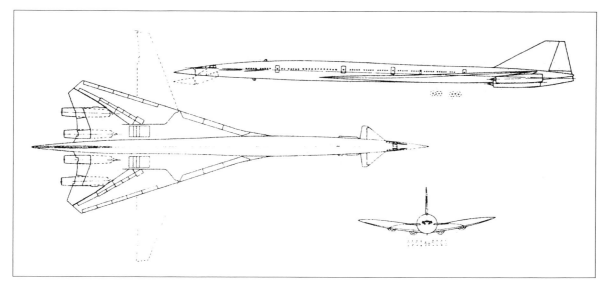

Three-view of an advanced 2707-200, basically a Dash-201 but with canards of delta shape mounted further forward carrying hinged flaps and with downstream strakes; droop snoot also added. (Boeing Company Archives)

pitch authority over the whole range of flight conditions, so a further change was to add delta canard foreplanes, with powered elevators, immediately aft of the flightdeck. Just downstream of these surfaces were 15 ft strakes on each side of the fuselage.

On 31 December 1966 the FAA announced that the winning team to build the SST was Boeing and General Electric. The crucial GE4 was always a single-shaft turbojet with afterburner, and in its J5 form had a nine-stage compressor handling 663 lb/sec. This may not sound much compared with the airflow through today's giant fan engines, but in the GE4 this was the flow through the core, including the combustion chamber and turbine. For comparison, today's widebody engines in the 55,000 lb class have core airflows of 260-280 lb/sec. The GE4/J5 even had hollow compressor blades. The original GE4/J4C first ran on 18 July 1966, and by October was running at 41,400 lb dry and 52,600 lb with afterburner. The new high-airflow nine-stage compressor for the J5 was tested in December 1967, and the first 63,200 lb prototype engine ran on 25 March 1968. By the time 633 lb/sec was reached, thrust had reached the later design target of 67,000 lb, and by 1970 the afterburning rating had been established at 69,900 lb. At Mach 2.7

this is equivalent to 333,000 hp. So far as I know, this is the most powerful aircraft engine of all time (though a case could be made out for the XLR99 rocket engine of the X-15A at over Mach 6).

Boeing and General Electric worked flat out to turn the challenging SST into hardware, well before President Nixon actually approved construction of two prototypes on 23 September 1969. The new designation of the aircraft was Model 2707-200, but by this time Boeing's agonizing doubts about the whole variable-sweep design were coming to a head. When you tool up to make an aeroplane it's the moment of truth. It's like writing a book: if you're going to alter anything, do it to the manuscript, because when it's set in type it costs real money. In the same way, it's bad enough (figuratively) to 'tear up the drawings', but that's a thousand times better than tearing up mighty steel jigs set in concrete and the titanium that comes out of them.

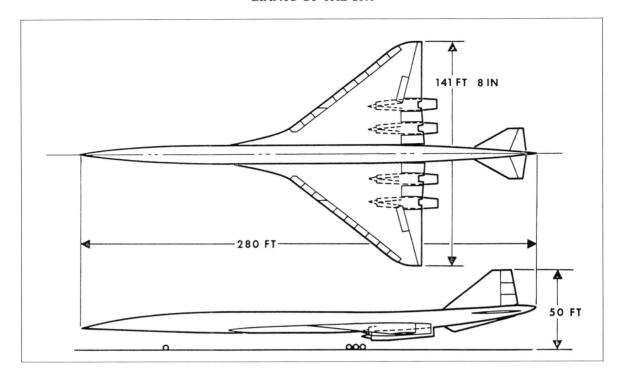

141 FT   8 IN

280 FT

50 FT

From the 318 ft 2707-200 Boeing developed the 2707-300 at 309 ft, then 298 ft and finally with the dimensions shown. Cancellation came soon after this stage was reached. (Boeing Company Archives)

In a nutshell, you can take the greatest bunch of aircraft design engineers in the world and, if you try hard enough, defeat them by giving them a task that is too difficult. The 2707-200 suffered from a multitude of problems, and in trying to cure it Boeing often made bits of it worse. The bigger aircraft needed more wheels, and after studying the retraction and ingestion problems the Dash-200 was designed with 16 main wheels folding into the inner wing, with the four mighty engines immediately downstream hung under the tailplane. But nobody liked this, especially when the weight estimates were refined. I visited the SST team in August 1968 and found them in deep gloom. The escalation in weight was officially deemed unacceptable. There were aerodynamic problems almost everywhere, and every fix brought forth worse problems. Aeroelastic flexure of both the wings and the fuselage appeared to pose 'the worst problems any design team has faced'. The sheer horsepower of the flight-control sys-

tem was increased four times in 1967-68 until it was 18 times as great as that of the 727. I was told 'Ignoring sonic boom and airfield noise, we face problems in many areas that we can't solve. Even with the planned reduction in cruise Mach to 2.65 we can't make it point in the right direction and fly where it's told without making it too heavy. We're already 26 tons overweight, short on range and still in deep aeroelastic trouble.'

In February 1968 it had been agreed to postpone the start of prototype construction by one year. Congress decided the planned $225 million for Fiscal Year 1969 would not be needed, and the sum was not voted. About 500 suppliers became desperate, asking Boeing how they could go ahead with their contributions when the aircraft was still in a fluid state. Privately I was told in August 1968 that there was little doubt the design would have to be abandoned again and replaced by a simpler concept. I saw numerous drawings and models of different ways to keep the landing gear away from the engines, improve flight control and, above all, reduce weight.

A year later, in the summer of 1969, Boeing announced the third revision of its SST, designated 2707-300. As predicted, it abandoned variable sweep and instead was a straightforward tailed delta, rather smaller than before (see data). Wing area was reduced, matched to a planned gross weight of 633,000 lb. Aerodynamically the wing had a root chord of 101 ft, giving a thickness ratio of 3.7 per cent, tapering to 3.0 at the tip, quarter-chord sweep of 50° and a gull-wing shape with dihedral at the root changing to anhedral at the outboard engines. Outboard of the root strake the leading edge comprised 10 sections of droop flap, while the trailing edge comprised small plain flaps, the sections outboard of the engines functioning as ailerons at low speeds. At high speeds roll control was in the hands of small spoilers. The tail comprised a small powered

tailplane and elevators and a vertical surface with three rudders, the uppermost being locked in high-speed flight. The canard was no longer needed, but the side strakes were retained.

The hinged nose was simplified into one unit. The engines, now of the J5P sub-type, were to be mounted directly under the rear part of the wing, each toed inwards and downwards. The main gear now comprised just two bogies, each with 12 wheels with carbon brakes, retracting neatly inwards into the fuselage. Cabin pressure remained 11 lb/sq in (a record), fuel capacity was almost unchanged at 440,000 lb (55,000 gal) and seating was reduced to about 210 mixed-class or 234 all-tourist. Unlike Concorde the fuselage was still visibly area ruled, the 11 ft 8 in maximum width being upstream of the wing. Not least of the changes in the Dash-300 was a switch from machined skins to titanium sandwich, which promised to reduce aeroelastic flexure and also reduce

Would you believe the mock-up of the Dash-300 was 38 ft shorter than its predecessor? (Boeing Company via Mike Hooks)

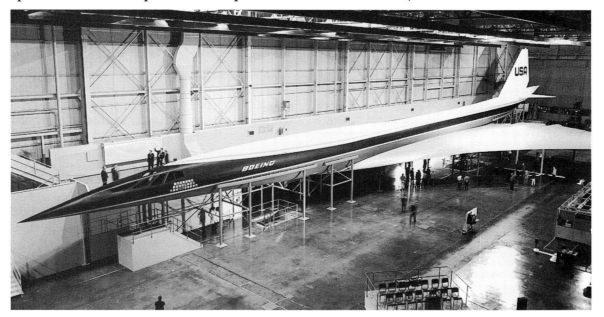

weight. Altogether it seemed a case of 'third time lucky' for the huge SST.

In his first Foreword as Editor of *Jane's All The World's Aircraft* John W.R. Taylor wrote in 1969: 'With delivery positions for 122 such aircraft already reserved by 26 of the world's airlines, Boeing are thinking in terms of an eventual sale of at least 500 aircraft...' However, the world was changing. It was partly the vociferous clamour of the rapidly growing lobby of environmentalists, who were convinced the SST would mean something like the end of the world. It was partly a growing antipathy of Congress towards aerospace, which was not helped by the bankruptcy of Rolls-Royce on 4 February 1971 and a close-run decision by Congress to vote federal funds to bail out Lockheed and the TriStar. Mainly, it was a general cooling of the national ardour with which the programme had been started, to the extent that, by the narrowest of margins, Congress voted to terminate the SST programme on 24 March 1971. The 318-ft Dash-200 mockup was sold to a Florida amusement park. Boeing still has the Dash-300 mock-up, and is still working on SST studies for NASA. Sir Frank Whittle believes — and I certainly agree with him — a future without an SST is unthinkable.

BOEING SST DATA

Designation	Model 733-390	Model 2707-200	Model 2707-300
Seating	150-227	250-350	210-234
Engines (4)	35,000 lb GE4-J4C	63,000 lb GE4-J5	67,000 lb GE4-J5P
Span	86 ft 4 in/173 ft 4 in	105 ft 9 in/174 ft 2 in	141 ft 8 in
Length	203 ft 10 in	318 ft 0 in	280 ft 0 in
MTO weight	430,000 lb	675,000 lb	633,000 lb
Wing area	(20°) 4,684 sq ft	(20°) 9,000 sq ft	7,900 sq ft

76 Lockheed HAPP

Throughout this book the giants have naturally tended to get, if not bigger, at least much heavier. So, just to prove there are exceptions to every rule, here is a giant which flies like thistledown! It rates as a giant purely on account of its span. So would a man-powered aircraft pedalled by 10 men, which (I calculate) could be built with a span of 500 ft, though it would need a very calm day to be brought out of the 500 ft hangar.

HAPP stands for high-altitude powered platform. It is just one of several species of VLEA (very long endurance aircraft), which for over 20 years have been studied in the USA and Soviet Union for their possible value in many kinds of surveillance. The objective is to carry a modest payload, such as optical cameras, return-beam vidicons, infra-red linescanners, sideways-looking radars and many other forms of sensor, climb to perhaps 70,000 ft and hold station for anything from days to years. Pictures or data would be relayed to an Earth receiver station. Obviously, one solution would be a low-power airship, filled with gaseous hydrogen under light pressurization and with a hydrogen-burning engine. But this has various drawbacks.

So do HAPP aerodynes, which have to weigh next to nothing despite having an enormous wingspan, and still be robust enough to survive take-offs and landings

This HAPP's span is 304 ft, but it would take more than 400 to equal the weight of an An-225!

and climbing up through, and descending back through, the dense and turbulent lower atmosphere. Wing loading would have to be much less than 1 lb/sq ft, yet loiter speed would have to be high enough to reach and maintain station in the face of any atmospheric disturbance or wind. Hydro-carbon-fuel engines are out. The only system that could fit the bill, with present technology, is electric propulsion using solar power. Solar cells have made tremendous strides in the past 30 years, but they are still poor performers. You need about an acre to power an electric light bulb. A typical installed power/weight ratio is 0.005 hp/lb; in other words you need 200 lb of cells, wires and motor to get 1 hp. The advantage is that it goes on for ever, except at night, because at 70,000 ft the Sun always shines all day.

The illustration shows a Lockheed Missiles & Space Co HAPP, developed in partnership with Astroflight for NASA Langley,

but there are dozens of others. Extensive research has shown that at heights varying from 65,000 to 75,000 ft there is hardly any place on Earth where wind would pose a major problem. The 304 ft wing and broad tailplane would be covered in silicon or (if we solve fabrication problems) higher-energy gallium arsenide cells. As well as driving the propellers the generation system would store electrical energy in batteries, or hydrogen/oxygen fuel cells, to feed the motors at night. The airframe would be mainly graphite-fibre composite and Mylar film. Weight (at take-off or landing) might be 3,000 lb.

Quite complex computer studies have been undertaken to see how far the ability to keep as many solar cells as possible square-on to the Sun is worth the extra complexity and weight. In the HAPP illustrated there are cells on the upper surface of the wing, on surfaces standing upright on the wing and on both sides of the outer wings, each about 60 ft long, which can hinge up through any angle to 90°. The podded sensors would weigh about 250 lb, and are expected to be designed to assist agriculture, though the range of beneficiaries could be almost open-ended.

77 An-124 *Ruslan* and An-225 *Mriya*

I am grateful to the chaps from Kiev, because they enable me to end this book — give or take a few paper projects — on a high note. For once, we have a 'biggest aeroplane in the world' with no ifs, buts or qualifications.

It all began in 1975 when the OKB (experimental construction bureau) of Oleg K. Antonov began work on a 'clean sheet of paper' heavy airlift transport. Oleg Konstantinovich sadly died in 1984, but he was not only a very genial man but on his trips outside the Soviet Union he was the most accessible of all Soviet General Constructors. He would even seek out people he knew, not to feed them propaganda but because he was an aviation enthusiast and loved to talk about his aeroplanes, and even those of other people. He knew Lockheed-Georgia had put up a sign saying THE AIRLIFT CAPITAL OF THE WORLD, and commented 'If that is based on payload multiplied by number of aircraft we ought to get that sign moved to Kiev'. Certainly the variety of Antonov's airlifters was far greater, and in 1975 it faced its biggest challenge.

The requirement was for the next-generation heavy logistic freighter to follow the very successful An-22 *Antei*. Like that aircraft, and the many versions of An-12 before it, the new transport had to meet the requirements of both the VTA (military transport aviation) and Aeroflot (the civil organization). The requirements were numerous, and often conflicting. Almost the only unanimous requirement was the ability to operate from remote isolated airfields with no servicing facilities, no ground equipment and no paved runway or apron. Apart from

that, the two customers differed in dimensions and types of cargo, the methods of loading, the need for low-level extraction or air-dropping of heavy loads, and many other thorny issues. One by one the problems were resolved, usually by talking the options through until complete agreement was reached. Never once was a design choice adopted in the face of any customer opposition. At last, after three years, the engine was a firm programme, there were no more disagreements, and construction went ahead on the prototype. Designated An-124, it was named *Ruslan*, a giant hero of Russian folklore. With civil registration SSSR-680125, it was flown by the bureau's chief test pilot, Vladimir I. Terski, on 26 December 1982.

Unlike its only foreign counterpart, the C-5, the An-124 never caused any problems, and has yet to give any indication of difficulty in meeting the design target of 8,000 full-load flights. Altogether it looks very much indeed like the Boeing and Douglas contenders for the C-5A contract, though in most respects it is considerably better. This is partly due to being 10 years later, which is reflected in superior aerodynamics, newer structures and later engines. The superior aerodynamics are manifest most clearly in the wing, where the deep supercritical profile enables the wing structure to weigh only 145 lb more than that of today's C-5A yet have an area of 6,760 sq ft, much higher aspect ratio, span of 240 ft 6 in and sweepback varying from 32° to 35°. Each wing carries six sections of leading-edge flap, covering the whole span, but these could

equally well be called slats because they translate forward as well as down to leave a slot when they are open. On the trailing edge are three enormous sections of Fowler flap, running out on six tracks. In the upper surface are (outboard) eight sections of spoiler and (inboard) four sections of airbrake, with slightly greater chord. Outboard of the flaps are two sections of aileron. Every movable surface is hydraulically driven, as are the four sections of elevator, hung on a fixed tailplane, and two sections of rudder.

The newer structure naturally means much greater use of composites. Carbon and glassfibre composites cover more than 16,150 sq ft of the skin, and total more than 12,125 lb in weight. The main cargo floor is titanium, and despite the tremendous (150-ton)

Top *The prototype An-124 was SSSR-680125. The second, named* Ruslan, *was 82002, since when most have followed in numerical order. Here 82007 taxies out at Farnborough. (Mike Hooks)*

Above *A slow flypast, with everything out and down. Antonov pilots can hold 200 km/h (124 mph). (Mike Hooks)*

loads it carries it is attached to the strong forged frames of the fuselage in such a way that relative movements are possible when there is, for example, a temperature difference across the skin of 70°C. The fuselage has a pear-shaped two-lobe cross section, the junction between the lobes and the huge wing/body fairings being all composite structures. The cargo hold is 118 ft 1 in long,

a complete relief crew. This was certainly needed on 6/7 May 1987 when Terski and two crews flew round the Soviet Union, over 12,521 miles, in 25 hr 30 min, landing with a 12-ton fuel reserve. Aft of the wing is a passenger compartment, typically with 88 seats. Hatches at various points in the upper deck open on to the tail or wing.

The engine that was one of the causes of the rather delayed start to prototype construction is the Lotarev D-18T. In many ways this shows its later design than the C-5's TF39, its overall dimensions being much smaller (for example, overall diameter 92 instead of just over 100 in, and overall length 212 instead of 271 in) despite the maximum airflow being 1,687 lb/s and take-off thrust 51,590 lb. The nacelles and pylon skins are glass or carbon composite, and incorporate a translating-cowl reverser attached to the rear of the fan case. The An-124 is fairly quiet, even on take-off.

The landing gear comprises left and right independently steered and retracted twin-wheel nose units and 10 twin-wheel main units, five in a row along each side, each individually retracted inwards and able to kneel in a controlled manner, the two front units on each side being steerable to enable the giant to turn round on a runway 148 ft wide. Avionics are predictably impressive, as is the difficulty of finding the 17 external antennas. Opening the nose leaves all cables and pipes unbroken. The flight-control system is as modern as the hour, a quadruply redundant FBW (fly-by-wire) system, with a fifth emergency mechanical channel to drive the surface power units directly. Deicing is by bleed air on the engines and wings, but the tail uses the unique Soviet electrical 'giant impulse' method, claimed to be more energy-efficient than any other system.

Altogether the An-124 seems to me an outstandingly good aircraft. With 507,063 lb of fuel in the 10 integral wing tanks the MTO weight is 892,872 lb. Height over the fin is 68 ft 2.3 in, which is a record among today's

An-124s maintain a regular shuttle bringing airframe components for the Airbus 330/340 programme from the Canadair plant at Montreal. (Canadair)

21 ft wide and over 14 ft 5 in high. Outstanding access is gained at both ends, though the nose takes 7 min to crank its way upwards, at the same time extending the front triply-hinged ramp which can take a 70-ton tank; the rear ramp doors open fully in 3 min. If necessary the An-124 can kneel nose-down, by retracting the nose gear so that the nose sinks on to two short supports, or nose-up by easing pressure in the rear main-gear oleos. Along the top of the lower deck run full-length rails carrying two electric travelling cranes each able to lift 44,090 lb. The lower deck is modestly pressurized to 3.55 lb/sq in, enabling the cross-section to be optimised with an almost flat underside and pronounced chine along the sides, while the upper deck is fully pressurized to 7.8 lb/sq in. The flight deck is arranged for a crew of six. Behind are very comfortable rest facilities, as well as accommodation of

Above *Spotless and polished, despite coming through a lot of bad weather, the Mriya taxies across the grass to get to its parking spot at the 1989 Paris airshow, with its Buran spacecraft on its back.* (Mike Hooks)

Right *Trouble is, whenever you try to show the size of the Mriya, you can't get it all in!* (Mike Hooks)

aircraft. Range varies from 10,250 miles with the normal maximum fuel capacity to 2,795 miles with the maximum payload of 330,693 lb. Commercial operations began in January 1986, and the first An-124s for the VTA — which are unarmed — were delivered a year later. By 1989 the number delivered had reached 22, and in conformity with the startling new commercial — indeed capitalist — policy in the Soviet Union, the Antonov OKB itself formed a special company to go after air cargo business all over the world. Antonov's successor as General Designer, Piotr V. Balabuyev, told me 'We believe the An-124 is the best air transport vehicle ever built. Greece, Moscow, West Germany, Spain, Iraq, anywhere — we are prepared both to export aircraft and also enter into wet-lease agreements to carry cargoes.' Brochures show such loads as 50 (normal) to 70 (small) cars, 100 tons of fresh meat or 176 head of bloodstock. The bureau's slogan: 'The 124 can carry anything anywhere'.

As the world's largest production aeroplane the *Ruslan* could hardly fail to be impressive, but in 1988 the Antonov bureau unveiled a development of it that was significantly larger! To be fair, they had an-

nounced such an aircraft was being built. The first picture showed the mighty An-225 on its ceremonial roll-out from the Kiev assembly plant in November 1988, towering over thousands of tiny humans. On 21 December it made its first flight, in the hands of a normal six-man flight crew headed by Aleksandr Galunenko, taking off in under 3,280 ft but keeping the landing gear extended.

In fact, there didn't seem a lot likely to go wrong, because almost all the difficult parts of the An-225, including avionics and software, are identical with those of the An-124. Work began in June 1985, mainly to provide an aircraft able to carry the *Buran* manned space orbiter and other loads, piggyback fashion. Stripped down *Buran* airframes and parts of *Energiya* launch vehicles had been carried in this way on the back of a greatly modified M-4 bomber, but this was far too limited in capability. The An-124 would have

At this moment the An-225 is straight and level, but what really impressed the Paris crowd was the way pilot Galunenko orbited the show at very low level in really tight steeply-banked turns. (Mike Hooks)

An-225 making a slow pass with take-off flap and slats extended.

been almost adequate, but it needed a new twin-finned tail to avoid having the fin and rudder in violently turbulent air in the wake of the giant payload. But instead of merely putting a new tail on an An-124 the Antonov designers wisely studied further possibilities, and found that with relatively little design effort and extremely low risk they could multiply the An-124 by roughly 1.5! Leader of this team, Deputy Chief Designer Anatoli G. Bulanenko, said, 'We found all the names from Greek mythology had been used, and in any case we are based in the capital of the Ukraine, so we used a Ukrainian word: *Mriya*, which means a dream'.

By far the biggest design effort was needed to add a new wing centre section. This, which carries an extra engine on each side, also requires a new carry-through central bridge in the fuselage. The extra centre section has a leading edge swept at the same

35° as the original inboard wing which is bolted on to its extremity, but the trailing edge is unswept. There is no flap/slat on the leading edge, but at the back is another section of flap and four more airbrakes, making a spoiler/airbrake total of no fewer than 32! The outer panels retain their pronounced anhedral, but the centre section is almost horizontal and pilots have experienced no difficulty avoiding wingtips contacting the ground. Two plugs were added to stretch the fuselage, and the modified central structure was further altered to accept the external-payload forces from above. Different loads require different attachments, and even the first aircraft, SSSR-480182, has provision for many enormous loads, some of the attachments being responsible for numerous blisters along the top of the fuselage. *Buran* is relatively short and carried well forward on the two large pylons

side-by-side above the wing; other loads need fixtures at the tail.

The inevitable redesigned tail starts with a modified rear fuselage, changed from a cone to a flat beaver tail, and continues with almost untapered tailplanes which, unlike those of *Ruslan*, have dihedral. Each carries three sections of elevator. On the tailplane tips are the fins, mounted at 90° and thus inclined inward. Behind each tailplane tip is a streamlined fairing which divides each rudder into upper and (smaller) lower sections. There is no change to the flight-control system or method of tail deicing. To carry the weight on the ground the main landing gear was modified. Two extra units were added on each side, making a total of 28 main wheels, and the steering was removed from the front two pairs on each side and transferred to the rear four pairs on each side. Thus, including the nose gear, the *Mriya* has 20 wheels with power steering!

Almost everything else was pure An-124, but the differences were still awesome. Span was increased by almost 50 ft to 290 ft, and wing area to approximately 10,280 sq ft. Length was increased to 275 ft 7 in, but the tail redesign reduced overall height to 59 ft 5 in and increased tailplane span to 107 ft 1½ in, both span and area being much bigger than the wing of a Lancaster. Length of the cargo hold was increased to 141 ft. There's room for 16 ISO containers or 80 family cars. The first *Mriya* was built without a rear ramp door, but obviously this could be restored if a need arose. MTO weight is

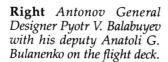

Left *Interior of* Mriya, *like a cathedral aisle.*

Below left Mriya *landing at the 1990 SBAC show at Farnborough, nose gears still off the ground.*

Right *Antonov General Designer Pyotr V. Balabuyev with his deputy Anatoli G. Bulanenko on the flight deck.*

at present set at 600 tonnes, or 1,322,750 lb. Maximum payload is tentatively put at 250 tonnes (551,150 lb), internal or external. Fuel capacity exceeds 300 tonnes, though I was told by Bulanenko 'So far we have never needed to put in more than 200 tonnes. Perhaps one day we will have time to take off with maximum fuel and set some more world records.' Carrying a payload of 200 tonnes internally the brochure range is 2,795 miles, the same as for *Ruslan* with 150 tonnes.

In summer 1989 the Antonov bureau was looking for export orders for the An-124 *Ruslan*, the world's greatest aeroplane except for the An-225, and was hoping eventually to get orders for four more An-225s. All the Antonov giants are assembled at Kiev from major parts often made elsewhere, and the complete wings are flown from Tashkent on top of an An-222. Unfortunately, Bulanenko said he could not see the Ministry of Avia-

tion Industry justifying a production order of *Mriyas* in order to fly in the wings of *Mriyas*! What's more he said 'The sky is a big place, but on the ground it's very different. I don't expect to see anything much bigger than the 225, at least not in my lifetime.' This is despite story 79.

I don't think anyone will argue if I say the An-225 will be the world's biggest, heaviest and most powerful aeroplane at least until the end of the century. And, unlike so many earlier giants, it is no lumbering plodder, needing all the strength of two pilots to make a Rate 1 turn. When it arrived at the 1989 Paris airshow, in quite poor weather and encumbered by the *Buran* on its back, I stood almost open-mouthed as it thundered round at a bank angle of about 45°, and occasionally greater, streaming white vortices from its wingtips and behaving like an overgrown fighter. Pilot Galunenko said 'No problem, you don't need both hands'.

78 Flying boat 2000?

It is self-evident that this book's interest is enhanced by the inclusion of projects, but

one has to be selective. I have quite a few lovely bits of artwork, some even bearing the

Left *Hinomaru (Rising Sun) markings adorn this project by the Japanese firm Shin Meiwa. At least they have recent experience of building flying boats. (Shin Meiwa via Mike Hooks)*

Below *Lockheed is the originator of this Sea Loiter Amphibian, which is intended to spend long periods in each mission sitting on the ocean listening for submarines. (Lockheed via Mike Hooks)*

names of famous aircraft manufacturers, which do not appear here because they were overtly impractical. For example, one is a twin-hulled freighter dreamed up by a company not a million miles from Burbank. The

hulls, which could have planing bottoms or air-cushion landing gear, are joined by a straight wing carrying five big fan engines. Fair enough, but then the two bows, or noses, are linked by a straight-across fore-

plane carrying four more engines, and I think the result would pose aerodynamic, structural and systems problems. There are lots more in the same vein.

One of the proposals which gets in by the skin of its teeth — because I don't believe a word of it — is a flying boat dating from 1978 drawn by Shin Meiwa of Japan. Once famed as the Kawanishi company, Shin Meiwa is one of the few builders of modern flying boats, so they know what they are talking about. Although they give the length of this leviathan of the skies as 'almost 300 ft' I can't help feeling it looks over-engined. Each of the six engines looks to be in the 100,000 lb thrust class. They are installed to provide USB (upper-surface blowing) across the top of the wing, with flattened jetpipes to squeeze out the flow across the wing to enhance lift, as in the Japanese Asuka STOL. Anhedral is adopted to bring the tip floats down to water level (the boat on the water is leaving wakes from both tips). The three-deck hull would have a lift to help the 1,200 passengers move around, the diameter of each pressure lobe being 27 ft 6 in. Small inlets serve auxiliary engines in the wing roots to blow across the flaps and other surfaces as in the company's STOL PS-1 and US-1.

Lockheed is the originator of the catamaran amphibian, with four 50,000-lb turbofan engines above a straight wing. Designed for ASW (anti-submarine warfare), it is in every sense a flying battleship. Features include a circular-section pressurized crew compartment and command centre riding on top of the two deep but narrow hulls which, when riding at speed over the waves, would generate surface-effect lift through the tunnel between them. The straight wing is 26 ft above the waterline, yet it was nevertheless deemed prudent to put the engines higher up still. Like some early flying boats this might result in big pitch changes when the throttles were opened or closed. Doubtless the V-type butterfly tail was adopted to avoid the engine wakes. Weighing 640,000 lb, this Sea Loiter Amphibian 'would be able to extend missions by sitting on the sea for 10-hr periods up to five times in any one mission'.

Another Lockheed, this is called a 'power-augmented ram wing' and is intended to fly only just above the water. Such things are not good at avoiding weekend sailors! (Lockheed via Mike Hooks)

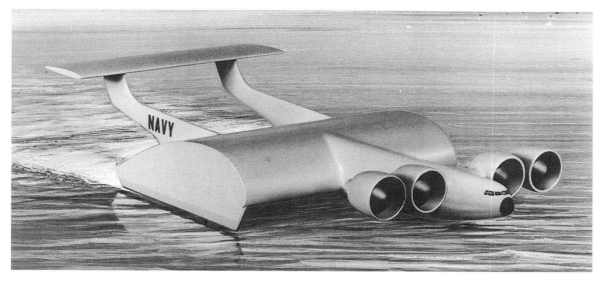

The last of these 'funnies' is another Lockheed, and it is more a surface-effect craft rather than an aeroplane. Called 'a power-augmented ram wing', it blows its jets across and also under the high-lift wing, the tailplane being for trim. It would carry a payload of 441,000 lb and might cruise at about 450 mph at 20 or 30 ft.

79 Soviet giant freighter

As the world's biggest country geographically, the Soviet Union might reasonably be associated with some of the world's biggest aircraft, and history has shown this to be the case. Today the vast undeveloped regions of the Central Asian republics and, especially, Siberia, are seen as needing not gangs of prisoners but the world's biggest earthmovers, pipelayers, diggers and other mechanical devices, and this in turn means enormous transport capability. Bearing in mind that we are talking about regions where there are, as yet, no railways and virtually no roads, the need for really capable air cargo aircraft is obvious.

Several ideas are being bandied about, and the requirement is seen as an obvious one for international collaboration. Already several Western companies have gone a long way in discussing joint programmes, to the mutual benefit of both parties. As a Brit, I would be delighted to see British Aerospace get a piece of the action, but to be frank I don't expect this. Where giant cargo aircraft are concerned we are talking about a vehicle to be certificated around 1996 which could really open up undeveloped regions without the environmental destruction that accompanies the building of motorways.

One of the Soviet ideas was displayed in the form of a model at the 1987 Paris airshow, and it is still a very active project today. The basic design has been drawn up by the Central Aerodynamic and Hydrodynamic Institute, the initials of which are usually rendered in English as TsAGI. This huge organisation carries out the basic work on aircraft configurations and aerodynamics.

When what seems to be the best possible basic design has been achieved, the requirement is put out to competitive tender and ends up with one (rarely two) OKBs, experimental construction bureaux. They do the detailed stressing and engineering and fly one or more prototypes. When ready, the accepted design is put into production at one of the Soviet Union's GAZ (national aircraft factories). This particular proposal is still being studied and refined at TsAGI, but I was told 'Several of the design bureaux have collaborated and are eager for the programme to go ahead, and that goes for the engine as well'. Engines are the responsibility of TsIAM, as noted later.

This cargo aircraft would be easily the biggest aeroplane in the world. It is a perfectly straightforward design, posing no particular problems, though a lot of work is still being done to decide which bits should be of composite construction and which bits metal. The basic twin-boom layout is obvious, the only controversial feature (which is not yet 'carved in stone') being the use of a separate detachable container for the payload. Such an idea goes back into the mists of time. I recall a sketch of such an idea by (I think) Curtiss-Wright in the 1920s. In 1947 Miles flew the delightful little M.68 Boxcar with its cargo carried in a detachable box. Without the box the rear fairing was simply attached directly behind the nose cockpit.

A much bigger example was the Fairchild XC-120 Pack-Plane, based on the C-119 and flown in 1950. A decade later Armstrong Whitworth failed in its prolonged attempts to launch detachable-container versions of

the AW.650. But today's Soviet project is something else.

Work really started with the payload container, which offers an unobstructed space about 215 ft long, 27 ft wide and 20 ft high. The idea is that there would be more containers than aircraft, so that they could be loaded and unloaded without holding up the flying. One problem in the past has been the sheer mechanics of moving the loaded container on the ground, getting it in the right position and attaching it to the aircraft. My belief is that this calls for a wheeled system that stays on the ground without the container. This huge pod is designed to be pressurized and to carry a load of 500 tonnes, 1,100,000 lb.

To leave room for the pod and keep the landing gear short the inner wings have acute anhedral. Most of the wing is untapered, only the outer panels having taper on the leading edges. Span would be about 400 ft and wing area 19,500 sq ft, matched to a take-off weight of 1,300 tonnes (2,866,000 lb). We now get an idea of just what kind of animal this would be, with double the wing area of the Hughes Hercules and double the weight of the An-225!

The eight engines are turboprops, each rated at 30,000 shp. They would drive contra-rotating propellers, each probably comprising two six-blade units, with a diameter of about 24 ft. TsIAM and the Perm MKB

An exhibition model of the giant cargo aircraft. (Via Flight International)

(engine design bureau) have studied an engine using the core of the PS-90A turbofan, the engine of the Tu-204. This could be developed with a new LP compressor and a five-stage LP turbine to meet the requirements, with very competitive fuel consumption, by far the biggest problem being the propeller gearbox. In 1989 a 30,000 shp gearbox was about to begin testing.

The crew might number as few as four, two pilots and two loadmasters, all accommodated in the short nacelle to which the freight container is attached. Of course, there could not be any conventional nose landing gear, which explains the large forward projections of the twin tail booms. Geometry of the landing gear is still a matter for study. The forward units, with multiwheel bogies, would of course be steerable. There would be about 32 main wheels, probably arranged in four main gears retracting into the boom. The size (168 ft span) of the tailplane/elevator is remarkable, and indicates the range of CG position that may have to be allowed for. To minimise structure weight and aeroelastic problems the vertical tails are canted outward to support the horizontal tail over a wider span. Overall length of the aircraft would be about 250 ft, of which about 235 ft would be accounted for by the pod.

All exciting and totally convincing. The Russians have a record of seldom talking about something unless they mean it, and of keeping quiet about their projects unless they really intend to build them.

80 Spanloaders

Throughout this book it has been evident that making aeroplanes larger than normal results in gains and losses. In theory one of the losses stems from the fact that, while areas (and thus wing lift) go up as the square of the linear dimension, the weights, and in general the necessary engine power, go up as the cube. But suppose we cheat and hold the vertical dimensions constant and merely spread out the aircraft horizontally? The Spanloader aims to do even better than this, in that it simultaneously spreads the weight across the span of the wing, as its name suggests, thus greatly reducing the wing bending moment. The possibilities are considerable.

In case anyone has failed to get a degree in structural engineering, the bending moment (BM) on a beam is equal to the transverse force on it multiplied by the perpendicular distance of the line of action of that force from the place where the beam is supported or fixed. Thus, the BM of a 150-lb man standing half-way along a diving board is the same as that of a 75-lb boy standing on the end. Wing spars are beams which are rigidly fixed at the roots. On the ground they sag down; in flight they flex up, and the BM is the total lift on the wing (which in straight and level flight, on each side of the centreline, is half the weight of the aircraft) multiplied by the distance of the centre of pressure of either half of the wing from the root, minus a small downward moment due to the wing's own weight. Obviously, the greater the BM, the more

This McDonnell Douglas Spanloader was planned in 1977. It would carry containers weighing 600,000 lb (just half its gross weight) inside a 300-ft wing. (McDonnell Douglas)

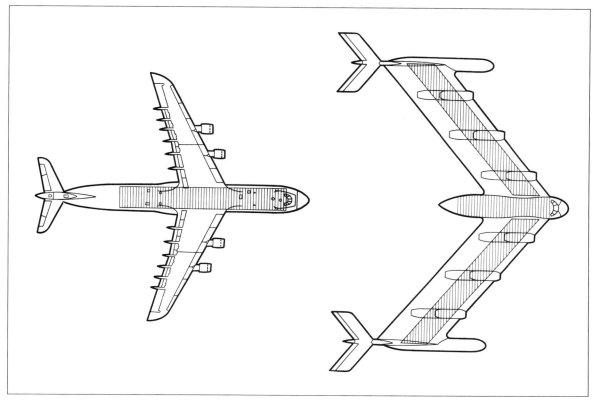

massive and heavy the wing has to be. We can now see the benefit of hanging engines along the wing, where they relieve the BM and also act as large masses to damp out flutter. The alternative is to hang them on the fuselage where they add to the BM, and do nothing to damp out flutter.

Thus the 747 and A340 do their best to minimise the structure weight. But they still carry all the payload inboard of the wing roots, so the spars still have a very severe time. You have only to look out of the window as the aircraft rotates on take-off to see BM in action. As the enormous lift forces come into play, and P2 says 'positive rate of climb established', the wing curves upwards dramatically towards the tip and we can almost hear the inboard structure groaning under the BM it is having to bear. Later, as we hit rough air, the tips flex up and down and the BM fluctuates wildly, often becoming negative. That's what causes fatigue

A Lockheed Spanloader project to the same scale as a C-5 Galaxy. Wingtip pods would house fuel. (Lockheed via Mike Hooks)

damage and shortens the life of the structure.

As we have seen, many designers of giants of the past have sought to put the passengers inside the wing, and use a vestigial fuselage merely to carry the tail. I don't think this idea is viable any longer, if indeed it ever was. Even if passengers aren't particularly keen to look out of the window — and you can count me in among those that are glued to the window, even when it's only a cloudscape — the structural problems of making a pressurized wing are considerable. V.J. Burnelli, G.T.R. Hill and others tried to solve the problem by 'quilting' the interior top and bottom skins so that the pressure loads were borne by portions of spherical

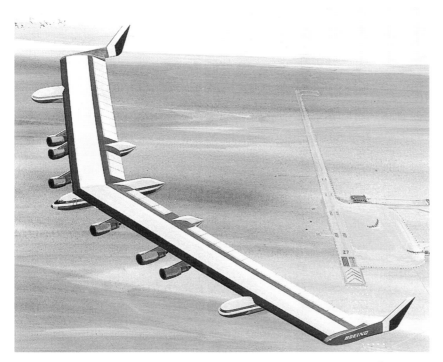

A Boeing Spanloader of true flying-wing type with a span of 500 ft. This could carry about 400 tons of containers at 500 mph. (Boeing via Mike Hooks)

surfaces, with their inwards-projecting extremities linked by vertical ties, somewhat like the rows of pillars between a cathedral's nave and aisles. This would be complicated and heavy, and nobody wants a nice big room to be filled with pillars, not even slender ones. So in my view passenger aircraft will continue to have conventional fuselages for as far ahead as we can see.

But the freighter is a different animal. Apart from the flightdeck, it does not necessarily need pressurization. One of the best things that ever happened to the movement of cargo was the agreement of the whole human race on a standardized family of cargo boxes, called ISO (International Standards Organization) containers. They are 8 ft wide, 8 ft high and 10, 20 or 40 ft long, and they fit specially tailored pick-ups on aircraft, trucks, trains and ships, and on cranes, straddle carriers, side-loaders and mechanised conveyors. So far as I know it has yet to be done, but I can see no problem in developing pressurized containers if necessary; we already have refrigerated ones, and a container giving, say, sea-level temperature and 8,000 ft pressure at 35,000 ft ought to be the proverbial cinch. In other words, tomorrow's giant cargo aircraft need not be pressurized. Thus, it can have a payload volume of any shape we like.

The obvious arrangement (I think) is the Spanloader, in which the containers are loaded into the wing and distributed across the span. This can be done in many ways. I myself took out a provisional patent back in 1963 for such an aircraft, loading each container through its own hatch (the front part of each hatch being a section of Kruger flap) so that at any airport it would be possible to transfer any container in or out without disturbing the others. At that time it was a novel idea (so was the HBPR engine, of which I mounted a row to blow across the wing) so nobody showed any interest. Today we are getting nearer to the stage where the world's air-cargo business might at last 'take off', as people have said it ought to do for 40 years. When it does, we might see some Spanloaders.

People are still playing about with different arrangements. One drawing shows a McDonnell Douglas suggestion, with six engines mounted like mine above the wing, and the tail carried on a very slim fuselage. Containers are loaded transversely through the full-depth wingtip, the three rows of containers being separated by the spars. A particular container thus might be locked in by others, but in any case the scheme is much more flexible than the traditional freighter fuselage seen in the background. Of course, and this goes for all Spanloaders, the entire load must always leave the CG close to the centreline, not offset to left or right, and every container must be locked in place.

Two of the drawings show what may be the ultimate layout in which the aircraft is an all-wing design. The Lockheed is contrasted with a C-5, showing the seemingly much greater floor area available for containers in the unconventional aircraft. This particular Spanloader has six engines with USB (upper-surface blowing), and all fuel and flight-control surfaces are at the wing-tips. A Boeing artwork shows a similar proposal, but with underslung engines and fuel in pods. The wing would have elevons, and Boeing has been trying to discover if there is the slightest possibility of loading containers from the trailing edge. To do so would involve each container, 8 ft by 8 ft, passing through the rear spar. You would say such holes could not be tolerated, but we are thinking in terms of conventional wings with large BM problems. If your payload is truly 'span-loaded' then the BMs are extremely small, except on the ground, so (perhaps) we can cut huge holes in our spars. Ideally we want to leave the aerodynamics and structure at the front of the wing alone, and loading through the back, perhaps by enabling each section of elevon to split into upper and lower halves, does seem a possibility. But each new break-

A fitting conclusion to this book is provided by a Boeing suggestion for a twin-fuselage cargo aircraft in the 2-Megapound (1,000-ton) class. Boeing suggest that the main wing box could be used for 'bulk shipments of minerals or oil'. I am unconvinced, but strongly believe such aircraft will be needed for urgent high-value containerised cargo. (Boeing via Mike Hooks)

through brings fresh problems. To minimise BM on the ground we want wheels not only at about one-third of the semi-span (note trailing-edge fairings) but also at the tips. Alternatively, ACLG (air-cushion landing gear) can spread the load. Either way, our flight-control system must take out every trace of bank as we hit the runway.

This all-wing Boeing might, like the Lockheed, have a span of 280-300 ft. But the final artwork shows an even bigger aircraft, with 12 engines in the 50-60,000 lb class, a span of some 350-380 ft and gross weight of 1,000 short tons. Fuel and landing gears would be housed in the two slim bodies, one of which contains the flightdeck (this reminds me of 'Timber' Woods' famous quote on the first take-off of the Beverley: 'My side's airborne, what about yours?') Bumps just visible under the leading edge could be further landing gears, to distribute the weight on the ground, but this raises the only obvious criticism of such aircraft: how can you taxi along a 50-ft taxiway if your outer wheels are over 250 ft apart? Air cushions could be

an answer. In this case there is a conventional tail, with the horizontal carried on inward-sloping fins. This enables the wing to be unswept, which in turn facilitates end-loading and unloading. But, however clever the computerised loading sequence, there will come a time when you want that urgent container in the middle, and with this aircraft there could be a row of 15 containers between it and either tip! One could also make the point that, even with quiet HBPR engines, 12 at full blast on take-off might make noise certification difficult, especially as airlines like to move cargo at night.

Enough of the problems! Such aeroplanes surely are enough to make at least one boy drop 'English Lit' or 'Social Sciences' and get down to solving the problems of tomorrow. If it ever gets built it will be quite closely a modern version of the biggest of the Adlershofs, but 10 times as heavy and 100 times as powerful. I can't help thinking they need a flightdeck in that other fuselage. The weather might be different.

Tables

Table of wing areas

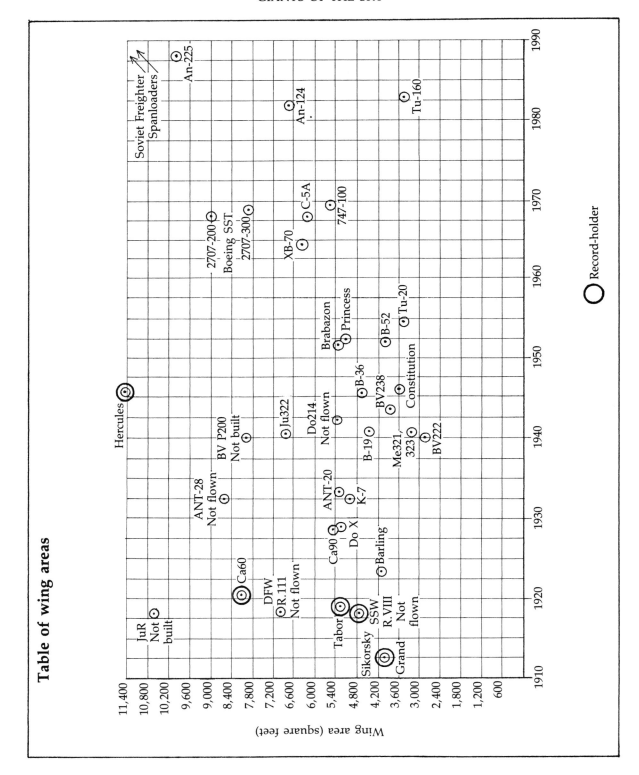

Wing area (square feet)

An-225

Soviet Freighter
Spanloaders

An-124

Tu-160

2707-200
Boeing SST
2707-300

XB-70

C-5A

747-100

Brabazon
Princess

B-52

Tu-20

B-36

BV238

Constitution

Hercules

BV P200
Not built

Ju322

Do214
Not flown

B-19

Me321,
323

BV222

ANT-28
Not flown

ANT-20

K-7

Ca60

DFW
R.111
Not flown

Ca90

Do X

Barling

JuR
Not
built

Tabor

SSW
R.VIII
Not
flown

Sikorsky
Grand

Record-holder

Table of wing spans

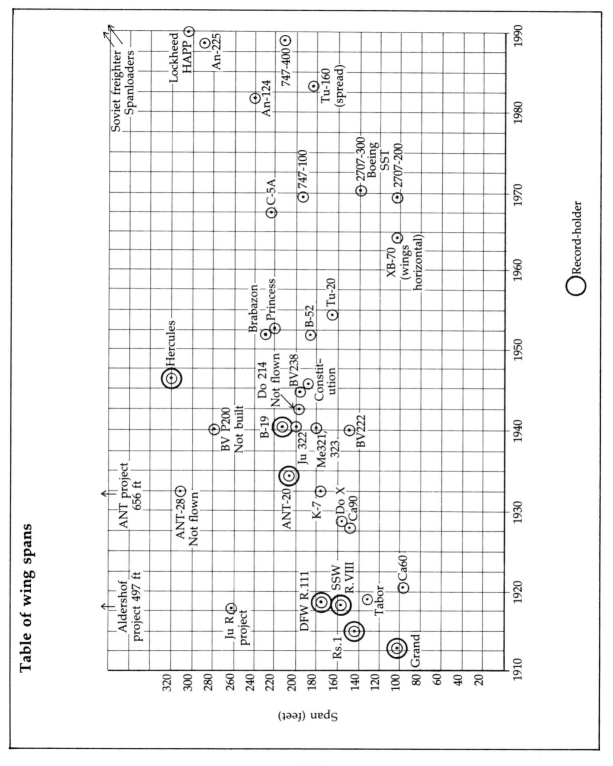

Table of horsepower/pounds thrust

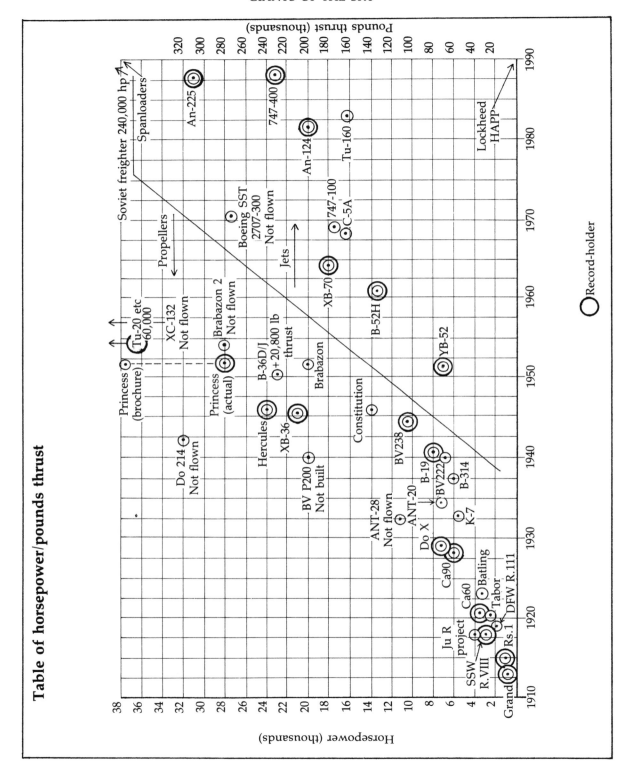

Table of maximum take-off weights

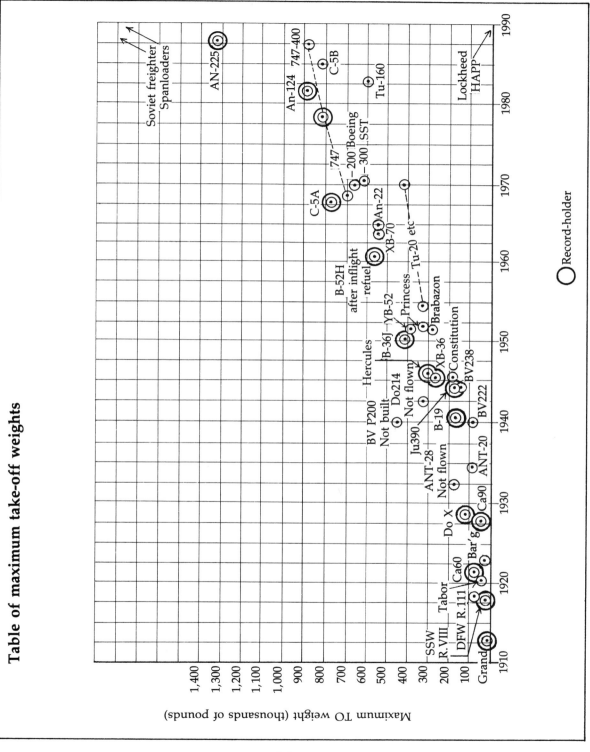

Maximum TO weight (thousands of pounds)

Index